Language in the Indian Diaspora

Language in the Indian Diaspora

Sociolinguistic Perspectives

EDITED BY RAJEND MESTHRIE AND
SONAL KULKARNI-JOSHI

EDINBURGH
University Press

Edinburgh University Press is one of the leading university presses in the UK. We publish academic books and journals in our selected subject areas across the humanities and social sciences, combining cutting-edge scholarship with high editorial and production values to produce academic works of lasting importance. For more information visit our website: edinburghuniversitypress.com

© editorial matter and organisation Rajend Mesthrie and Sonal Kulkarni-Joshi, 2024, 2025
© the chapters their several authors, 2024, 2025

Edinburgh University Press Ltd
13 Infirmary Street
Edinburgh EH1 1LT

First published in hardback by Edinburgh University Press 2024

Typeset in 9/12 pt Noto Serif
by Cheshire Typesetting Ltd, Cuddington, Cheshire

A CIP record for this book is available from the British Library

ISBN 978-1-4744-7835-9 (hardback)
ISBN 978-1-4744-7836-6 (paperback)
ISBN 978-1-4744-7837-3 (webready PDF)
ISBN 978-1-4744-7838-0 (epub)

The right of Rajend Mesthrie and Sonal Kulkarni-Joshi to be identified as the editors of this work has been asserted in accordance with the Copyright, Designs and Patents Act 1988, and the Copyright and Related Rights Regulations 2003 (SI No. 2498).

Contents

List of Figures, Maps and Tables	vii
Notes on Contributors	x
Acknowledgements	xiv
Abbreviations	xv
List of Main Symbol Equivalences	xvii

	Introduction: Diversity and Diaspora Rajend Mesthrie and Sonal Kulkarni-Joshi	1
1	Resistance and Reconciliation: Language and Identity Construction among the Internally Displaced Bhils in the Narmada Valley Sonal Kulkarni-Joshi	12
2	Narratives of Displaced Kashmiri Pandits: Mobility, Diasporic Morbidity and the Chronotope of Victimhood Rakesh M. Bhatt	29
3	Patterns of Language Use in the Diaspora Communities in Kolkata Aditi Ghosh	48
4	Diasporic Adjustments and Indian Languages in South Africa Rajend Mesthrie	68
5	Language in the South Asian Diaspora in Britain Devyani Sharma and Lavanya Sankaran	89
6	Symbolic Value as a Catalyst for Language Maintenance: Sanskrit in the US Diaspora Rajeshwari V. Pandharipande	108
7	Indian Languages in Singapore Ritu Jain and Rajesh Rai	125
8	East Indian Languages in the Caribbean Diaspora Surendra Gambhir	143

9	A Sociolinguistic Investigation of the Retention of Ancestral Dialect Features in Kokni Spoken in Cape Town *Ruta Paradkar*	167
10	The Dialect Roots of Varieties of Gujarati in South Africa *Rajend Mesthrie and Vinu Chavda*	186
11	South African Gujarati Literature: An Inventory and Critical Commentary *Mrunal Chavda and Rajend Mesthrie*	205
12	Performing Language Alternation in Multilingual Mauritius: The Conversational Significance of Song Interludes in Everyday Interactions *Tejshree Auckle*	227
	Index	251

Figures, Maps and Tables

Figures

1.1	Languages spoken in Nandurbar district (based on Census of India 2011)	14
2.1	The Pir Panjal range, visible from Srinagar, Kashmir	30
2.2	Ticket to (forced) exile	34
3.1	Language preference of respondents showing language choice with interlocutors across generations	57
3.2	Language preference of respondents for communication across age groups	57
3.3	Most preferred languages of respondents in official domains	58
3.4	Language choice in other domains	60
4.1	Schematic presentation of North Indian continuum relevant to South African indentured diaspora (1860–1911)	70
5.1	Main language other than English, as reported in the 2011 UK Census	91
8.1	Letter written in Hindi showing influence of Sarnami	155
9.1	Average Kokni use in the family domain across young, middle and old age groups	172
9.2	Kokni, English and Afrikaans usage in various social domains among the young, middle and old age groups	173

Maps

1.1	The Sardar Sarovar Project and its surrounding areas	13
4.1	South Africa, showing main cities referred to in text	81
8.1	Sketch map of regional use of stem + -e verb forms in the North Indian continuum by frequency of usage	150
8.2	Sketch map of distribution of future endings in modern Indo-Aryan	151
9.1	Sending areas in the Kokan, Maharashtra State, India	169
10.1	The main districts of Gujarat today	189
10.2	Four fieldwork sites for Gujarati in South Africa	190

Tables

1.1	Villages sampled for the present study in the Narmada area	16
1.2	Host villages surrounding Narmadanagar	17
1.3	Host villages surrounding Rewanagar	17
1.4	Villages surrounding Rozwa	17
1.5	Resettled and original villages in the Narmada project sample	18
3.1	Reported mother tongues of respondents	54
3.2	Respondents' mother tongues – modified in relation to Hindi as cover term	55
3.3	Language preference of respondents in the home domain	56
3.4	Language choice: official domain	58
3.5	First language in schools attended by respondents	59
3.6	Language choice with friends, in the neighbourhood and in other domains	60
3.7	Mother tongue of most friends	61
3.8	Percentage of second-most preferred language in home domain	62
3.9	Percentage of second-most preferred language in official domain	62
3.10	Percentage of second-most preferred language in other domains	62
3.11	Choice of language for inter-linguistic communication by respondents	62
3.12	Choice of language by other speakers while speaking to the respondents	63
3.13	Language choice in scripted media	63
4.1	Summary of initial diversity and koine outcomes in seven South African Indian languages	79
5.1	General Certificate of Secondary Education GCSE entries over time	93
5.2	Bilingual language use in daily life in the Panjabi community	96
5.3	Bilingual/multilingual language use in daily life in the Sri Lankan Tamil community	99
7.1	Census data on Indians by ethnic group, 1957–2010	132
7.2	Census data on predominant household languages by ethnic groups, 1980–2010	133
7.3	Number of venues for community schools in 2021	136
7.4	Student enrolment for non-Tamil Indian languages, 2010–18	137
8.1	Indian diaspora in the Caribbean area	145
8.2	Variation in the future endings in different transplanted varieties	152
8.3	Comparison of the *b*- and *h*-future in Guyanese Bhojpuri and India's regional varieties in India	152
9.1	Differential features in the ancestral village-based varieties in KCT Kokni	176
9.2	Variants in the KCT Kokni attested in the *LSI* samples from Raigad and Ratnagiri districts	181
10.1	Variable dental–retroflex interchanges in colloquial nineteenth-century Gujarati and present-day Cape Town that differ from the standard	192
10.2	The most common tokens that show some retroflex for dental realisations in Cape Town Gujarati by consonant type and environment	193

Figures, Maps and Tables

10.3	A skeletal summary of the *s*-shift in four Gujarati dialects and the standard	196
10.4	The *s*-shift in Surti and Kathiawadi dialects and its uptake in Cape Town	197
10.5	Miscellaneous consonant features in dialects of Gujarat	200
10.6	Miscellaneous vowel features in dialects of Gujarat	201
11.1	Phases of Gujarati literary history	206
12.1	Font styles used to represent code-switching to specific languages	233

Notes on Contributors

Tejshree Auckle is a senior lecturer in the Department of English Studies at the University of Mauritius. Her research interests include multilingualism and language contact phenomena as well as issues of language planning and policy (with particular reference to Mauritius). Her most recent publication is the article 'Orthography, ideology and the codification of Mauritian creole: The implications of decreasing linguistic abstand', published in the *Journal of Pidgin and Creole Languages* (2023).

Rakesh M. Bhatt is a professor of sociolinguistics at the University of Illinois, Urbana-Champaign. He specialises in sociolinguistics of language contact, and in particular issues of migration, minorities and multilingualism, code-switching, language ideology, and world Englishes. The empirical focus of his work has been on South Asian languages, particularly Kashmiri, Hindi and Indian English. His book *Verb Movement and the Syntax of Kashmiri* (Kluwer Academic Press, 1999) was published in the Studies in Natural Language and Linguistic Theory series. He was co-author of *World Englishes* (Cambridge University Press, 2008) with Rajend Mesthrie, and has had articles published in numerous international journals. He is currently working on a book-length manuscript, under contract with Cambridge University Press, on the sociolinguistic patterns of subordination of Kashmiri language in diaspora. Other manuscripts in progress, both co-authored with Agnes Bolonyai, deal with code-switching (Routledge and Edinburgh University Press). He is also currently the editor of the volume *Handbook of South Asian Englishes* (Oxford University Press).

Mrunal Chavda holds a PhD in Drama from the University of Exeter. He was a postdoctoral research fellow at the University of Cape Town (South Africa) working on a research project entitled 'A Sociocultural Documentation of South African Gujarati'. His publications include 'If only Bollywood ... The case of British Asian theatre', 'Performing Garba (the clap dance): Choreographic and commercial changes', 'The rhetoric of Gandhi and Ambedkar' and 'Rhetoric of Sustainability in Academic Research', in addition to a teaching case study entitled 'Difficult conversations at YuVim's boutique' (Sage Business Case). His forthcoming publications include '1000 Anamikas: Rangoli's attempts to break the glass ceilings' in *The Case for Women*, and 'Rangoli group of institutions: Expanding preschool franchise business post-Covid-19 pandemic and national education policy' (2020) with Ivey Publishing.

Contributors

Vinu Chavda holds a PhD in Linguistics from Gujarat University. She was a postdoctoral research fellow at the University of Cape Town (South Africa) and worked with Rajend Mesthrie on a research project entitled 'A Sociolinguistic Documentation of South African Gujarati'. She has co-authored a book, *Bhartiya Bhasha Jyoti: Gujarati*, published by the Central Institute of Indian Languages (CIIL), and she has extensive industry experience as a linguist, including within organisations such as CIIL, American Institute of Indian Studies, Education Initiatives, Lionbridge Technologies, Playhouse Production, Oxford University Press and Oxford Gujarati Language Initiative. Her article publications include 'Cape Town Gujarati and its relation to Gujarati dialectology: A study of retroflex boosting' (with Rajend Mesthrie) and 'Do NRGs require government support to retain the Gujarati language? A discussion on the South African Gujarati language'.

Surendra Gambhir is an emeritus distinguished member of the South Asia Faculty at the University of Pennsylvania. He holds an MA (Sanskrit) from Delhi University and a PhD in sociolinguistics from the University of Pennsylvania. His research work extended across Guyana, Trinidad, Suriname, Guadeloupe, Mauritius, Fiji, India and the United States. He has authored eight books and more than 100 research articles published in books, encyclopaedias and international journals. He is the recipient of many awards, including the President of India award for his research contributions to India's diaspora. He was a visiting professor at Cornell University, University of Wisconsin, and the Humanities Foundation, a consultant to National Foreign Language Center and Center for Applied Linguistics, chair/member of various national and international committees, and a keynote speaker in national and international conferences. As Chair of the Language Committee of the American Institute of Indian Studies from 1998–2007 he directed thirteen language programmes in India.

Aditi Ghosh is a professor in the Department of Linguistics, University of Calcutta. She completed her MA and PhD in Linguistics in the same department. Previously she has been a faculty member of the Department of Linguistics, Assam University Silchar, and a research fellow at the Asiatic Society, Kolkata. Her current research interests lie primarily in different areas of sociolinguistics, including different aspects of multilingualism, interactional sociolinguistics, language policies, and language politics, language choice and language use, language attitude, and the study of the relationship between the city and the languages. She has led major research projects on these topics and has published extensively in them.

Ritu Jain is a senior lecturer in the Language and Communication Centre and Assistant Chair of the School of Humanities at Nanyang Technological University, Singapore. She is editor of the Routledge volume *Multilingual Singapore* and has published in journals such as *Language Policy* and *Current Issues in Language Planning*. In her research, Ritu examines the impact of language policies/language management on the maintenance of minority languages in immigrant settings. Her current large-scale research explores the rapidly escalating shift to English among Indians in Singapore. She is also part of a global study investigating factors that influence/impede home language transmission.

Sonal Kulkarni-Joshi is Professor in Linguistics and Head of the Linguistics Department at Deccan College (Deemed to be University), Pune, India. She received a PhD in Linguistics from the University of Reading, UK. Her research interest is in the field of language variation and change. She headed a multiversity major project on the sociolinguistic aspects of displacement in the Narmada Valley (2010–12). She was coordinator of a Special Assistance Programme on Language Contact in India, funded by the University Grants Commission of India (2011–16). Since 2017 she has headed a government-funded project for the creation of a digital database of Marathi dialects (www.sdml.ac.in). Her publications include journal articles in *Indian Linguistics*, *International Journal of Dravidian Linguistics* and *Journal of South Asian Languages and Linguistics*. She was treasurer of the Linguistic Society of India (2005–14).

Rajend Mesthrie is Emeritus Professor of Linguistics at the University of Cape Town. He has researched Indian languages, African languages and English since the 1980s, with special – but not exclusive – reference to South Africa. He was Head of the Linguistics Section (1998–2009), President of the Linguistics Society of Southern Africa (2002–9) and President of the International Congress of Linguists (2013–18). He is an elected honorary member of the Linguistics Society of Southern Africa and the Linguistic Society of America. Among his book publications are *Language in Indenture: A Sociolinguistic History of Bhojpuri-Hindi in South Africa* (Routledge, 1992; reprint 2019), *Language in South Africa* (ed., Cambridge University Press, 2002), *A Dictionary of South African Indian English* (UCT Press, 2010) and *World Englishes* (with Rakesh Bhatt, Cambridge University Press, 2008).

Rajeshwari V. Pandharipande, is Professor Emerita of Linguistics, Religion, Sanskrit, and Comparative and World Literature at the University of Illinois at Urbana-Champaign, USA, and a permanent member of the South Asia Committee at the University of Chicago. She holds two PhD degrees, in Sanskrit Literature (from India) and in Linguistics (from the University of Illinois). Her research and teaching focus on the language of religion, sociolinguistics, structure, and the literature of South Asian languages (Sanskrit, Hindi and Marathi), Hinduism in India and diaspora, and Asian mythology. She is recipient of the Chancellor's prestigious award with the permanent title, 'University Distinguished Teacher Scholar'. In addition to more than 100 articles, she has published a number of books, including *A Descriptive Grammar of Marathi* (Routledge), *Sociolinguistic Dimensions of Marathi* (Lincom Europa Publications), *The Eternal Self and the Cycle of Samsara* (Ginn Press), three co-edited volumes and two collections of Hindi poems.

Ruta Paradkar is a postdoctoral research fellow in 'South Asian Migration and Sociolinguistics' at the University of Cape Town, working with Rajend Mesthrie. She obtained her PhD from the Deccan College (deemed to be University), India (2022) on sociolinguistic characteristics of Kokni spoken in Cape Town. She has written on the Padye variety of Goa (2014) and has co-authored a paper on the Korlai Creole Portuguese (2015) – both language contact varieties spoken on the western coast of India. She has been an Infosys fellow at the Bhandarkar Oriental Research Institute (August–October 2022), where she worked on the varieties of Konkani spoken in Mangalore, Karnataka, and she has taught Konkani to second-language adult learners of the language at WRLC, Pune. Her research interests include languages in migration, language contact, and dialectological and sociolinguistic aspects of the Konkani and Marathi language varieties.

Rajesh Rai is Associate Professor and Head of the South Asian Studies Programme (SASP), National University of Singapore (NUS). His research interests are in the fields of Indian diaspora and heritage studies. Rai has authored and edited several major works including a five-part book series titled *Hidden Heritage: Minority South Asian Communities in Singapore* (2022); *Singapore Indian Heritage* (2017); *Indians in Singapore, 1819–1945* (2014); *Religion and Identity in the South Asian Diaspora* (2013); and *South Asian Diaspora: Transnational Networks and Changing Identities* (2009). Rajesh was also assistant editor of the *Encyclopedia of the Indian Diaspora* (2006), which has gained global recognition for its contribution to Indian diaspora studies. His articles have been published in premier academic journals such as *Modern Asian Studies*. He is recognised for his excellence in teaching for which he has won several awards at the National University of Singapore.

Lavanya Sankaran PhD Cantab, works as a lecturer in language education at King's College London. She teaches on both undergraduate and postgraduate programmes on modules related to language structure, culture, ideology and qualitative research methods. Her research interests lie in the field of sociolinguistics, specifically in the areas of multilingualism, diaspora and migration, drawing on concepts from linguistic ethnography. Two research projects that she has been involved with include a Leverhulme-funded project on multilingual development amongst Sri Lankan Tamil adults in London (2015–18) and an ESRC-funded project on dialect development and style in the Punjabi community in Southall, London (2008–10). Her publications include journal articles in *Language in Society* and the *International Journal of the Sociology of Language*. She is currently researching conflict-generated diasporic identities.

Devyani Sharma is Professor of Linguistics at Queen Mary University of London. She conducts research in the areas of sociolinguistics, bilingualism, language contact, language and dialect typology, and syntactic and phonetic variation. She studies postcolonial and diaspora varieties of English and has also worked on syntactic variation and typology of Indian languages, including ergativity and agreement systems in Indo-Aryan languages (published in *Language Typology*) and the syntax of Hindi and Kashmiri. Recent publications include *From Deficit to Dialect: The Evolution of English in India and Singapore* (Oxford University Press, 2023), *Research Methods in Linguistics* (Cambridge University Press, 2013, co-edited), the *Oxford Handbook of World Englishes* (Oxford University Press, 2017, co-edited) and *English in the Indian Diaspora* (Benjamins, 2014, co-edited).

Acknowledgements

We thank the authors of the chapters for their endurance through the COVID-19 period and their patience in working through the review, revision and copy-editing process. Thanks are due to the National Institute for the Humanities and Social Sciences (NIHSS, South Africa) and the Indian Council for Social Science Research (ICSSR, India) for funding the project 'Language Change and Identity among Indian South Africans, with special reference to Gujarati and Konkani' as part of a BRICS initiative (Reference number NIHSS/ICSSR 201514.) These agencies covered the main running expenses of the research and editing leading to this book project. We also acknowledge the NRF (National Research Foundation) South Africa for a SARCHI (South African Research Chair) grant no. 64805, *Migration, Language and Social Change*, which covered Rajend Mesthrie's research activities over fifteen years as SARCHI chair.

We gratefully acknowledge capable research assistance provided by the following individuals: Dr Ruta Paradkar for help in preparing the front matter for the volume and the index, Dr Yolandi Ribbens-Klein for assistance with maps and tables, and Ms Fatima Sadan for general administrative cover. We thank Dr Connie Israel for supplying the cover photograph of Sanskrit Road, Tongaat, South Africa. We thank Laura Williamson at Edinburgh University Press, who first expressed interest in publishing the research after the initial workshop at the International Congress of Linguists (2018), and Sam Johnson and colleagues at EUP for their patience throughout this publishing project.

Abbreviations

ACTFL	American Council on the Teaching of Foreign Languages
BTTSAL	Board for the Teaching and Testing of South Asian Languages
CMIO	Chinese – Malay – Indian – Other
CPT	Cape Town
CS	Code-switching
DAT	Dative
EMPH	Emphatic
ERG	Ergative
F	Feminine
GB	Guyanese Bhojpuri
GCSE	General Certificate of Secondary Education
GEN	Genitive
IB	Indian Bhojpuri
IMP	Imperative
IMPV	Imperfective
INF	Infinitive
JKLF	Jammu Kashmir Liberation Front
KCT	Koknis of Cape Town
KP	Kashmiri Pandit
KZN	KwaZulu-Natal
LOC	Locative
LSI	*Linguistic Survey of India*
LT	Literary Tamil
M	Masculine
MT	Mother Tongue
NTIL	Non-Tamil Indian Language
OBL	Oblique
P/PL	Plural
PEN	Personal Experience Narrative
PERF	Perfective
PRES	Present
S/SG	Singular
SA	South Africa

SADHU	South African Dravidian Hindi-Urdu
SIL	Summer Institute of Linguistics
SLT	Sri Lankan Tamil
ST	Spoken Tamil
SUB	Subjunctive
TUPS	Transvaal United Patidar Society

Main Symbol Equivalences

Indological	Alternatives	IPA
Long vowels:		
ā	aa	[aː]
ī	ii	[iː]
ū	uu	[uː]
Nasal vowels:		
ã	aN	[ã]
ĩ	iN	[ĩ]
ũ	uN	[ũ]
Consonants:		
Retroflex:		
ṭ	T	[ʈ]
ḍ	D	[ɖ]
ṛ	R	[ɽ]
ṇ	N	[ɳ]
ḷ	L	[ɭ]
ṣ	S	[ʂ]
Dental:		
t	t	[t̪]
d	d	[d̪]
r	r	[r̪]
Aspirate and other:		
kh	kh	[kʰ]
ś	sh	[ʃ]
c	ch	[tʃ]
ch	chh	[tʃʰ]
h	h	[ɦ]
ḥ	h	[h]

Introduction: Diversity and Diaspora

Rajend Mesthrie and Sonal Kulkarni-Joshi

We begin with a glimpse of the human stories behind migration and diaspora, drawing on Hajratwala (2009), who provides a compelling account of the spread of the Hajratwalas from a small Indian village to Fiji and thence to six different continents. The first migrating ancestor of the family journeyed to Calcutta [Kolkata] from his home village in Navsari, Gujarat (see Map 10.1) in 1909 to join indentured workers bound on a ship to Fiji. A calamitous famine of 1899 had made conditions close to impossible in Navsari district. As a passenger Motilal paid his own fee, but essentially was consigned to joining the indentured 'coolies' on board. With his weaver background (claiming former Khatri/warrior caste status) he took up employment as a tailor in a European firm in the clothing business. (Motilal went on to eventually open a tailor shop of his own in Suva.) Visits to family in Gujarat were few, but he did enable relatives to come to Fiji as chain migrants. When the plague hit Fiji in 1918, Motilal was one of its many victims.

Motilal's brother and brother-in-law continued to run the shop, while his eldest son came over to Fiji for the first time at the age of fourteen to work with his uncles. The business M. Narsey & Co. grew into one of the largest department stores in the islands (Hajratwala 2009: 40). The importance of Motilal's wife, known as *Maajee*, cannot be overestimated: while she may not have gone over to Fiji in his lifetime, she was the rock that kept the family and homestead (mortgaged to pay for Motilal's first trip) together in Navsari. She was eventually persuaded to join her sons and grandsons in Fiji in the 1960s, motivated by an upcoming wedding. *In our yard a lot of paan is growing*, wrote her grandson on the back of a photograph, *and Maaji is collecting paan and the wedding was also performed in the yard* (Hajratwala 2009: 44). Collecting paan ('betel leaf') in the Navsari homestead was a job Maaji would not allow anyone else to do. No doubt this was her tangible link with India. The family's diaspora with different members extended to Natal (South Africa) and later to the UK, Canada, Hong Kong, Australia and New Zealand. In each territory is a human and economic story to parallel the efforts of Motilal Narsey.

This book attempts to foreground the sociolinguistic adaptations of such migrants in diasporas. We adopt a practical definition of diaspora as a loose collection of peoples living outside an historical homeland and fully immersed in their existing places of residence, who retain some cultural and historical links with the homeland, resulting in an identity partially defined by the historical migration. While a strong transnational consciousness characterises the first group of immigrants and its immediate descendants, with subsequent generations this may become more of a heritage identity than one that is actually bi-national. Social networks in diasporas tend to favour people of similar background, but the quest for economic livelihood and new living arrangements often make this multi-ethnic. Matters of identity may thus become fluid, permeable to context and sometimes contradictory (see Cohen 1997). Vertovec (2000) stresses three meanings of diaspora: (1) as a social form (the process of becoming dispersed, cementing of social ties arising from migration, new economic strategies, etc.); (2) as a type of consciousness (based on common experiences, and an outlook leading to a common identity); and (3) as a mode of cultural production (of objects, images, and meanings – back and forth, which may transcend, change and even creolise according to circumstances).

The prototype is the Jewish diaspora (leaving aside the political complexities of the homeland question); one can speak of any other diaspora; but the ones most frequently evoked are the African diaspora (though one may speak of more specific Nigerian or Zimbabwean diasporas too), the Indian diaspora, the Chinese diaspora, etc. At the outset it must be acknowledged that the Indian diaspora overlaps with a broader South Asian diaspora. While migrants from present-day India, Bangladesh, Pakistan, Sri Lanka, Nepal and so forth may initially consider themselves distinct in terms of culture and identity, they may be ascribed a broader identity by the host society based on cultural and physical similarities. Moreover, social interaction in the new host countries does increase the sense of community and solidarity, despite significant differences. This book therefore sometimes refers to the broader South Asian diaspora (most notably in Chapter 5 by Sharma and Sankaran on the UK) rather than just the Indian case. However, most chapters focus specially on migrations out of India or from one territory within India to another as a kind of internal diaspora.

India has had a long history of travel, trade and settlement within other parts of Asia, Africa and the West and in fact now maintains a palpable global presence. India's Ministry of External Affairs estimates that there are just over 32 million Indians residing outside India. A document tabled to the Lok Sabha (one of the two Houses of Parliament) in 2020 lists numbers of Indians in the diaspora across 210 countries (https://mea.gov.in/images/attach/NRIs-and-PIOs_1.pdf).

The totals cited below and excerpted from the document include numbers irrespective of their reflecting temporary migrants or permanent settlers abroad. In Indian government terminology these include both *non-resident Indians* (NRIs) and *people of Indian origin* (PIOs). The former are citizens of India living abroad, the latter are citizens of other countries, some of whom actively claim the status of *overseas citizens of India* (OCIs).

Of the 210 countries listed, eight have over a million Indians:

USA	4,460,000
UAE	3,425,144
Saudi Arabia	2,594,947
Malaysia	2,987,950
Myanmar	2,009,207
Canada	1,689,055
UK	1,764,000

Introduction

Sri Lanka	1,614,000
South Africa	1,560,000
Kuwait	1,029,861

Another six countries have numbers exceeding half a million Indians:

Mauritius	894,500
Oman	781,141
Qatar	746,550
Singapore	650,000
Nepal	600,000
Trinidad & Tobago	556,800

Numbers in excess of 200,000 are listed for Australia, Bahrain, Fiji, Guyana, Italy, the Netherlands, New Zealand, Reunion Islands and Suriname. Over 100,000 are reported for (mainland) France, Germany, Indonesia, Thailand and the Philippines. These numbers are impressive; though raw numbers should not be taken as the sole or even main indication of importance. Numbers in Mauritius, for example, mean that Indians form a majority and have wielded major political and cultural influence since independence. Likewise, Indians are demographically and proportionally very significant in Guyana, Suriname, Fiji and Trinidad & Tobago, despite not falling into the upper echelons of the numbers above. The numbers and proportions of Indians living and working in the Gulf States are also very striking in raw numbers and proportionate to the entire population. All the more so since these numbers are greatly amplified by other South Asians, especially from Pakistan.

The South Asian diaspora has attracted much recent scholarship from a variety of perspectives: historical (Kondapi 1951, Fisher, Lahiri and Thandi 2007), sociological (Brown 2006, Mawani and Mukadam 2014), anthropological (Oonk 2007), and interdisciplinary with an economic theme (Parekh 2001). The number of references is now too great to be listed here; we have accordingly limited ourselves to one or two references per area. One key highly recommended work that has achieved both scholarly and popular status is the *Encyclopedia of the India Diaspora* (Lal, Reeves and Rai 2006). Where language in diaspora is concerned an early pioneering work was that of Agnihotri (1979) who studied the use of Panjabi amidst the adaptations of the Sikh communities in Leeds, England. A number of works dealt with indenture and its effects on Bhojpuri-speaking migrants worldwide as supplied in the references to Chapters 4 (on South Africa) and 8 (on the Caribbean). Outside this, the number of detailed studies informed by mainstream linguistics is relatively small. English in the Indian diaspora has also attracted a fair bit of attention – see e.g. the edited collection of Hundt and Sharma (2014) and the work of Mesthrie (e.g. 1992, forthcoming) on South African Indian English and Marianne Hundt on Indo-Fijian English (e.g. Hundt 2014). This is a strand of work that we have decided not to include in this work, since our aim is to highlight Indian languages themselves. But the topic of changes in speech repertoires in diaspora (see Canagarajah 2017) across South Asian/Indian communities is indeed worthy of future comparative studies. Work on the internal movement of language in India has attended to factors which catalyse the endurance of home languages in diaspora. This work includes the following case studies: Saurashtri in Tamil Nadu (Pandit 1972), Marathi in Cochin, Kerala (Ghatage 1967), Konkani in Kasargode, Kerala (Ghatage 1970), Punjabi diaspora (Sachdeva 1981), Kannada in Delhi (Satyanath 1982), thirteen migrant linguistic groups in a slum in Mumbai (Rajyashree 1986), Bengali and Punjabi in Delhi (Mukherjee 1996), and Sindhi across India (Iyengar and Parchani 2021). These studies attribute the resilience of the migrant languages in the home and the extended kinship community largely to the ability of the bilingual speakers to adapt the form and function of the home language to harmonise with the ambient languages – a striking feature of Indian/South Asian bi/multilingualism. But we witness a shift in scholarly understanding of the Indian multilingual experience. Earlier studies emphasised the non-competitive bilingual, horizontally diglossic Indian experience (Pandit 1972, Khubchandani 1983), and the continuity of migrant languages in the home domain, especially in the second and third generations, presumably motivated by the importance ascribed to the ethnic separateness of the home domain in South Asian/Indian society (Gumperz and Wilson 1971). However, more recent work highlights that minority languages survive by exhibiting 'anti-predatory' sociolinguistic behaviour and by becoming inconspicuous in the public domains of the competitive, hierarchical linguistic ecosystem (e.g. Mohanty 2010).

With India being a country of well over 400 languages on most counts, and a geographical terrain that matches the size of Europe, there is little reason to expect homogeneity in the diaspora. There are also historical considerations like the time of migration, which may lead to different senses of India and of being Indian or 'overseas Indian'. Among the background issues that have to be considered are whether the migrations were: (a) from pre- or post-partition India, (b) from India or South Asia more generally, (c) semi-forced or voluntary, and (d) if they resulted in rootedness in a new terrain or ability to maintain a transnational presence via circular migration.

While an increasing sense of unity does develop amongst Indians overseas, a sense of regional and ethnic diversity inherited from the homeland may persist for several generations. Following Mesthrie (2008 and updated in 2021) we may identify four kinds of movements out of India in different periods: (1) early historical exploration and trade in Southeast Asia and East Africa between the fifth to seventh centuries CE – see e.g. Horgevorst's (2015) intensive account of the influence of Sanskrit and Tamil in maritime Southeast Asia, especially on Malay, (2) labour migrations of mainly the nineteenth and early twentieth centuries CE under indenture, (3) free economic migration of mainly the late nineteenth century and all of the twentieth century CE, and (4) a new globalised e-generation (of global business personnel and 'computer-wallahs'), who are not as tied to the country of migration as the previous diasporas. Paradoxically – in view of their global status – they are able to retain stronger links with the homeland via jet travel, and the possibility of regular visits and stays (pre-COVID-19, anyway). They are aided in language maintenance by the new instantaneous communicative affordances of their generation. These sub-diasporas are not of course entirely discrete. In particular, the migration of Gujaratis as economic migrants overlapped considerably in time and space with that of indentured labour in the British colonies of the nineteenth and twentieth centuries CE. At the time of writing, the plight of Indian (and Pakistani) migrant workers in the Middle East, especially Qatar, is under scrutiny. Since they do not

Introduction

have permanent citizenship rights, they form yet another strand of Indian migration, whose sociolinguistics amidst radical inequality has still to be treated comprehensively (a compelling general account occurs in Nehra Vohra's strikingly titled book *Impossible Citizens: Dubai's Indian Diaspora*). What research exists has focused on the learning and the growth of L2 or even pidgin varieties of Arabic among immigrants (e.g. Smart 1990, Almoaily 2014). In some ways this labouring class strand of the diaspora shares some similarities with the relatively elite e-generation in being able to return on an annual basis to India, via the affordances of jet travel. They are aided by the relatively quick journey of around five hours from the Middle East to, say, Mumbai or Bengaluru, enabling immersion in two different worlds within a day. This is a far cry from the two-to three-month journeys by sailing and later steamship of indentured labourers from, say, Kolkata to Port of Spain, Trinidad.

In this book we also include the sociolinguistic results of internal migration within India itself. This is meant to enhance the comparative study of Indian languages outside of their earlier established habitats. For example, one may speak of a Kashmiri diaspora, whose members may be found in the USA, the UK, Canada and Australia, but also significantly within parts of India like New Delhi, after the political uncertainties and atrocities of the 1980s. This kind of 'internal diaspora' differs from that of international migratory contexts insofar as the immigrants are still immersed in an Indian cultural and historical environment. However, in terms of the dilemmas and difficulties of home language maintenance and changes in speech repertoires they share many of the issues facing international migrants. Three of the opening chapters in this volume set the scene in their treatment of sociolinguistic developments within India of an 'internal diasporic' nature.

A socio-historical approach is of necessity the broad frame of reference for this book, with all studies focusing on changes wrought in communicative needs and practice, new socio-psychological realities, and changes in language and language repertoires over space and time. Within this unity, individual authors were left free to adopt an eclectic approach depending on their focus, with a composite picture emerging from these different 'conversations'. Sonal Kulkarni-Joshi's poignant study (Chapter 1) of the relocation of speakers of Bhili to make way for the Narmada Dam project is a salutary exemplar of the ecology of language in a socio-historical context. Kulkarni-Joshi shows the effects of the change from living with a degree of freedom in a mountainous, forested and riverine terrain to a more constrained plains environment with new housing arrangements. This drastic loss of eco-freedom has an impact of how people live and talk about their experiences.

A parallel is to be found in Chapter 2 in Rakesh Bhatt's focus on the displacement of Kashmiri Pandits, which confronts the history of contestation, conflict and misrepresentation. From his study in Delhi, Bhatt argues that Kashmiri language and rituals have become limited to private and sacred spaces there, whereas local languages of Delhi and Hindu festivals like Holi and Diwali are associated with public and secular spaces. This dynamic echoes diglossic-like cultural arrangements that develop in international diasporas too. Its linguistic methods include the recording of stories and memories of conflict and displacement, subject to a strong chronotopical analysis, emphasising how time and space are re-presented in language and discourse, with particular poignance in this case. Both opening chapters show how people subject to displacement and the formation of an internal diaspora try to come to terms sociolinguistically with their 'inheritance of loss' (to use the words of Booker Prize-winning novelist Kiran Desai 2006).

Likewise, Chapter 3 by Aditi Ghosh covers the learning of new languages and degree of retention of older languages of their repertoires by immigrants in Kolkata from other parts of India. While largely affirming the assimilatory trends among migrant groups noted in previous studies of urban contact (e.g. Satyanath 1982, Iyengar and Parchani 2021), Ghosh reports that immigrants invest in their own languages and the official language Hindi more than the local language Bengali, which commands less prestige.

The next three chapters focus on diasporic themes from South Africa, the United Kingdom and the United States of America. Chapter 4 by Rajend Mesthrie summarises the history of Indian languages in South Africa from the perspective of migration, contact and koineisation. In South Africa Tamil, Telugu and Bhojpuri (or Bhojpuri-Awadhi-Hindi-Urdu as a continuum) are largely connected to the experience of indentureship from 1860 to 1911, while Gujarati and Kokni (the local term for Konkani) are largely connected to the 'free' migration of people seeking work and trading opportunities since the 1870s. Mesthrie summarises his earlier research on Bhojpuri and shows that its history in South Africa is fairly similar to that in the Caribbean, Fiji and Mauritius, insofar as a robust koine developed out of the initial dialect and language diversity of the North Indian continuum. By contrast he finds a moderate degree of koineisation in South African Telugu, as studied by Varijakshi Prabhakaran (1996). Relying on earlier work by Mesthrie (2007), he notes that South African Tamil is largely a carry-over of the Northern dialect of Indian Tamil, and hence not a koine. This accords very well with records from the extensive ships' lists of the time. Koineisation is the linguists' term for the amalgamation of features from several antecedent dialects and closely related languages to form a new vernacular, that is subsequently transmitted to the next generation. It goes beyond structural interest to being of social and historical importance in showing how diasporic communities undergo internal linguistic changes that reflect the first layer of adaptation in diasporas. The chapter also covers a second layer of changes in the language repertoires of migrants as they adapt to new linguistic realities of the host country. Mesthrie's chapter also summarises the position of Hindi, Urdu, Gujarati and Kokni in relation to the theme of language adaptation in South Africa.

Chapter 5 by Devyani Sharma and Lavanya Sankaran presents case studies of two languages of the South Asian diaspora in the UK/London – Panjabi and Tamil. Their multigenerational project reveals common patterns of stable bilingualism and cross-generational code alternation in both communities. Multilinguality (cf. Agnihotri 2006, 2009, Khubchandani 1988) which characterises language practice across South Asia indexes fused cultural orientation and hybrid identities in the diaspora too. The study also highlights interesting differences in the speech repertoires and language practices that are contingent upon the distinct migration trajectories (e.g. double migration in the Tamil diaspora), demographic size, social class and language ideologies.

The unifying role of Sanskrit in the USA among recent Indian migrants is the subject of Chapter 6 by Rajeshwari Pandharipande. Jayanathan Govender (2022) noted that some diasporic religions tend to sacralise their respective homelands. This is partially true of their languages too. In his study of the Tamil language in Guadeloupe (West Indies), Murugaiyan (2019) noted how Tamil had become a sacred

Introduction

language of this community of indentured descent going back to the late nineteenth century. It is not just that the colloquial form of the language eventually gave way to the local Creole and French, but that the H form became sacralised. Murugaiyan notes how priests encourage the notion that Tamil is not a language for ordinary mortals; it is a language of the gods, for whom priests are a necessary intermediary. Pandharipande argues strongly that Sanskrit has the edge over other Indian languages in the USA in being transparently linked to a single and sacred function as the transmitter of traditional Hinduism. Her chapter traces the earlier history of Sanskrit in US theosophical thought, and reminds us of its linguistic and spiritual importance even before the presence of a substantial Indian diaspora in the country. That role is now supplemented by the ubiquity of yoga practices in the country, which exhibit varying degrees of use of Sanskrit as a medium.

The Indian diaspora community in Singapore and an assessment of their languages are the focus of the chapter by Ritu Jain and Rajesh Rai (Chapter 7). They employ Moag's (2003) detailed 'feature factor matrix' (reproduced in the appendix to their chapter) to describe the shifting linguistic landscape in Singapore. They show how the popularity of Tamil within the ethnically and linguistically diverse South Asian diaspora has declined since colonial times and the early post-colonial period. The language has yielded to the other official languages in Singapore (English, Malay and Mandarin) as well as other non-official Indian languages (Gujarati, Punjabi, Sindhi, Bengali, Urdu and, especially, Hindi). The authors attribute the shift away from Tamil in the 21st century mainly to the use of English, a language of high status. Other factors include the absence of ethnic enclaves, ongoing immigration, the adoption of the high variety of Tamil in education and increased state support for the other Indian languages in the diaspora.

Chapter 8 by Surendra Gambhir covers the use of Bhojpuri and Hindi in the Caribbean, with its main focus on Guyana, Trinidad and Suriname. Gambhir traces the early history of these varieties and the growth of a koine in Guyana, the primary focus of his earlier fieldwork and influential PhD thesis (Gambhir 1981). A koine reflecting demographic emigration patterns among Indians had its heyday for over eighty years in each territory. Gambhir describes a salient feature which survived in the Caribbean and in other Bhojpuri diasporas and which has receded in India, viz. a verb stem + -e pattern which has both subjunctive as well as indicative uses. The widespread adaptation to the host country led to the adoption of Creole and English in Guyana and Trinidad, and the eventual decline of Bhojpuri. Nevertheless, the cultural value of Hindi remains strong, even if it too is not much spoken. Gambhir shows the symbolic value of using a few catchphrases from these heritage languages in community as well as political domains. Overall, Suriname seems to have had a stronger tradition of Indian language maintenance, though Gambhir cautions that even here there are warning signs about incipient shift among younger people.

South Africa features again in the next three chapters, a reflection of the continuing interest of researchers on its languages, despite their diminishing use today. It is also a reflection of the robustness of the research, which continues to turn out new insights on both Indian and South African sociolinguistics. Chapter 9 by Ruta Paradkar focuses on Kokni in Cape Town, where it has been in existence since the 1870s. The small size of the community belies the interests it holds for studies of migration, transnationalism and diasporic dialectology. Paradkar demonstrates that circular migration and more than occasional visits to the Konkan coast of India by subsequent generations have fostered a sociolinguistic consciousness that noticeably differs from that of the indentured Indian communities of South Africa. Thus, while there is an overall identity attached to being a Cape Town Kokni, some village dialect features persist and are above the level of social consciousness. Paradkar's work shows that this correlates with a strong awareness of village roots among Cape Town Koknis, well beyond the original groups of migrants.

Chapter 10 by Rajend Mesthrie and Vinu Chavda continues this theme of a diasporic dialectology, with a focus on the dialect spread of Gujarati in South Africa. The authors examine certain key features of Gujarati in relation to differential use in three cities: Cape Town, Port Elizabeth (now Gqberha) and Durban. These features include interchanges between dental and retroflex consonants, consonant doubling and a salient consonantal shift involving k, kh, c, ch, s, $ś$, h, $ɦ$ and $ø$. The main differentiator is the place of origin of migrants, with two dialects becoming prominent in diasporas: Surti of the Surat and neighbouring districts and Kathiawadi of the Kathiawad peninsula. Settlement patterns and relative demographics prove salient in establishing Surti as the main Gujarati dialect in Cape Town and to a lesser extent Port Elizabeth. In Durban the two dialects co-exist with a slight majority favouring the Kathiawadi form. The chapter thus shows that diasporas can enable a double dialectology not just for linguists but for speakers themselves. While the chapter is a study of Gujarati as heritage language in South Africa, it also contributes to Gujarati linguistics of India in that it brings to attention linguistic properties that have not been given their full due there. Moreover, the authors argue that the properties of retroflex usage for dentals and the chain shift from k, kh all the way to $ø$ are old ones that invite a revisit of Indo-Aryan norms.

Gujarati is also the subject of Chapter 11, this time from a literary perspective. Although this book has a linguistic focus, it was felt that at least one language deserved attention to its written output in diaspora. And here Gujarati in South Africa springs easily to mind for the role of Mahatma Gandhi in writing in both Gujarati and English and in his role as a progenitor of a modern Gujarati prose style. Gandhi's twenty-year stay in South Africa and the influence of his newspaper *Indian Opinion* (1903 to 1961) made Gujarati the most important written language in diaspora for that time. Mrunal Chavda and Rajend Mesthrie's chapter examines some of the creative use of language in the newspaper. It also gives voice to the many Gujarati writers in South Africa whose works have been neglected by Gujarati specialists in India and by scholars in South Africa, where much of their 'popular' writings in magazines have not been translated before. The authors thus make a case for the diasporic segment to be incorporated into the established Gujarati canon.

The final chapter (12) by Tejshree Auckle presents a cogent account of Bollywood-inspired song interludes as a conversational truss in hybrid (Bhojpuri-Kreol-Hindi) code-alternation in the Mauritian diaspora. The author exemplifies the playful yet conversationally meaningful role of popular forms of cultural expressions accompanied by dance steps inspired by the original choreography. She explores and explains the pragmatic implications, the social and stylistic effects of creative embedding of Bollywood pop songs in a Kreole matrix ('vocal instrumentalising', Coupland 2011) in relation to popular forms of local entertainment such as the Mauritian Sega.

A note on symbols

In this book we have tried to give a flavour of different conventions used in practice for the languages being described, rather than attempting one uniform standardisation. Thus the reader will see a few texts given in the original script (e.g. Devanagari or Kaithi), with transliteration and translation. Most commonly, data is given in transliteration at the outset. For practical reasons different transliteration conventions have arisen and remain in use in reporting on Indian languages. The reader will see some chapters using the Orientalist/Indological orthography and others departing from it for practical purposes (avoiding complex symbols on typewriters of old and using capital letters for certain retroflex consonants or doubling of vowel symbol for length) or for phonetic fine-tuning. Most writers stick to one set of conventions while acknowledging the others. Sometimes a mixed set of symbols is used, as in the more readable Orientalist symbols for spellings and IPA (International Phonetic Alphabet) for fine-tuning of phonetics. For the reader's convenience the main correspondences are provided in a separate list in the book's prelims.

There is one other matter of variation in the presentation of data that involves code-switching. Here too we have given individual authors licence to use the conventions of their choosing (bold, italic, roman, underlining) for different languages, with the proviso that they provide a key in the relevant section.

Conclusion

We conclude with a wish-list of sociolinguistic topics we would like to have covered but must leave for future research and researchers. The language practices among internally displaced populations in India, both in borderland contexts and marginal, inaccessible settings, are under-researched. Policy-making in the country (e.g. the emphasis in the New Education Policy (2020) on school education in the mother tongue/local language/regional language) will be better informed if such research is taken up in the future. The most striking part of the contemporary diaspora is the very large proportions of Indian workers in the Gulf States. Some work on the learning of Arabic has been cited above; but we would like to see more work on the Indian languages themselves in these territories. What is this strand of socio-historical experience and contact with colloquial Arabic adding to the lexicon of modern Indian languages of migrants and their families back home? A further and related topic concerns the experiences of the fourth diaspora – to what extent are people with global mindsets in the business and computer worlds able to maintain Indian languages in diasporas, especially with the expectation of regular travel back to India and cultural maintenance for their children? We sometimes hear of the possibility of new hubs being formed via the economic and electronic possibilities for some Indian languages in the USA. While the intentions and optimism are to be supported, previous diasporic research suggests that adjustments to new livelihoods and social networks in diasporas are a counter-influence that optimists must face. Other topics awaiting future research include the phenomenon of the double diaspora (but see the case of onward migration among Sri Lankan Tamils resulting in a hybrid diasporic repertoire, reported in Chapter 5 in this volume). A large number of Indians have migrated from India to a British colony and thence on an individual basis to another part of what used to be a 'dominion' territory. Thus there are Indo-Caribbeans in Canada and the USA; Indo-Fijians in Australia and New Zealand; Indo-South Africans in Australia, New Zealand, Canada and the USA, and so forth. Issues of sociolinguistic identity and accommodation become interesting when interacting with first and subsequent generations of migrants from India. We trust that the diversity of research presented in this volume will stimulate such new research in the future.

References

Agnihotri, R. K. 1979. *Processes of Assimilation: A Sociolinguistic Study of Sikh Children in Leeds.* D. Phil thesis, York University, UK.

Agnihotri, R. K. 2006. Identity and multilinguality: The case of India. In Amy B. M. Tsui and James, W. Tollefson (eds), *Language Policy, Culture, and Identity in Asian Contexts.* New Jersey: Lawrence Erlbaum Associates, pp. 185–204.

Agnihotri, R. K. 2009. Multilinguality and a new world order. In A. K. Mohanty, M. Panda, R. Phillipson and T. SkutnabbKangas (eds), *Multilingual Education for Social Justice: Globalizing the Local.* New Delhi: Orient BlackSwan, pp. 268–77.

Almoaily, Mohammad. 2014. Variation in Gulf Pidgin Arabic. In Isabel Buchstaller, Anders Holmberg and Mohammad Almoaily (eds), *Pidgins and Creoles Beyond Africa-Europe Encounters.* Amsterdam: Benjamins.

Brown, Judith. 2006. *Global South Asians: Introducing the Modern Diaspora.* Cambridge: Cambridge University Press.

Canagarajah, Suresh (ed.). 2017. *The Routledge Handbook of Migration and Language.* New York: Routledge.

Cohen, Robin. 1997. *Global Diasporas – An Introduction.* London: Routledge.

Coupland, N. 2011. Voice, place and genre in popular song performance. *Journal of Sociolinguistics*, 15 (5): 573–602.

Desai, Kiran. 2006. *The Inheritance of Loss.* New York: Grove Press.

Fisher, Michael, Shompa Lahiri and Shinder Thandi. 2007. *A South-Asian History of Britain: Four Centuries of Peoples from the Indian Sub-Continent.* Oxford: Greenwood World Publishing.

Gambhir, S. 1981. *The East Indian Speech Community in Guyana: A Sociolinguistic Study with Special Reference to Koine Formation.* Doctoral dissertation in Linguistics, University of Pennsylvania.

Ghatage, Amrit M. 1967. *Cochin: A survey of Marathi Dialects.* Bombay: The Maharashtra State Board for Literature and Culture.

Ghatage, Amrit M. 1970. *Marathi of Kasargod.* Bombay: The Maharashtra State Board for Literature and Culture.

Govender, Jayanathan. 2022. Indian problem, Indian menace, Indian ubiquity: Indian South Africans at the intersections. In Shanta Balgobind Singh (ed.), *Indians in South Africa: Perspectives from 1860 to the 21st Century.* Pietermaritzburg: AASBS (Alternation African Scholarship Book Series), Vol. 11, pp. 145–71.

Gumperz, John J. and Robert Wilson. 1971. Convergence and creolization: A case from the Indo-Aryan/Dravidian border in India. In A. S. Dil (ed.), *Language in Social Groups, Essays by John J. Gumperz.* Stanford, CA: Stanford University Press, pp. 251–73.

Hajratwala, Minal. 2009. *Leaving India: My Family's Journey from Five Villages to Five Continents.* Boston, MA: Houghton Mifflin Harcourt.

Horgevorst, Tom. 2015. Lexical influence from North India to Maritime Southeast Asia: Some new directions. *Man In India*, 95 (4): 293–334.

Hundt, Marianne. 2014. Zero articles in Indian Englishes: A study of primary and secondary diaspora situations. In Marianne Hundt and Devyani Sharma (eds), *English in the Indian Diaspora*. Amsterdam: Benjamins, pp. 131–70.

Hundt, Marianne and Devyani Sharma (eds). 2014. *English in the Indian Diaspora*. Amsterdam: Benjamin.

Iyengar, Arvind and Sundri Parchani. 2021. Like community, like language: Seventy-five years of Sindhi in post-partition India. *Journal of Sindhi Studies*: 1–32.

Khubhchandani, Lachman. 1983. *Plural Languages, Plural Cultures: Communication, Identity and Socio-political Change in Contemporary India*. Honolulu: University of Hawaii Press.

Khubhchandani, Lachman. 1988. *Language in a Plural Society*. Delhi: Motilal Banarasidass and Shimla IIAS.

Kondapi, C. 1951. *Indians Overseas 1838–1949*. Oxford: Indian Council of World Affairs.

Lal, Brij, Peter Reeves and Rajesh Rai. 2006. *Encyclopedia of the Indian Diaspora*. Singapore: Editions Didier Millet.

Mawani, Sharmina and Anjoom Mukadam (eds). 2104. *Globalisation, Diaspora and Belonging: Exploring Transnationalism and Gujarati Identity*. Jaipur: Rawat Publications.

Mesthrie, Rajend. 1992. *English in Language Shift: The History, Structure and Sociolinguistics of South African Indian English*. Cambridge: Cambridge University Press.

Mesthrie, Rajend. 2007. The origins of colloquial South African Tamil. *Oriental Anthropologist*, 7 (1): 17–38.

Mesthrie, Rajend. 2008. South Asian languages in the second diaspora. In Braj Kachru, Yamuna Kachru and S. N. Sridhar (eds), *Language in South Asia*. Cambridge: Cambridge University Press, pp. 497–514.

Mesthrie, Rajend. 2021. Contacts and contexts: Varying diasporic interactions and koineisation outcomes for Indian languages in South Africa. *Journal of Sociolinguistics*, 25 (5): 703–19.

Mesthrie, Rajend. Forthcoming. Indian South African English. In Raymond Hickey (ed.), *The Cambridge History of the English Language*. Vol. 6.

Moag, Rodney F. 2003. Language loss versus language maintenance in overseas Indian communities. In R. Sharma and E. Annamalai (eds), *Indian Diaspora in Search of Identity*. Mysore: Central Institute of Indian Languages, pp. 1–39.

Mohanty, Ajit. 2010. Languages, inequality and marginalization: Implications of the double divide in Indian multilingualism. *International Journal of the Sociology of Language*: 131–54.

Mukherjee, Aditi. 1996. *Language Maintenance and Shift: Punjabis and Bengalis in Delhi*. New Delhi: Bahri.

Murugaiyan, A. 2019. *Langues de l'Inde en Diasporas*. Paris: Scitep Editions.

Oonk, Gijsbert (ed.). 2007. *Global Indian Diasporas: Exploring Trajectories of Migration and Theory*. Amsterdam: Amsterdam University Press.

Pandit, Prabodh. 1972. *India as a Sociolinguistic Area*. Poona: University of Poona.

Parekh, Bhikhu. 2001. *Integrating Minorities*. London: Institute of Contemporary Arts.

Prabhakaran, Varijakshi. 1996. Sociolinguistic analysis of South African Telugu: History and structure. *South African Journal of Linguistics*, 14 (4): 118–27.

Rajyashree, K. S. 1986. *An Ethnolinguistic Survey of Dharavi, a Slum in Bombay*. Mysore: CIIL.

Sachdeva, Rajesh. 1981. *A Study of the Punjabi-Hindi Bilinguals*. Pune: Poona University.

Satyanath, T. S. 1982. *Kannadigas in Delhi: A Sociolinguistic Study*. Unpublished doctoral dissertation. Delhi: University of Delhi.

Smart, J. R. 1990. Pidginization in Gulf Arabic: A first report. *Anthropological Linguistics*, 32 (1/2): 83–119.

Vertovec, Steve. 2000. *The Hindu Diaspora: Comparative Patterns*. London: Routledge.

CHAPTER 1

Resistance and Reconciliation: Language and Identity Construction among the Internally Displaced Bhils in the Narmada Valley

Sonal Kulkarni-Joshi

1. Introduction

This chapter presents a sociolinguistic account of the early history of displacement and resettlement of the Bhils, a conglomeration of tribal communities in the Narmada Valley in west-central India. The chapter draws on a study which was designed to assess the impact of internal displacement on language and cultural practices of the displaced population following the construction of dams across the Narmada River in central India in the 1990s.[1] Displacement and resettlement lead to disintegration of community structure, social and kinship networks, as well as adaptation in terms of social identity, all of which have linguistic consequences. The migration of the Bhils out of the villages in the forests in the Satpuda mountains to the plains at the foothills of the Satpuda in central India (in the Nandurbar district in the state of Maharashtra) is about thirty years old today.

Within studies of migration, displacement is a fairly recently recognised phenomenon, where people flee from their local environment to another location inside their own country, rather than to another country as refugees (Heugh 2017). India has one of the highest rates of development-induced displacements in the world and dam building is one of the main contributors to such displacement (Negi and Ganguly 2011). Although tribals constitute only 8 per cent of the Indian population, about 40 per cent of persons affected by development-related activities are tribals. The construction of dams in post-Independence India has led to forced eviction of people, especially tribals. Arguably one of the most controversial development projects in the world, the Narmada Valley Development Project led to the displacement of about 4,300 families from thirty-three villages, out of villages in the Satpuda hills and relocation in the plains of Nandurbar district in north-west Maharashtra. (The Sardar Sarovar Project (SSP) affected families in the states of Gujarat and Madhya Pradesh too; the specific sociolinguistic fallout of these migrations is not discussed in the present chapter.) While the economic and socio-political impact of the SSP on the afterlife of the displaced people is fairly well-documented (e.g. Baviskar 2004, Dhagamwar 2006, Whitehead 2010 and Thakur 2014), its linguistic consequences have not received academic attention. The present chapter will draw on fieldwork in

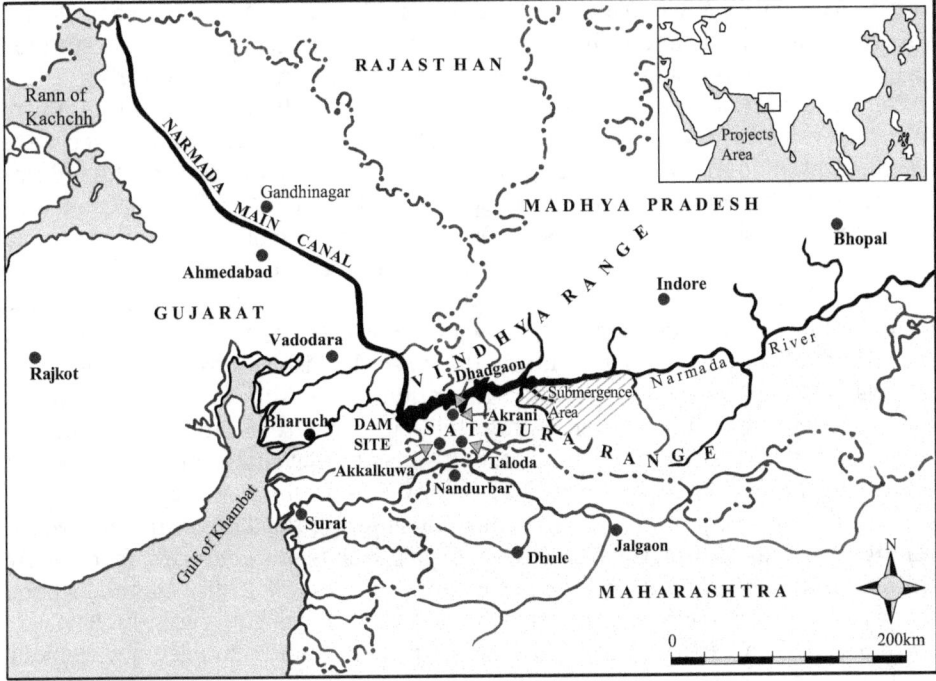

Map 1.1 *The Sardar Sarovar Project and its surrounding areas*

partially submerged and resettled villages in Nandurbar district, written records as well as oral archives to understand the relationship between internal displacement and language practices among the affected communities. Our focus will be on assessing the social semiotic resources used by the Bhil community to index their existence before and after the displacement.

2. The social-historical background

Khandesh in central India

The research sites included in this study are situated in the westernmost district on the northern border of Maharashtra State, Nandurbar. It is bounded on the west and the north by Gujarat State; on the north-east and north by the state of Madhya Pradesh and to the south and south-east by the district of Dhule. (Dhule and Nandurbar constituted East Khandesh, a part of the Bombay Presidency in British colonial India.) The region is flanked by two rivers – the Narmada to the north and the Tapi to the south. Both rivers drain into the Arabian Sea on the western coast. The northern frontier of this region is bounded by the Satpuda mountain range. (We shall see in section 4 that these aspects of the Khandesh topography are culturally salient and find an important place in the folklore of the region.)

The region is predominantly tribal (the Indian term being *adivasi* = 'original inhabitant'). Today the term 'Bhil' is used to refer to a conglomerate of tribal communities –

Barda, Dangchi, Dhanka, Dhorepi, Gavit, Khotil, Mathvadi, Mavchi, Nahal, Pavra, Vasava, Bhilala, Nirdhi and Tadvi. (See Mohanty, Kulkarni-Joshi and Hasnain 2013 for an overview of literary sources to address the question, 'Who are the Bhils?')

The various tribal groups are speakers of a variety of Bhili dialects (around fifty of them) which form a continuum (Phillips 2012). Contemporary Bhili dialects are classified as Indo-Aryan (belonging to the Rajasthani-Gujarati-Marathi-Khandeshi continuum), though the presence of speakers of Austro-Asiatic languages and Dravidian language(s) in prehistoric times is postulated by a number of scholars (see Southworth 2005, Mohanty, Kulkarni-Joshi and Hasnain 2013).

This study focuses on examining the effect of the forced migration of the Bhils from their natural habitat in the Satpura mountains to the plains in the Khandesh in the last decade of the twentieth century. However, the historical record reveals that this was neither the community's first migration nor was it the Bhil community's first experience of confrontation with hegemonic powers. In fact, the community has been in a constant state of flight at least since the eleventh century. The region has been taken over and dominated by several rulers who have kept the Bhils in a state of flight; beginning with the Mughals entering the Deccan in the twelfth century, the Rajputs from Gujarat in the fifteenth to sixteenth centuries, followed by the onslaught of the Marathas in the eighteenth century, the British colonial rulers, moneylenders, forest officers, land surveyors and the police until recently (Baviskar 2004: 54–65). The particular social history of the community moulded a 'rebellious consciousness' among the Bhils (ibid.).

The SSP (Sardar Sarovar Project), which resulted in the displacement of the tribal communities in Nandurbar, was a part of the NVP (Narmada Valley Project), the single largest river valley project in India (Baviskar 2004: 199). Thirty dams were proposed in the NVP in order to provide drinking water, irrigation and electricity in

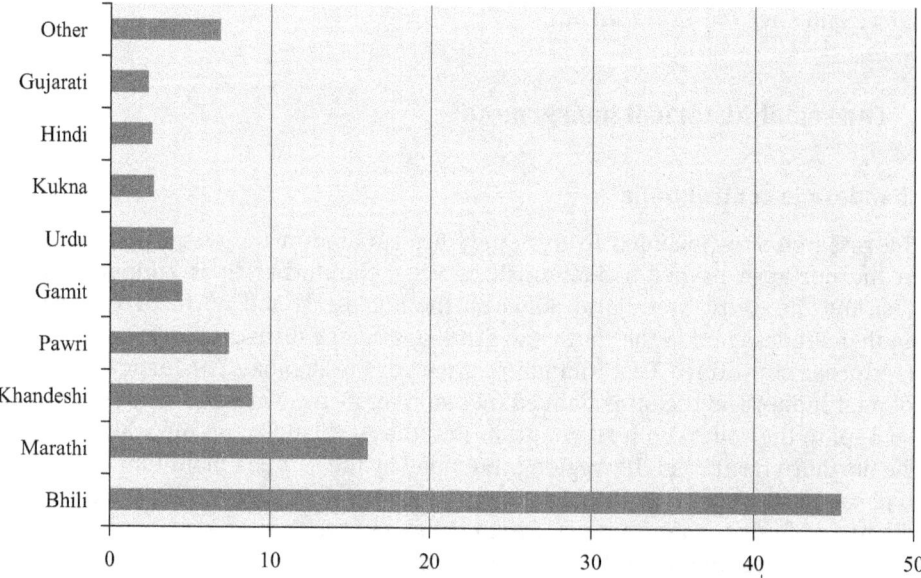

Figure 1.1 *Languages spoken in Nandurbar district (based on Census of India 2011)*

the region. In terms of extent of area submerged and families displaced, the SSP was the second-largest construction within the NVP. Thirty-three villages in Nandurbar district were partially or fully submerged due to the construction of the SSP. Even after a tenacious long-drawn out resistance by the affected villages under the leadership of the Narmada Bachao Andolan (NBA, Save Narmada Movement, led by the activist Medha Patkar), the government did not relent and the height of the dam walls was increased. Eventually the villagers were compelled to accept compensation offered by the government and to move from *muḷgav* (original villages) in the Satpuda to *punərvəsən* (resettlement) in the plains around the town of Taloda. As we shall see in section 6 of this chapter, both *muḷgav* and *punərvəsən* refer not only to spaces in markedly different physical ecologies, but also to constructs created out of the shared experiences of the affected persons/families.

The impact of the displacement on the social, cultural and linguistic practices of the Bhils can be gauged only with an understanding of the difference between the 'old world' and the 'new world' (Kulkarni-Joshi, Hasnain and Mohanty 2015 for details.) The *muḷgav* (original village) of the Bhils were sparsely populated *paḍas* (hamlets) on mountain slopes. Each *paḍa* was an extended clan or kinship network. The forests in the Satpuda mountains and the Narmada River had fulfilled the Bhils' daily needs. Sustenance-based shift and slash farming was practised in the mountain villages. Clan members assisted each other in farming activities in exchange for a meal of *kukḍu* (chicken) and *huru* (wine prepared from *mahua* flowers). The Bhils rarely felt the need for money transactions. Farm produce was usually bartered for salt, matches, etc. At times grain from the farm or *tendul* leaves from the forest were sold in the market in the neighbouring towns (Kavat in Gujarat or Dhadgaon in Nandurbar). The little cash that they earned in the market was used occasionally to buy clothes or oil from the village *Bhoi* (caste of petty traders). In times of illness, help was sought from the village *buḍva* (wise-man or god-man) who was well versed in the medicinal uses of plants growing on the Satpuda mountain. If the soil quality deteriorated or if the family was looking for a change, they shifted their home made of bamboo to another location on the mountain. The home language was adequate to fulfil all communicative needs in the *muḷgav*. There is no evidence of a prestigious language or a link language among the various Bhil tribes or among the Bhils and non-tribals in the *muḷgav*. Most villagers reported that they heard about the construction of a dam across the Narmada and the possibility of their displacement only after the activists started arriving in the village.

Twenty years on, the resettled families talk about their painful realisation that their resistance to government diktats had come to nought. Each family shared vivid memories of how the entire *paḍa* wept on a day in the mid-1990s when they uprooted and stacked their bamboo homes along with their animals and other belongings in trucks organised by government officials and left for an uncertain future in an unfamiliar region. Most SSP-affected villages along the Narmada were vacated between 1991 and 1998. The resettlement villages were created by clearing about 4,000 hectares of forest land in the plains of Nandurbar (Taloda and Shahada tehsils). Each resettled village or *punərvəsən* houses families of several submerged villages (*paḍas*). The housing pattern in the resettled villages differs from that in the original villages. While the houses in the old villages were few and scattered on the mountains, the houses in the resettled villages in the plains are very closely packed.

Such a close-knit residential pattern has facilitated maintenance of the original home language (cf. section 5). Many resettled villages are provided with infrastructure and facilities, which is uncommon for a developmental project. The facilities included residential schools, a fair-price shop and a Primary Health Care Centre. The elders in the resettled villages, however, talked of the hardship they faced in the new world: the farming techniques they used in the mountains were not useful in the plains and they had to learn new farming practices suited to the plains; old crops were given up and new crops had to be cultivated. They were particularly unhappy that water and electricity had to be paid for and that they had to buy salted fish – since they no longer had easy access to fresh fish in the Narmada or to the berries and other produce of the forest in the Satpuda. (See the personal narration in section 4 which alludes to the Narmada river as mother and Satpuda mountain as father.)

3. The research sites and data collection

Data for the present study were collected in three resettled villages in Taloda tehsil as well as in the partially submerged villages of origin in Akrani and Akkalkuwa tehsils[2] in Nandurbar district. (See Map 1.1.)

The resettled villages

The resettled villages sampled for the study included one predominantly Bhil and one predominantly Pawra village (Narmadanagar and Rewanagar respectively) and a third, Bhil-Pawra mixed village, Rozwa.

Narmadanagar
Narmadanagar village is in Taloda *taluka* of Nandurbar district. It was the first resettlement in the year 1990–1 (hence also referred to as *Punarvasan* – 1 or Resettlement No. – 1). The total population of the village is 3,353 and the total number of households is 578 (Census of India 2011). The Bhils in Narmadanagar speak various Bhili dialects (e.g. Noiri, Bariwti, Dehwali). Of these, the Noiri variety is spoken by a majority. The villagers also speak Dehwali which is the language spoken by Bhils in the neighbouring host villages. Farming is the main occupation of the villagers.

Rewanagar
This is a predominantly Pawra village (resettlement number 3). It is also probably better-developed among the resettled villages. Agriculture is the main local occupation; modern methods of cultivation are used by farmers. Farming is practised by the

Table 1.1 *Villages sampled for the present study in the Narmada area*

S. No.	Resettled villages	Tehsil	Year of settlement	Resettled communities
1	Narmadanagar	Taloda	1990–1	Bhil
2	Rewanagar	Taloda	1992–4	Pawra
3	Rozwa	Taloda	1994–5	Bhil + Pawra

Source: The local primary health centre in each village.

Table 1.2 *Host villages surrounding Narmadanagar*

Direction	Villages	Home language of the villagers
East	Rajveer	Dehwali
West	Sora	Dehwali
North	Waaleri	Dehwali
South	Chhota Somawal	Dehwali

villagers not only to cultivate their own food but also as a source of income: excess produce is sold in the local market. Cash crops including sunflowers are cultivated locally. The total population of the village is 3,211. The village is divided into six *paḍas* (colonies, each corresponding to a village of origin): Warwali paḍa, Keni paḍa, Sadri paḍa, Patil paḍa, Uddya paḍa, and Bharai paḍa. Pawri is the dominant language of interaction in the village.

Table 1.3 *Host villages surrounding Rewanagar*

Direction	Villages	Home language of the villagers
East	Rozwa	Pawri
West	Amoni	Bhili
North	Chaugaue	Bhili
South	Dohrbir	Pawri and Bhili

Rozwa

The total population of Rozwa according to the 2001 Census was 1,838 and 2,900 in 2013. The village was resettled in 1994–5. About 75 per cent of the Rozwa population is Pawra and 25 per cent is Bhil. Unlike Narmadanagar and Rewanagar, Rozwa is divided into seven *paḍas*. We observed that marriages between Bhils and Pawras in this village were common. There were two Bhoi families in the village at the time of data collection. Unlike the resettled Rozwa, the demography of old Rozwa (which is the host village in the vicinity in which the new Rozwa village has been resettled) is predominantly Bhil; the Pawra population of the old village was negligible. Villagers reported that the Sarpanch and Police Patil (administrative officers) of Rozwa were almost always from the local Pawra community. The village has both a Primary Health Care Centre and a school.

Table 1.4 *Villages surrounding Rozwa*

Direction	Village	Resettled/original village	Home languages of the villagers
East	Gopalpur	Resettled village	Pawra and Bhili
West	Rewanagar	Resettled village	Pawra
North	Kothar	Original village	Bhili
South	Old Rozwa	Original village	Bhili

Selection of original villages

Our fieldwork in the resettled villages, Narmadanagar and Rewanagar, determined our choice of the original villages. Since we had collected data from inhabitants of the Patil *pada* in Rewanagar, we selected the original villages of these Pawra respondents viz. Uddya, Bhusha and Khardipada in Akrani tehsil along the backwaters of the Narmada. Similarly, the Bhils interviewed in Narmadanagar originally came from the villages of Danel and Mandhwa in Akkalkuwa tehsil. The original villages were located along the Narmada backwaters in the Satpuda mountains. The project team, including the author, travelled from the town of Taloda first in a shared jeep, then by boat and then on foot to reach the scattered households in the original villages on the mountain. The project team stayed with families in the partially submerged villages; observation of village life and interactions among the villagers was possible during these short stays.

Table 1.5 *Resettled and original villages in the project sample*

Resettled village	Villages of origin
Narmadanagar	Danel, Mandhwa
Rewanagar	Uddya, Bhusha, Khardipada
Rozwa	Sikka

Research tools and data collection

Data were elicited using a sociolinguistic questionnaire, a word list of approximately 1,200 words (arranged into semantic fields such as body parts, kinship terms, numerals, names of seasons, months, colours, plants, crops, fruit, birds, animals, clothing, topography, etc.) and a list of basic sentence structures. In addition to these, folk songs, descriptions of wedding rituals and festivities were recorded. Daily village activities, practices and cultural artefacts were recorded during the project team's stay in the villages and in Taloda over six field trips. These included farming equipment, storage of farm produce, cooking practices, cooking utensils, healing practices, clothing, dressing habits, brewing *mahua* liquor at home, socialisation practices, entertaining relatives and strangers in the home, gatherings of neighbours and friends in the evenings, public gatherings, interactions with social activists, interactions among students, interactions between students and teachers in the school, interactions in the market, etc.).

4. Data analysis

An attempt will be made here to understand the forced displacement of the Bhils in terms of continuities and discontinuities in the community's linguistic and social practices. These practices are closely interwoven with the belief system and the epistemology of the Bhils. We will begin by examining selected examples of folklore and personal narrations of displacement to illustrate the 'meaning making processes' employed by members of the community to come to terms with the process of displacement itself and life in the resettled world.

Religious practice, nature and the oral tradition of the Bhils

The oral tradition of the tribals in Khandesh is closely intertwined with religious practice and their belief system draws on the rural, pastoral lifeworld. The tribal gods include *Waghdeo* ('tiger god' or the god of animals), *Nandkho* (god of grains), *Hirkulya* (god of agriculture), *Malyadev* (god of vegetables), *Govaldev* (god of cowherds), etc. Most revered of all is the goddess *Devmogra* (*Yahamogi*). Waghdeo continues to be worshipped at the entrance to the resettled village while the worship of *Indal* (Lord Indra, a deity) begins on the farm, proceeds through the home and culminates in the flowing river. The place of worship was outside the house, at the village entrance in the old villages. By contrast, a separate 'god-house' or place of worship is commonly observed inside the house in resettled villages. The tribal deities (photographs of Mother Mogi, Raja Pantha, etc.) share this space with mainstream Hindu gods like Shankar and Ganesh.

Indal remains a very important religious festivity in the new world. Three young, unmarried men accompanied by drummers walk to the family farm a week before Indal worship to 'tell' the *komba* tree in the farm by tying three of its branches together that these will be cut the following week to be offered in worship. Traditionally *huru* brewed from *mahua* flowers is offered along with grain to Indal. *Mahua* wine is also consumed as a part of the celebrations. But *mahua* trees do not grow in large numbers in the resettlement area. A small bottle of *mahua* wine is brought from one of the old villages and mixed with beer; this concoction is used both for worship and consumption. But our collaborators in the resettlement told us in dismay that, after worshipping Indal, they were compelled to disperse their offerings in the stagnant pond outside the village as there was no flowing body of water close by.

Worship of a tribal god includes narrating stories related to the god. Various kinds of stories are narrated by different narrators: the *pujari, bhagat, goywale, roḍali* and *maṇḍvi*. The storytelling and singing to the accompaniment of *ḍhol* (drums) in a gathering of villagers after sunset was a regular activity in the old village. In contrast to the old villages, we noted a dearth of storytellers and a decline in storytelling as a practice in the resettled villages. Our collaborators suggested the following reasons: fishing had been replaced by agriculture as the primary means of livelihood and long hours had to be spent by all family members on the farm. Further, television and recorded programmes on mobile phones were preferred by the younger members of the family.

Singing and dance, however, have remained important cultural practices. Wedding songs and farming songs were recorded by the project team in the old villages. *Songaḍja parṭi* which involves song, dance and humour is a form of entertainment presented by groups of artists in the plains in the Dehwali speech variety and is enjoyed by all tribals in the region. (Video recordings of such events are watched on the mobile phone even in the old villages. Thus, the speech variety of the plains is understood even by the *məthwaḍe* (mountain dwellers) – an instance of reverse migration of a speech variety mediated by technology.)

A number of resettled collaborators reported that impromptu protest songs were sung to the tunes of traditional songs in protest marches in the valley or outside government offices in Taloda/Mumbai/Delhi during the resistance. The author recorded the following song sung in an informal gathering of collaborators in Taloda in 2012. The song was composed by the tribal activist, Jhilabai Vasave who was then aged about eighty-eight years. (The song is in the Dehwali variety of Bhili.)

    khube pawəra hɛ ma pawu
    khube pawəra hɛ
    amu mortsawala ra pawu
    amu dilli bombe dzai:ne
    kaydo pas keyo
    khube pawəra hɛ

[Free translation: 'O brothers, we are very strong (powerful); we lead protest marches to Delhi and to Mumbai [centres of political power] and get laws passed [in favour of the evicted tribals]. We are very powerful.']

The other local participants in our gathering joined in, singing a song they were familiar with. While singing protest songs before meetings on environmental and other social issues is a common practice, the role of such music went beyond simply mobilising people for the Save Narmada Movement; it bound people with a sense of a common loss, hope and solidarity. Even today the songs are sung and are accompanied by reminiscences from the village elders of the long resistance. 'Very simply this music tells the story of a community' (Rathore 2021).

Bhil epistemology, cosmology and language practice

The resettled Bhils and Pawaras (especially the younger community members) assert a shared identity – *adivasi* (which refers both to their tribal status and tribal language). The common 'tribal consciousness' fits well with a story of common origin of the Bhils and Pawras collected by the author in the resettled village of Rewanagar from a Pawra (male, aged about seventy; see Naik (1956) for similar and other stories of origin). The region was struck by a deluge. When the water started receding, Dedla and Dedli, Harijan (downtrodden or a member of an untouchable caste) brother and sister, moved to Pavagad (in Gujarat state). Various peoples originated from their secretions: Gujars (a nomadic community) from their phlegm, Mahars (a downtrodden caste) from their urine and faeces, and both Bhils and Pawras from their tears. This 'origin myth' underscores the brotherhood of the Bhils and Pawras in the region. The slogan *amu akha ek he* ('We are all united') which charged the anti-dam movement in the Narmada Valley is heard in political rallies, public gatherings and in schools even today.

    The Narmada and the Satpuda (mountain) as well as the Tapi (river) and *ɖuɖa dərya* (Arabian sea) indexed the villagers' existence in the old world. They feature in a number of folk stories we received in the old villages. We received the narration below in the Noiri variety of Bhili in Danel from a speaker of the Vasava community. The two rivers, Narmada and Tapi, which mark the northern and southern limits respectively of the tribal territory in Nandurbar are portrayed as sisters vying with each other to reach their beloved, *ɖuɖa dərya*. The story alludes to the quiet flow of the mighty Narmada in this region and contrasts it with the gushing Tapi.

Narration 1:

Noiri	Free English Translation
1 tapi an nərməda i: benu bohini hautya	Tapi and Narmada are sisters.
2 benu bohīha aridz niklina ugtal dekhiya budtal dzatinya	Both sisters go from the east to the west.
3 dzatinya tehnam tiya ki ṭhərʋino ki səmudran dzai:nha milhu: tenhamaye bhago bhago dʒahu bhago bhago dʒahu məndʒe khədko aʋe sad aʋe dəgdə aʋe ṭaltya dʒahu	They decide that they will not disturb anyone on their way to the (Arabian) sea. They decide to avoid the stones and pebbles on the way as they run (towards the Arabian sea).
4 palhne dzata dzata kay huyo ki tapi dze huye te sadbid dəgəd bado dʒi huye harkidʒ ti goini	But in reality, Tapi does not spare a single stone or pebble in her path. She carries all of them with her as she rushes in a hurry to win the race.
5 an nərməda huye ti khədko sad ṭalti ṭalti goi:ni	As for Narmada, she took care to avoid the stones in her path.

(This narration was recorded by the author in the Noiri speech variety in the original village, Danel in December 2013.)

Naming practices too reveal the community's close relation with its natural ecology. Children born before migration were named in various ways: (a) after the day on which the child was born (e.g. *Somya* – child born on a Monday), (b) after mountains (e.g. *Doŋgrja*), (c) after natural phenomena (e.g. *Dəgdja* 'stone'), (d) after holy periods – e.g. *Dəsrja* (child born during Dasara) or *Holya* (child born during Holi), etc. Children born after the resettlement were given more mainstream names: e.g. *Dilip, Keshav*, etc.

Conceptualisation of the old world was hinged on two salient aspects of the local topography – the Narmada River and the Satpuda mountain. Narmada was mother and Satpuda was father to their tribal children. In spite of the villagers' long struggle and obstinate refusal to leave their homes in the original villages, the height of the walls of the dam was increased and the waters of the Narmada flooded their homes. The first of two narrations of the lived experience cited below recounts the villagers' response to the predicament of losing the homestead.

Narration 2:

Sl. No.	Narrative clause
1	Actually people consider Narmada like a Devi (= goddess).
2	Because to pray to Narmada or to merely see her ...
3	... people from across the country come opposite (sic) our village to Jalsindhi
4	Or come opposite Jalsindhi where we worship Akhada
5	Ranikajal who is our Devi and her full name (sic) we recited sitting in the Akhada
6	... and the Akhada is located on the sands of the Narmada
7	Beloved to be such a holy/pure Narmada River ...
8	... and we who live on her banks, feel in a way that we are Narmada's sons, children

9	When the waters of the Narmada came to my house, the Sardar Sarovar (Dam) waters, ...
10	... at that time I literally performed *pooja* (of Narmada)
11	This is because such a far off River ... to reach the River it took us at least 45 minutes, climbing down.
12	The River came to my house today and that is why I performed her pooja.
13	In a way we had the feeling of a mother towards the River. I cannot describe her at all.
14	Today too I am at a place like Vadchil (resettlement village)
15	Because all the pictures that I have seen before my eyes, I can see those pictures today.
16	... (i)t seems as if I have seen a dream ... but what do we do?
17	Finally the government made us helpless/compelled us to live a life like this.
18	We fought for 20–33 years to live there, to stay there.
19	It is not as if we did not receive anything after having fought.
20	Whatever we received we got because of our struggle/battle.
21	Had we not struggled, we would not have received that also. But we had to do all this to save the River.
22	Water remained in my house for nearly eight days.
23	The whole house drowned but: 'Narmada, now you are to drown my house' ...
24	I did not say that but performed her *Pooja* and broke a coconut.
25	And we remained in that water for eight days.
26	That is Narmada! Who can describe Narmada? It is difficult to do that.

(*Source*: https://oralhistorynarmada.in/impact-of-submergence-and-displacement/kevalsi ngh-vasave-short-clip/. Narrator: Kevalsingh Vasave, Nimghavan, Nandurbar.)

This poignant narration is the shared experience of an entire community; the community had worshipped Narmada when she had blessed them from a distance like a benevolent goddess. For more than twenty years they had resisted government authorities in order to save their mother and their home. Even when she entered the village and threatened to engulf her children's homes, far from feeling angered or betrayed by the mother's malevolent behaviour, the children felt overwhelmed by her holy presence in their homes and they worshipped her by breaking a coconut.

But this affinal relation was soon transformed. In the narration below the speaker describes how the benevolent Narmada was choked by the construction of the dam. The giver of life and sustenance is now portrayed as a 'bloated carcass'.

Narration 3:

Sl. No. **Narrative clause**
1	I sold 13 goats and a bullock to buy a buffalo.
2	It went to the river to drink water and got stuck ...
3	... in the silt and dies. I lost a cow also ...
4	... in this way. She had a calf ...
5	... in her stomach. That too died.
6	We had sixty goats and only four to five now remain.

7	Crocodiles caught and ate the rest. We had not seen anything like this before, nothing at all.
8	The River was flowing freely; animals were happy and so were the people.
9	Now we go to the River to bathe in fear. We have to constantly keep track of our children.
10	Our farms have been submerged. We used to get vegetables and tubers from the forests.
11	The forest is our father and we call the River our mother.
12	We settled here by clearing the forests, praying …
13	… to the Gods and taming the tigers and bears.
14	Why has the government lied to us in such a big way? Is this not a lie?
15	The River has been choked (damned); a noose has been tied around her neck (with the dam) …
16	… and so it has bloated like a carcass.
17	It used to flow so freely earlier. Who will see that?
18	You choked her. Where will she go? How many things were in her belly? And what all died!
19	Now the river is dead and along with it we are also dying.

(*Source:* https://oralhistorynarmada.in/impact-of-submergence-and-displacement/pervi-short-clip/. Narrator: Pervi, Jalsindhi, Madhya Pradesh.)

In this narrative too, far from portraying Narmada as the inflictor of suffering, the river and her children are portrayed as victims of an act of the government. The construction of the dam itself is presented as 'choking' the mother by 'tying a noose' around her neck. This act of violence transformed the free-flowing river which had nourished life along her banks into a body of stagnated water infested with life-taking animals. The affected villagers are portrayed as disoriented, fearful orphans.

5. Language maintenance and language shift: the emergence of link languages in the new world

Here we pick up a more direct examination of the migrants' linguistic repertoire in relation to the changed circumstances in the new, resettled world. The resettled tribals are referred to locally as the *mathwaḍe* ('those from the mountain top') while the tribals who lived in the plains before the resettlement began are referred to as the *dehwale* (< *deṣwale* 'belonging to the plain region'). The Bhil and Pawra communities in the villages of origin were predominantly monolingual (in Noiri and Pawri respectively). Our collaborators reported that a few village elders spoke some Gujarati or Hindi if they had contacts in Gujarat or in Madhya Pradesh. Narrations of personal reminiscences revealed that the villagers had come in contact with a host of outsiders before they migrated out of the Satpuda: (a) Hindi-speaking pilgrims from neighbouring Madhya Pradesh who stayed for a few days with host families in the villages before continuing the *Narmada parikrama*; (b) Hindi-speaking forest officers; (c) Marathi-speaking police officers deployed by the state government to maintain law and order during the resistance; and (d) Marathi- and Hindi-speaking activists who often spent months in the village and themselves eventually learned enough Pawri to interact with the villagers. Our male collaborators described their interactions as boys with the police officers stationed in the old villages whom they helped to catch crabs or turtles in the river, brought special knives from their homes to clean the crabs with, etc. In the course of these interactions they picked up some Marathi words, but they were often amused that the policemen used similar but unfamiliar words (e.g. Marathi *kasəw* for Pawri *kəʧaj* 'tortoise'). They also came in contact with other *məthwaɖe* who were speakers of other Bhil dialects in the market towns – Dhadgaon in Akrani tehsil or Molgi in Akkalkuwa tehsil in Nandurbar or in Kavat in Gujarat. Pawri was the language of interaction in Dhadgaon and Noiri/Bhilori in Molgi. But there is no evidence for either a tribal link language or for language shift before migration. Although the sending areas in Akrani and Akkalkuwa tehsils were multilingual (in a wide range of varieties of Bhili and Ahirani), the villagers themselves were by and large monolingual. Our collaborators reported that they used their own home variety when they came in contact with tribals belonging to other groups: they understood each other's languages (cf. Watters 2012 for a discussion of mutual intelligibility among the Bhil dialects). When the activists from the cities of Mumbai and Pune first arrived in the original villages in the late 1980s, they met with resistance from the villagers and were asked to leave. Over time the activists (especially Medha Patkar, the leader of the Save Narmada Movement) learned Pawri, which was perceived as being the easier of the Bhil dialects. The speeches were made by the activist leaders in this region using a mix of Pawri and Marathi. This intervention by the activists resulted in the rescaling of Pawri (cf. Blommaert 2007) before the displacement out of the original villages.

As with the inhabitants of the original villages, the first generation of resettled migrants and women remain largely monolingual in the home variety. We noticed a strong maintenance of the home language within the family and within the *paɖa/*village. This was also the language of interaction with the village *sarpanch* and *police patil* (local administrators) who usually belonged to the dominant community in the village. An important factor which facilitates maintenance of the heritage language in the resettled villages is the residential pattern in these villages. Whereas the houses in the original, partially submerged Bhil and Pawra villages were scattered on the mountain sides or arranged in loose clusters, the houses in the resettled village samples for the present study were arranged in tightly knit, rectangular clusters. Each such cluster or *paɖa* in the village consisted of houses belonging to families from a single original village, speaking a single home language.

Ahirani (or Khandeshi, the home language of non-tribals including the Bhoi (trading) community in the plains) is used in interactions with non-tribals while Dehwali and Kotla (spoken by Bhils in the plains) are used in inter-tribal communication in the Taloda – Shahada region. After migration to the resettled villages in the plains, a structurally variable, village-based multilingualism of the original villages was gradually replaced by a wider societal, functional multilingualism. The migrants encountered domains of communication and communicative needs which were unknown before migration – the health care centre, the *aʃrəmʃala* (residential school) which was staffed by Marathi-speaking teachers from different parts of Maharashtra, the large market in Taloda, etc. Children of the first-generation migrants who were sent to local schools formed the first generation from these families to receive formal education (Thakur 2019 mentions a couple of Marathi-educated youth from an earlier time.) The language of instruction in these schools is exclusively Marathi.[3] The teachers in these schools spoke of the need for 'mainstreaming' the migrants' children through the Marathi language. Children were discouraged, even reprimanded, for using home languages in the classroom. Our efforts to coax class eight and class nine students to narrate stories or sing songs in the home language were met with silence. Outside the classroom during playtime or recess, the children interacted with each other mainly in Dehwali; the children also used their home varieties. The high schools are located in the towns of Taloda – Shahada; here the children learned Ahirani as the contact language. Young college-going boys from migrant families in a college in Taloda reported that they used Ahirani as a shared language in the college. The use of Ahirani among young female students in the college in Taloda seemed to be more restrained. Like the monolingual older members of their families, they spoke in their home variety even to interlocutors from a different Bhil community. They confirmed a good understanding of each other's home varieties. Almost without exception, school-educated migrant children and adolescents reported 'Adiwasi' to be their home language; our interaction with the resettled communities revealed that 'Adiwasi' referred to Noiri, Pawri, Dehwali and other speech varieties of the tribal communities individually as well as collectively as an umbrella term. The term excludes the local privileged varieties, Ahirani and Marathi.

The resettled villages are equipped with health care centres but the migrants were wary of being examined by Marathi-speaking health workers who asked questions about internal body organs. These questions caused discomfort to the first-generation migrants, especially women, who preferred to go back to the *buḍwa* in the partially submerged villages of the old world; these wise men would chant prayers in the home language to ward off illness.

Although exposure to the resettled, new world has expanded the speech repertoire of the educated Bhils, proficiency in the languages of opportunity is often limited. The project team met with a large number of graduates and postgraduates, especially in the discipline of social work, from resettled families. Marathi is the language of higher education in the region. We made two observations in these interactions: a low level of fluency in Marathi (which is nevertheless perceived to be the language of opportunity and employment) and a high level of unemployment. In the course of our fieldwork in Narmadanagar over four or five days, for instance, we noticed a large group of about thirty men in their twenties who played cricket in the village from morning until dusk even on weekdays. On making enquiries we were told that these young degree holders found themselves in limbo – they were unable to find jobs that paid at least more than what their fathers paid the farm hands and they were reluctant to help the family in farming activities now that they were so well-educated.

The use of multiple languages was observed in public spaces. Interactions with activists and government officials were mainly in a mix of Dehwali/Pawri and Marathi. The marketplace was the most multilingual domain. The shopkeepers come from the neighbouring states of Rajasthan and Madhya Pradesh too. They speak a mix of Ahirani, Dehwali and Pawri to their customers.

Lexical attrition

We view the lexicon of a language as closely tied with the ecology, culture and social organisation of the community that speaks it. A comparison of semantically organised lists of lexical items between the original and resettled villages led to observations of both continuities and change in socio-cultural practices. While semantic fields such as kinship and body part names showed complete maintenance, other semantic fields such as numerals, colour terms, clothing, food items, etc., revealed the influence of Ahirani/Marathi. For example, the previously used vigesimal numeral system is increasingly being replaced by the decimal system of Marathi. Bamboo was used widely in the original Bhil villages for multiple purposes including construction of houses and household objects including baskets for various kinds of storage. A loss of the lexical terms used to refer to various kinds of bamboo baskets which had distinct functions was noted in the resettled village.

Table 1.6 Words denoting 'types of basket' in original and resettled Bhil villages

	Original village (Danel)	Resettled village (Narmadanagar)
Lexical Item	Gloss	Gloss
ṭupli	Basket	Basket
muṭi	Basket for storing grain	Basket for storing grain
hiku	Basket hung from the roof to stop animals from eating food	Iron rack for storing containers, etc.
otə	Basket for hanging over the kitchen fire to dry grain, etc.	(Was not identified by young Bhils)

The changed soil conditions and cultivation practices in the resettlement have impacted the types of grain cultivated before and after migration. After migration, fishing is no longer an important activity and fresh fish is not a part of the daily diet. Respondents in the resettled village reported that *vərai*, *āŋgri* and *hal* were no longer cultivated; however, because of their contact with the partially submerged original village, they still recognised these lexical items.

6. Conclusion

In this chapter we presented a sociolinguistic description of the tribal community, the Bhils, in west Khandesh who were compelled to leave their villages in the Satpuda mountain for a life of compensation in resettled villages. Our focus was on understanding the social semiotic resources (linguistic and social practices) which indexed their identity in various phases of the displacement. We juxtaposed the structural multilingualism of the old world with the functional multilingualism of the new world and investigated factors which have catalysed such an outcome in the Narmada Valley in central India. Increased geographic mobility has, on the one hand, made the resettled social groups more aware of and reflexive of their language and group identities. On the other hand, the link between the language and the social group has become unstable leading to the enregisterment (cf. Agha 2007) of Pawri, Dehwali, Ahirani and Marathi as link languages. The expansion of the linguistic repertoire in response to communicative contexts in the new world is increasingly leading to a hierarchical marginalisation of the traditional languages of the old world.

The narrowly circumscribed scope of this study allowed observation of language and social practices in a handful of villages. Collaborators in this study had multi-locale origins (Danel, Mandhwa, Uddya, Bhusha, Khardipada, etc., in Mathwad). The resettlement too is multi-sited (Narmadanagar, Rewanagar, Rozwa, etc.). Yet, an important finding in this study of internal displacement is the shared, symbolic construction of *muḷgav* (the homeland) and *punərvəsən* (the new world). 'Being adivasi' in the old world was indexed by a lifestyle based on an ideology of subsistence and self-sufficiency, a belief system and religious practices which reaffirmed their intimate relation with nature. The benevolent perception of nature and an anchoring in indigenous knowledge were implicit in adivasi practices (e.g. agriculture, fishing, medicine, etc.), the myths surrounding the tribal deities, ubiquitous narratives weaved around the local natural habitat (river, mountain, forest, animals, etc.), and in self-expression through song and dance. Collectively these experiences index the idea of a 'homeland' in the migrant's memory. This self-sufficiency was also evident in the use of the home language which fulfilled all their communicative needs.

Equally, the study demonstrated that, despite the multi-sited resettlement, the migrant experience is shared across the resettled villages. It is underscored by a sense of loss, betrayal and resentment, and a coming to terms with the new world. Adjustments and adaptation in the new world are indexed on the one hand by attempted continuities in cultural and religious practices of the old world; on the other hand, there is a gradual reconciliation with a new ideological stance premised on surplus. This was evidenced, for example, in the cultivation of cash crops, digital modes of entertainment as well as an expanded linguistic repertoire.

Notes

1. 'Internally Displaced Populations and Multilingual Spaces: A Sociolinguistic Perspective' Major Research Project awarded by the University Grants Commission of India (2012) to S. Kulkarni-Joshi (Principal Investigator, Deccan College, Pune), S. Imtiaz Hasnain (Aligarh Muslim University) and Panchanan Mohanty (Hyderabad Central University). The assistance of Ms Jayashree Bharambe, Dr Vivek Kumar and Mr Satish Bangar is duly acknowledged.
2. The terms *tehsil* and *taluka* are used in India to refer to a sub-district or cluster of villages.
3. The present discussion does not include the NBA-run ashramshala we visited in Danel (an original, partially submerged village) in which teachers use and encourage the children's home speech varieties in the classroom.

References

Agha, Asif. 2007. *Language and Social Relations*. New York: Cambridge University Press.

Baviskar, A. 2004. *In the Belly of the River: Tribal Conflicts over Development in the Narmada Valley*. New Delhi: OUP (1st edition 1995).

Census of India. 2011. Population by Mother Tongue. https://www.censusindia.gov.in/2011census/C-16.html

Dhagamwar, V. 2006. *Role and Image of Law in India: The Tribal Experience*. New Delhi: Sage Publications.

Heugh, Kathleen. 2017. Displacement and language. In S. Canagarajah (ed.), *Routledge Handbook of Migration and Language*. Abingdon: Routledge, pp. 187–206.

Kulkarni-Joshi, Sonal, S. Imtiaz Hasnain and Panchanan Mohanty. 2015. *Internally Displaced Populations (IDPs) and Multilingual Spaces: A Sociolinguistic Perspective*. Report submitted to the University Grants Commission of India, New Delhi.

Mohanty, Panchanan, Sonal Kulkarni-Joshi and S. Imtiaz Hasnain. 2013. Prolegomenon to Bhil-Pawra relations in West Khandesh: Evidence for an early substratum. *Indian Linguistics*, 74: 95–104.

Naik, Thakorlal. 1956. *The Bhils: A Study*. Delhi: Bharatiya Adimjati Sevak Sangh.

Negi, Nalin Singh and Sujata Ganguly. 2011. Development projects vs. internally displaced populations in India: A literature based appraisal. In J. Schade and T. Faist (eds), *COMCAD Working Paper Series*. Series on Environmental Degradation and Migration.

Phillips, Maxwell. 2012. *Dialect Continuum in the Bhil Tribal Belt: Grammatical Aspects*. PhD thesis submitted to SOAS, London.

Rathore, Vaishnavi. 2021. Jal-Jangal-Jameen ke Geet: An earful of environmental protest music in India. *The Bastion*. https://thebastion.co.in/politics-and/jal-jangal-jameen-ke-geet-an-earful-of-environmental-protest-music-in-india/ (accessed 20 November 2022).

Southworth, Franklin. 2005. *Linguistic Archaeology of South Asia*. Cambridge: Cambridge University Press.

Thakur, Vikram. 2014. Logjam: Peasantization caused deforestation in Narmada Valley. In Mahesh Rangarajan and K. Sivaramakrishnan (eds), *Shifting Ground: People, Animals, and Mobility in India's Environmental History*. Oxford: Oxford University Press.

Thakur, Vikram. 2019. Learning and leading: Resistance, subaltern leadership and the making of two Bhil community leaders from the Narmada Valley, Western India. *South Asia Multidisciplinary Academic Journal*, 21: Representations of the 'Rural' in India from the Colonial to the Post-Colonial.

Watters, Stephen. 2012. *A Sociolinguistic Profile of the Bhils of Northern Dhule District*. Dallas, TX: SIL International Publications.

Whitehead, Judith. 2010. *Development and Displacement in the Narmada Valley*. Delhi: Pearson.

CHAPTER 2

Narratives of Displaced Kashmiri Pandits: Mobility, Diasporic Morbidity and the Chronotope of Victimhood[1]

Rakesh M. Bhatt

1. Introduction

The term 'diaspora', beyond its biblical usage, has been used to refer to groups of people who live in one place but have – and express – ancestral ties to another, an 'idealised' homeland (Cohen and Fisher 2019). The diasporic experience is generally considered one of ambivalence, of a double presence: nostalgia for home (then and there) and a possibility of opportunity in a new space (now and here). Rather than studying diaspora as a simple move between two sedentary time-spaces, I study Kashmiri diaspora from a slightly different perspective: I follow the sociolinguistic tropes of their 'diaspora becoming', the struggles in their acculturation to the 'local', in becoming the 'other'. The conflicts that shape their cultural transformation become audible in the narratives of their new location, in the 'peripheries'. These narratives provide insights into the ways in which dispersed populations express their diasporic identifications, the various linguistic resources and practices they recruit to instrumentalise Kashmiri diaspora in action; an irreversible, ongoing process of identity transformation, from *káshir* (Kashmiris) to 'migrants'.

In this chapter, I examine narratives of displaced Kashmiris within a chronotopic framework that offers a uniform analysis of the dis-embedding from the homeland, the forced migration to different peripheries, and the consequent discontinuity of their experience. Specifically, I argue that these narratives provide metapragmatic evidence of the inextricable linkage of space and time in the production of diaspora identities, captured through the concept of chronotope: the intrinsic connectedness of temporal and spatial relationships that are rhetorically – metapragmatically – expressed (cf. Bakhtin 1986, Agha 2007, Blommaert and De Fina 2017, Karimzad and Catedral 2021). A chronotopic analysis, I will show, offers a view of diaspora identities that is dynamically constituted as social practices that refer to different space-time condensations – there and then, here and now, and yet-to-be futurity – as experienced in mobility and displacement. For Kashmiris, displaced under violent conditions – victim diaspora (Cohen 1999) – the doubled chronotopic interpellation, home and host, is weaved into a dominant diasporic chronotope of victimhood, linking their identity resources to those of the Jewish diaspora.

2. Kashmiri Pandits: a contextualisation

This chapter focuses on the catastrophic displacement of Kashmiri Pandits in 1990 that set into motion a process of rebuilding, in a space – the liminal space – between a home, which is inaccessible, and a host, which is undesirable. In order to understand the displacement narratives of Kashmiri Pandits, it is important to understand their genealogy, and in so doing the first obvious step is to acknowledge, within the local cultural politics of Kashmir, their unique identity as Kashmiri Hindus, Shaivites, Saraswat Brahman by caste. The word Pandit in the traditional, local sense means a 'learned' person or a priest. It is perhaps important to point out that the religious beliefs and practices of Kashmiri Pandits is part of their personal experience, central to their spiritual life, and to their community identity, even in dislocated, unfamiliar socio-cultural geographies (cf., especially, Pant 1987, Holloway and Valins 2002).

Given the geopolitical history of post-partition India, Kashmir has appeared in our national conscience either as a place that is linked to an imagined paradise (referred to as 'heaven on earth'), for the valley of Kashmir is indeed full of lakes, springs, rivers and waterfalls cascading down the Pir Panjal mountain range (see Figure 2.1), or it appears as a contested space, claimed both by India and Pakistan. The contested nature of this space follows from the dominant socio-cultural and political discourses that appear along two tropes: one that foregrounds the issue of plebiscite,[2] and the other that discusses Kashmir ahistorically, as never being a part of India. Both of these tropes are, unfortunately, short-sighted and partial, and they present a *parti pris* view of Kashmir – of its history and of its people. With respect to the plebiscite, the UN Security Council Resolution 47 (1948) had clearly presented a framework

Figure 2.1 *The Pir Panjal range, visible from Srinagar, Kashmir*

for the administration of a plebiscite that involved three sequential and conditional steps: first, the Government of Pakistan secures the withdrawal from the State of Jammu and Kashmir of tribesmen and Pakistani nationals not normally resident therein who have entered the state for the purposes of fighting; once this first step was undertaken and completed, then, second, the Government of India withdraws its own forces from Jammu and Kashmir, reducing them progressively to the minimum strength required for the support of the civil power in the maintenance of law and order; and after this was established, then the third step was to be undertaken: the administration of the plebiscite. Since the Government of Pakistan failed to take the first required step, the plebiscite never took place.

As for the other issue, of whether Kashmir was ever a part of India, a quick reading of the Nilamatapurana,[3] a seventh-century local Sanskrit text, provides evidence of how old, and integrated with India, the story of Kashmir is, as Kumari [Ghai] informs us:

> The Nilmata opens with Janamejaya's enquiry from Vaisampayana as to **why the king of 'Kasmira' did not participate in the war of Mahabharata** although his kingdom was not less important than any other in the country. Vaisampayana states that some time before the Mahabharata war was fought, king Gonanda of Kasmira had been invited by his relative Jarasandha to help him in a war against the yadavas. Gonanda complied with his request and was slain on the battle field by Krsna's brother, Bala. In order to avenge his father's death, Gonanda's son Damodara went to Gandhara to fight with Krsna who had gone there to attend a Svayamvara. Krsna killed Damodara in the fight but taking into consideration the high sanctity of Kasmira, he coronated his rival's pregnant widow Yasovati. Damodara's Posthumous son Bala Gonanda was a minor at the time of the great war, so he did not join either the Kauravas or the Pandavas. ([1973] 2007: 1, bold font added, for emphasis)

In other words, the discussion of the representation of Kashmir in the epic battle of Mahabharata points to how long Kashmir, a Hindu state, has been part of India. Specifically, with reference to Kashmiri Pandits, I would like to point out that the Almanac of Kashmiri Pandits (known to us as 'Janthri'),[4] also called *Saptrishi samvat*, is in its 5,098th year in continuation – that is how old the Kashmiri Pandit tradition has been of keeping time, that is how long the Kashmiri Pandit community had been living in Kashmir, until it was catastrophically destabilised by the 1990 event. This destabilisation, qua ethnic cleansing, however, wasn't the first. I discuss the various mass movements of Kashmiri Pandits next.

3. Kashmiri Pandits in diasporas

There have been several mass movements of Kashmiri Pandits (hereafter, KPs) out of Kashmir, mostly during eighteenth and nineteenth centuries, for reasons of both economic mobility and religious persecution. The first migration of KPs from Kashmir, however, took place much earlier, due to religious persecution during Sultan Sikandar's reign (1389–1413). It is believed that during his reign, only eleven

KP families in Kashmir were left: others were killed, converted to Islam or were forced to flee from the valley (Koul 1924, Kilam 1955, Parimu 1969).[5] Later, during Sultan Zain-ul-Abidin's reign (1420–70), some KPs are believed to have returned under the Sultan's guarantees to them of religious freedom and government appointments so long as the KPs – a sociolinguistically important language policy decision – learned Persian, which had become the new official language.[6] The bulk of the later migration of KPs out of Kashmir appears to have been during the repressive Afghan rule in Kashmir in the late eighteenth and early nineteenth centuries (1753–1819), when Hindus were persecuted for following their religion (Hangloo 2000). Those KPs who were able to flee from later (eighteenth-century) persecution settled down mainly in cities of Northern India, working primarily in government services (Koul [1924] 1991, R. Kaul 2005) and living together in *mohullas* ('locality, residential area'; cf. Pant 1987) – a reconstitution in dispersion, as it were![7] The *mohullas* became critical in not only maintaining their distinctive ethno-linguistic identity but also served as a physical, community place for the exercise of their exclusive social and cultural rituals (cf. Pant 1987: 32, and passim). These *mohullas* also served as safe interactional spaces that carried in their memory the violence of the past. The prominent KP political activist of the time, Bishan Narayan Dar (1864–1916), a migrant settled in Lucknow (Uttar Pradesh) recalls, in an Urdu verse, the brutal circumstances of the KP who refused to convert to Islam:

> Young and old, rich and poor, men and women
> The hearts of all overflowed with attachment to religion
> Let us lose our lives, they said
> But not our Brahman name[8]

The verse above invokes the exilic condition, what makes the home no longer safely habitable. Such acts of imagination feed the memories of the past and bring to the present the narratives of exile – the painful banishment from their *watan* ('homeland'). The capacity of exilic condition to produce compensatory fantasies and longing is best captured in the (Urdu) words of the late nineteenth-century KP lawyer-poet of Lucknow, Brij Narain Chakbast (1882–1926):

> Ages have passed since this garden was abandoned
> Yet the story of its love is still fresh

While the structures of *watan* that memory built for these KPs are often recalled in poetic metre, these displaced KPs, according to Pant (1987), did not necessarily express a strong desire to return to Kashmir, and remained largely unaffected by the social and political movements there.[9] Yet, almost paradoxically, those KP migrants who settled in North India were quick to rally around the sufferings of KPs in Kashmir, raising funds for relief work after the 1892 fire that devastated Srinagar and the cholera outbreak in Kashmir, or later during the floods of Kashmir in 1903 (ibid.). The restoration of place, the homeland and the people still there, arguably served as a collective imaginary identification for these diasporic KPs, who made efforts in their exilic conditions to be always symbolically connected to their place of origin – Kashmiri Hindu Brahmins, distinct from North Indian Hindu Brahmins (cf. also Pant 1987).[10] In other words, the longing for Kashmir may have subsided in these earlier migrants, but a strong sense of belonging – a romantic attachment – to the place always remained entrenched in the psyche of the KP.

To summarise the discussion so far in the words of Kaul (2005: 7):

> [S]ince the advent of Islam in Kashmir in 1339 AD, the Hindus, who are the original inhabitants of the Valley, have from time to time faced tyrannies of the Muslim rulers in various forms who imposed heavy taxes, perpetrated the most barbaric methods of torture, brutalized and killed them in thousands, forced their females into marriage and males into conversion, desecrated and demolished their temples and forced the remaining Hindus into exile.

Turning now to the latest KP mass exodus, in January 1990, we see similar tropes that defined some of the earlier exoduses: fleeing from religious persecution, although the enemy was not a foreign ruler this time, but (part of) a global Islamic jihad aided and abetted by extremist actors in Pakistan (cf. Reynolds 2008, Fair 2014). This last exodus was inevitable:[11] unhappy with the outcome of the 'rigged' state assembly elections on 23 March1987, the Jammu Kashmir Liberation Front (JKLF) established itself as the leading organiation that Muslim youth rallied around.[12] JKLF provided the youth with the means (guns and ammunition) to engage in a demand for *azadi* (freedom) by first claiming responsibility for the bomb explosions on 31 July and 1 August 1988, and subsequently training the Muslim youth for an armed insurgency in the state with the help of Pakistan (Madan 2008, Reynolds 2008). While initially presenting itself as a secular democratic organisation, JKLF soon developed a communal and fundamentalist orientation around mid-1989, targeting and killing KPs as *mukhbirs* ('informers' [to the Indian government]), while clarifying their concept of *azadi* as Nizam-i-Mustafa, Islamic rule, and 'the call went out: "If you wish to do god's work, go and pick up a Kalashnikov"' (Madan 2008: 25) – a sea-change from the deeply pacifist Sufi-Rishi Islamic traditions practised by the local Kashmiris during the early to mid-twentieth century.

Witnessing the selective killings of KPs in broad daylight during the late autumn of 1989, and the terror campaign that was unleashed on them – through warnings in letters, posters, pamphlets, newspapers, and on neighbourhood public address systems asking them to accept Islam or leave the valley – created an environment of fear and insecurity in the KP community (Madan 1998, R. Kaul 2005; *inter alia*). After the administrative collapse in early January, and no guarantees of protection for them from the government, the KPs started to leave their homes – a risk-averting strategy – beginning as a trickle in November 1989. According to some estimates (Evans 2002), eventually about 200,000 (mainly) KPs left the valley of Kashmir after the onset of attacks, and *en masse* soon after 19 January 1990 (see Figure 2.2 below) – the date on which KPs memorialise the death, destruction and displacement of the community as their holocaust day.

The ticket below, dated '20-1-90' (20 January 1990), recalls the abrupt disruption of the KP community, and the disorder and social disintegration that such sudden ruptures engender: becoming a foreigner in a homeland. The ticket signifies the canonical 'Road' chronotope (à la Bakhtin 1981: 243–52), representing the

Figure 2.2 *Ticket to (forced) exile*

experience of mobility and migration. More specifically, it occupies the liminal space between a stable, familiar, sacred space of the past (home chronotope) and an unfamiliar cultural geography of the future (host chronotope):[13] it thus serves at once a politics of nostalgia and a politics of uncertainties (see excerpt (1) below).

The excerpt in (1) below is part of the discussion of the events of 19 January 1990, when, according to 'BN', mosques in the entire valley issued declarations that the KPs were *Kafirs* ('infidels') and that they had to either *leave* Kashmir, *convert* to Islam or *be killed*. Almost overnight, those who chose to leave became stateless people displaced within their own country, occupying a paradoxical position of refugees in their own country. Affected by violence and conflict, they present a testimonial of their condition of uprootedness: from deportation to exile, and to, as it turns out, alienation.

(1) BN, [M, 53] Camp Muthi, Phase 2, Jammu (3 March 2007)[14]

1. *pat yelyi asyi booz laawud sapikaran pyeTh tI:* 'Later when we heard on the loudspeaker also
2. *raliv, tsaliv ya galiv,* convert (to Islam), leave, or perish
3. *me kar phaTaphaT TikiT (2.0)* I got the tickets quickly
4. *tI draayi (6.0)* and (we) left
5. *asyi gayi mahraa beghhar* we-HON became homeless
6. *vanyI chI yimnayi silaman manz paymit* now we are dwelling in these slums
7. *kaDaan doha doha* living from one day to the next'

The key expressions, *raliv, tsaliv ya galiv* ('convert, leave/run away, or perish/die') in line 2 above, recall the past tyrannical orders of Sultan Sikander to the KPs during his reign in the late fourteenth century that, according to local KP legend, left only eleven KP families in the valley. The echo of the violent narratives of the past lead the KPs quickly to a familiar path (lines 3 and 4) of nomadic subjectivity (line 5). The 'dwelling in these slums' (line 6) indicates the nomadic predicament, living from one day to the next (line 7) – similar subjectivity tropes appear in various different guises throughout the interview process of different respondents.

The socio-historiography of KPs discussed above, of repeated and religio-politically enforced evictions, presents the interpretive context of recent identity narratives of internally displaced ('new migrant') KPs – post-January 1990.[15] The narratives of new migrant experience, of dis-possession and dis-location, show an amnesia-in-action as these KPs recompose and repurpose the old habits of thought to a new syntax of social relations and their symbolic representations.

4. Data and analysis

The narrative data comes from a larger ethnographic study of internally displaced KPs that includes a total of twenty-nine hours of audio recordings of open-ended/casual conversations and semi-structured interviews. Using a socially-situated, discourse-analytic methodology (Wodak and Meyer 2016), for this chapter I closely examine three metapragmatic commentaries (128 minutes) with respect to the conflict, and its negotiated hybridity, between the time-space constructions of subjectivity in the 'home-land' and in the 'host-land'. These commentaries, I will argue, illustrate the inextricable linkage of space and time in the production of diaspora identities.

But before I begin the description and analysis of data, a quick comment on the theoretical constructs I use is in order. The contextual lens used to frame an understanding of the KP narratives is that of the chronotope – which allows a useful framing that assumes that (1) all social(-linguistic) practices have a spatial and a temporal dimension, (2) different time-space configurations are linked to different specific forms of personhood, and (3) all meaningful action takes place in a temporalised space (Bakhtin 1981, Giddens 1995, Agha 2007, Blommaert 2015, Karimzad and Catedral 2021). The unity, as well as polycentricity and polyphony, of time-spaces inheres in every narrative text analysed for this study, making it sufficiently possible to read the KP experiences through the chronotopic imagination. Just as Bakhtin declared, and as discussed exhaustively by Karimzad and Catedral (2021: 18–20), the conceptualisation of chronotope is not homogenous: its descriptive and analytic uses have been revised over the years. Yet Bakhtin's central claim stands firmly on its original formulation: 'every entry into the sphere of meaning is accomplished only through the gates of the chronotope' (Bakhtin 1981: 258).

In this chapter, I mainly follow Blommaert's (2015: 111) conceptualisation of chronotopes 'as aspects of contextualization through which specific chunks of history [spatiotemporally organized] can be invoked in discourse as meaning-attributing resource' (cf. also Blommaert and De Fina 2017, Karimzad and Catedral 2021). As a way to understand the contemporary process of deterritorialisation, of the new migrant KPs, I frame the methodological and theoretical approach in terms of a dominant chronotope, the biographical chronotope:[16] a discursive-practical heuristic that reflects symbolic memories of individual biographies. It is within the scope of this large-scale dominant chronotope that the various small-scale chronotopes become discursively recognisable. The individual biographies show clearly the KP migrants caught between different temporal registers: a past that is unavailable and a future that is uncertain! With this brief theoretical introduction, I now turn to the analysis of data.

4.1 Narrative 1: the diasporic chronotope

The following excerpts (2a and 2b) show how migrant KPs in their diasporic location seem to have lost their 'home' but are unsettled and uncomfortable in the 'host' context. Removed from a time-space of social-linguisic practices (home chronotope) to a time-space of displacement (host chronotope) that is often associated with contrastive values, the diaspora chronotope of KP migrants is a constant negotiation between the two: home and host chronotopes. As the data below will show, it is in the negotiation that an analysis of diaspora as *Third Space* (Bhabha 1994) emerges, constituting its own interpellation in the process of representation – opening up the possibility, in the displacement, of different, even incommensurable, cultural practices and priorities to appear.

In the first part of the excerpt, (2a) below, a fifty-nine-year-old male KP (S) presents in his first two turns a home chronotope as a synthesis of time (his memory of the past) and space (culturally meaningful place, peopled by a network of relationships). The home chronotope represents for this KP a tension between belonging and exclusion: a place to which he cannot return, as there is *now* nothing *there* that belongs to him, and there is no desire for return as that *place now* hosts 'muslim militants'. The scattering away of his kith and kin from homeland to distant places and the new and unrecognisable moral orders and values (violence, disorder, militancy) there now leads to the ambivalence of belonging. In his third turn, S switches to the host chronotope, which is also presented as unacceptable since it entails adoption of an unfamiliar – local, Hindi/Punjabi – sociolinguistic habitus, that results in some loss of agency to altered sociolinguistic practices ('why don't you use Hindi?'). The resulting indeterminacy, expressed in terms of anxieties and uncertainty of his (S's) own subjective positioning, is explained as the indexical mismatch between the immediate chronotopic context (host) and the brought along images of himself (cf. Karimzad and Catedral 2021: 22) – the conflict between the chronotopes of normalcy (Karimzad 2020, Blommaert 2017).

(2a) The diasporic chronotope (M, 59)

S: *asyi cha-na vanyi yatshaan vaapas gasun*	S: We don't want (desire) to go back now
I: *ti kyaazyi*	I: Why's that?
S: *ahhansa, atyi kyaa ruud vanyi yi son chu, saaryi rishtedaar aayi taetyi tsalith, keNh gayi jemyi, keNh gayi bamyi, kafii cha yeti [9 secs) tatyi cha vanyi musalman miltants, asyi ma haikav gasith*	S: Well, what is left there now that is ours, all the relatives have left from there, some went to Jammu, some to Bombay, some are here(9 sec] now there are only muslim militants, (so) we can't go (there)
I: *ta vanyi*	I: So, now?

Narratives of Displaced Kashmiri Pandits

S: *vanyi kyaa, phaTnas cha aamityi, kath karhaav, kamsiith,* **ab bacche haendi meN baat karte haiN aapas meN** *kashur cha-na karaan*
I: *kyaazyi*
S: *hamsaayi chu panjeb, timan siith ma karan kashur, sakulas manz tI cha haendi, asyi cha <u>husband wife</u> panavay karaan kashur tath tI cha yim shuri vanaan asyi* **aap haendi meN baat kyun nahiN karte**

I: *yi kyaazyi*

S: now what, we have reached a breaking point, we'd like to talk, but with whom, now the children talk in Hindi among themselves, not Kashmiri
I: Why?
S: Neighbors are Punjabi (Hindi speaking), they are not going to use Kashmiri with them, in School it is Hindi, We husband wife speak Kashmiri with each other, even for that the kids say why don't you use Hindi
I: Why's that?

The loss of agency in new time-space configuration is more poignantly presented in excerpt (2b) below by this speaker, (M59), as he grapples with indeterminacy while making sense of his current predicament. In response to my question in the last turn in excerpt (2a) above, the speaker in his very first turn in excerpt (2b), see below, expresses his *subject* position as being placed in relation to local socio-cultural practices. In fact, (2b) captures all the trappings of diaspora becoming, the intergenerational loss of symbol-laden rituals and customs replaced by socio-cultural and sociolinguistic participation necessary for local belonging. Whilst KP parents are sequestered inside a *panDaal* ('festive tent') engaged in a holy ritual of the pooja-celebration of Lord Shiva (S's turn 4), their children speak Hindi [mixed with Punjabi], not their mother tongue, Kashmiri, while playing outside with other kids (S's turn 2). Kashmiri language and rituals are thus circumscribed to private and sacred spaces, whereas local (non-Kashmiri) language and the Hindu festivals of Holi and Diwali are designated to public and secular spaces, flagged by S's last turn with a switch to Hindi, the dominant local language. The transformation in becoming local – the acquisition of the habitus of the host chronotope – is, however, incomplete, producing hybridities that are only grudgingly accepted, as revealed by the sarcastic laugh that accompanies the mention of a diasporic identity of '*Punjabi Kashmiri*' at the end of this excerpt.

(2b) The diasporic chronotope (M, 59) (cont.)

S: *asyi ruud na paanas taanyi ki yiman hechnaavhav saaNyi panin sanseskaar*
I: *hmmn*
S: *utra aas herat, tamaam shuryi, kashir shuryi yim aaNganas manz gindaan aasyi, tim as saaryi karaan panjeb*

I: *panjeb?*
S: *na sa, um, haendi, ta panjeb ti aasyi mix karaan.*
I: *parents katyi aasyi*
S: *tim ha sa aasyi shamyaanas manz yetyi na pooza aas sabdaan*

S: it didn't remain up to us, to teach them our own rituals/values
I: hmmn
S: Day before was Herat (Shiva's day), all the kids, Kashmiri kids were playing in the courtyard, they were all speaking Punjabi

I: Punjabi?
S: No, um Hindi, but they were also mixing Punjabi
I: Where were the parents?
S: They were in the tent where the prayers were taking place

I: *shuryi kyaaz aas na pooza pyath* S: *(4 secs) yiman cha-na, saanyan shuryan herath phikri khasaan (3 secs)* **lekin agar holi hogi, ya Diwali hogi, man lagaa kar selbrate karte hai,** *yiman chu panun sooryi mashit gomut asyi tI, Punjeb Kashir* (sarcastic laugh)	I: Why were the kids not at the prayers S: (4 secs) These, our kids don't understand (significance of) Herat (3 secs), but if there is Holi or Diwali, they celebrate with passion, they have forgotten everything that was their own, we too, Punjabi Kashmiris (sarcastic laugh)

To summarise, the tensions between belonging and exclusion, loss of traditional values and the discovery of new ones highlights a diasporic experience of dis-orientation. An orientation to home (or homeland) evokes unpleasantness – a place that is not culturally meaningful anymore (now), as all the networks of kinship, family and friends are absent, and their absence is filled now by the presence of 'muslim militants'. Thus, home is 'rechronotopized' (à la Karimzad 2021) by the KP (S) in (2a) as an unappealing, in fact unsuitable, option. An orientation to host, however, is undesirable, too, as new socio-cultural scripts of the host chronotope demand radical revisions of the older habits of thought, leading to cultural moribundity and, eventually, morbidity: not only the loss of social, cultural and linguistic practices but also a loss of the capacity to retain Kashmiri folklore, myths, values and beliefs.

What appears in the biographical narrative in (2) is a chronotopic clash, between home and host. What emerges in this clash, I hypothesise, is a *Third Space* chronotope, a chronotope that accommodates the rejection of both the old and the new, what is left behind and what lies ahead: a chronotopic identity that resides in-between the two, expressing, simultaneously, both and neither; a hybridity described mockingly by the subject in (2b) as *Punjabi Kashmiris*.

4.2 Narrative 2: chronotopic instability

The other trope of Kashmiri diasporic identity is impermanence/instability, which carries the echoes of the previous speaker. The excerpt in (3a) below comes from a fifty-three-year-old KP woman, an English schoolteacher at a local school in Mayur Vihar, New Delhi. The diasporic identity, as this excerpt shows, is the inability to be connected in the host community, now and here, left with only memories of the homeland, then and there. It is not only the home landscape and climate that is missing (see turn 2 of R), but also the freshness and the beauty condensed in that time-space that is recalled, which is especially brought into sharp focus when contrasted with the present living conditions, here and now. And, as also discussed above in (2b), the absence of family and other networks of relationships is repeated, highlighting the specific rupture that migration engenders.

What is striking, however, is that the respondent, R, skillfully incorporates contrasting landscapes as a symbolic resource for group identification; landscapes, in other words, become one of the most important symbolic representation of diasporic identity, a representation that allows her to morally (superior, pure, beautiful) incorporate the physical space – invested with moral-cultural meaning – into a definition of who we are. And yet, this morality is contested and negated in the local, host chronotope when her children remind her of the moribundity of their ethno-linguistic identity. The location of diaspora identity is thus arguably a *Third Space* – neither here and now nor there and then, between (the romantic recollections/memories of) home and (the material and symbolic challenges of) host: a home time-space that is lost, unreachable, only invokable and imagined, and a host time-space that has to be put up with, lived and tolerated. And yet it is in the local geographies that she citationally comments (end of last turn of R) on the loss of historical-linguistic practices, the routine use of Kashmiri in interpersonal interactions. The two irreconcilable chronotopes, home and host, paradoxically constitute together a new kind of subject: 'Punjaeb Kashir', a hybrid Kashmiri (see also 2b above) that straddles the two chronotopes (home-host) on a regular basis, unanchored to either one of them. In extracts (3a) and (3b) code-switching to English is indicated by underlining.

(3a) Chronotopic instability

R: **ham ab yahaaN solaa saal se haiN,** used to **ho gaye haiN**
R: We are here now for 16 years, we have become used to (this place)

I: used to kyaa]
I: Used to, what]

R: [kashiir-uk shehjaar ma melyi yeti, saaph havaa, yi garm mazhar oos na, panin zabaan, panin lookh aasan, dal lake, chahmeshahi (2 secs) tohyi chuvna kashiir gamatyi, yath chaa kaNh comparison, vanyi chu yohoi bughtun,
R: [(we won' get) the calmness of Kashmir, clean air, this hot-hell wasn't (there), our own language, our own people there, Dal Lake, Chasmashahi, (2 secs) haven't you been to Kashmir, is there any comparison, now we have to tolerate this

I: hmmn, yi chu]
I: Hmmn, this is]

R: [saanyan shyuryan gav sooruyi mashith, vanyi cha myan kuur me vanaan, '**meri** friends **mujhe kehti haiN, "tu Kashmiran hai", toh tujhe Kashmiri kyuN nahiiN aati**', van kyaa vanas
R: [our kids have forgotten everything, now my daughter says, 'my friends tell me, "you are Kashmiri", why don't you know Kashmiri', what can (I) say (to her)

I: tohyi kyaa vonuv
I: What did you say

The narratives of 'here and now' (host chronotope) express cultural instability; especially, the loss of their most important symbolic resource, language (identity and practice), in response to new relations of power and domination. The answer to my question in the last turn in excerpt (3a) above is presented as a moral failure in parenting (see first turn of R in 3b, below). This failure is quickly repaired by placing the material constraints of diasporic existence; especially, the burden of being dislocated and deeply affected by conflict, and the struggles to sustain a semi-durable diasporic habitat. Her struggles reference a compromised dignity, appearing in repeated statements such as 'living in a small/little apartment' (compared, presumably, to a comfortable life, 'leaving everything there'); or, in situationally ironic statements as finding a teaching position, 'full time, English teacher ... I am MSc in Botany.' The nostalgia, juxtaposed with current ironies, leads to the experience of aporia (internal contradictions) and uncertainty.

But, it is the impermanence that defines her diasporic condition (her last turn) – the host locale is not home, 'home is (back there) in Srinagar'; in other words, home is now carried in memory and in acts of imagination. However, the desire to belong to it now is forbidden by the reality that exits there now. Home, as she describes it, is temporary, transient, ephemeral – 'we may not be here next time when you come!' The impermanence is then concretely expressed as their present socio-cultural disposition, *khanabadosh* ('Nomads') as the KP diasporic habitus. To be sure, nomadism, in her biographical account, refers to a lack of home-site, untethered; feeling a sense of homelessness![17]

(3b) Chronotopic instability (cont.)

R: *kyaa vanhaas, yi cha saanyii galtii, I take phul responsibility. She was two when we left Kashmir, leaving everything there, his brother gave us shelter, then we found a small apartment here, we were struggling, my husband worked, I found a teaching position, full time, English teacher, I am MSc in Botany (laughs) so we were both working full time and we are living in this little apartment, and we have lived here for some time*	R: what could I say, this is our fault, I take full responsibility. She was two when we left Kashmir, leaving everything there, his (husband's) brother gave us shelter, then we found a small apartment here, we were struggling, my husband worked, I found a teaching position, full time, English teacher, I am MSc in Botany (laughs) so we were both working full time and we are living in this little apartment, and we have lived here for some time
I: So, this is home now?	I: So, this is home now?
R: *No, No, No, Home is in Srinagar, this is not home (5.0) who knows where home is, next time, when you come, we may not be here*	R: No, No, No, Home is Srinagar, this is not home (5 secs) who knows where home is, next time, when you come, we may not be here
I: Kashmir?	I: Kashmir?
R: [a big deep sigh] *who knows, gatshaa, magar me chu-na basaan vanyi (3.0) asyi cha vanyi gamityi khanabadosh*	R: [a big deep sigh] who knows, (I wish to) go, but I don't think so now (3 secs), we have now become nomads

To summarise the discussion so far, a conceptualisation of chronotopic instability refers to the inability of migrant KPs to connect securely to a place, fused with time: it follows a time-space logic that is inevitably tied to an imagined identity that is locked in a *place* between *then* (not available) and *now* (only barely tolerated). Home is still desirable, but not a possibility anymore, '(I wish I could) go, but I don't think so now'. Host, on the other hand, is not home, only to be tolerated, 'now we have to tolerate this (hot temps, and absence of all things familiar)'. The reference to a nomadic life shows how stability is undetermined, as place is imagined between temporal registers of past and future – the present is still up for grabs, not fixed; arguably, as also discussed above, a *Third Space Chronotope*.

4.3 Narrative 3: victim chronotope

Finally, I present excerpt (4) below, to demonstrate a particular affective dimension of the Kashmiri diasporic chronotope, of victimhood, as the narrative relates the experiences of morbidity in the past, and the unstable living conditions of the present, to the familiar, and the dominant, chronotope of the Jewish diaspora. In most KP narratives, and in several KP publications,[18] the KP exoduses are invariably expressed in hyponymic relationship to the paradigm case of Jewish diaspora – the successive scattering and reconstitution-in-dispersion. And much like the exilic yearning for a return to Jerusalem, the recent KP experience of diaspora has expressed a similar yearning for return to Kashmir, where 'home' is![19] And, yet, paradoxically, much like the Jewish diaspora's lack of pathos of exile, there is now a similar lack of pathos of exile in migrant KP communities, though in public spheres there are still calls for a return to Kashmir. On 5 August 2019, the abrogation of Articles 370 and 35A[20] has renewed a possibility of return, now a political imperative, for displaced KPs, lifting their burden of homesickness.

The excerpt in (4), narrated by a forty-eight-year-old male KP (MK), shows the systematicity with which the historical self-image of Kashmiris is interdiscursively calibrated, citationally, and measured affectively, with other larger (time-space) events leading up to the holocaust.

(4) Victim chronotope and scaling holocaust

MK: **dekhiye**, ba vanoov, **aap ko bhii samajh aayegaa, aap puuchte hai na ki vahaaN kyaa hua hamaare saath**
I: na mahraa [me
MK: [**mai bataauNgaa vahii, Jewz ke saath kyaa hua, ek kaum jo bahut hardworking Thii, paRhii likhii Thii, bahut successful Thii, economically,**
I: aahnsa
MK: timan kyaa taavan pyav, sui taavan pyav asyi tI
I: you mean
MK: they faced holocaust, we faced our holocaust (3 secs) January 19
I: January 19?
MK: holocaust day, Kashmiri holocaust day
I: January 19, me aas-na patah
MK: Yes, they had started murdering prominent Hindus long before, there were demonstrations dohay has-a, dohay, jaloos hasa neraan, threatening slogans, to burn Pandit homes, screaming raliv, tsaliv, ya galiv, asyi gasyi panunayi Pakistan, baTav rostui, baTni saan

I: yi kam aasyi?
MK: JKLF, (4 secs), we left our homes in the middle of night, lost everything (9 secs) sooruyi gav mahraa khatam, khabar vanyi kyaa banyi, jewz gayii kamsekam bajah, asyi kyaa banyi vanyii, asyi gayi darbadar

MK: See, I'll tell you, you will also understand, you ask (don't you) what happened there with us
I: No Sir [I
MK: [I will tell you that(–only), what happened to the Jews, a community that was very hardworking, educated, was very successful, economically
I: yes (honorific)
MK: What hell befell on them, that very hell befell us (idiomatic use, Kashmiri)
I: you mean
MK: They faced holocaust, we faced our holocaust (3 secs) January 19
I: January 19?
MK: holocaust day, Kashmiri holocaust day
I: Jan 19, I did not know that
MK: Yes, they had started murdering prominent Hindus long before, there were demonstrations, everyday(hon), every day, parades of demonstrators, threatening slogans to burn Pandit homes, screaming convert (to Islam), leave (the land), or die, we want our Pakistan, without KP men, but with KP women.
I: Who were they?
MK: JKLF, (4 secs), we left our homes in the middle of night, lost everything (9 secs) everything has finished, don't know what will happen now, at least Jews prospered, what will happen to us now, we've become homeless

The excerpt (4) is a response to my question, what happened to KPs there in Kashmir during the time leading up to the mass exodus in January 1990. MK frames the KP experience of exodus within a familiar – and the dominant – chronotope of Jewish diaspora, contextualising right in the beginning, in his second turn, the FRACTAL connection (cf. Blommaert 2017, Gal 2018): 'what happened to us is precisely what happened to the Jews'. These comparisons, in slightly altered forms, appeared frequently in KP migrant narratives, as they presented a description of their predicament before, during and after their exodus. The fractal comparisons, I argue, create scalar differences of encompassment – two tokens (large-small) of the same type (holocaust) – the more encompassing category (Jewish Holocaust) is interpretable in an ideological frame as of greater scale than the KP holocaust. The two minority communities, KPs and Jews, are constructed on two different time-spaces interpreted within the same moral and ideological order – hardworking, highly educated and economically successful – and positioned against an evil 'that put them/us through hell'. As with the Jews, the KP homes were marked, and they were given three choices: *raliv* (convert to Islam), *tsaliv* (leave the land), *ya galiv* (or die). KPs, as in this particular excerpt, are thus projected as victims, suffering violence; uprootedness leading up to their holocaust, 19 January, memorialised as the Kashmiri holocaust day. And, in the end, in the last turn, the speaker presents a retrospective on Jews in positive terms, while his prognosis for Kashmiri is one of 'inconstant homeland' (Duschinski 2008).

5. Conclusion

In this chapter I analysed the diaspora identity of migrant KPs, forced out of their homes and homeland, and rehabilitated – either through personal networks or, mainly, through inadequate government intervention – in distant and new, unfamiliar places. Situating the current exodus in terms of previous ones afforded a contextualisation for the migrant narratives that repeatedly draw from those time-spaces. The biographical narratives I have analysed here show that the displacement of KPs is both geographical and conceptual, unable to belong where they are or return to where they belong – they simultaneously occupy two incommensurable time-spaces!

What seems to emerge from these narratives is a subject position that carries the familiar tropes of victim diaspora (à la Cohen 1999): expelled from home and unable to return; interpellated as 'migrants' yet self-consciously identifying themselves as victims of genocide perpetrated on them by 'muslim jihadists' who are branded as 'militants' fighting for *azadi* ('freedom' from India). It is in this, and through this, web of contradictions that the migrant KPs link, narratively, their identity resources to the Jewish experience of expulsion. The analytic-conceptual surprise, however, in the KP data is the frequent reference to the pathos of an exile consciousness; not a settled distinction between homeland and exile that is expected in diasporic imaginations (cf. Stierstorfer and Wilson 2018). So while aligning themselves with the Jewish diasporic subjectivities, in order to make sense of their own, KP migrants are unable to come to terms with a settled order that secures their sense of belonging. This seems to me to be an important theoretical finding of the analysis.

The other important finding is an insistence on a theoretical methodology: chronotope – a lens that yields a resolution of data that brings into sharp focus the sociolinguistically significant generalisations that remain obscure otherwise. Inspired by recent works on chronotopes (Blommaert 2015, Blommaert and De Fina 2017, Karimzad and Categral 2021), the analysis of diaspora experience as chronotope presented in this chapter offers a number of favourable consequences. First, it presents a synthesis of time (memory of the past) and space (culturally meaningful place) as the central organising principle in articulating the diaspora identity; second, it captures a theoretically more nuanced understanding of diaspora existence: a transformation from dwelling-in-displacement (Clifford 1994) to a dwelling-in-dischronotopicality (Peeren 2006); third, it shows how the doubled interpellation – home and host – is weaved into a dominant diasporic chronotope of victimhood, characterised by expressions of conflict, hybridity and doubleness; it establishes memorial links with other chronotopes through acts of citationality; the fractal comparisons of KP holocaust (small) with Jewish Holocaust (large) – a matter of scale difference; and, finally, it offers an explanation of the Kashmiri diaspora as *Third Space* Chronotope: nomadic, unsettled, homeless, unanchored – subjects lacking agency, being in a constant state of structural disequilibrium and ambivalence, and creating a new area of negotiation of representation (that is unrecognisable from standard/received measures of perception).

Notes

1. This is the story of my people, Kashmiri Pandits, a personal story in some ways. This chapter is a modest effort to give a hearing to the broken spirits of their victimised souls.
2. This discourse usually, and erroneously, takes the form that India did not administer the UN-authorised plebiscite in 1948, or soon after.
3. The Nilamata is a Kashmiri purana considered as one of the most authentic sources of the ancient cultural history of Kashmir. According to this purana, Kasmira was occupied by a vast lake called Satisar and inhabited by a demon Jalodbhava. The Vishnu (the supreme god in the Vaishnava tradition) along with other gods and goddess ordered Ananta to drain off the lake so as to eliminate Jalodbhava, invincible in waters. Ananta made an outlet with a plough and thus the valley came into existence (Kumari [1966] 1988: 16). Furthermore, mention should be made of Kalhana's Rajatarangini, a twelfth-century text that describes a 3,698-year history of Kashmir in 7,830 slokas. Although Rajatarangini was written in Sanskrit, Kashmiri was the popular mother tongue of many Kashmiris at that time, as evidence most clearly in the works of the eleventh-century poet, Ksemendra (cf. Trivedi 1996).
4. Janthri has an important communal function, of structuring important events – births, marriage, birthdays – and it also provides a calendar of important religious days (e.g. Ashtami, Ekadashi, Shivratri) and even auspicious dates for travel, etc.
5. According to Pant (1987: 12), even today it is possible to divide KPs into those who descended from families who left Kashmir during Sikandar's reign (known as *Bhanmasis*) and those who stayed (known as *Malmasis*).

6. The official language of Kashmir until then was Sanskrit – and this new language policy introduced a switch from one diglossic situation (Sanskrit [High]; Kashmiri [Low]) to another (Persian [High]; Kashmiri [Low]), with obvious implications for the cultural and economic capital of Kashmiri.
7. The successive scattering and reconstitution-in-dispersion is not very different from the diasporic condition of the Jews after the Assyrian, Babylonian and Roman conquests – a reference point for contemporary KP migrants discussing their own condition. This point is discussed later in the chapter.
8. Cited in Kaul and Raina (1931: 52–3), original verse written in Perso-Arabic script.
9. It is quite possible to hypothesise here that perhaps the difference between *diaspora* and *exile* may have to do with the fact that the former lacks the pathos of exile, a need to return, having grown comfortable in the new networks of compatriots. The exile consciousness carries the pathos of displacement and a yearning for returning home.
10. Some of the cultural-religious practices of Kashmiri Brahmins had developed independently from North Indian Brahmins, especially in the rituals associated, for instance, in the celebration of Shivratri, Janamashtami and other religious festivals.
11. Although the political-social events leading up to the mass exodus of KP in January 1990 are more complicated than as I present them, the main actors and events directly responsible for the KP exodus are summarised here.
12. The KP discourse is premised on the claim that rejects the suggestion that the militant movement resulted from the political alienation or economic deprivation of Kashmiri Muslims. As Teng and Gadoo (1991: 31) claim in their *White Paper on Kashmir*: 'The militant violence in Kashmir is an ideological struggle which is fundamentalist in outlook and basically communal in character ... The terrorist violence is not a local eruption of political dissent or discontent, nor is it a political movement geared to objectives which involve change in the instruments of power or processes of political participation. It is a religious crusade, the continuation of the Muslim struggle for the separate Muslim homeland in India, to complete the partition of India by securing the Muslim majority state of Jammu and Kashmir for the Muslim State of Pakistan.'
13. While road is one of five major agora chronotopes, Bakhtin does assume an unlimited number of 'minor chronotopes', those that emerge from the dialogical imagination ('created chronotopes of imagination').
14. Transcription notes: the data are not transcribed closely, following IPA. In the data extracts, Kashmiri is shown in *italics*, Hindi in ***bold italics*** and English in *underlined italics*. Furthermore, capital N represents nasalisation of the preceding vowel, capital T represents retroflex sound, and capital I represents unrounded high front lax vowel. Vowel length is represented by doubling the same vowel.
15. The term new migrant' was used often as an identifier for those KPs who had moved en masse after January 1990 to New Delhi, the site of my ethnographic work, to mark them differently to those who had moved out of Kashmir in the 1950s and 1960s for mainly economic reasons.
16. I use biographical chronotope not in the sense of Woolard (2013), but as an analytic portal that connects events, times and memories of migrant KPs, enabling

their individual biographies to assume semantic coherence across different time-space configurations. It also serves to identify the genre of 'Victim Diaspora' (à la Cohen 1999).
17. Nomadism in KP narratives does not refer to dispensing altogether with the idea of a fixed home or centre. Rather, nomadism for KPs is about repurposing the old habits of thought to negotiate and navigate 'cultural difference', to come to terms with a new meaning and representation in displacement.
18. Publications such as *Koshur Samachar* (Kashmiri News) and *Naad* (The Call) have a wide presence in the homes of the KP diasporas in Delhi and other major cities in India. These monthly magazines have been regularly publishing articles, editorials, appeals and first-hand accounts highlighting the plight of KPs in Delhi (and elsewhere) and demanding a safe space for the return of KPs. But, mainly, these magazines offer a continued effort to preserve and protect the distinctive identity of the diaspora community.
19. 'Next year in Kashmir' echoes the Jewish yearnings in exile: next year in Jerusalem!
20. Article 370 of the Indian Constitution gave special status to Jammu and Kashmir (J&K), conferring it with the power to have a separate constitution, a state flag and autonomy over the internal administration of the state. The net effect was that Jammu and Kashmir state's residents live under a separate set of laws, including those related to citizenship, ownership of property and fundamental rights, as compared to residents of other Indian states. Article 35A of the Indian Constitution empowered the J&K state's legislature to define 'permanent residents' of the state and provide special rights and privileges to them. These privileges included the ability to purchase land and immovable property, the ability to vote and contest elections, to seek government employment and to avail themselves of other state benefits such as higher education and health care. Non-permanent residents of the state, even if Indian citizens, were not entitled to these 'privileges'. (Source: https://en.wikipedia.org/wiki/Article_370_of_the_Constitution_of_India#Change_of_status_of_Jammu_and_Kashmir; https://en.wikipedia.org/wiki/Article_35A_of_the_Constitution_of_India).

References

Agha, A. (2007). *Language and Social Relations*. Cambridge: Cambridge University Press.
Bakhtin, M. M. (1981 [1935]). *The Dialogic Imagination*. C. Emerson and M. Holquist, trans.; M. Holquist, ed. Austin: University of Texas Press.
Bakhtin, M. M. (1986). *Speech Genres and Other Late Essays*. Austin: University of Texas Press.
Bhabha, H. (1994). *The Location of Culture*. New York: Routledge.
Blommaert, J. (2015). Chronotopes, scales, and complexity in the study of language in society. *The Annual Review of Anthropology*, 44: 105–16.
Blommaert, J. (2017). Commentary: Mobility, contexts, and the chronotope. *Language in Society*, 46 (1): 95–9.
Blommaert, J. and A. De Fina (2017). Chronotopic identities: On the time-space organization of who we are. In A. De Fina and J. Wegner (eds), *Diversity and Super-Diversity*. Washington: Georgetown University Press, pp. 1–14.
Clifford, J. (1994). Diasporas. *Cultural Anthropology*, 9 (3): 302–38.
Cohen, Robin (1999). *Global Diasporas: An Introduction*. London: Routledge.

Cohen, R. and C. Fisher (eds) (2019). *Routledge Handbook of Diaspora Studies*. London: Routledge.
Duschinski, H. (2008). 'Survival is now our politics': Kashmiri Hindu community identity and the politics of homeland. *International Journal of Hindu Studies*, 12 (1): 41–64.
Evans, A. (2002). A departure from history: Kashmiri Pandits 1990–2001. *Contemporary South Asia*, 11 (1): 19–37.
Fair, C. C. (2014). *Fighting to the End: The Pakistan Army's Way of War*. Oxford: Oxford University Press.
Gal, S. (2018). Visions and revisions of minority languages. In P. Lane, J. Costa and H. De Korne (eds), *Standardizing Minority Languages: Competing Ideologies of Authority and Authenticity in the Global Periphery*. New York and Abingdon: Routledge, pp. 222–42.
Ghai [Kumari], V. (2007 [1973]). *The Nilamata Purana: A Brief Survey*. https://ikashmir.net/nilmatapurana/doc/nilmatapurana.pdf.
Giddens, A. (1995). *A Contemporary Critique of Historical Materialism*. Stanford, CA: Stanford University Press.
Hangloo, R. L. (2000). *The State in Medieval Kashmir*. New Delhi: Manohar.
Holloway, J. and O. Valins (2002). Editorial: Placing religion and spirituality in geography. *Social and Cultural Geography*, 3 (1): 5–9.
Karimzad, F. (2020). Metapragmatics of normalcy: Mobility, context, and language choice. *Language & Communication*, 70: 107–18.
Karimzad, F. (2021). Multilingualism, chronotopes, and resolutions: Toward an analysis of the total sociolinguistic fact. *Applied Linguistics*. https://doi.org/10.1093/applin/amaa053.
Karimzad, F. and L. Catedral (2021). *Chronotopes and Migration: Language, Social Imagination, and Behavior*. New York: Routledge.
Kaul, R. (2005). *Migration and Society: A Study of Displaced Kashmiri Pandits*. Jaipur: Rawat Publications.
Kaul, B. K. and J. N. Raina (1931–2). *Bahar-e-gulshan-e-Kashmir*. Allahabad: Indian Press.
Kilam, J. L. (1955). *A History of Kashmiri Pandits*. Srinagar: Gandhi Memorial College, Managing Committee.
Koul, A. (1991 [1924]). *The Kashmiri Pandit*. Calcutta: Thacker & Spink.
Kumari, V. (1988 [1966]). *The Nilmatpurana: A Cultural and Literary Study*. Srinagar: J & K Academy of Art, Culture and Language.
Madan, T. N. (1998). Coping with ethnicity in South Asia: Bangladesh, Punjab, and Kashmir compared. *Ethnic and Racial Studies*, 21 (5): 969–89.
Madan, T. N. (2008). Kashmir, Kashmiris, and Kashmiriyat: An introductory essay. In A. Rao (ed.), *The Valley of Kashmir: The Making and Unmaking of a Composite Culture?* New Delhi: Manohar Publishers, pp. 1–35.
Pant, K. (1987). *The Kashmiri Pandit: The Story of a Community in Exile in the 19th and 20th centuries*. New Delhi: Allied Publishers.
Parimu, R. K. (1969). *A History of Muslim Rule in Kashmir*. New Delhi and Kolkata: Capital Publishing House.
Peeren, E. (2006). Through the lens of the chronotope: Suggestions for a spatio-temporal perspective on diaspora. In M. Baronian, S. Besser and Y. Jansen (eds), *Diaspora and Memory*. Amsterdam: Brill Rodopi, pp. 67–77.
Reynolds, N. (2008). Revisiting key episodes in modern Kashmiri history. In A. Rao (ed.), *The Valley of Kashmir: The Making and Unmaking of a Composite Culture?* New Delhi: Manohar Publishers, pp. 563–604.
Stierstorfer, K. and J. Wilson (eds) (2018). *The Routledge Diaspora Studies Reader*. New York: Routledge.
Teng, M. K. and C. L. Gadoo (1991). *White Paper on Kashmir*. New Delhi: Joint Human Rights Committee for Minorities in Kashmir.

Trivedi, V. (1996). *The Heritage of Kashmir*. New Delhi: Manohar.
Wodak, R. and M. Meyer (eds) (2016). *Methods of Critical Discourse Studies*. London: Sage.
Woolard, K. (2013). Is the personal political? Chronotopes and changing stances toward Catalan language and identity. *International Journal of Bilingual Education and Bilingualism*, 16 (2): 210–24.

CHAPTER 3

Patterns of Language Use in the Diaspora Communities in Kolkata

Aditi Ghosh

1. Introduction

The traditional perception of diaspora, developed in connection with the history of traumatic displacement, and subsequent migration and dispersion of the Jewish community, carries with it an intrinsic assumption of an ineffaceable allocation of geographical space to groups of people, assigned to them by birth. It assumes that human groups, categorised according to social-cultural markers, have only one legitimate homeland and all the other places for settlement for the said group are temporary dispersions, often associated with an inference of trespass, with the ultimate aim being to return to the homeland.

In this sense, the concept of diaspora feeds into that of the nation-state which presumes the natural habitat of a socio-culturally homogenous population within a political boundary, sharply contrasted with other human groups bounded by other political boundaries. This conceptualisation of diaspora appears untenable and out of date in the current time where the movements of people are increasingly the norm rather than the aberration. As the assumptions of a pre-determined homeland and an absolute nation-state have been called to question (Anderson [1983] 2006), works on diaspora has also evolved to incorporate the changing nature of human mobility and loosening ties of groups with geographical spaces (cf. Clifford 1994, Gilroy 1994, Hall 1990). This change has often led to an expansion of the meaning of 'diaspora' in academic studies as well as media representations to include a wide range of cases including those of immigrants, expatriates, refugees, guest workers, exile communities and overseas ethnic communities. This leads to the notion of 'long-distance diaspora' (Anderson 1998), i.e. communities with emotional and social ties to the idealised homeland, often offering support to ultra-nationalist movements. This 'diaspora explosion' (Brubaker 2005: 1), with a tendency to incorporate every dispersed community under the extended meaning of the term, risks compromising the distinctiveness and utility of the term altogether. Tölöyan (1996) had earlier cautioned that the term ran the risk of becoming a 'promiscuously capacious category'. Consequently, the focus of current studies moves away from defining diaspora in terms of 'homeland' as a geographical space, to that of an overall attitudinal orientation. Here homeland is constructed, to quote Said (1978), in terms of 'imaginative geography and history... to intensify its own sense of itself by dramatising the difference between what is close to it and what is far away'. The diaspora communities in such cases are understood as dynamic categories involving a stance and an orientation towards a homeland as reflected in their attitudes, ideologies and practices. Brubaker (2005), following the leading works on Diaspora, draws up three core criteria for the constitution of a diasporic community.

1. *Dispersion in space.* This is the most basic criteria for defining any diasporic community, but unlike the classical understanding of diaspora, here dispersion includes voluntary movement, often motivated by social or economic upward mobility, and it also includes movements within borders of nation-states.
2. *Orientation towards a real or imagined homeland.* This may be the most pertinent criteria for defining diasporic communities in today's context. The orientation (or a stance or attitude towards) a homeland (and its symbolic and cultural representation) as existing in collective memory or myth with loyalty and commitment towards maintenance and betterment gives a diasporic community a distinctiveness from the host culture.
3. *Boundary maintenance.* This involves adopting a non-assimilative identity and maintenance of distinctiveness vis-à-vis neighbouring cultures of the host space.

In the Indian context, language constitutes an indispensable criterion in the construction of diaspora communities. Cases of language-based groups of Indian citizens settled within India – but away from the geopolitical regions historically, politically or conventionally assigned to their language and linguistic communities – constitute the most common diasporic population in India. The historical association of different languages to different geographical areas in India was reinforced in the linguistic reorganisation of states (or the State Reorganisation Act of (1956) which tried to enforce some linguistic homogeneity within the state boundaries. This validation of linking language to regions tends to assign the status of 'outsiders' or 'migrants' to non-dominant linguistic groups settled (often for generations) in different localities in India. For a detailed analysis on the impact of linguistic reorganisation with special focus on issues in the border of Maharashtra and Karnataka (see Kulkarni-Joshi forthcoming).

The homeland orientation of such communities is strongly associated with the language associated with the homeland. However, rather than a communication medium, here language tends to assume the position of a collective cultural marker or a symbolic representation. Such communities may comprise people who have limited competence in their home language and have rather restricted use of those languages. Yet, even in such cases, the language of the homeland remains a marker of the community and people.

Kolkata is the capital of West Bengal, where Bengali is the official state language, and where the majority of the state speaks Bengali as the primary language. The city is intrinsically associated with Bengali people, language and culture. Kolkata's stereotypical association with Bengali often overlooks the fact that the city has been the home for many languages and cultures for centuries (cf. Clark 1956, Raj 2011, A. Ghosh 2015). Bengali is the numerically dominant regional language, and according to 2001 Census data the Bengali speaking population constitutes 62 per cent of the total population of the city. There are other estimates which give a lower percentage of Bengali residents in the city. For example, according to a report placed in the parliament in 2003, the Bengali speaking population in Kolkata is about 37 per cent (Sarkar 2005) In any case, the numbers show the presence of a large diasporic population of Kolkata residents who speak various other languages (other than Bengali).

The multilingual situation in Kolkata is of course not unique, since most modern cities are multilingual as a result of dispersion, migration and long-term settlements of groups of people caused primarily by voluntary movements due to social, occupational and various other objectives. At the same time, in spite of their natural diversity, cities exercise various pressures towards homogenisation. These may be overt (in the form of incentives, discriminative policies, etc.) or covert (in the form of social or cultural alienation, etc.). Cumulatively they have the effect of discouraging non-dominant languages to develop or to be maintained. Even when the promotion of a language is not overtly backed by the administration, the non-dominant languages may face what Bourdieu (1991) calls 'symbolic domination'. Studies on the relationship between city and languages (cf. Cassesnoves and Sankoff 2003, Chriost 2007, Chand 2011, Siemund 2013) focus on diverse outcomes of the inter-language dynamics in the cities including language dominance, uneven distribution of language-based power and resources, real or perceived pressure on the non-dominant or non-majority language speakers to shift or 'assimilate' to the dominant and majority language(s).

One of the key approaches to understanding language dynamics in multilingual spaces is to look into how individual languages are distributed by their use across the spectrum of human communication. Fishman's (1965) concept of the domain-based functional distribution of languages is a pertinent tool to investigate the functional relevance of particular languages in multilingual scenarios. Based on this framework, Parasher (1980) investigated English and mother tongue usage among educated urban bilinguals residing in the cities of Hyderabad and Secunderabad. He showed that English is often in a diglossia-like distribution with the mother tongues in Indian cities. Not unexpectedly for the times, the mother tongue dominates in the home domain and English dominates in all domains of formal/official communication.

This chapter explores the pattern of language choice, in different domains, among the population who are residents of Kolkata and do not have the host language of the city, i.e. Bengali, as their mother tongue. Though the study started with the aim to study the language usage of the 'long-term migrants' of Kolkata, a large section of the respondents (409 out of the total 495) interviewed for the study, was born and brought up in Kolkata. Additionally, more than 60 per cent of the respondents reported that they consider Kolkata as their 'home' and given a choice they would like to settle in Kolkata in their future (for details see A. Ghosh 2019). In such cases, the term 'migrant' even in its inclusive sense of the term (Carling n.d., *Glossary on Migration* 2019: 132–3) does not do justice in describing the population under survey. On the contrary, 'diaspora', in the modified sense of the term (a population living away from the real or imagined homeland with a distinctive orientation towards it) appears better suited. The respondents in this study represent multiple diaspora communities distinguished in terms of their orientation towards homelands along with the languages of homelands.

The aim of the study is to examine the use and influence of three dominant languages of the city (viz., Bengali – the official state language and the language of the majority of the population of the city; English – one of the two official languages of India and a language that carries great functional, social and utilitarian value for upward mobility; and Hindi – the official language of India with a history of several attempts to be promoted to the status of a national language and a symbolic representation of the nation-state of India) and their mother tongues in the lives of the target populations.

2. Theoretical framework

As mentioned earlier, the study will analyse the data based on Fishman's (1965) framework of language distribution across different domains of communication in the setting of a widespread stable multilingual context. Apart from providing an explanation of the socio-cultural organisation of language choices in a spectrum of multilingual communication context, up to now it has been one of the most successful frameworks in explaining the system of relationship between language choice in multilingual communication and various social, cultural and other factors, including setting or context of communication, the topic of conversation, and the relationship between the interlocutors.

In this study the respondents are asked to report their choice of language in different communication contexts and with different interlocuters. As expected in a multilingual urban space like Kolkata, many of them have reported use of more than one language or switching between languages in those situations. In such cases, they were asked to rank those languages in order of preference. In this study primarily the first preference is used for analysis (see section 4).

Fishman's original theorisation of domain-based distribution of language use was primarily directed to communication patterns in the multilingual in-groups, rather than communication in contact situations. The approach though is extremely useful in studying language-use patterns in language contact situations. In contact situations communication requires a shift away from the native language for at least one (and sometimes both) of the interlocutors. Here the language towards which the interlocutors choose to shift is of particular interest. In multilingual communications, the languages chosen for communication as a matter of common agreement by diverse linguistic groups may be indicative of several factors (for the politics of using a so-called lingua franca see Phillipson 2008). Usually, the chosen language in such cases is the one associated with prestige and power (or the H language (Ferguson 1959)). However, there may be various other factors that influence such choices. For speakers with a non-dominant native language in a multilingual city like Kolkata, such choice is indicative of the system of language behaviour required for them to develop an appropriate communicative competence in the city.

3. The background of the respondents

The respondents for this chapter were 495 educated long-term residents of Kolkata, who do not have Bengali – the major regional language – as their mother tongue (a term discussed in the next section). Only those respondents were selected whose parents do not have Bengali as a mother tongue. To ensure that the respondents were long-term residents of Kolkata, only those who had lived in the city for at least nine consecutive years at the time of the interview were included in the survey. Secondly, only those with at least ten years of formal education were selected to ensure relatively uniform exposure to the English language which can only be learned in this way. The responses were collected via structured questionnaire schedules.

The composition of the sample interviewed for the survey is as follows. The length of stay in Kolkata for the respondents ranges from nine years to seventy-eight years (mean 27.82 and mode 20); a large majority of the informants (82.6 per cent) have lived in Kolkata all their lives. Many have expressed their deep attachment to the city (for a detailed discussion see A. Ghosh 2019).

A larger section of the sample (73.3 per cent) is made up of women. Respondents for this study are from the area under Kolkata Municipal Corporation surrounded by Howrah, North 24 Parganas and South 24 Parganas. Though some of these border districts are considered to be under Greater Kolkata and share the Kolkata Postal Index Number, these districts are not included in the study.

The age range of the residents is from fifteen to eighty-one with a mean of 33.89 and a mode of 18 (smallest value of multiple modes). Among the respondents 34.3 per cent (N = 170) have completed graduation, 34 per cent (N = 168) have completed higher secondary or equivalent (class XII), 8.3 per cent (N = 41) have completed secondary or school-leaving exams (class X) and the rest have various higher degrees including postgraduate, MPhil., PhD, post-doctorate. Occupation-wise, the data consisted of a large number of students (44.2 per cent, N = 218). Other than that, the data consist of housewives (16 per cent, N = 79), teachers and other educationalists (15 per cent, N = 74), professionals (13.8 per cent, N= 65), businessmen (4.9 per cent, N = 24), retired persons (2.4 per cent, N = 12), and the rest are in various other occupations.

3.1 Mother tongue

As discussed already, the language background of the diaspora communities, particularly in the Indian context, is a vital part of their homeland orientation. In this survey, the most commonly used term 'mother tongue' (henceforth MT) was used during the interview with the respondents to elicit their language background, as this term is the only one firmly established in common knowledge as indicative of one's language affiliations. Needless to say, the term has its own complexities (cf. Gupta 1997: 499, Le Page and Tabouret-Keller 1985: 189ff., Skutnabb-Kangas 2008: 105ff.). Apart from the universal problem associated with determining MTs, in India there are a few specific problems. The division and grouping of language varieties into different languages is quite controversial in India. In the Indian census, smaller or minor language varieties that are grouped under larger languages are named mother tongues. In this sense MTs parallel what is traditionally understood by linguists as dialects. There are some well-documented problems in the system of grouping these varieties under languages as well. For example, a large number of genealogically divergent language varieties are grouped under Hindi in the Indian census (for a detailed discussion see A. Ghosh 2012: 436ff.). On the other hand, in spite of the extreme structural similarity between languages like Hindi and

Urdu, they are firmly established as separate languages in the census as well as in general perception. Additionally, in certain areas of India, the nature of language affiliation is 'fluid' (Khubchandani 1983, 1974). This means that as the individuals or communities are proficient in several languages or language varieties as well as in the linguistic culture, they can project any or all of them as part of their regular language repertoire. In such repertoires the boundary between the languages and language varieties becomes 'fluid' or flexible. This often leads to some fluctuation in the reporting of MTs during language surveys and censuses.

Predictably, recording the language background of the respondents in this survey was a complex matter and has produced a range of diverse responses. Some respondents claimed affiliation to multiple MTs, either because their parents have different MTs, or because they feel that they have a stronger allegiance to a different language than that of their parents. Other respondents reported varieties that do not have language status in the Indian Constitution (e.g. Khortha, Pahari, etc.). Some respondents named both the variety and the recognised standard language under which they are grouped as their MTs (for example, Khari Boli and Hindi.)

In Table 3.1 all entries are presented as they are reported by the respondents. The multiple MT responses are presented with forward slashes (e.g. Haryanvi Hindi/Marwari) and alternative spellings and pronunciations are given in brackets. Overall, the respondents interviewed in this survey reported forty-one different MTs or MT combinations (Table 3.1), not all of which constitute separate languages or MTs. A large section of respondents (N = 88) said that they have more than one MT. Such responses were most consistently reported with some of the languages and language varieties associated with Hindi.

As Table 3.1 shows, the Hindi MT respondents constitute the largest section of the sample at 30.9 per cent. However, the categorisation of MTs taken as reported by the respondents posed some problems. Apart from reporting more than one MT (Hindi as one of the MTs in all cases), some reported Bhojpuri, Awadhi, Marwari, etc., as their MT. However, these are classified as MTs under the Hindi language in the Indian census. In Table 3.2 all the multiple mother tongue responses (with Hindi as one of the MTs) and those MTs which are classified under Hindi in the census are taken together as 'Hindi(s)' or kinds of Hindi. There were twenty-three such responses in total. The percentage of the Hindi(s) group then becomes much higher at 64.6 per cent and the total number of MT categories comes down to eighteen (see Table 3.2).

4. Methods and findings

The responses were collected by fieldworkers through interviews which lasted for about forty-five minutes on average by a carefully designed questionnaire schedule, which was pre-tested in a pilot study (Ghosh, Dan and Bhadra 2009). The questionnaire was designed to elicit self-reports from the respondents about their language usage in different domains, situations, and with different interlocutors. As the data is drawn from self-reports, there remains a chance of respondents misjudging their actual usage. There may also be a tendency to provide more socially appropriate answers. However, even in such cases, the choice of language – or at

Table 3.1 Reported mother tongues of respondents

	N	%
Hindi	153	30.9
Marwari	39	7.9
Malayalam	37	7.5
Hindi/Bhojpuri	37	7.5
Hindi/Marwari	32	6.5
Tamil	26	5.3
Bhojpuri	25	5.1
Urdu	24	4.8
Gujarati	19	3.8
Punjabi	19	3.8
Maithili	15	3.0
Oriya	9	1.8
Nepali	7	1.4
Telugu	5	1.0
Konkani	5	1.0
French	3	0.6
Braj	3	0.6
Angika	3	0.6
Hindi/Bhojpuri/Awadhi	3	0.6
Hindi/Maithili	3	0.6
Marathi	2	0.4
Hindi/Khari Boli	2	0.4
Awadhi	2	0.4
Hindi/Urdu	2	0.4
Hindi/Bihari	2	0.4
Hindi/Magahi	2	0.4
Hindi/Punjabi	2	0.4
Lisan ul-Dawaat	1	0.2
Kannada	1	0.2
Chinese	1	0.2
Magahi	1	0.2
Rajasthani	1	0.2
Kachchi (or Kutchi) Gujarati	1	0.2
Khotta (or Khortha)	1	0.2
Sindhi	1	0.2
Kalwar	1	0.2
Haryanvi Hindi/Marwari	1	0.2
Hindi/Kumauni	1	0.2
Pahari/Kumauni	1	0.2
Pahari/Kashmiri	1	0.2
Hindi/Bengali	1	0.2
Total	495	100

least what is considered to be the ideal choice of language by the respondent – is represented. This reflects the ideological standpoint of the respondents towards the languages.

The domains here are based primarily on the socio-cultural setting of the communication and are broadly categorised into three categories. These were (1) home, (2) official – including workplace and schools, and (3) other domains – including neighbourhood, friendship, and locales of regular communications such as banks,

Language Use in the Diaspora Communities in Kolkata

Table 3.2 *Respondents' mother tongues – modified in relation to Hindi as cover term*

	Frequency	Percent
Hindi (s)	319	64.6
Malayalam	37	7.5
Tamil	26	5.3
Urdu	24	4.8
Punjabi	19	3.8
Gujarati	19	3.8
Maithili	15	3.0
Oriya	9	1.8
Nepali	7	1.4
Konkani	5	1.0
Telugu	5	1.0
French	3	.6
Marathi	2	.4
Sindhi	1	.2
Kachchi Gujarati	1	.2
Chinese	1	.2
Kannada	1	.2
Lisan ul-Dawaat	1	.2
Total	495	100

post offices, markets, etc. Within these settings, the respondents were asked to report their choice of languages for communicating with different addressees. As the respondents are all multilingual urban residents, with various degrees of mastery over at least four languages – Bengali, Hindi, English, and their MTs (or three languages if the MT is Hindi), they often reported that they would choose more than one language for the same setting and the same addressee. In such cases, they were asked to rank the languages that they would use in order of preference. As mentioned in section 2, in this chapter, the primary analysis is of the first preference for language for communication in the three categories outlined above. In section 4.2, the results of the second-most preferred languages per individual are also analysed to further reveal the extent of multilingual communication.

4.1 Language use

In the following sections, the most preferred languages in different domains, as reported by the respondents, are presented. The data collected showed a large number of languages as first preference in different domains of use. In some domains, the total number of languages elicited was as high as ten. However, in all cases, the four most reported languages are the MT, Bengali, English and Hindi. In the following charts, the choice of these four languages is presented by the actual number and their valid[1] percentage.[2]

4.1.1 Language choice: home domain

The home domain is crucial for issues relating to language maintenance for non-dominant languages and for the MTs of diaspora populations. Table 3.3 shows that the MT dominated as the preferred language for communication in almost all cases at home, except for communication with domestic help, most of whom are presumably

Table 3.3 *Language preference of respondents in the home domain*

Interlocutor	MT		Hindi		Bengali		English	
	N	%	N	%	N	%	N	%
Grandfather	216	84.0	21	8.2	1	0.4	3	1.2
Grandmother	263	84.3	24	7.7	1	0.3	1	0.3
Father	376	82.6	51	10.3	5	1.0	8	1.8
Mother	387	83.2	46	9.9	6	1.3	10	2.2
Father-in-law	155	82.9	17	9.1	11	5.9	1	0.5
Mother-in-law	164	81.6	20	10.0	12	6.0	0	0
Husband	101	71.1	29	20.4	4	2.8	6	4.2
Wife	74	83.1	8	9.0	4	4.5	1	1.1
Brother	311	74.2	52	12.4	8	1.9	36	8.6
Sister	271	75.1	41	11.2	7	1.9	30	8.2
Son	106	68.4	30	19.4	7	4.5	11	2.2
Daughter	99	66.4	33	22.1	8	5.4	8	5.4
Other relatives	368	76.0	72	14.9	12	2.9	9	1.9
Household helps	99	29.2	74	21.8	158	46.6	2	0.9

from a different linguistic background than the respondents. Hindi comes second as the most preferred language followed by English and Bengali respectively. However, there is also a noticeable shift in preferred language across generations. Figure 3.1 is based on the data of most preferred language for communication with grandparents, parents, siblings and children (as presented in Table 3.3) and shows that there is a minor but consistent decline in the choice of MTs across generations, with a simultaneous increase in preference for Hindi. Among the other two languages, there is a sharp increase in the preference of English as a preferred language for communicating with generations below the parent's generation. Bengali is the least preferred among these languages, though there is a minor increase in its use in communication with sons and daughters.

Figure 3.1 represents the language choice of the respondents for communication with members from different generations within the family and it shows some decline in the choice of MT. Figure 3.2 is based on the respondents' perception of language preference among different age groups within their linguistic community for intra-age group communication. They were asked to report their understanding about the most preferred language of communication for people who were older, younger and the same age as them, for communicating among themselves.

Here we found a sharper decline (compared to Figure 3.1) in the choice of MT for communication across age groups and an almost equally sharp increase in preference for Hindi and English for communication with the younger generation (see Figure 3.2). It may be concluded that at least ideologically even if not in actual use, English is accepted as much as Hindi as a language for younger people. Bengali, though it also shows an increase with age of the interlocuters, again appears to be the least preferred language in all the cases, except for communication among the older age group where it is preferred (by 2.1 per cent) over English (0 per cent).

4.1.2 Language choice: official domain

Under the official domain, two main formal areas of interactions are included, i.e. school and workplace. If we look at the highest percentage in language choice,

Language Use in the Diaspora Communities in Kolkata 57

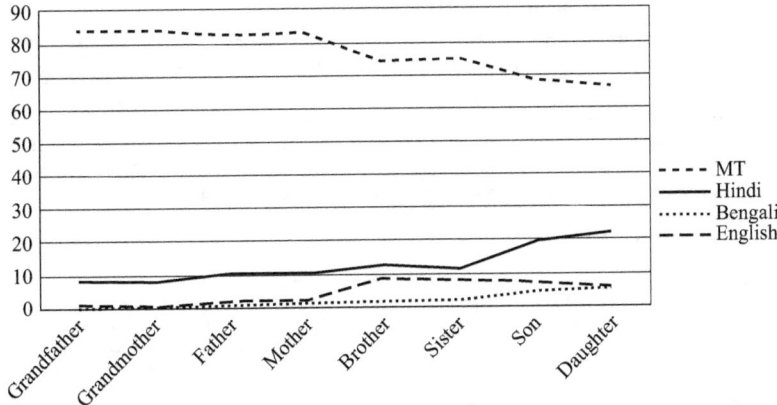

Figure 3.1 *Language preference of respondents showing language choice with interlocutors across generations*

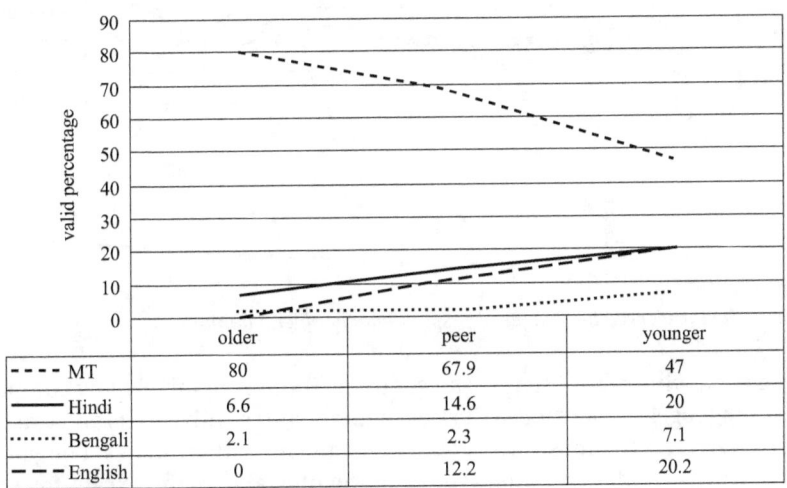

Figure 3.2 *Language preference of respondents for communication across age groups*

English, as expected, emerges as the most preferred language for communication with those ranked higher than the respondent communication (teacher and boss) and for formal interactions (with clients and other official interactions). For peer-group communication MT is the language of choice in schools (classmates), but Bengali is the choice of most for the workplace (with colleagues). Hindi is chosen for communication with lower-ranked colleagues. It was also noted there are some differences in the pattern of language preference in schools and workplaces.

It can be seen from Figure 3.3 and Table 3.4 that the preference for English is highest in most formal and high prestige interactions (during interaction with authority figures in school and office, such as teachers and bosses, and during other official interactions). Conversely, a preference for English is lower in intimate, informal and low-prestige domains – such as in interacting with classmates and

Table 3.4 Language choice: official domain

	MT		Hindi		Bengali		English	
	N	%	N	%	N	%	N	%
Teachers	154	35.3	69	15.8	27	6.2	180	41.3
Boss/authority	38	20.8	29	15.8	34	18.6	81	44.3
Other official interactions	76	17.1	51	10.5	54	10.9	263	59.1
Colleague	49	26.6	39	17.4	64	34.8	39	21.2
Client	25	18.7	31	23.1	26	19.4	51	38.1
Classmate	210	50.1	102	24.3	24	5.7	72	17.2
Subordinate	52	10.5	58	31.8	53	28.7	20	4
Others	155	34.0	106	23.2	89	19.5	94	20.6

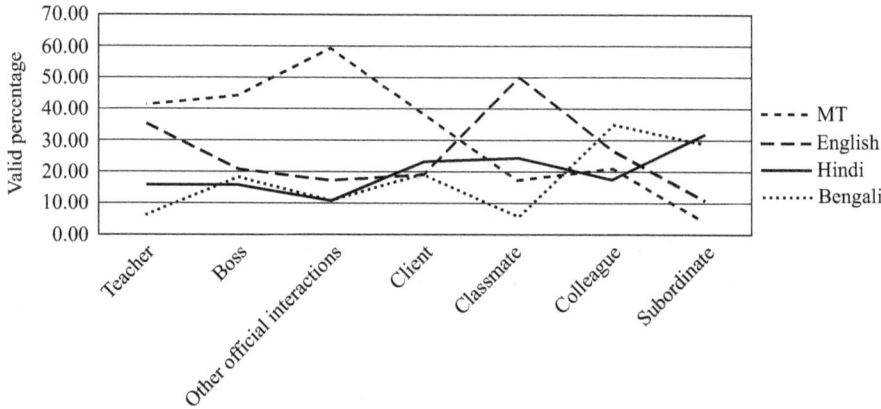

Figure 3.3 Most preferred languages of respondents in official domains

colleagues and with subordinates. The choice of Hindi is relatively low compared to the other languages. Nevertheless, it rises in interactions with clients and classmates, and turns out to be the most preferred language with subordinates. Bengali scores even lower than Hindi in all interactions in the official domain, except for communication with colleagues. Like Hindi it also scores highly in interaction with subordinates. This shows that in the official domain both Hindi and Bengali are preferred for informal and low-prestige communication. Bengali is preferred more than any other language for communication with colleagues in informal communication. The preference for Hindi in communication with subordinates indicates its association with low-prestige contexts. The MT is preferred by most for interaction with classmates. It is also preferred by a high percentage (second highest after English) as the language for communication with teachers. Bengali is the least preferred language for communication in school (6.2 per cent with teachers, 5.7 per cent with classmates). This may be explained by the other languages being used as the first language in schools previously attended by the respondents. Table 3.5 shows that most respondents had attended schools where they had MT as the first language (47.7 per cent) with only 1.4 per cent having had Bengali as the first language.

Some differences may be noted in the pattern of interaction in schools and workplaces. In both places English is the preferred language of communication with

Language Use in the Diaspora Communities in Kolkata 59

Table 3.5 *First language in schools attended by respondents*

	N	%
MT	236	47.7
Hindi	103	20.8
English	139	28.1
Tamil	3	.6
Kannada	4	.8
Malayalam	1	.2
Bengali	7	1.4
Assamese	1	.2
Oriya	1	.2
Total	495	100.0

authority figures (boss and teacher). However, for communication with peer groups (colleagues and classmates) some interesting differences emerge. A preference for the MT is notably higher in school (50.1 per cent) than in workplaces (26.6 per cent. This is a likely reflection of the relatively multilingual environment of workplaces compared to schools, which were more MT dominated. A preference for Bengali for peer-group communication in workplaces is significantly higher in workplaces (34.8 per cent) than in schools (5.7 per cent). A preference for Hindi over English also seems to reverse in peer-group interaction in schools versus workplaces. Whereas Hindi (24.3 per cent) is preferred over English in schools (17.4 per cent), English (21.2 per cent) is preferred over Hindi (17.2 per cent) by about the same percentage of respondents in workplaces.

4.1.3 Language choice in other domains

Other than home and official domains the different contexts of regular interaction can be classified into four major categories.

1. Relatively formal and non-intimate interactions in different governmental and similar institutions, such as: bank, post office, government offices, and hospitals.
2. Informal interactions for daily necessities in local shops, fish/vegetable markets, and with neighbours, taxi drivers, etc.
3. Intimate interaction such as with friends and in social occasions.
4. Interactions in relatively high-prestige social contexts, such as shopping malls and restaurants.

The results, as found in the survey are given in Table 3.6 and Figure 3.4.

Here Bengali appears as the most preferred language in almost all the interactions of the first category, viz., post offices, banks, government offices, hospitals. In the second category as well, Bengali emerges as the most preferred language in local shops (36 per cent in local shop, 47.4 per cent in fish and vegetable market), but not for interaction with taxi drivers (MT 36.6 per cent and Hindi 36.3 per cent) and neighbours (MT 43.8 per cent). Bengali is least preferred in the fourth category, showing a more or less consistent decline for its preference from low-prestige to high-prestige communication. The MT is the most preferred language for communication in the third category – with friends (52.6 per cent) and for socialising

Table 3.6 Language choice with friends, in the neighbourhood and in other domains

	MT		Hindi		Bengali		English	
	N	%	N	%	N	%	N	%
Friends	257	52.6	119	24.3	52	10.6	58	11.9
Neighbours	211	43.8	116	24.1	134	27.8	14	2.9
Taxi driver	174	36.6	173	36.3	127	26.7	1	0.2
Post office	129	28.4	86	18.9	219	48.1	20	4.4
Bank	116	24.6	77	15.3	178	37.7	106	22.5
Restaurant	137	29.4	112	24.0	83	17.8	131	28.1
Local shop	168	35.4	119	25.1	171	36.0	14	2.9
Fish/vegetable market	149	32.0	96	20.6	221	47.4	--	--
Shopping mall	126	27.2	95	20.5	86	18.5	157	33.8
Parties and social gatherings	179	38.6	96	20.7	41	8.8	137	29.5
Hospital	140	29.6	84	17.8	151	31.9	96	20.3
Government offices	122	27.9	51	11.7	192	43.9	69	15.8

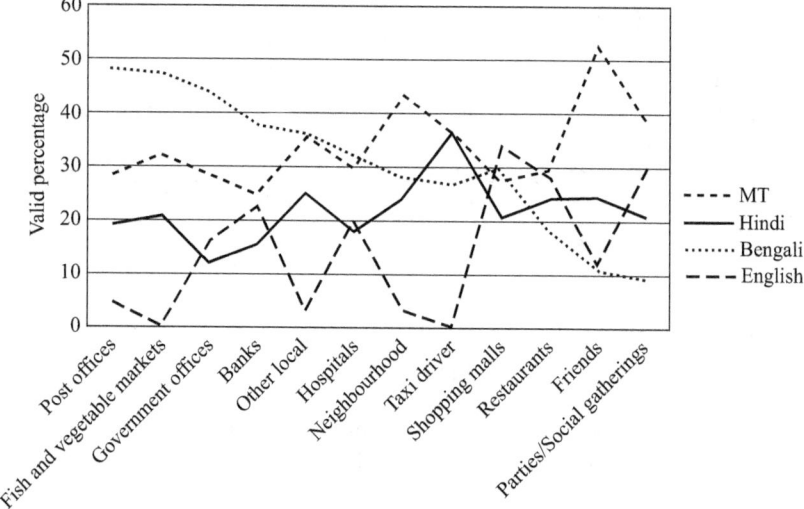

Figure 3.4 Language choice in other domains

(38.6 per cent). For the relatively high-status contexts of shopping malls and restaurants, English is the most preferred language (33.8 per cent and 28.1 per cent respectively).

A high preference for the MT for communication with neighbours, with friends and while socialising contrasts with a preference for other languages in workplace interactions (Table 3.4). This pattern reflects a tendency to live and socialise mostly within one's own linguistic community. This is confirmed by the responses in Table 3.7 regarding the MTs of most of the friends of each respondent. The large number of non-responses in the second-most preferred language for communication in different contexts (discussed in section 4.2) also indicates that communication in a particular domain and context is predominantly done in one language.

Language Use in the Diaspora Communities in Kolkata 61

Table 3.7 *Mother tongue of most friends*

	N	%
MT	257	52.3
Bengali	109	22.2
Hindi	78	15.9
Marwari	12	2.4
Bhojpuri	8	1.6
Gujarati	7	1.4
Tamil	5	1.0
Punjabi	4	0.8
Oriya	3	0.6
English	2	0.4
Urdu	2	0.4
Malayalam	1	0.2
Kannada	1	0.2
Bihari	1	0.2
No Preference	1	0.2

4.2 Second-most preferred languages in all domains

In this section, the percentage of the second-most preferred languages for communication in different domains, including 'no answers', are analysed to see if more than one language is involved in individual cases of communication. The results in the home domain (Table 3.8) show a high percentage of 'no answers', which indicates that, for each context of communication, one primary language is preferred. In the official domain (Table 3.9), the percentage of 'no responses' is comparatively lower. Here, except for communication with colleagues and subordinates, where Bengali is highest, English is the second-most preferred language in all cases. In other domains (Table 3.10), there are fewer non-responses and Bengali appears to be the second-most preferred language for communication in almost all contexts. The exceptions are parties and social gatherings, where English is preferred, and in hospitals where Hindi is preferred. In two other contexts of communication Bengali is preferred by slightly fewer numbers than other languages. For interaction in shopping malls, preference for Hindi is slightly greater than for Bengali, and for interactions with friends, English is preferred by a marginal number.

4.3 Language choice: inter-linguistic communication

To ascertain the choice of language for inter-linguistic as well as intra-linguistic situations, the respondents were asked to report the language most preferred by them when speaking to speakers of their own MT, when speaking to Bengali and Hindi speakers, and when speaking to speakers of other languages. The results (given in Tables 3.11 and 3.12) show that, while speaking to speakers of Bengali, Hindi and speakers of their own MT, the most preferred language is the language of the addressee. This remains the same when the respondents are the addressees, i.e. while communicating with Bengali and Hindi speakers the language of communication is predominantly Bengali and English irrespective of the MT of the respondents. When speaking to speakers of languages other than these three, they reported a

Table 3.8 Percentage of second-most preferred language in home domain

Interlocutor	MT	Hindi	Bengali	English	No Answer
Grandfather	2.0	1.0	0.0	1.0	95.6
Grandmother	1.6	1.2	0	0.2	96.2
Father	3.2	3.6	3.0	6.5	83.4
Mother	4.2	3.8	1.8	3.6	85.9
Husband	9.0	9.0	2.6	4.2	89.3
Wife	3.0	0.6	0.6	2.0	96.2
Brother	6.5	4.6	2.2	10.1	75.8
Sister	5.9	4.0	1.2	7.9	80.8
Son	1.8	2.0	1.2	7.1	87.5
Daughter	2.4	2.4	1.2	7.1	86.7
Other relatives	7.3	6.3	5.3	9.3	71.1

Table 3.9 Percentage of second-most preferred language in official domain

	MT	Hindi	Bengali	English	No Answer
Teacher	6.1	5.3	8.9	15.4	63.4
Boss	2.4	2.8	5.5	6.9	63.8
Colleague	4.0	5.1	7.5	5.7	77.8
Classmate	6.3	7.3	7.1	16.8	61.6
Client	2.2	4.6	3.0	6.1	84.0
Subordinate	1.4	4.0	6.5	3.2	84.8
Other official interaction	4.4	6.7	7.9	8.7	72.3

Table 3.10 Percentage of second-most preferred language in other domains

	MT	Hindi	Bengali	English	No answer
Friends	8.7	10.1	13.1	13.7	47.7
Neighbour	7.5	8.5	11.1	4.8	66.9
Taxi driver	4.4	8.9	19.8	0.6	34.4
Post office	1.8	2.6	14.1	3.6	76.8
Bank	4.4	8.7	15.6	10.7	60.6
Local shop	4.2	8.1	12.5	2.6	72.5
Fish/vegetable market	3.0	7.5	12.5	0.6	76.2
Shopping mall	5.3	12.9	12.5	12.1	57.2
Parties and social gatherings	10.1	11.7	14.1	16.8	47.1
Hospital	4.8	12.5	11.7	11.1	59.8
Government offices	3.0	6.7	11.1	9.7	69.5

Table 3.11 Choice of language for inter-linguistic communication by respondents

	MT		Hindi		Bengali		English	
	N	%	N	%	N	%	N	%
Own MT speakers	394	80.4	63	12.9	5	1	7	1.4
Bengali speakers	51	10.3	40	8.1	377	76.9	22	4.5
Hindi Speakers	221	44.6	241	50.8	1	0.2	11	2.3
Other language speakers	108	23.0	109	23.2	13	2.8	222	47.3

Table 3.12 Choice of language by other speakers while speaking to the respondents

	MT		Hindi		Bengali		English	
	N	%	N	%	N	%	N	%
Own MT speakers	381	77.8	59	12.0	8	1.6	11	2.2
Bengali speakers	41	8.4	38	7.8	397	81.2	11	2.7
Hindi speakers	229	47.4	240	49.7	3	0.6	11	2.2
Other language speakers	88	19.9	112	25.3	22	5.0	197	44.5

Table 3.13 Language choice in scripted media

	MT		Hindi		Bengali		English	
	N	%	N	%	N	%	N	%
Reading newspaper	105	21.2	41	8.3	15	3.1	328	66.9
Reading books	162	32.7	68	13.7	9	1.8	244	50.4
Writing letters	129	27.7	45	9.1	5	1.0	285	61.2
Other documents	39	8.5	24	5.2	3	0.3	394	85.7
Films	222	45.5	176	36.1	16	3.3	71	14.5
Songs	240	49.4	160	32.9	26	5.3	56	11.5
TV programmes	249	52.4	163	34.3	19	4.0	42	8.8

preference for English (47.3 per cent while addressing them and 44.5 per cent while being addressed), which shows a preference for English as the lingua franca.

4.4 Language choice in other spheres

Language choice in other spheres can be categorised into two main types. Firstly, the choice of language for reading and writing is overwhelmingly English, followed by Hindi. Secondly, the choice of language for most entertainment media is dominated by the MT and Hindi. Bengali is least preferred in all these spheres.

5. Conclusion

The principal trends of language choice, as found in the survey, are as follows.

The MT is predominantly preferred for communication within the family. However, there is a slight but consistent decline in this preference across the generations. This is also confirmed by the respondents' reported patterns of language use among different age groups. Hindi is the most preferred language as the replacement by showing an overall increase in preference across generations. English is also perceived as the language of youth, as its preference almost equals Hindi for the younger age group.

In the official domain, English is expectedly preferred in high-prestige and formal communications. Hindi is preferred in low-prestige situations. The preferred language for intimate communication varies in schools and workplaces. The MT is most preferred in school, whereas Bengali is preferred in the workplace – which is presumably more diverse than schools. Preference for Bengali is lower than Hindi in all contexts of communication within the official domain except for communication with colleagues.

Bengali is preferred for everyday non-intimate, obligatory interactions in various government offices and local shops, but for communication in the more up-market contexts the preferred language is English. For most other kinds of voluntary social interactions, the MT is the preferred language.

English is the preferred lingua franca in inter-linguistic situations. Hindi and MT are preferred languages for entertainment whereas English is dominant in written communications.

If we try to establish a functional distribution of Hindi, English, Bengali and MTs, it may be seen that the MT is dominant in intimate, voluntary and informal communications – within the family, among classmates in schools, and in other voluntary social interactions including communication with friends. Along with Hindi, it is also the most preferred language for entertainment and media. MT is also preferred for intra-community interaction among various age groups, though there is a decline in its preference among younger age groups.

Bengali is mostly dominant in regular, local and obligatory communications including banks, post offices, etc., for communication among colleagues in workplaces, and for communication with household help. It is also the second-most preferred language in almost all contexts other than family and official domains.

English is most preferred for formal communications and for communication in high-prestige settings, including shopping malls and restaurants. And it is also the most preferred for written communication and for inter-linguistic communication. It is also preferred as much as Hindi for communication among younger age groups. This shows that even though the actual number of contexts in which English is preferred most for communication is restricted, English remains a coveted language.

A preference for Hindi is increasing among younger age groups within the family and in some other intimate communications. However, the preference for Hindi in low-prestige communication in the workplace indicates its relatively low status. Hindi (along with English) is also dominant in entertainment media.

As in Parasher's (1980) study, a diglossia-like distribution is noticed here too as the languages from their repertoires are distributed across different domains of usage in the overall data. However, the data in the home domain, especially across generations, show other dominant languages, i.e. Hindi and English, replacing the erstwhile home languages, reflecting a gradual 'leak' (Fishman 1967) into the stability of the diglossic situation. It may be concluded that a slow shift is in progress among educated non-Bengali speakers residing in Kolkata. And this shift is towards Hindi from MT, not to the local language of Bengali.

Talking about language adaptation of the Indian diaspora in the international context, the writer Amitav Ghosh (2002) points out that the uniqueness of the Indian diaspora lies in the fact that the links between India (the 'homeland') and the diaspora population are that of a culture that does not necessarily carry the two most important factors usually associated with culture – viz., language and religion. He argues that the major religions, including Hinduism in the Indian diaspora, are marked by their diversity of practice. As for language, Ghosh opines that India has exported not the language, but the 'process of adaptation to heteroglossia'

(p. 246). Citing examples of creoles used by Indians in Fiji, Trinidad and Guyana, where Hindi is at best a domestic solidarity language, Ghosh argues that unlike French, British or Chinese, the Indian diaspora appears to be more 'linguistically adaptable'.

Recent papers on language choices among the Indian diaspora show there is a consistent tendency to delink the language of the homeland from the diaspora identity (Jain and Wee 2018, Cook and David 2020). Jain and Wee's paper shows a tendency to choose Hindi from all language communities in Singapore, where Indian identity is historically represented by Tamil language and culture.

In cases of the internal diaspora in India, the choice of languages may be influenced by several factors including the host state and MT background of the speakers. Das Gupta and Fishman's (1971) paper, exploring subsidiary language claiming among migrants and non-migrants, shows a dominant pattern of language claiming based on the MT background of the claimant and the host state. Overall, among non-migrants there is a tendency to claim English as a subsidiary language, whereas for migrants there is a tendency to claim Hindi as a subsidiary language, though there is a north-south divide.

In showing the patterns of shifts in the language preferences in different contexts of communication, this study demonstrates the kind of 'linguistic adaptability' Ghosh (2002) had pointed to in the international diaspora community. The results uncover the community's competence in navigating the multilingual nature of the city. At the same time, an increasing influence of Hindi is notable in the community, echoing the findings of Das Gupta and Fishman (1971) and Jain and Wee (2018).

Acknowledgements

I gratefully acknowledge the support from the University Grants Commission (extended under the University with Potential for Excellence scheme) with which this research was conducted. I sincerely appreciate the insightful comments and suggestions by the editors towards finalising this chapter.

Notes

1. In the data presented in this chapter, valid percentage is used over actual percentage which excludes missing data from the calculation. For example, those who do not have a sibling are excluded from the calculation of the percentage language choice with brother and sister.
2. In all the tables the response 'MT' represents cases where the MT of the respondents matches the particular response; for example, a Tamil speaker giving Tamil in response to a question. If a Hindi speaker gives 'Hindi' in response to a question, that is enumerated under MT. The data of 'Hindi' only represent cases where the respondents of a MT other than Hindi give Hindi in response to a question; for example, a Tamil speaker giving Hindi in response to a particular question.

References

Anderson, B. (1998). *The Spectre of Comparisons: Nationalism, Southeast Asia and the World*. London: Verso.

Anderson, B. (2006 [1983]). *Imagined Communities: Reflections on the Origin and Spread of Nationalism*. London: Verso.

Bourdieu, P. (1991). *Language and Symbolic Power*. Cambridge, MA: Harvard University Press.

Brubaker, R. (2005). The 'diaspora' iaspora. *Ethnic and Racial Studies*, 28 (1): 1–19.

Carling, J. (n.d.). The Meaning of Migrants. Retrieved 21 March 2021 from The Meaning of Migrants: https://meaningofmigrants.org/.

Cassesnoves, R. F. and D. Sankoff (2003). Identity as the primary determinant of language choice in Valencia. *Journal of Sociolinguistics*, 7 (1): 50–64.

Chand, V. (2011). Elite positionings towards Hindi: Language policies, political stances and language competence in India. *Journal of Sociolinguistics*, 15 (1): 6–35. Retrieved from http://onlinelibrary.wiley.com/doi/10.1111/j.1467-9841.2010.00465.x/abstract.

Chriost, D. M. (2007). *Language and the City*. Hampshire and New York: Palgrave Macmillan.

Clark, T. W. (1956). The languages of Calcutta. *Bulletin of the School of Oriental and African Studies*, 18: 453–74.

Clifford, J. (1994). Diasporas. *Cultural Anthropology*, 9 (3): 302–8.

Cook, M. A. and M. K. David (2020). Language shift and identity reproduction among diaspora Sindhis in India and Southeast Asia. *Modern Asian Studies*, 1–30. doi:10.1017/S0026749X20000013.

Das Gupta, J. and J. A. Fishman (1971). Inter-state migration and subsidiary-language claiming: An analysis of selected Indian census data. *International Migration Review*, 5 (2): 227–49.

Ferguson, C. (1959). Diglossia. *Word*, 15 (2): 325–40.

Fishman, J. (1965). Who speaks what language to whom and when? *La Linguistique*, 1: 67–88.

Fishman, J. A. (1967). Bilingualism with and without diglossia; diglossia with and without bilingualism. *Journal of Social Issues*, 23 (2): 29–38. Retrieved 3 October 2019 from https://spssi.onlinelibrary.wiley.com/doi/abs/10.1111/j.1540-4560.1967.tb00573.x.

Ghosh, A. (2012). Bhojpuri as a non-dominant variety of Hindi. In R. Muhr (ed.), *Non-dominant Varieties of Pluricentric Languages: Getting the Picture*. Frankfurt am Main, Berlin, Bern, Bruxelles, New York, Oxford, Wein: Peter Lang, pp. 435–52.

Ghosh, A. (2015). Bengali as a pluricentric language. In R. Muhr and D. Marley (eds), *Pluricentric Languages: New Perspectives in Theory and Description*. Frankfurt am Main, Berlin, Bern, Bruxelles, New York, Oxford, Wien: Peter Lang, pp. 143–54.

Ghosh, A. (2019). Kolkata and Bengali for the 'others': A sociolinguistic Analysis. *Journal of the Asiatic Society*, 61 (4): 19–42.

Ghosh, A., M. Dan and B. Bhadra (2009). Multilingualism, modern metropolis and youth: A sociolinguistic profile of a section of students of Calcutta University. *The Dhaka University Journal of Linguistics*, 2 (3): 1–18. doi:10.3329/dujl.v2i3.4140.

Ghosh, Amitav (2002). The diaspora in Indian culture. In Amitav Ghosh (ed.), *The Imam and the Indian*. Delhi: Ravi Dayal Publication, pp. 243–50.

Ghosh, Amitav (2015, June). kakhonoi bangalir shahor chilo na kolkata (Kolkata was never a Bengali City). *Ei Samay*: 8.

Gilroy, P. (1994). Diaspora. *Paragraph*, 17 (3): 207–12.

Glossary on Migration (2019). Retrieved 21 March 2021 from International Organisation for Migration: https://publications.iom.int/system/files/pdf/iml_34_glossary.pdf.

Gupta, A. F. (1997). When mother tongue education is not preferred. *Journal of Multilingual and Multicultural Development*, 18 (6): 496–506.

Hall, S. (1990). Cultural identity and diaspora. In J. Rutherford (ed.), *Indentity: Community, Culture, Difference*. London: Lawrence and Wishart, pp. 222–37.

Jain, R. and L. Wee (2018). Cartographic mismatches and language policy: The case of Hindi in Singapore. *Language Policy*, 17: 99–118. doi:https://doi.org/10.1007/s10993-016-9429-8.

Khubchandani, L. M. (1974). Fluidity in mother tongue identity. In A. Verdoodt (ed.), *Applied Sociolinguistics*. Heidelberg: Groos, pp. 81–102.

Khubchandani, L. M. (1983). *Plural Languages, Plural Cultures: Communication, Identity, and Sociopolitical Change in Contemporary India*. East-West Center: University of Hawaii Press.

Kulkarni-Joshi, S. (forthcoming). Broken arcs of a circle: The sociolinguistics of linguistic reorganisation of states in India. In A. Ghosh (ed.), *Broken Arcs of a Circle: The Sociolinguistics of Linguistic Reorganisation of States in India* (pp. 311–44). Kolkata: The Asiatic Society.

LePage, R. B. (1988). Some premises concerning the standardization of languages, with special reference to Caribbean Creole English. *International Journal of the Sociology of Language*, 71: 25–36.

Le Page, R. B. and A. Tabouret-Keller (1985). *Acts of Identity: Creole-Based Approaches to Language*. Cambridge: Cambridge University Press.

Parasher, S. V. (1980). Mother tongue-English diglossia: A case study of educated bilinguals' language use. *Anthropological Linguistics*, 22 (4): 151–60.

Phillipson, R. (2008). Lingua franca or lingua frankensteinia? English in European integration and globalisation. *World Englishes*, 27: 250–67. doi:https://doi.org/10.1111/j.1467-971X.2008.00555.x.

Raj, K. (2011). The historical anatomy of a contact zone: Calcutta in the eighteenth century. *Indian Economic Social History Review*, 2 (48): 55.

Said, E. W. (1978). *Orientalism*. New York: Pantheon Books.

Sarkar, K. (2005, 3 March). So disdained. *The Statesman*, p. 9.

Siemund, P. I. (2013). *Multilingualism and Language Diversity in Urban Areas: Acquisition, Identities, Space and Education*. Amsterdam and Philadelphia, PA: John Benjamins Company.

Skutnabb- Kangas, T. (2008). *Linguistic Genocide in Education or Worldwide Diversity and Human Rights?* New Delhi: Orient Longman.

Tölöyan, K. (1996). Rethinking diaspora(s): Stateless power in the transnational movement. *Diaspora*, 5 (1): 3–36.

CHAPTER 4

Diasporic Adjustments and Indian Languages in South Africa

Rajend Mesthrie

1. Introduction – socio-historic mobility in the Indian diaspora

In this chapter I provide an overview of the sociolinguistics of indenture and the allied movement of trading class 'passenger Indians' to South Africa in the period 1860–1911. I also bring the South African story up to date by considering new migration of a more diffuse nature since the 1990s, when immigration from India became legally possible again. Indenture was the main part of a great movement of Indians to the British colonies like Mauritius, Fiji and various Caribbean territories between 1839 and 1926. Indenture tied migrants to fixed contracts with a specific employer, with the choice of re-indenting or even staying on after the five- or ten-year period on a small free plot of land. The latter was an option that the vast majority exercised. Under this scheme a very large number of people (154,184) arrived in Port Natal (now Durban) from the ports of Calcutta (now Kolkata) and Madras (now Chennai). The origins of migrants usually lay much further into the interior. For 'North Indians' the present-day states of West Bengal, Bihar, Uttar Pradesh, Jharkhand and Uttarkhand were the main recruiting areas (corresponding to the Bengal Presidency and Agra and Oudh of the British period). For 'South Indians' the present-day states of Tamil Nadu and Andhra Pradesh (corresponding to the Madras Presidency of the period) were the main recruiting areas.[1]

The migration records kept by the British-Indian authorities are impressive. The ships' lists mention all of the following details of each migrant systematically, if not always with total accuracy: *Name* (= first name); *Father's name* (= his first name); *Sex*; *Age*; *Caste*; *Zillah* (= district of origin); *Thanna* (= administrative sub-district having a police station); *Village*; *Arrival* (= date, name of ship, port of embarkation); *employer* (= to whom first indentured); *deceased/returned* (rarely filled); and *remarks* (on any bodily marks or illness etc. – also rarely filled). These records have been digitised at the Documentation Centre of the former University of Durban-Westville (now part of the University of KwaZulu-Natal). A single line of entry per person may seem laconic but it allows us to infer a world of details (see Bhana 1991, Gubili 2018, Mesthrie in preparation). No specifically linguistic information is given in these records. However, given other detailed records of the time such as Grierson's *Linguistic Survey of India* (1903) and the *Imperial Gazetteer of India* (1881–1931) it is possible also to deduce the likely languages and even the likely regional variety of each language spoken by migrants (Mesthrie [1991] 2019). It is also possible to guess at the degree of their multilingualism. Complementing this historical record with oral history interviews undertaken since the 1980s with descendants of the second and third generation and even beyond allows a rich appreciation of language in migration, indenture and post-indentured life. Space allows only a brief discussion of the linguistic outcomes of working and living together on plantations, internal language and dialect contacts, the formation of distinctly South African varieties, and the changes, additions and subtractions from the linguistic repertoires of individuals and groups.

The older diasporas of pre-jet travel were very different from modern instantaneous travel and communication. These differences pertain to aspects of the journeys made to the holding depots in the port cities, the three or so week-long wait there for the next sailing ship, and the ten-to-twelve-week journeys on open sea. All of these would encourage solidarity and speech accommodation at various levels, as migrants looked to each other for support. Social distinctions and hierarchical niceties so important in Asian societies would have to make way for an egalitarianism in the depots and ships that would have been previously unthinkable to most.

In Mesthrie (1991) I showed how the study of newly coined words can give us insights into matters of social history and changing identities. The port cities of embarkation became not just a vivid memory, but a shorthand for two new parallel identities. Migrants from the vast north-eastern to north-central area called themselves *Kalkatiyā lõg*, while from the south the label *Madrāsi kāre* emerged. These translate as *Calcuttias* and *Madrasis* or 'people from Calcutta' and 'people from Madras'. Migrants thus made it clear that these two new common identities were bound up with one of the port cities. These ports were not to be confused with their actual areas of origin, which the first two and sometimes three generations remained knowledgeable of, from first-hand experience or by word of mouth. Areas of origin sometimes played a role in the new identities too, in matters of choosing a surname. Within time there was pressure on Indians born in South Africa to go the bureaucratic route of choosing and fixing a surname, in contrast to more fluid traditional methods (see Mesthrie 2020). One might say that this opened up a choice of indexicalities as to whether one selected one's father's first name, a caste or other title, or a religious deity as surname. Some individuals chose a surname that indexed a place: surnames like *Bangal, Bihari, Parthab, Ajodhya* and *Mathura* all echo a place in the old homeland. This practice was uncommon among South Indians, among whom I have only the place surname *Madurai*. Surnames have taken on a fixed and iconic status; leaving first names more open to experimentation with Western names (*Dylan*), hybrid names (*Shernice*) and neo-Indian names (*Kimasha*), in addition to the retention of traditional Sanskrit, Tamil or Arabic-based names (Mesthrie 2020).

Allied to indenture was a voluntary and looser migration process in which Indians mainly from the Gujarat and Konkan areas sought a passage to South Africa. They settled in different parts of the country, including KZN (the colony of Natal, now KwaZulu-Natal province). Many of them worked in menial (but 'free') positions in factories, docks and the like, and moved up as petty traders (Dhupelia-Mesthrie 2009). Some Gujaratis came over as established, internationally connected merchants. A key difference for this chapter is the greater degree of mobility among these passenger Indians, who could visit India at will if they could afford it. In effect this was often after a period of three years or so, to visit their home villages, rest, recover and try and bring over at least one or more relatives to South Africa. This migration can thus be described as *circular* (since a migrant could make several 'round trips') and *catenaic* (since it could initiate a 'chain' of migration within a village or family circle, with one family member after another slowly joining in). Home villages and towns were commemorated even more strongly among the newly adopted surnames of passenger Indians. To take a few examples: the surnames *Randeria, Valodia, Karodia* index a village or town in Gujarat (with the suffix *-ia* (or *yā*) meaning 'pertaining to, of'); *Karjieker, Murudker* and *Harneker* index a village in the Konkan (with *-ker* being a suffix denoting 'village of origin').

2. Repertoire changes in diaspora

Inevitably migrants had to learn new ways of communicating in KZN, which led to significant adjustments in their speech repertoires. Villagers in India tended to be stronger on vernacular modes of communication relying on localised forms of Indo-Aryan languages (if from the north) and Dravidian languages (if from the south). The traditional distinction between horizontal and vertical communication is useful in describing language use in the new plantation contexts of KZN. At the horizontal level people made dialect adjustments to accommodate others from the same language belt, but whose speech was slightly different. For North Indians the closely related languages or dialects in the melting pots were: Hindi, Urdu, Bhojpuri, Bengali, Awadhi, Chattisgarhi Magahi, Maithili and, to a much lesser extent in terms of numbers, Panjabi, Braj, Rajasthani, Oriya, etc. These form a speech continuum (as emphasised by Grierson 1927: 141) and apart from Bengali are all mutually intelligible.[2] Figure 4.1 provides a schematic representation of the geographical relation of these 'named varieties' to each other.

Given the plantation context and the limited opportunities of education, a local lingua franca for this group emerged, which was most often called *Kalkatiyā bāt*. This means 'language of those associated with Calcutta'.[3] It thus referenced the port

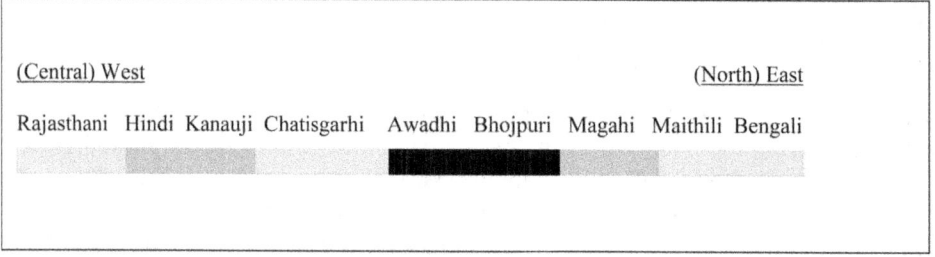

Figure 4.1 *Schematic presentation of North Indian continuum relevant to South African indentured diaspora (1860–1911)*
Key:
■ – major contributing varieties
▨ – moderately contributing varieties
▫ – other contributing varieties

of embarkation as the most important form of heritage. The agentive -*yā* suffix, is characteristically Bhojpuri and offers a subtle reminder that these migrants were from the Bhojpuri-speaking area, and not from Kolkata itself.[4] Implicit in the new name was the rider that these migrants were *not* from Madras. A new two-way contrast was set up in diaspora between *Kalkatiyā* and *Madrāsī* people, who ordinarily would not have been in contact in India. United in common Indian heritage (including religions) and the new plantation contexts (including long rows of barracks housing) the two terms nevertheless encapsulated significant differences. These differences pertained to languages (Bhojpuri and Tamil not being mutually intelligible and in fact from different language families) and cultures (involving differences of a fine-grained nature including certain food preferences, certain aspects of marriage customs, favoured religious ceremonies within Hinduism and so forth). Food preferences also became encapsulated linguistically in jocular terms among the young in the 1950s and 1960s for *porridge people* (said teasingly of South Indians) versus *roti people* (said teasingly of North Indians, who preferred home-made round flatbread over porridge or rice). The distinction lingers on: in a radio interview of 2016 a singer of Zulu and Tamil background called herself in slight jest, *a porridge ou*.[5] Thus a new linguistic and social division arose in KZN that wasn't quite characteristic of India. People of North Indian and South Indian background seldom intermarried until the 1970s, over a century after the first migrations and a half-century after the last. Only now is a closer identity emerging in which the linguistic and regional heritage of the past is not as salient as a current common identity of being 'Indian South African'.[6] This dynamic was not the same in India, where the proscriptions on marriage were traditionally by caste, not language group per se. Furthermore, the north–south difference in India is a continuum rather than a stark discrete set.

Another facet of horizontal communication was the need to communicate with local Zulu people, some of whom worked on the plantations with Indians. Particularly important in this regard was the emerging pidgin Fanakalo, which combined a basic Zulu lexis with a basic English-like S-V-O syntax (Mesthrie 1989). This would have been the first new code to be learned in KZN. It also proved useful in cases where Indians could not communicate with each other up to the 1980s, though this was only as a last resort. (The preferred ways of communicating among Indians were via Hindi or Tamil, either as first language or second language picked up by some in the barracks.) M. K. Gandhi also observed as early as 1909 that young people soon started using 'a smattering' of English if they had had sufficient schooling. But Fanakalo was an important code in the early period, since it was also a mode of vertical communication with white employers. Exceptions were formed by some British employers who knew Hindi (Hindustani) from service in India. And a few Zulu people learned Hindi and Tamil if they had had close contacts with Indians.

Blommaert's (2008) notion of scaling and rescaling is a useful one in migration. By virtue of numbers Bhojpuri and Tamil were upscaled as the main Indian languages of migration. In contrast, Hindi – which was to become a national language after Indian independence in 1947 – was not so commonly spoken on an everyday level; though it retained its status for meetings, public functions and literacy. Important languages of the home country became downscaled if the number of migrants was low. Kannada, Malayalam and Bengali speakers would have been absorbed within a generation by the more numerous Tamil and Bhojpuri speakers. For Malayalis some research is now emerging that suggest a sense of group identity in the period of indenture, despite their small size. There were also stereotypes about Malayalis having special magical powers which they were said to be not reluctant to use (Israel 2020: 216). Malayali speakers appear to have been keener to return to India than other indentured Indians (though this proportion was quite high too). This might explain why a Malayali identity never gelled in South Africa, until a much later diaspora of the 1980s onwards comprised of teachers and professionals.

Telugu is an interesting intermediate case of rescaling. At the time of migration, it was the one of the largest Dravidian languages in India (with Tamil, which it may even have outnumbered slightly). In South Africa, it was large enough to survive till today, but always in a minority compared to Tamil (Prabhakaran 1996). And given good relations between the communities, which in this case didn't prohibit marriages from the earliest period, Telugu in South Africa did come under the sway of Tamil, in terms of naming practices and structural influences (Prabhakaran 1996). One dimension not discussed by Prabhakaran is the retention of Telugu by people of Christian faith. An early Christian teacher was John Rungiah who arrived from India (or possibly Sri Lanka) in 1903 (Brain 1983: 222). He was an influential missionary who composed hymns in Telugu. There is a collection of handwritten Telugu hymns in possession of one or two families associated with Rungiah's Baptist Church. Sermons and services were conducted entirely in Telugu up till the 1990s (Israel 2020: 197–8).

Other instances of linguistic realignments of interest concern religion. Small numbers of Muslims from the south who might have spoken Tamil or Telugu moved generationally into Urdu as family language, under the influence of Muslim compatriots from the north of India.

The presence of the Gujarati language among Muslim traders and their offspring brought some rescaling too, since they were considered of higher social standing than the indentured labourers. Thus, colloquial Urdu became to some extent socially downscaled in KZN as a language associated with indenture, having lower status than Gujarati among Muslims. However, it retained its high status as a language of musical and cultural heritage. Contrarily, Kokni in Cape Town remained a spoken but largely unwritten language. It received an upscaling in becoming the most spoken Indian language in Cape Town, but in truth it was overshadowed not just by English and Afrikaans but also by Arabic in religion and Urdu in music and poetry. But as we shall see its community status remained high.

3. Internal dialect contacts in diaspora

In this section I provide a relatively brief overview of the characteristics of seven Indian languages that survived in South Africa, in terms of what can be gleaned about how they changed from their antecedents in India. In this overview I rely on my own previous work as well as that of scholars cited below. In Mesthrie (2021) I report on Bhojpuri, Tamil, Telugu, Gujarati and Kokni, which is repeated here in slightly adapted form. To this I now add information on Hindi and Urdu in both their L1 developments as well as L2 forms learnt by other Indians on the plantations and beyond. The main focus will be on initial dialect diversity for each language spoken by immigrants, subsequent contact and the resulting degree of koineisation. This sociolinguistic and structural enquiry thus speaks to the relative demographics in terms of speaker numbers, migration patterns, areas of origin, new speaker identities and relations in the new diasporic varieties that emerged. *Kalkatiyā bāt* (as cited above) resulted from dialect accommodations among speakers as they grew accustomed to one others' slightly different ways of speaking. These differences were largest in morphology, much less so in vocabulary, phonetics and syntax.[7] A koine would have developed initially as an 'interdialect' (Trudgill 1986) – i.e. a loose compromise dialect that people used as a second dialect rather than as their original vernacular. The latter would have remained in force when communicating with people from their own district of origin. In time the interdialect would have become the new vernacular norm, presumably stabilised by the second generation of South African-born Indians.[8] My understanding of the accommodations that led to koine formation has not changed since 1993:

> The process of accommodation between adult speakers will result in the neutralization of the social meaning attached to linguistic variants. That is, the variation in the early stages of koine formation will no longer correlate clearly with non-linguistic factors like region, function, and social status (Samarin 1971: 133). More salient variants will be retained, while minority and marked forms will be 'accommodated out' (Trudgill 1986). Forms that are more regular, and therefore more easily learnable (by adults), stand a better chance of being retained. Where several variants occur, frequency of a particular form must assume some importance: the more dialects a form occurs in, the greater its chances of survival in the koine. In determining who accommodates to whom, and what forms win out, demographic factors involving proportions of different dialect speakers and relative prestige of groups will clearly play an important role. (Mesthrie 1993: 39)

As these claims are expounded in detail in Mesthrie ([1991] 2019, 1993), only a light exemplification is given here:

1. Variation in **early** stages of input: These can be guessed at from some minor free variation in third-generation speech in my interviews: e.g. present participle forms in *-it* among a few speakers (*jāit* 'going') instead of the more usual *-at* (*jāt*). The former is characteristic of migrants from the Eastern Hindi area; the latter is more widespread in the Bhojpuri areas.
2. Survival of **forms** that are frequent across dialects: This holds especially for the various tense formations. Taking just one example: future forms in the first- and second-person sg. with *-b* and third sg. in *-i* win out because they occur in five of seven input varieties. Such forms occur in Bhojpuri, Magahi, Maithili, Eastern Awadhi and Western Hindi but not among Western Awadhi or Western Hindi varieties.
3. **Demographic** factors: For the example in (2) above the vast majority of migrants were from the Bhojpuri-Awadhi areas – see schematic Figure 4.1. This gave these two varieties a predominance in the koine – Bhojpuri in the majority coastal dialect of KZN and Awadhi in the Uplands variety (Mesthrie [1991]) 2019: 41–55).

4. **Neutralisation** of older regional linkages: The forms that win out no longer index a regional identity from within India, but pass unremarked as unmarked vernacular forms of the second and third person in the new country. For example, the frequent variant for third sg. past tense -*lak* no longer marks a narrow Magahi-speaking identity, but is the main variant of the coastal areas of KZN.
5. **'Accommodating out'** of some forms: Here marked forms with no widespread surface equivalent are lost. For example, a fused negative copula form *naikhĩ* 'is not', which is characteristic of the contiguous Bhojpuri, Magahi and Maithili but is unusual in the wider area, did not survive.

Bhojpuri in South Africa (and in fact all the colonies to which it was taken) is thus a koine that can be characterised as having high initial dialect diversity, high internal contact, and a high degree of koineisation.

Tamil, the other important language of indenture, shows a different contact trajectory. Tamil of South India is divided into four dialect areas, more-or-less corresponding to the cardinal points, though of course determined by geographical features and socio-historical factors.[9] Thanks to the ships' lists and a properly constituted statistical selection by Swan (1985) we can make an educated estimate of the numbers of speakers of each of these dialect areas who travelled to South Africa. North Tamil, centring around North Arcot and Chingleput districts – the latter containing the port city of Madras – provided around 85 per cent of incoming migrants in South Africa. Speakers from the remaining dialect areas were much fewer in comparison: West Tamil 6 per cent, East Tamil 5 per cent, and Southern Tamil 3 per cent. In Mesthrie (2007) I undertook an analysis of dialect features of Tamil in India cited in the literature to see how many of these were to be found in the Tamil that had survived into the third and fourth generation of the South African offshoot of the late 1980s. These typically involved variants of high vowels /i u/, variants of the palatal phoneme /c/, variants of each of dental /l̪/, alveolar /l/ and retroflex /ɭ/, occasional variant forms of pronouns and auxiliaries, and miscellaneous lexical items. Of these, no form reported to be idiosyncratic to Southern or Eastern Tamil is to be found in South African Tamil (out of seven and three possibilities respectively).

My survey turned up two of ten features reportedly characteristic of the Western dialect. These were the form *peranta* 'having been born' showing an [e] before /r/ instead of the expected [i]; and shortening of some vowels before verb endings. However, the dialect literature is possibly not quite accurate, since both characteristics are also found in the northern dialect (Ron Asher, personal communication October 1991). In contrast to the paucity of dialect survivals above, the four features claimed to be diagnostic of the northern dialect of Tamil do indeed occur in South Africa. The most salient of these is the frequent change of /l/ to [j], e.g. *keyvi* 'old woman', where the educated colloquial form is *kiḷavan*. There may be more similarities, since a description of the Vellore sub-variety of the northern dialect (Ghandigachalam 1980) turns up many more dialect possibilities and similarities (Mesthrie 2007). All in all, South African Tamil accords with colloquial Northern Tamil, the dialect area that produced a large majority of the original migrants. So, in contrast to the Bhojpuri sector of migrants in South Africa, Tamil had low initial diversity and hence low internal contact and is not a koine, but is an offshoot of one particular colloquial dialect.

The third language of indenture to be considered briefly is Telugu, spoken to the immediate north of the Tamil-speaking area in India, and showing Tamil-Telugu bilingualism in the border areas. As with the Tamil case, there are four dialect areas, which are given as northern, eastern, central and southern (Prabhakaran 1996).[10] I have calculated from Swann's lists that the proportion of speakers per dialect area over the full fifty-one-year period of indenture was approximately as follows: southern 64 per cent (North Arcot), eastern 19 per cent (Visakhapatnam), central 16 per cent (Godaveri), and northern 1 per cent (Hyderabad). In parentheses I have provided the district with the most speakers within each dialect area.[11] I am indebted to Prabhakaran (1996) for collating the dialect literature on Telugu and establishing which features remain in South Africa. That she found no features characteristic of the northern dialect in her study is no surprise given the paucity of migrants from this area (1 per cent). Of the twenty-one dialect features that remain in South Africa, eight are from the southern area, seven from the eastern area and six from the central area. To give one example each, Prabhakaran finds a word-final morpheme *-mu* for the future (surviving from the south), a future habitual morpheme with *-a + -di* (e.g. *pilustāḍi* 'he/she will habitually call') from the east, and interrogative forms like *ēndi* 'what', *ōru* 'who' and *eppḍu* 'when' from the central dialect (Standard Telugu *ēmi*, *evam* and *eppuḍu* respectively). The percentage survival of dialect features can be said to be roughly 80 per cent of the ten diagnostic features from the southern dialect, 67 per cent of the nine features from the central dialect, 64 per cent of the eleven features from the eastern dialect, and 0 per cent of the eight features from the northern area. We may conclude that Telugu in South Africa is a koine – a moderate contact variety of three dialects.[12] It also shows influences from bilingualism with Tamil, both in India (in its southern dialect) as well as in South Africa (Prabhakaran 1996).

For the 'passenger Indians' and their immediate descendants, social networks with ancestral villages were not entirely lost. There were at least weak ties (Milroy 1980) with Indian villages and towns, which reinforced the ways of speaking associated with the village and district of origin. Slightly different sociolinguistic patterns emerged among the descendants of passenger Indians.

In South Africa, Kokni speakers and their descendants reside largely in Cape Town, as a fairly close-knit community since the late nineteenth century. Mesthrie, Kulkarni-Joshi and Paradkar (2017) provide an initial overview of the sociolinguistics of Kokni transnationalism, work that is being taken up by Paradkar (2022, and in this volume). The most striking feature is how a memory and consciousness of village identity have survived into the third generation of urban dwellers in fashionable Cape Town! This will be discussed in the concluding session in greater detail. Cape Town Kokni identity can best be described as basically South African, with a strong transnational awareness. Their main languages are in fact English and Afrikaans, with Kokni as heritage language, that is receding among the youth of today (Mohamed 2019). Paradkar indicates that while there is a general variety that can be labelled Cape Town Kokni, it is not a homogeneous one. There are strong traces of three such village-based sub-varieties in her Cape Town database. For reasons of space only one example will be given taken from Mesthrie, Kulkarni-Joshi and Paradkar (2017). A Cape Town-born speaker associated with Latvan area of the Konkan used *-av* for the first-person sg. verb ending, while another associated with the Kalusta area use *-aj*. That variation like this still correlates with ancestral dialects is remarkable and places the variety at the opposite end of the koineisation scale. The correlation can be explained by the fact that many community members more often speak Kokni to relatives on visits to India, whereas Afrikaans and English now tend to dominate in Cape Town (and prevent a total degree of levelling or koineisation).[13] To summarise, Cape Town Kokni involves moderate initial regional diversity, moderate internal contact, and differential persistence of village features. It is not a koine and appears to continue to be close to three different village varieties of India (with Latvan, Habsan and Kalusta as foci).

Gujarati in South Africa presents still more different patterns. Dhupelia-Mesthrie (2009) notes that transnational village linkages are commemorated and celebrated far more frequently by the Muslim Indians who came from Konkan areas of Maharashtra, than by the Gujarati Hindu community. Of thirty-three districts of modern Gujarat State, migrants to South African tended to come from two broad areas – Kathiawad peninsula in the west (including the towns and districts of Porbander, Rajkot and Janagadh) and south-eastern districts like Navsari, Surat and Valsad. (The central and northern dialects of Gujarati are not really represented in South Africa.) Although many families are in touch with their villages, it is the broader regional identity that has gelled in South Africa. Till today there are Surat and Kathiawadi associations in Durban and Johannesburg, the cities with a large concentration of Gujarati descendants. People from these two regions called themselves *Kathiawadis* and *Surtis* respectively, while also honouring a broader *Gujarati* identity.

In Cape Town and Port Elizabeth, the next largest cities, the Gujarati population is descended almost entirely from Surat and neighbouring districts. Mesthrie and Chavda (2020) show that Cape Town Gujarati is not a koine, but is closely related to the Surti dialect of Gujarat as described by Grierson (1908) and Sampat (1973). Briefly these dialect features involve: (a) a predilection for changing dentals to retroflexes, (b) use of voiceless [h] where Standard Gujarati has [s], (c) [l] in place of standard /n/ in some words, (d) some gemination of medial consonants, and (e) metathesis of medial diphthong and consonant. A brief example of each of these in respective order is: (a) *ḍāḍā* 'grandfather', (b) *hāru* 'good', (c) *nāllo* 'little', (d) *tājjā* 'fresh' and (e) *lāigo* 'began', where Standard Gujarati has *dādā*, *sāru*, *nāno*, *tājā* and *lāgyo* respectively. In summary, Cape Town Gujarati shows little initial regional diversity; hence little internal contact; it is not a koine, but is identifiable with Surti dialect. (Durban and Johannesburg are hypothesised to be different, showing the continuing co-existence of both Surti and Kathiawadi dialects, with minor modifications).

We now turn to varieties of Hindi and Urdu. Hindi has status as an official language of India and is therefore taught as an option in some schools. The spoken form of Hindi has not to my knowledge been analysed. People educated in India, or who have spent a reasonable amount of time there do have control over Hindi, though this is exceptional today. More often people without these advantages as far as language acquisition are concerned, and with moderate exposure in part-time classes, achieve at best a kind of Hindi much shaped by Bhojpuri. (It may even be said to be a kind of Bhojpuri with superstratal Hindi influence – see Mesthrie and Hashami 2021.) In this variety some of the obvious markers of Bhojpuri morphology are given up in favour of Hindi endings, especially *-tā/tī/te* in the present, *-egā* in the future and *-a* in the past. This also applies to suffixes like *-yā* and *-wā* topic/familiarity/denigration. Such speakers may make gender distinctions lost in SA Bhojpuri, and substitute more obviously Hindi lexis – e.g. *lekin* instead of *bakī* 'but', *chāhiye* instead of *honā* (a local form adopted from Dakkhini Urdu). Some shibboleths have developed in this way: Hindi *do* 'two', *sab* 'all' *bhojan* 'food' are held to be more appropriate than Bhojpuri *dū*, *sob*, *khānā* etc. However, the adoption of Hindi by such speakers was never complete. In particular, ergativity in the past tenses is not used, and the Bhojpuri/Eastern Hindi system of subject – agent equivalence remains (*ham dekhlī*, not *maine dekhā* for 'I saw'). Thus Hindi (as opposed to Bhojpuri) of KZN is a synthesis between South African Bhojpuri and Hindi, avoiding the sociolinguistically marked forms of Bhojpuri (cited above) and the grammatically marked structural property of ergativity. This foreshadowed developments in India itself, where the Hindi that is replacing Bhojpuri in parts of Bihar is itself a synthesis of the two varieties (Hashami 2015, Mesthrie and Hashami 2021). Hashami (2015) labels this variety of India 'Contact Hindi'.

A second language variety of Hindi was developed on the plantations and residential barracks by speakers of Tamil and Telugu whose characteristics are discussed in Mesthrie (2000) – hence a kind of Contact Hindi too. I originally labelled this South African Dravidian Hindi, though the appellation South African Dravidian Hindi-Urdu (SADHU) might be more appropriate. Unusually, the invariant form *rātā* (from Hindi and Bhojpuri *rah-* 'to live') covered both past and present tense for some speakers. Some forms which this variety shares with Bhojpuri but not Hindi are *ham* for the first-person sg. pronoun (pl. equivalent *ham lōg*). Some Dravidian influences occur in the phonology, e.g. *h*-dropping (*usiār* for Bhojpuri *husiār* 'clever', final *-um* becoming a nasal vowel (e.g. *mālõ* for Bhojpuri *mālum* 'know'). In some ways the variety uses forms that are closer to Hindi-Urdu in South Africa, rather than Bhojpuri: e.g. the oblique forms *iske* (proximal) and *uske* (distal) for third-person pronouns, where Bhojpuri has *eke* and *oke*. Thus, SADHU shows that inter-language forms developed out of the plantation experience in South Africa. Desai (1997: 36–7) suggests that Gujarati traders also had a second language form of Hindi as part of this communicative-contact mix. She cites the name *Naitali* for SADHU as used in communication with Gujarati traders (though the term was probably broader than this to include L1 usage of Hindi too). SADHU was used mainly by Hindus whose first language was Tamil or Telugu. In contrast, people of Islamic descent emanating from Hyderabad and its environs spoke a form of Dakkhini Urdu described below (plus Tamil or Telugu). Comparisons with Fijian Dravidian Pidgin Hindi described by Siegel (1987: 178–9) make it clear that SADHU was linguistically close enough to its target (colloquial Bhojpuri and Hindi), with not much 'off track' innovative grammatical forms (see Mesthrie 2000: 56–7) to be considered a pidgin (or new linguistic system). The same applies to the second-language variety of Hindi spoken by Gujarati traders, despite being labelled a pidgin by Desai (1997: 37). This is perhaps the place to mention that in rare cases Bhojpuri and Hindi were used by Zulu speakers brought up and working among Indians and by English-speaking whites with experience of India under the Raj.

Farooqi (1967: 225) cited in translation by Aziz (1988: 139) writes in Urdu verse of the diversity within South Africa's Muslims:

We brothers are divided thus:
Some are Bohras and others Hyderabadis

Some are Memons and others Koknis
Some are Mia Bhais and others Thais

Aziz (1988) outlines three main varieties of Urdu spoken in South Africa: Shimali – the standard variety; Gujri – characteristic of some Muslims from Gujarat who had Urdu as their L1 rather than Gujarati; and Deccani (Dakkhini) – characteristic of Muslims from mainly the Hyderabad area. Unfortunately for our purposes Aziz did not elaborate further on these varieties, as his main interest was in matters of education and promotion of the language. We may in fact add a fourth variety – Mashriqi – which is the name in India for the Urdu of the Bhojpuri- and Awadhi-speaking areas. Aziz notes – without exemplification – that 'the features of [...] Urdu dialects in this country have the tendency to converge as a result of the different dialect users mixing together'. However, my own passing acquaintance with colloquial Urdu suggests some diffuseness rather than the focusing characteristic of koineisation. Some features of Dakkhini Urdu remained strong among those Muslims of South Indian background. A regular feature of my interviewees was the form *meriko* 'my', where Standard Urdu has *merā/ī/e* and Bhojpuri has *hamār*. One Dakkhini form *honā* 'to want, wish' survives robustly and has in fact passed on to Bhojpuri speakers in South Africa, replacing *chāhatā* as noted above (hence *Oke thorā pānī honā* 'He wants some water'). Some speakers emanating from the Bhojpuri area noticeably use *-tā* and *-ā* forms in the present and future, avoiding Bhojpuri *-at* and *-li/le/lak* forms respectively. Some speakers were bi-dialectal, using both the South African Bhojpuri koine as well as Urdu. In one interview an elderly Muslim couple spoke Urdu to me and gave Urdu forms in elicitation/translation tasks. Yet, as I turned to leave after the interview, they spoke to each other in Bhojpuri. In this perhaps unusual situation of code divergence, they spoke Urdu to a Hindu out-group member, but Bhojpuri to each other. Since our relations were cordial, it is probably more a case of judging Urdu to be more appropriate in a formal context than Bhojpuri. Perhaps the term Bhojpuri-Urdu would be appropriate for their colloquial variety. Unfortunately, no information on the Gujri variety of Hindi-Urdu is available to me. Again, one would have to draw a distinction between the L2 variety spoken by traders (Hindu or Muslim) with Gujarati as L1 and the Muslims from Gujarat who specifically had Gujri Urdu as L1. But based on Aziz (1988) and my own experiences, my impression is that Urdu may well be relatively diffuse in South Africa, showing weak convergence at best. Table 4.1 summarises the different outcomes for the seven languages discussed in this chapter.

4. Nuances of heritage and identity in transnational third spaces

In this section I explore further, via discursive rather than structural evidence, the nature of Indian sociolinguistic identity in South Africa. There is particular interest in the extent to which people identify with the new land, the ancestral homeland or the third space between (see Bhabha 1994). This is not a straightforward issue. Some individuals comment that in South Africa they consider themselves Indian, but in travelling to India 'become', or realise themselves to be, South African. Indian citizens making overseas visits sometimes comment that Indians

Table 4.1 Summary of initial diversity and koine outcomes in seven South African Indian languages

Variety	Input Diversity	Koine?	Remarks
KZN Bhojpuri	+++	+++	robust koine
KZN Tamil	+	-	not a koine
KZN Telugu	++	++	moderate koine
KZN Hindi	+	+	Bhojpuri-Hindi synthesis
KZN Urdu	+	-	diffuseness
CPT Kokni	++	-	village-aligned varieties continue
CPT Gujarati	-	-	Surti dialect continuation
DBN Gujarati	+	-	weak convergence of two dialects

Key: + Moderately strong; ++ Strong; +++ Very strong; CPT – Cape Town; DBN – Durban; KZN – KwaZulu-Natal.

in the diaspora are 'more Indian than the Indians'. Such issues can be resolved by considering identity not as an 'either/or' category but as a nested sequence or something even more open ended and dynamic. Identity also goes beyond the ethnicity so often overemphasised in past South African law, ideology and discourse. Many Indians in KZN have a sense of being ethnically Indian South African (calling themselves 'Indian' for short), with a local sense of place – of belonging to a rural locale, a small town or township/suburb in a larger city. These are nested within an identity of belonging to the province and country. These identities can be well illustrated from the game of cricket. When the Indian national cricket team plays in the UK, the Caribbean and elsewhere they attract local Indian support that in some grounds easily outweighs the 'home' support.[14] Sporting relations between India and South Africa had been curtailed in 1947 when India attained its independence, a period that coincided with the ascent of apartheid in South Africa (see Desai et al. 2002). Only in the post-apartheid era were normal diplomatic and sporting relations resumed. When the first Indian (male) cricket team arrived in 1994 to take on South Africa, a question on most sports lovers' lips was *Who are you supporting – India or South Africa?* It was a complex question, since although South Africa had attained a non-racial democracy, its first post-apartheid cricket team still drew on sportsmen who had benefited from the opportunities of their youthful apartheid days. Notably at that stage, the South African national team had no one from the Indian community in it. I used the opportunity to gauge a sense of identity by questioning numerous friends and relatives at the time and listening to strangers' discussions. Opinion was divided: some plumped for South Africa, but a slight majority of those I observed unhesitatingly chose India. Older people generally opted for India, younger ones were more ambivalent. One young relative gave me an interesting answer that supports the idea of a nested sequence of identities. When asked whom he supported in the upcoming tour, he said excitedly, 'Jonty Rhodes, Natal and India'. He was citing a local/provincial white cricketer who was a national sporting hero at the time, and his home provincial team (mostly white at that time) while overall rooting for India. Cricket thus foregrounds a postmodern view of identities in diaspora and a global world – multiple, diffuse, fragmented and sometimes contradictory.

Where language specifically is concerned, there is what I term a 'diasporic gap' between ancestral land and new homeland practices. The speech repertoires of the second generation in diaspora of necessity change in response to a new nativity. While an ancestral language remained with this generation, it had to be realigned in relation to new local varieties, interactions, concepts and realities. Borrowings, code-switching and the kinds of selections and levelling associated with koines add to the diasporic gap. Interesting mixes also developed like speaking say Kokni with an Afrikaans intonation; or conversely (and more frequently) English with, say, a Tamil accent. One example that attained legendary status within some families known to me and passed down to one or two generations of oral tradition and humour involved a local loanword. A second-generation South African Bhojpuri speaker had managed to save up funds for a visit to the homeland. In excitedly telling the tongawalla (oxcart driver) in her ancestral district that she had come back *bagāshā kare ke* ('for a visit') she was met with uncomprehending silence.[15] Only then did she come to realise that *bagāshā* was not a Hindi word but a loanword from Zulu *ukuvakasha* 'to go for a visit'. Another salient episode in the 1970s that speaks of the diasporic gap from both sides made its way into the newspapers of the time and was quoted in a play (*The Lahnee's Pleasure*, Ronnie Govender 1972). At a time when the cultural boycott of South Africa meant that very few Indians were allowed into the country (by both governments), an exception was made on religious grounds for the classical devotional singer, Pithukuli Murugudas. By the 1970s Tamil was receding as a home language and South African Indian English was a social dialect with norms of its own that differed from the English of India (and the rest of South Africa). The singer, Murugudas, was understandably piqued when local Indian audiences, finding his English accent amusing, often laughed out loud. His response is immortalised in the play (Govender 1972: 35): 'Y'all laughing because I'm talking English this way. Just imagine how I'm laughing when y'all talking Tamil.'[16]

A language identity in diaspora often outlasts the actual use of the language. Whereas shift is now a reality in most Indian South African homes, many families still think of themselves as 'Tamil' or 'Hindi', etc., or even 'Tamil-speaking' and 'Hindi-speaking'. When undertaking sociolinguistic work in the late 1980s, a young consultant in her twenties said, 'I am Tamil-speaking.' Since this seemed unusual and refreshing in an age of shift, I probed further. Was she fluent in Tamil, then? 'Oh no', she replied 'I can't talk Tamil. But I am Tamil-speaking.' What she meant was that the family still upheld the customs associated with Tamil. I further surmised that having at least one senior member in the household or wider family who was fluent in the ancestral language was enough to 'licence' a 'Tamil-speaking' identity for the whole family.

5. Regional differences among Indians in South Africa

It is not the case that language alone is a differentiator among Indians in South Africa: region matters too. New senses of being Indian and/or Indian South African came into play as Indians settled in parts of the country that allowed them to. This subtle change of identity is a result of two aspects: (a) adaptations to local places, settings, peoples and cultures, and (b) internal demographic proportions amongst Indians per region.

Diasporic Adjustments and Indian Languages in South Africa

Map 4.1 *South Africa, showing main cities referred to in text*[17]

For the first set (a) the following can be noted:

(i) Agriculture and rural life for Indians was quite common in KZN province but not so in the other provinces.
(ii) Rugby as a sport was little followed in KZN but was popular in Gauteng and Cape Town.
(iii) Foods such as *phuthu* 'stiff, dry porridge', *kobe* 'samp' and *tebe* 'leaves of arum lily' were common among descendants of indentured Indians in KZN but are largely unknown by Indians outside the province. These foods show the influence of living among the Zulu population. Together with *mealie rice*, 'rice substitute made of crushed maize', these may now be considered as having the status of 'soul food' within the Indian community there. Conversely *gatsbys* and *snoek* are associated more with Cape Town.

With regard to (b) above differences in local demographics have had subtle effects on multilingual speech repertoires:

(i) Amongst Indians Tamil predominated in KZN but was less prominent in the other provinces.
(ii) Gujarati was the most spoken Indian language in the Eastern Cape and Gauteng regions.

(iii) Kokni was the most spoken language in Cape Town, and almost unknown outside the Western Cape.
(iv) Indians of Muslim descent are demographically larger in Cape Town than Hindus. The opposite is true of KZN.
(v) In KZN province Indians are proficient in Fanakalo (a pidgin lexified by Zulu) and sometimes in Zulu too. Outside this province it is Afrikaans that is known as a second language by Indians (and sometimes even L1).
(vi) Where English is concerned, KZN has a variety easily identifiable with the Indian community. In other provinces Indians speak a variety of English, sharing much in common with the coloured communities (see Mesthrie 2012).

6. Nuances of contact between new migrants and the older diaspora

My final theme concerns interaction between the older diaspora and the newer migrants of a more globalised era, based partly upon Mesthrie (2021). Here a newer Bengali-speaking diaspora has to be factored in that has come into being since 1994.[18] New Bengali-speaking migrants of Hindu background are mainly from West Bengal, India, coming over as students, lecturers and professionals, mainly in IT. Those of Muslim background tend to be from Bangladesh and are involved in small-scale trading.

Different orientations to heritage and local integration can be discerned between the old and new diasporas. The first of the illustrations pertains to cricket again. In 2012-13 I was invited to attend a local sporting event in Rylands, Cape Town, run over two weekends. The event was meant to encourage young Muslims of the area to participate in sport and as a social activity for their families. It was run as a cricket tournament and festival that attracted family members of all ages and sexes out their homes. To my surprise team identities were built around villages of the Konkan: Kalusta Super Chargers, Latvan Lions, Habsani Royals, Sangameshwar Super Kings, Khed Badshahs, Morba Challengers, Karji Knight Riders, and Furus Phantoms. The first part of these names spoke volumes about the importance of the village identity 140 years after the initial migrations.[19] The second part evoked an awareness of globalisation, echoing the big teams of the Indian Super League, which are globally famous (Knight Riders, Super Kings, etc). A year later I attended a sportsday of the newer migrants from Bangla Desh. Unlike the Kokni community, they are of necessity more spread out as migrants who were still trying to establish themselves in different parts of Cape Town. It was therefore a rare occasion to be able to see them all together. Their attire – including barefoot soccer – contrasted with those of the well-kitted, older diaspora Kokni youngsters. A greater contrast lay in the names they selected for themselves: the Mitchell's Plain Bangla Deshis, the Rylands Bangla Deshis, the Athlone Bangla Deshis, the Landsdowne Bangla Deshis, the Muizenburg Bangla Deshis, etc. The local suburb or township names coupled with the country of common origin rang out loud and clear on the loudspeakers, with a clear sense of pride in their new surroundings. The onomastics of these sporting events thus spoke volumes about aspects of heritage and identity. For the older diaspora it was important to commemorate the names of villages of the Konkan left behind a century ago. For the newer diaspora, identity was being forged by claiming allegiance to the residential places of the new homes.

My observations in Cape Town show that new migrants from South Asia find in the older diaspora a ready-made resource for cultural and religious integration and general support. The Hindu Bengalis are given access to the local temple run by Gujaratis, holding prayers and services of their own in a separate adjoining hall. The Muslim Bengalis initially integrated into one of the three local mosques (which traditionally drew on a Kokni majority of worshippers). They now seem large enough to convene a prayer and meeting place of their own, with signage in Bengali. Occasional visiting and migrating Indians and Sri Lankans of Tamil background integrate within the local Tamil community and the temple associated with it. These linkages are perhaps to be expected. However, one further example of cooperation is of particular note. Sikhs from India were also welcomed into the Gujarati Hindu space running a school and *gurudwār* (Sikh prayer place) within the temple premises. This is a very positive development considering the deterioration of Hindu-Sikh relations in India since the early 1980s. And generally Hindu-Muslim relations remain good in South Africa, given their common experiences under indenture and trading, as well as South Africa's apartheid restrictions. (Here they wisely do not appear to follow the divisive pathways of present-day India.) One diasporic development is that temples become associated not with Hindus from the locality, but of particular regional ancestries from India. Friends from India once expressed surprise that one could talk of a 'Tamil temple' and a 'Gujarati temple', professing that temples in India did not have this particular sociolinguistic nuance (but are characterised by the predominant deity). In diaspora with language always under potential threat of diminution and loss, temples play a social role too.

The integration of new Gujarati migrants and the older diaspora is culturally almost seamless. At religious and cultural occasions differences are not particularly noticeable. The new migrants have strengthened the local musical, cultural and religious traditions. They have also strengthened the position of the Gujarati language, taking it into public spaces like shops and streets, beyond the previously diglossic restrictions to home, temple and cultural gatherings. Young people (first-generation migrants) can now be heard playing cricket at one recreational field with Gujarati as medium. But there are limits to the degree of linguistic resuscitation. I turn to the matter of Gujarati brides from India. This practice though not very common is valued as a source for cultural continuity and renewal. In recent times under incipient language shift, it was hoped that young brides would be able to speak Gujarati in the homes and be a source of input to children. Anecdotal evidence suggests that this is easier in theory than practice. Young husbands prefer such a wife to speak Gujarati but to be 'modern' in outlook (which assumes a good command of English too). Moreover, while the young brides do speak Gujarati to elders and to other new migrants from India, and their own children, they also need to fit in with the norms of their new peers in diaspora. Here the language of prestige is English. Sociolinguistic interactional nuances involving prestige, speech accommodation and new senses of identity in diaspora provide surprises to community elders as they witness greater accommodation of the few (new migrants) to the many (of the older diaspora).

7. Conclusion

Of necessity, this chapter has had an historical emphasis in charting out how Indian communities and their speech resources unfolded in the South African plantation and later apartheid and new global contexts. Sadly, the heyday of Indian languages as vibrant spoken idioms has long passed, peaking in the 1950s and 1960s, a century after the initial indentured immigrations. Young Indians have had a stronger sense of internal unity since then, especially in KZN, with the ancestral ties to particular communities in India less important today. In this modern story the language of culture and community is English, though quite firmly English in a distinctly Indian incarnation (see e.g. the *Dictionary of South African Indian English*, Mesthrie 2010).

Appendix

An example of South African Bhojpuri of the Midlands (with Awadhi influences).

The speaker Mrs Ramsarak (pseud.), aged 104 when interviewed in 1981, had been born in India, arriving in South Africa at the age of six, with her mother. (English loanwords in italics).

> Hamar janam India me rahal, Ajamgarh me. Hamar bap khetī ke kām karat rahā … jate rāhī, nā? … Aur sānj ke āte. Hamar bāp nahī hyā āyā … ū gujar gis Ajamgarh me. Hamar māī jāt rahin, tīn aure aurat sanghe *ṭaun* ke. Nahī mālum, kuch lewe jāt rahin. Ham to ghare rahā. Ta ek ṭhagwā, taun thagat lage, bole kauno caur *klīn* karnā, kauno dāl, aur sob *groserī klīn* kare ke, acchā darmahā-paisā milī. Tā phir kal ke aona – eise mange.

[**Gloss**: 'I was born in India, in Azamgarh. My father used to do agricultural work – he would go (by morning) and return in the evening. My father didn't come to South Africa – he (had) died in Azamgarh. My mother was going with three other women to town. I'm not sure, they were going to buy something. I was at home. Then a crook – those who recruit people – said (to them) "Some (can) clean rice, some dāl, and all the groceries – a good reward/ payment will be had. Then you can come again tomorrow" – that's how he asked'.]

Annotated gloss of first two lines:

> hamar janam India me rah-al,   ajamgarh me.
> my   birth India in was-PAST Azamgarh in
>
> hamar bap   khetī ke   kām   karat rahā … jat-e rāhī,   nā? …
> my   father farm DAT work doing was   go-ing would   no
>
> aur sānj   ke   āte.
> and evening DAT would-come.

hamar	bap	nahī	hyā	āy-ā ...	ū	gujar	gis	ajamgarh	me.
my	father	not	here	come-PAST ...	he	die	go-PAST	Azamgarh	in

Notes

1. To complete the story we need to acknowledge very small number of migrants from what are now Madhya Pradesh, Odisha, Kashmir, Kerala and Karnataka. Even Gujarat and the Maharashtra, usually associated with 'free' rather than indentured movement, provided small numbers of labourers.
2. Bengali provided very few migrants apart from the very first year of migrations and does not feature much in the socio-historical linguistic account of the period of indenture.
3. This form of speech went by many names: Hindi (officially), Hindustani, and sometimes *Naitālī*. As I show below it was a koine that could just as well be called Bhojpuri-Awadhi-Hindi. In my technical writings I called it *Bhojpuri* (a name remembered by only a few) to stress that this wasn't a poor form of Hindi as often suggested, but was related more to the closely related neighbouring variety/language Bhojpuri.
4. The [ɑ] vowel of the first syllable is also from Bhojpuri, Awadhi and Hindi and not Bengali which substitutes [ɒ] here, as in the modern rendition of the city's name *Kolkata*.
5. Lungi Naidoo in an interview on Radio Lotus, 2018. The term *ou* is a slang term for 'person'.
6. 'Indian South African' and 'South African Indian' are more-or-less synonymous, apart from a nuance over heritage and political stances. The former carries a slightly (though not always appreciated) stronger message of being South African first and of Indian heritage next.
7. I have no information on possible differences in speech acts and pragmatics within this continuum.
8. In my interviews of the 1980s I managed to find one survivor of the first migrating generation in KZN, whose speech – to my surprise – was very much like that of the second and third generations, rather than being clearly distinguishable from them. She must have had to slowly abandon her original vernacular in favour of the local koine.
9. Steever (1990) identifies five dialects, the fifth being a central dialect drawing on some centres considered 'Eastern' (Tanjore and Tiruchirappalli) and 'Western' (Madurai) by others. On the other hand, Ron Asher (personal communication, October 1991) considered there to be just three main dialect areas (north, south and central). My selection of four dialect areas is thus not cast in stone. Since the northern dialect remains distinct in all scenarios, my analysis of the dialect input to South Africa is not affected.
10. See the references in Prabhakran (1996), some of which collapse the central and eastern dialects into one coastal dialect.
11. The inclusion of North Arcot might strike the specialist reader as strange, since it is a district in what is now Tamil Nadu. However, the records of the time (notably the *Imperial Gazetteer*) make it quite clear that it is a multilingual area,

with large-scale Tamil-Telugu bilingualism. A pro rata calculation leads to an estimate of 274 (i.e. 39 per cent as indicated by the *Imperial Gazetteer*) arrivals being Telugu-dominant.
12. The characterisation of 'moderate' koineisation is made by comparison with Bhojpuri in which many more languages, dialects and linguistic features were involved.
13. Such is the two-way transnationalism that several people report learning Afrikaans phrases in the Konkan area of India in preparation for a stay in Cape Town.
14. At the World Cup of 2019, at Lord's Cricket Ground in London, the commentator spoke with obvious irony about the English cricket team needing to 'start well to silence the crowd'. The irony was that they were playing at home, but the support for the visiting Indian team outweighed that for the England team.
15. This is a story that runs in my family, referring to an incident from around the 1950s. It used to be recounted with great humour and relish, perhaps delighting in the ignorance of the relatively well-off visitor to the homeland.
16. I have edited Govender's spelling of *you'll* to *y'all*, as the former is ambiguous.
17. Since completion of the fieldwork Port Elizabeth has come to be officially known as Gqberha.
18. Bengalis feature in the early slave records of the Cape and in the earliest shiploads of indentured workers to Natal. However, no Bengali identity had emerged from these movements.
19. It needs to be stressed that this is not a parochial Indian identity, since the community is active in other spaces involving liberation politics of the 1980s and 1990s and local social causes. There is also a tradition of occasional intermarriage with other Cape Town Muslims.

References

Ships' Lists 1860–1911. Gandhi_Luthuli Documentation Centre, University of KwaZulu-Natal. http://scnc.ukzn.ac.za/doc/SHIP/shipndx.html.

The Imperial Gazetteer of India. 1881–1931. Digital South Asia Library. https://dsal.uchicago.edu/reference/gazetteer/.

Aziz, Ahmed. 1988. *An Investigation into the Factors Governing the Persistence of Urdu as a Minority Language in South Africa.* Unpublished MA thesis, Pretoria, University of South Africa.

Bhabha, H. K. 1994. *The Location of Culture.* London and New York: Routledge.

Bhana, Surendra. 1991. *Indentured Indian Emigrants to Natal 1860–1902 – A Study Based on Ships' Lists.* Delhi: Promilla.

Blommaert, Jan. 2008. *The Sociolinguistics of Globalisation.* Cambridge: Cambridge University Press.

Brain, Joy. 1983. *Christian Indians in Natal.* Cape Town: Oxford University Press.

Desai, Ashwin, Vishnu Padayachee, Krish Reddy and Goolam Vahed. 2002. *Blacks in Whites – A Century of Cricket Struggles in KwaZulu-Natal.* Pietermaritzburg: University of Natal Press.

Desai, Usha. 1997. *Investigation of Factors Influencing Maintenance and Shift of the Gujarati Language in South Africa.* Unpublished PhD thesis, University of Durban-Westville.

Dhupelia-Mesthrie, Uma. 2009. The Passenger Indian as worker: Indian immigrants in Cape Town in the early twentieth century. *African Studies*, 68 (1): 111–34. doi:10.1515/ijsl-2017-0025

Farooqi, M. A. 1967. *Takhayyulat-e-Farooqi* (Reflections of Farooqi). Johannesburg: Buzme Adab Transvaal.

Gandhi, Mohandas K. 1909. Editorial. *Indian Opinion*, 30 January 1909.

Ghandigachalam, N. 1980. The Vellore Tamil dialect – a brief study. In S. V. Subramanian and I. K. M. Irulappen (eds), *Heritage of the Tamils – Language and Grammar*. Madras: International Institute of Tamil Studies, pp. 287–94.

Govender, Ronnie. 1972. *The Lahnee's Pleasure*. Johannesburg: Raven Press.

Grierson, Sir George. 1903–27. *Linguistic Survey of India*. Delhi: Government of India. 1903. Vol. V, Part 2: *Bihari and Oriya Languages*. 1908. Vol. IX, Part II: *Rajasthani and Gujarati*. 1927. Vol. I, Part I: *Introductory*.

Gubili, Krishna. 2018. *Viriah*. Chennai: Notion Press.

Hashami, Sabiha. 2015. *Contact Hindi in Bihar and Jharkhand: Structure and Use*. Unpublished PhD thesis, Jawaharlal Nehru University.

Israel, Connie (ed.). 2020. *Sāyiṅkālaṁ – Life Songs and Stories of Noah Moses Israel*. Durban: Self-published.

Mesthrie, Rajend. 1989. The origins of Fanakalo. *Journal of Pidgin and Creole Languages*, 4 (2): 211–40.

Mesthrie, Rajend. 1991. *Language in Indenture: A Sociolinguistic History of Bhojpuri-Hindi in South Africa*. Johannesburg: Witwatersrand University Press (international reprint edition: Routledge, 2019).

Mesthrie, Rajend. 1993. Koineization in the Bhojpuri-Hindi diaspora with special reference to South Africa. *International Journal of the Sociology of Language*, 99: 25–44.

Mesthrie, Rajend. 2000. Dravidian Hindi in South Africa: An historical variety. *The Yearbook of South Asian Languages & Linguistics*, pp. 49–59.

Mesthrie, Rajend. 2007. The origins of colloquial South African Tamil. *The Oriental Anthropologist*, 7 (1): 129–55.

Mesthrie, Rajend. 2010. *A Dictionary of South African Indian English*. Cape Town: University of Cape Town Press.

Mesthrie, Rajend. 2012. Ethnicity, substrate and place: The dynamics of Coloured and Indian English in five South African cities in relation to the variable (t). *Language Variation and Change*, 24 (3): 371–96.

Mesthrie, Rajend. 2020. Onoma and anomie. In Dorothy Driver (ed.), *A Book of Friends: In Honour of J. M. Coetzee on his 80th Birthday*. Melbourne: Text Publishing, pp. 127–35.

Mesthrie, Rajend. 2021. Contacts and contexts: Varying diasporic interactions and koineisation outcomes for Indian languages in South Africa. *Journal of Sociolinguistics*, 25 (5): 703–19.

Mesthrie, Rajend and Vinu Chavda. 2020. Cape Town Gujarati and its relation to Gujarati dialectology: A study of retroflex boosting. *Journal of South Asian Languages and Linguistics*, 7 (1): 43–56.

Mesthrie, Rajend and Sabiha Hashami. 2021. Connecting the Contact Hindi of Bihar with the Bhojpuri-Hindi diaspora. In Tariq Khan (ed.), *Alternative Horizons in Linguistics: A Festschrift in Honour of Prof. Panchanan Mohanty*. Munich: Lincom (*Lincom Studies in Linguistics & Culture 01*), pp. 150–8.

Mesthrie, Rajend, Sonal Kulkarni-Joshi and Ruta Paradkar. 2017. Kokni in Cape Town and the sociolinguistics of transnationalism. *Language Matters*, 48 (3): 73–97.

Milroy, Lesley. 1980. *Language and Social Networks*. Oxford: Blackwell.

Mohamed, Naasira. 2019. *Investigating the Retention of Kokni Lexicon among the Youth of Cape Town's Kokni Community*. Unpublished MA thesis, University of Cape Town.

Paradkar, R. (2022). *Language and Transnational Identity: A Sociolinguistic Account of the Kokni Diaspora in Cape Town*. Unpublished PhD thesis, Deccan College Post-Graduate and Research Institute, Pune.

Prabhakaran, Varijakshi. 1996. Sociolinguistic analysis of South African Telugu (history and structure). *South African Journal of Linguistics*, 14 (4): 118–28.

Sampat, Madhu. 1973. *Comparative Study of Three Gujarati Dialects (Surti, Charotari, and Kathiyawadi)*. Unpublished PhD dissertation, Poona, Deccan College.

Siegel, Jeff. 1987. *Language Contact in a Plantation Environment*. Cambridge: Cambridge University Press.

Steever, Sanford. 1990. *Tamil and the Dravidian Languages*. In Bernard Comrie (ed.), *The Major Languages of South Asia, the Middle East and Africa*. London: Routledge, pp. 231–52.

Swan, Maureen. 1985. *Gandhi – The South African Experience*. Johannesburg: Ravan Press.

Trudgill, Peter. 1986. *Dialects in Contact*. Oxford: Blackwell.

CHAPTER 5

Language in the South Asian Diaspora in Britain

Devyani Sharma and Lavanya Sankaran

South Asian migration to Britain

South Asian languages have been present in the United Kingdom for centuries. Dozens of South Asian languages have a substantial presence in the country, most significantly Bangla, Gujarati, Panjabi, Hindi and Urdu. In addition to these Indo-Aryan languages, there are large numbers of speakers of other South Asian languages, such as Tamil, a Dravidian language spoken in South India and Sri Lanka.

South Asians started migrating to Britain during the British colonial rule of India. 'Lascars', or Asian crewmen on European ships, started settling in England as early as the seventeenth century, and then in increasing numbers with the establishment of the East India Company (Visram 2015). The early twentieth century saw increased migration from Bengal and other parts of Eastern India, due to shipping routes, as well as an increase in Panjabi-speaking merchants and labourers (Agnihotri 1987). These migrants were primarily from rural backgrounds, with limited education and resources.

Mid-twentieth-century migration saw more varied populations arriving in Britain. The first wave was in the immediate post-war period, 1940s–1960s, when the United Kingdom faced severe labour shortages and actively facilitated labour migration from former colonies. The British Nationality Act of 1948 converted former 'British subjects' to 'Commonwealth citizens' and permitted such citizens to enter the United Kingdom without restriction. In the late 1960s and 1970s, policies of Africanisation in East Africa (Kenya and Uganda) forced South Asians to migrate, and the large majority moved to the United Kingdom. The majority of these migrants were Gujarati speakers (Dave 1991: 90). In socio-economic terms, the East African immigrants were typically highly educated with professional and commercial occupations.

The Asian population grew substantially until 1971, when a series of immigration acts began to restrict numbers. The increased migration had generated growing political hostility (CARF 1981, Oates 2002), which took the form of national anti-immigration rhetoric (e.g. Enoch Powell's 1968 'Rivers of Blood' speech), political rallies by far-right parties, riots and race-related deaths, forced bussing (sending Asian children to schools far from home to reduce the concentration of Asians in local schools, a policy implemented by white British parent groups), and language reception classes that separated non-European children from others. These inter-ethnic tensions abated in later years.

In this chapter, we review the status and use of heritage languages in South Asian communities in the UK, and focus on a few case studies in more detail. There is very limited research on the linguistic structure of South Asian languages in the UK, a major lacuna in diaspora linguistics. A few notable exceptions in the UK include Stuart-Smith and Cortina-Borja's (2012) examination of change in lexical tone among heritage users of Panjabi in the UK, and McCarthy, Evans and Mahon's (2013) documentation of the acquisition of Sylheti phonology among bilingual children in the London Bengali community. Given the lack of such work, we do not review changing phonological or grammatical systems of South Asian heritage languages, but rather focus on qualitative and quantitative descriptions of the maintenance and use of these languages. For new varieties of British Asian English in these communities, see Sharma and Wormald (forthcoming) for a detailed overview.

Heritage languages

Studies in language and migration have noted the uneven ways in which language hierarchies get organised and influence linguistic practices in diaspora (Rosa and Trivedi 2017: 330). Globalisation and the movement of people to metropolises can lead to heritage languages being 'reduced' to home languages, as migrants are pressured to adopt the languages of their host countries as their working languages (Tan 2017: 470–1). Maintaining these languages with limited institutional embedding and resources can be challenging.

This can be compounded by conservative interpretations within the community of what a heritage language is. It is often romanticised in terms of ancestry, nativeness, origin and homeland (Baker 1995, He 2010), emphasising its status as inherited from a past ideal and connoting a fixed essence and origin. This notion of an idealised ancestral language often emerges due to anxiety about rapid social and intergenerational change post-migration. The target of heritage language acquisition can therefore quickly become a 'correct' ancestral version, a conservative position that ironically often hastens language shift away from the heritage language in younger generations.

Scholars have urged a move away from these dominant and limiting views of heritage language as fixed and unchanging. They suggest recognising these languages as fluid and always in flux with ambient socio-cultural factors, particularly for younger individuals in diaspora groups (Tan 2017: 468–9, Canagarajah and Silberstein 2012: 82). This is echoed by Garcia's (2011: 7) concept of 'sustainable languaging', which focuses on language shifts and transformation of the heritage language through interaction with other languages in specific socio-cultural contexts. Instead of treating heritage language as a cultural tradition to be inherited, Garcia (2011) and Blommaert (2010) argue that we should see it as mobile and contextually shaped, a process that evolves over time (see also Britain (2016) on a shift from sedentarist to nomadic perspectives in sociolinguistics). The present chapter will show, both through patterns of language uptake in education and patterns of language use in the community, that South Asians in the UK maintain and develop complex language repertoires that do not always correspond straightforwardly to inherited ethnic, cultural or national identities.

South Asian heritage languages in Britain

The number of South Asians in Britain has grown significantly since the 1960s, increasing from to 4.4 per cent (2.6 million) in 2001 to 6.9 per cent (4.4 million) in the 2011 Census (ONS 2011). In 2001, just under half of this group were listed under the Census ethnic category 'Indian'; by the 2011 Census, this proportion had dropped to a third, with proportional increases in the categories of 'Pakistani', 'Bangladeshi' and 'other Asian'. Just over half of the top three Asian categories – Indian, Pakistani and Bangladeshi – are now represented by individuals born in the UK; in earlier decades the proportion of individuals born in South Asia was higher. The South Asian population is growing at a faster rate than the white majority.

London is the largest hub of South Asian settlement in the UK. According to the 2011 Census, 35 per cent of the South Asian community lives in London (over 15 per cent of the city's total population), with major concentrations in West and East London. South Asian languages are concentrated in different neighbourhoods of London, e.g. Gujarati in North London (Wembley), Bengali in East London (Tower Hamlets) and Panjabi in West London (Southall and Hounslow).

Five South Asian languages were found to be the most commonly spoken languages in the UK after English and Polish in the 2011 Census (Figure 5.1). Several other South Asian languages are also well represented in the UK, in particular Tamil (a Dravidian language spoken in South India and Sri Lanka), Sylheti (under-reported, since it is frequently reported as and grouped with Bengali, as in the census data in Figure 5.1), Pashto (speakers from Afghanistan and Pakistan) and Malayalam (another Dravidian language).

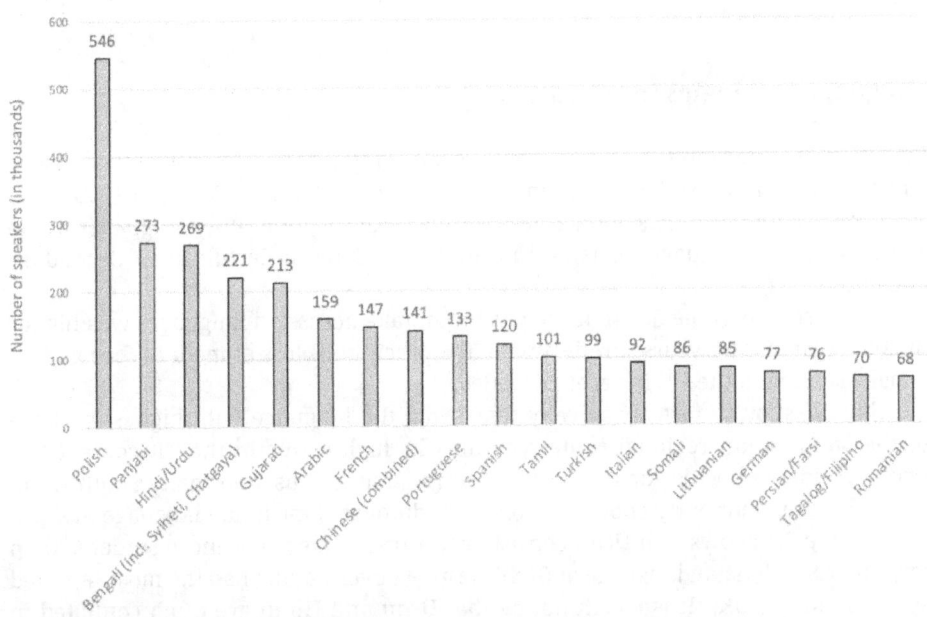

Figure 5.1 *Main language other than English, as reported in the 2011 UK Census (ONS 2011)*

Until 2011, the British national census gathered no language-related information at all. Borough- or council-level information data was somewhat informative but was not consistently gathered over time and across regions. Even now, the census offers only limited information. In 2011, the census introduced just a single question asking for a respondent's main language, a monolingual framing that was retained in the 2021 Census. By asking for just one 'main language other than English' and relying on broad ethnic categories of 'Indian', 'Pakistani' and 'Bangladeshi', census data tend to erase and simplify complex language practices and speech communities.

A large majority of South Asians in Britain are multilingual and participate in patterns of 'embedded diglossia' (Calvet 1987) overlooked by census statistics. South Asian communities often recognise one or more high prestige (H) South Asian languages, that is distinct from the lower (L) prestige language that the majority of community members speak in the home. For example, the majority of Bangladeshis in Britain come from the Sylhet province in north-east Bangladesh and speak Sylheti as their home language, rather than standard Bangla. Bangla is nevertheless the language that is promoted in terms of prestige and literacy (Lawson and Sachdev 2004) and that is reported in the census. Similarly, the Pakistani community sees Urdu as a language of literacy and of very high prestige across the entire northern part of the Indian subcontinent. However, here again, Urdu is often not the primary home language for Pakistanis in Britain, nor indeed in Pakistan. Panjabi is widely used as a home language, and a substantial number of Pakistani immigrants are from the Mirpur province and speak Mirpuri, a variety of the Potwari language that shares features with Panjabi and Pahari. Some Pakistani migrants speak Pashto as their home language. Many Pakistani households will therefore follow a layered form of 'triglossia', with Mirpuri, Panjabi and Urdu layered across social situations and social networks.

Language ideologies in education

Evidence of differential status of South Asian languages in the UK is very clear when we look at these languages in the context of education. Table 5.1 (JCQ 2021, Vidal Rodeiro 2009) shows entry rates for a number of community languages in the 'Other Modern Languages' category in the GCSE (General Certificate of Secondary Education).

Note, firstly, in Table 5.1, that the level of uptake across all languages was higher in 2007 than in later years, a reflection of the precipitous loss of modern foreign language learning in the UK in recent decades.

Table 5.1 shows more specifically that Urdu, the language with highest prestige in the South Asian regional context, retains its high status in the UK context too. Urdu is widely selected for its cultural and religious status, and many South Asian schoolchildren currently choose Arabic or Urdu over their home language at GCSE level. Table 5.1 shows that Urdu consistently attracts five times more students than any other South Asian language at GCSE, despite never having had the most reported speakers in the UK. (It is worth noting that Urdu and Hindi are often conflated in British statistics, but despite its high status within India, Hindi has struggled more to gain the level of recognition of Urdu in the UK; Table 5.1 specifically refers to the

Language in the South Asian Diaspora in Britain 93

Table 5.1 *General Certificate of Secondary Education (GCSE) entries over time*

Language	2007 GCSE entries	% of students whose mother tongue is that language (2007)	2011 GCSE entries	2021 GCSE entries
Urdu	5410	43.3	3960	3203
Panjabi	1088	75.0	885	643
Gujarati	1028	74.7	565	248
Bengali	1469	95.3	996	361

Urdu GCSE, as the Hindi GCSE was discontinued some years ago.) Urdu is also an exception in that all other South Asian languages have significantly lower uptake than other major foreign languages – Arabic, Chinese and Polish – despite their large community sizes. This is because they are largely seen as home languages and not as languages for educational or professional advancement.

This difference in status between Urdu and other South Asian languages is also clear when we look at the data in columns 2 and 3 in Table 5.1. The data in these two columns are from one of very few detailed examinations of GCSE language statistics beyond the three main European languages (Vidal Rodeiro 2009). The table shows that 95 per cent of GCSE students of Bengali had the language as a home language (this of course treats Sylheti speakers as Bengali speakers, a layer of ideological erasure). This is in contrast to only 43 per cent for Urdu. Although this might suggest that a high proportion of Bengali speakers are taking their language at GCSE level, it only means that few *other* people take Bengali. In fact, only 45 per cent of Bengali speakers took Bengali at GCSE (and only 15 per cent of Panjabi speakers), in contrast to 46 per cent of Urdu speakers, the highest of all the South Asian languages.

In sum, uptake of South Asian languages in British secondary schools offers a stark illustration of language ideology in action: high uptake of Urdu by Urdu speakers *and* by speakers of other languages, in contrast to low and declining uptake of Bengali by either Bengali speakers or by others. Panjabi and Gujarati pattern broadly like Bengali, being treated as only community-relevant and tending to lose out to higher prestige languages.

In the next sections, we explore language maintenance and language practices in more detail in three communities: the Panjabi community, the Sri Lankan Tamil community, and briefly the Sylheti/Bengali community.

The Panjabi community

Panjabi speakers are an excellent example of how problematic a one-to-one mapping of language and speech community is when dealing with South Asian communities. The geographical area called the Panjab (East and West) in South Asia predates the partition and creation of India and Pakistan. As a result, the ethno-linguistic group described as 'Panjabis' are sub-categorised into Panjabi Sikhs, Panjabi Hindus and Panjabi Muslims based on religious affiliations, all very large demographic groups in South Asia. The region is united by a common language, Panjabi, which forms a bond between these three groups now divided by religious and national boundaries.

Another interesting complexity across the Panjab region – and reflected in British Panjabi communities – is their distinct ideologies regarding languages of prestige for education and government. Panjabi Sikhs consider Panjabi to be their mother tongue, but also the symbolic language of their culture. Its role therefore has been formalised as the language of literacy via the Gurmukhi script and has been embedded institutionally, e.g. in education and politics. Hindu Panjabis and Muslim Panjabis, by contrast, also use the language as their mother tongue but generally ascribe it the status of a colloquial language, associated with their home culture and vernacular folk culture. These two communities choose different languages as their language of prestige for educational and other official functions: (Sanksritised) Hindi and Urdu respectively. Some Panjabis are competent in multiple literacy traditions, but for the most part the three Panjabi-speaking religious communities adopt distinct educational and prestige ideologies, both in South Asia and the UK. At the same time, the language facilitates strong bonds of friendship across religious sub-communities and among Panjabi-speaking second-generation British Asians from different cultural traditions (Sharma and Rampton 2015). This will be shown later in the example in (1).

The data presented in this section come from a large multigenerational project in one of the oldest and largest Panjabi communities in the UK, in Southall and surrounding boroughs in West London (Sharma, Rampton and Harris 2008–10). Particularly due to its proximity to Heathrow airport, where migrants arrived (e.g. the government arranged temporary housing in the vicinity of the airport when thousands of East African Indians arrived), the area received substantial numbers of South Asian migrants in the post-war period. By the late 1970s, 30 per cent of the population of Southall was Asian – still a minority but a large and highly visible one – and the town had become a lightning rod for racial tension (CARF 1981, Oates 2002). Far-right, anti-immigration parties held rallies in the town, leading to violent riots and racially motivated deaths. British Asian anti-racist political activism developed in response, combining Gen 1 and early (older) Gen 2 participants. School policies also reflected anxiety about shifting demographics, with bussing and remedial classes for Asian heritage children.

Although racial tension continued through the 1990s, the more recent decades in Southall have been characterised by a striking reduction of overt hostility. This change in race relations corresponds to the South Asian population in Southall becoming the majority (Oates 2002). Southall schools became dramatically more multiracial, with the proportion of minority ethnic origin students in Ealing schools now ranging from 40 per cent to 99 per cent (Ealing JSNA 2010). This later period also coincided with greater societal acceptance of British Asians. Today, many public signs in Southall are in English and Panjabi, even at the local pub, and the town's lively Panjabi atmosphere – bhangra music, Indian restaurants, clothing and jewellery shops – has become something of an institution in London. Children born and raised during the 1980s and 1990s grew up in a climate in which wider British society accepted an increasingly visible, legitimated, even celebrated, middle-class British Asian culture. In stark contrast to the older group, the younger Gen 2 participants in our data rarely offered any narratives of racial tension.

Table 5.2 illustrates the robust maintenance of Panjabi across generations in Southall and Hounslow, West London. (For early studies of language maintenance, see Husain 1991, Mahandru 1991, Choudhury and Verma 1994, Saxena 1995, Sneddon 2000, and Verma et al. 2001.) Bilingual usage is indicated for Panjabi 'P' and English 'E', as well as secondarily Hindi/Urdu 'H'. 'PE' indicates equal use, but 'P(E)' indicates more Panjabi use in that situation. A wide range of contexts of language use are reported for each individual. The column entitled 'Migration' indicates whether individuals are Gen 1 (migrated to UK as adults) or British-born (Gen 2 and above). Active bilingualism can be seen across generations, with particularly active code-switching among Gen 1 individuals and older Gen 2 individuals, i.e. the first British-born generation. Younger Gen 2 individuals tended to also be actively bilingual, but with more situation-based alternation and a reduced prevalence of 'PE' usage.

Table 5.2 also shows an inevitable shift from Panjabi dominant bilingualism to English dominant bilingualism (cf. Extra and Yağmur 2004; Sevinç 2016 for similar patterns across generations in the Turkish-Dutch community). However, the table shows that with almost no exception, individuals of all ages and generations are active bilinguals. This is partly due to the substantial size and sustained in-migration in such communities. Stable bilingualism of this kind can in turn be an important source of continuing influence on the English spoken by later generations, with development of a local ethnically marked variety of British English too (Sharma and Sankaran 2011).

This high degree of active bilingualism, and particularly of unmarked code-switching among older Gen 2 individuals, is illustrated in the long conversational extract in (1). The extract is from a phone conversation between a middle-aged Muslim British Asian businessman (Participant 26, Panjabi/Urdu/English trilingual) who was born and raised in West London and his childhood friend from the neighbourhood, a middle-aged Sikh man. Only the businessman's speech is included in the extract. In the extracts below Panjabi use is given in italics with brief translations included in square brackets immediately thereafter. Code-switching to English is in Roman font.

(1)
Solidarity-building
o kiddaan bhai? Thik hai? [what's up brother? you okay?] how's i' going man?   1
nah phone aa gayaa si- o bande daa phone aayaa si haan. [i got a call. that guy's call
   came.]   2
hor kiddaan? [what else?] everythin' alrigh'?   3
yeah listen listen righ'? you started up in business   4
and e::h i though' i'd give you a li'l head start as well   5
yeah i give you the yeah you take the balloon orders from me   6
all the balloon orders the arches and tha'   7

Tough haggling Asian businessman
tu kuchh changi job *kariye da jab-* fuck about *na kari* [do a good job. don't fuck about.]   8
changa sahi sahi kaam kari [do a good, proper proper job.]   9
to m- dassi phir [so tell me] how much is i' a balloon?   10
come on *yaar! sastaa kar! achhaa Thik* [man, make it cheaper! good okay]   11
alrigh' then okay tha's fine. nice one. yeah yeah. tha's good yeah yeah   12
yeah we need these balloons you know   13

Table 5.2 Bilingual language use in daily life in the Panjabi community

Name	Migration	Generation	Age	Gender	Years in UK	Grandparent generation	Grandparents	Aunties	Mother	Father	Siblings	Spouse	Early Life	Friends	Kids	Work	Counting	Writing	University	Grandchildren	Swearing/Anger
Participant 1	1	Mid	45	F	19	P(F)	P(F)	PU	P(U)	P(U)	UP	PU	U(P)	P		U(E)	UP(E)	UP(E)	U	E(P)	-	U(E)
Participant 2	1	Mid	52	M	18	P	P	P	P	P	P	P	P(E)	P(E)	P(E)	E(P)	P	E	P(E)	-	P(E)
Participant 3	1	Mid	49	F	27	P	P	P	P	P	P	P	P(E)	P(E)	P	E(P)	P(E)	E	P(E)	-	P(E)
Participant 4	1	Mid	37	M	7	P	P	P	P	P	P	P	P(E)	(P)(U)(E)	P	(P)(U)(E)	P	E	-	-	P
Participant 5	1	Mid	47	F	27	P	P	P	P	P	P	P	P,B(E)	P	PE	P(E)	E(P)	E(P)	-	-	E
Participant 6	1	Mid	52	F	31	P	P	P	P	P	P	P	PE	P(E)	P(E)	E(P)	E	E(P)	E(P)	-	E(P)
Participant 7	1	Mid	47	M	23	P	P	P	P	P	P(E)	PE	PH	P(E)	PE	PE	E(P)	E	E(P)	-	P
Participant 8	1	Mid	49	F	33	P	P	P	P	P	P(E)	P	P(E)	P(E)	PE	P(E)	P	E(H)	-	E(P)	P
Participant 9	1	Mid	34	M	7	P	P	P	P	P	P	P	P(E)	PE(H)	P(E)	PE	P(E)	E	E(P)	-	E
Participant 10	1	Mid	45	F	24	P	P	P	P	P	P	PE	P(E)	P(E)	PE	PE	P(E)	E(P)	P(E)	-	PE
Participant 11	1	Mid	36	M	17	P	P	P	P	P	P	PE	PE	P(E)	PE	PE	PE	E	E(P)	-	E
Participant 12	1	Mid	45	F	10	PH	P	HP	P	P	H	HE	PE	HE	-	PEH	E	E	PE	-	E
Participant 13	1	Old	57	M	41	P	P	P	P	P	P	P	P(E)	P	P	P(E)+	P	E	E	E	P(E)
Participant 14	1	Old	64	F	37	P	P	P	P	P	P	P	P	P	P(E)	E(P)	E	E	-	E	E
Participant 15	1	Old	65	F	35	P	P	P	P	P	P	P	P(E)	P(E)	PE	E(P)	E	E(P)	-	E(P)	P
Participant 16	1	Old	63	F	45	P	P	P	P	P	P(E)	P	P	PG(E)	E(P)	PE	E	PE	-	-	PE
Participant 17	1	Y	31	M	1	P	P	P	P	P	P	P	P	P	P	P(E)	P(E)	PE	P(E)	-	PE
Participant 18	1	Y	25	M	1	P	P	P	P	P	-	P	P	P	P(E)	P(E)	PE	E	-	-	PE
Participant 19	1	Y	29	F	2	P	P	P	P	P	P	P	P(E)	P(E)	P(E)	P(E)	P(E)	P(E)	E(P)	-	P(E)
Participant 20	1	Y	21	M	0.5	P	P(E)	P	P	P	P	PE	P(E)	PE	-	E	PE	E	E(P)	-	P(E)
Participant 21	1	Y	20	M	2	P	P	P	P	P	P(E)	-	P(E)	PE	-	PE	E	E(P)	E	-	EH
Participant 22	1	Y	24	M	2.5	HP	H(E)	H	H(P)	H(P)	H(E)	HE	PE	H(E)	-	(H)(E)(P)	E	E(H)	E(P)	-	-
Participant 23	1	Y	23	M	7	P	P	P(E)	P	P	PE	-	PE	E(P)	-	E	E	E(P)	E	-	(E)(P)(H)
Participant 24	1.5	Mid	49	F	38	P	P	P	P	P	P	P(E)	PE	PE	E(P)	E(P)(H)	P(E)	E	-	-	P(E)
Participant 25	1.5	Mid	48	F	37	P	P(U)	P	P	P	E(P)	PE	PE	E(P)	-	(E)(P)(U)	E	E	-	-	E
Participant 26	2	Mid	41	M	41	P(U)	P	P(U)	P	P	E	U	E(P)	(E)(U)(P)	E	P(U,E)	P(U,E)	E(U)	-	-	-
Participant 27	2	Mid	48	F	42	HP	P	HP	P	P(E)	PE	P	E(P)	P(E)	PE	E	E	-	-	E
Participant 28	2	Mid	42	F	42	P	P	P	P	P	E	PE	E(P)	PE	PE	EH	E	E	-	-	PE
Participant 29	2	Mid	37?	M	37	P	PH	P	P	P	E	-	E(P)	PE	-	HP(E)	E	E	E	-	-
Participant 30	2	Mid	48	M	44	PU	PU	P	P	P	E(U)	EU(P)	E	E	EU	(E)(P)(U)(I)	E	E	E	-	P
Participant 31	2	Mid	41	F	35	P	P	P(E)	P(E)	E(P)	-	E(P)	E	-	E(P)	E	E	E	E	-	PE
Participant 32	2	Mid	41	F	41	P	P	P	P(E)	PE	E	E(P)	E(P)	E	E(P)	E	E	E	-	-	E(P)
Participant 33	2	Mid	40	M	40	P	P	P(E)	P(E)	P(E)	E(P)	P(E)	E(P)	E	E(P)	E	E(P)	E	E	-	E
Participant 34	2	Mid	41	M	35	P	P	P(E)	PE	PE	E(P)	E(P)	E(P)	E	E(P)	E	E	E	E	-	PE
Participant 35	2	Mid	43	F	43	P	P	P(E)	P(E)	P(E)	E(P)	E(P)	E(P)	E	E	PE	E	E	-	-	PE
Participant 36	2	Mid	39	M	39	P	P	P(E)	E(P)	E(P)	E	E(P)	E(P)	E	E(P)	E	E	E	-	-	PE
Participant 37	2	Mid	35	F	34	P	P	P(E)	E(P)	E(P)	E	E	E	E	-	E(P)	E	E	E	-	P
Participant 38	2	Y	22	M	20	P	P	P	P	P	PE	-	E(P)	E(P)	-	E	E(P)	E(P)	E	-	E(P)
Participant 39	2	Y	23	M	23	P	P	P	P	P	E(P)	E(P)	E(P)	E(P)	-	E	E	E(P)	E	-	PE
Participant 40	2	Y	23	M	20	P	P	P	P	P	E(P)	-	E(P)	E(P)	-	E	E(P)	E(P)	E	-	E(P)
Participant 41	2	Y	23	M	23	P	P	P	P	P	E(P)	E(P)	E(P)	E	-	E	E(P)	E	E	-	E
Participant 42	2	Y	22?	M	22	P	P	P	P	P	E(P)	-	E(P)	PE	-	E(P)	E(P)	E	-	-	PE
Participant 43	2	Y	22	M	22	P	P	P	P	P	E(P)	E(P)	E(P)	E	-	E	E(P)	-	-	-	PE
Participant 44	2	Y	25	F	25	P	P	P	P(E)	E	-	E(P)	E(P)	E	E(P)	E	E	E	-	-	E
Participant 45	2	Y	23	F	23	P	P	P	-	E(P)	E	E(P)	E(P)	E	-	E	E	E	E	-	P
Participant 46	2	Y	22	M	22	P	P	P	P(E)	P(E)	E	E(P)	E(P)	E	-	E	E(P)	E(P)	E	-	PE
Participant 47	2	Y	29	F	29	P	P(E)	P(E)	P(E)	E(P)	E(P)	E(P)	E(P)	-	E(P)	E(P)	E(P)	E	-	-	E(P)
Participant 48	2	Y	21	M	20	P	P(E)	P(E)	P(E)	E(P)	-	E(P)	E	-	E(P)	E	E(P)	E(P)	-	-	P
Participant 49	2	Y	19	M	19	P	P(E)	P(E)	P(E)	E(P)	E(P)	E(P)	E(P)	-	E(P)	E(P)	E	E	E	-	PE
Participant 50	2	Y	19	F	19	P	P(E)	P(E)	E(P)	P(E)	E(P)	E(P)	E(P)	E	E(P)	-	E(P)	E(P)	E	-	E
Participant 51	2	Y	23	F	23	P	P	P(E)	P(E)	E(P)	E(P)	E	E(P)	E	-	EGm	E	E	E	-	P
Participant 52	2	Y	18	M	18	P(U)	P	P(E)	P	E(P)	E(P)	-	E(P)	E	-	E	E	E	E	-	P
Participant 53	2	Y	27	F	27	U(P)	U(P)	U(E)	E(U)	E(U)	E(P)	-	E(P)	E	-	E(P)	E	E	E	-	PE
Participant 54	2	Y	21	M	21	P	P(E)	E(P)	E(P)	E(P)	-	E(P)	E	-	E	E	E(P)	E	-	-	E
Participant 55	2	Y	26	F	26	P(H)	P	E(P)	PE	PE	E	-	E(P)	E	-	E	E	E(P)	E	-	E(P)
Participant 56	2	Y	19	M	15	P	P(E)	E(P)	E(P)	E	E	E(P)	E(P)	-	E	E	E	E	-	-	E
Participant 57	2	Y	17	M	17	P	P(E)	E(P)	E(P)	E(P)	-	E	E	-	E	E	E	E	-	-	E
Participant 58	2	Y	23	F	23	P	P(E)	E	E(P)	E(P)	E	E (P)	E	-	E	E	E	E	-	-	P(E)
Participant 59	2	Y	25	M	25	P	P(E)	E(P)	E	E	E	E	E(P)	E(P)	-	E	E	E(P)	-	-	-
Participant 60	2	Y	22	F	22	P(E)	P(E)	E(P)	E	E	E	E	E	E	-	E	E	E	E	-	E
Participant 61	2	Y	23	F	23	E(P)	E(P)	E(P)	E(P)	E(P)	E	E	E	E	-	E	E	E	-	-	P(E)
Participant 62	2	Y	10	M	10	E(P)	E	E	E	E	-	E	E	E	-	E	E	E	E	-	E
Participant 63	2.5	Y	20	M	20	U	UE	U(E)	E(U)	E(U)(P)	E	-	E	E(U)(P)	-	(E)(P)(U)	E(U)	E(U)	E	-	E
Participant 64	3	Y	12	F	11	P	P(E)	PE	E(P)	E(P)	E(P)	E	E	E(P)	-	E	E(P)	E(P)	-	-	E
Participant 65	3	Y	14	M	14	P(E)	P(E)	PE	E	E(P)	E	-	E	E	-	E	E	E	-	-	E

Shared cultural knowledge
jiddaan tin balloon honde a ik tree *de ich* [the one where three balloons are in one tree]	14
yeah *haan kar le idda phir. Thik hai. acchha* [yes do it like this then. okay good]	15
yeah do i' like tha' then. i don't mind	16
they gotta look nice you know with nice pre'y colours you	17
know sometimes you ge' pinks and blues and r:reds and yellows	18

Shared cultural knowledge:
byaah de rang jeDe honde a. tennu pata hai yaar [wedding colours, you know the ones]	19

Solidarity-building:
hor kiddaan? [what else?] what's going down man everything cool?	20
how's things a' the yard? the old lady alrigh'?	21
you're no' giving her any trouble are you?	22
yeah be'er behave yourself man. kick your arse in otherwise	23
yeah don't want any more complaints from you yeah?	24
yeah don't go ou' my home pissed. telling you	25
yeah you gon regre' it man i'm telling you bloody behave yourself righ'	26

Tough Asian wife:
nahin te tennu jutiyaan maar ke bahar kar denaa tennu [or she'll throw shoes at you and kick you out of the house]	27

Honourable Asian masculinity:
banda ban jaa [be a man]	28
nah nah nah seriously man look listen hear me ou' man look [continues with advice]	29

Devyani Sharma

The extract shows a rich cycle of stance alignments and indicates a wide range of functions of code-switches in the British Asian community. It also illustrates the role of Panjabi as a bridge between religious and national divides. The broad stances, acts and personae that this speaker evokes through Panjabi include: in-group solidarity-building, a haggling Asian businessman, shared cultural knowledge, a tough Asian wife, and honourable Asian masculinity. In each case, affiliation rather than denigration is asserted: these voicings build solidarity, reduce social distance, and unidirectionally affiliate the speaker positively with recognisable aspects of Asian culture. More generally, this particular speaker has crafted a flamboyantly alternating linguistic repertoire – he combines elements of Panjabi, Standard English, vernacular London dialect (glottal replacement of /t/ is indicated informally), and Caribbean Creole – to index a composite meaning of bi-cultural authority, claiming each culture as his own. This deep bi-cultural orientation is replaced in the younger second generation with a more fused British Asian and more English-dominant style of bilingualism (Sharma 2011).

The Sri Lankan Tamil community

The 2011 census (ONS 2011) showed that slightly over 127,000 people born in Sri Lanka lived in England and Wales, with 70 per cent of Tamil speakers living in London (Jones 2020). This represented an 88 per cent increase since 2001, which itself saw a 72 per cent increase since 1991. Given the context of the Sri Lankan civil war, the majority of these Sri Lankan-born people are Tamils (Jones 2020). Figure 5.1 also indicates the level of maintenance of Tamil use.

Like the Panjabi community, the Tamil community similarly defies a simple national or religious cultural profile, with a large Sri Lankan Tamil (SLT) population, as well as an Indian Tamil group that includes the movement of mostly skilled workers and higher education students. While it is not possible to separate this latter group of Tamils from the broad category 'Indian', the rise in recent years in student visa applications from South India, and the status of Chennai as a hub of India's hi-tech economy, suggest that Tamils may well be represented within these migration streams (Jones 2013: 25).

The Tamil community in the UK and particularly in London is somewhat different from the Panjabi community for a number of reasons. First, it is a smaller community, which can compromise language maintenance, with fewer opportunities for language use and fewer resources for community language teaching. A number of smaller or more dispersed South Asian language communities (e.g. Nepali, Malayali, Sindhi, Pahari, Konkani, Balochi) also struggle with language maintenance.

Second, there are two different primary sources of Tamil speakers, a larger group of SLT speakers and a smaller group of South Indian Tamil speakers. SLTs came to the UK in distinct waves: first with middle-class professional migration in the mid-twentieth century, then in larger post-independence numbers, especially after Sinhala was made the official language in Sri Lanka in 1956, and finally a particularly large number of refugees after the onset of civil war in 1983. SLTs are therefore a very diverse group in terms of nationality, caste, class, education, religion and motivations for migration (Sankaran 2022). Recent studies indicate fairly similar language maintenance to other South Asian languages, though, interestingly, Canagarajah (2019) suggests that the South Indian dialect spoken in Tamil films may influence the Tamil spoken by younger SLTs in the diaspora.

The significant SLT diaspora in the UK was formed as a direct result of the political conflict in Sri Lanka, which lasted twenty-six years and caused a mass exodus of Tamils (Ganesh 2018). Sri Lanka was among the top countries of origin for asylum claimants in Britain in the 1990s and early 2000s. By 2002 it was estimated that 110,000 SLTs lived in the UK, of which 60,000 were refugees (Zunzer 2004).

In the mid-1980s, the British government started to place restrictions on asylum migration to the UK, which caused SLT asylum migration to shift to countries in continental Europe (Pirouet 2001), in particular Germany, Switzerland, Norway, Denmark, Sweden and the Netherlands (Velamati 2009). Many SLT refugees acquired citizenship in EU member states after waits of over a decade, thus laying down roots in the local linguistic ecologies but also gaining the ability to move within the EU. A large number relocated to the UK (Lindley and Van Hear 2007). SLT migration patterns to Britain thus shifted from direct asylum migration from Sri Lanka towards onward migration from Europe (David 2012, Sankaran 2021). According to Lindley

Language in the South Asian Diaspora in Britain 99

and Van Hear (2007: 17), this relocation or 'onward migration' was mainly motivated by the 'greater perceived economic opportunities, for reasons of education and language, to re-group with family and friends, and because of the greater critical mass of Tamils in parts of the UK and therefore the greater possibility to lead a familiar life'. The numbers were large enough to sustain temples, Tamil language classes, Saturday music and dance schools, and other cultural needs.

This section will consider heritage language use in this diaspora group, focusing on SLTs living in London (Rampton 2015–18), specifically forty-two participants from concentrated Tamil populations in the boroughs of Harrow, Ealing, Redbridge and Kingston upon Thames. The participants represent a range of biographies – as spouses, students, refugees, elderly parents – and migration trajectories. They are also varied in terms of their length of stay in the UK; newcomers who had lived in the UK for less than ten years, Gen 1 SLTs who had been living in the UK for at least twenty-five years, and Gen 2 Tamils either born in the UK or who arrived as children.

Table 5.3 outlines patterns of language use in the sample of speakers. The table includes information about when 'onward' migrants arrived from Europe.

Table 5.3 *Bilingual/multilingual language use in daily life in the Sri Lankan Tamil community*

Name	Migration	Generation	Age	Gender	Years in EU	Years in UK	Temple	Grandparents Generation	Aunties/Uncles	Mother	Father	Sibs	Spouse/partner	Early life	Friends	Children	Youth (friends/cousins)	Work	Counting	New Media (writing)	Highest level education	Playing sports	Grandchildren	Swearing/Anger
Participant 1	1	Old	64	F		25	T	T	T	T	T	T	T		TE	T	T(E)	T	T		E	E	T	NA	
Participant 2	1	Mid	34	F		8	T	T	T	T	T	T	T		T	T(E)	T	NA	E(T)		E	T	T	NA	T
Participant 3	1	Mid	46	F		25	T	T	T	T	T	T	T		T	T	T	T(E)	T		E	T	T	NA	T
Participant 4	1	Mid	46	F		25	T	T	T	T	T	T	T		T	T(E)	TE	NA	T		E	T	T	NA	E
Participant 5	1	Old	65	F		28	T	T	T	T	T	T	T		T(E)	T(E)	T(E)	ET	T		NA		E	E(T)	T
Participant 6	1	Mid	44	F		26	T	T	T	T	T(E)	T(E)	T(E)	T	T	E(T)	E	E	TE		E	E	ET	NA	TE
Participant 7	1	Old	69	M		34	T	T	T	T	T	T(E)	TE		TES	E	E	E(T)(S)	ET		E(T)	E	ET	E(T)	T
Participant 8	1	Mid	51	F		30	T	T	T	T	T(E)	T(E)	T		T(E)	T(E)	T(E)	E(T)	T(E)		E(T)	E	T	NA	E
Participant 9	1	Y	22	M		4	T	T	T	T	T	ET	NA		E(T)	NA	E	T(E)	T		E(T)	E	T	NA	T
Participant 10	1	Old	65	M		34	ET	T(E)	ET	T	T	T	ET(S)		ET	E	E	E	E		E(T)(S)	E	E	E	E
Participant 11	1	Mid	55	F		34	ET	T	ET	T	T	T	T		ET	E	E	E	E		E	E	E	E	ET
Participant 12	1	Old	85	F		17	T	T	T	T	TM	T	E		TE	E(T)	E	NA	TE		NA	E	NA	E(T)	TE
Participant 13	1	Old	75	M		49	T	T(E)	T	T(E)	NA	T	E(T)	T(E)	E(T)	E(T)	E	E(T)	E(T)	T(E)	NA		E	T	E	TE
Participant 14	1	Old	60	F		35	T	T	T(E)	TE	TE	TE	TE		TE(S)	E(T)	E(T)	E	E(T)	E(T)	E(T)	E	E	NA	E(T)
Participant 15	1	Old	66	F		33	T	T	T(E)	E(T)	E	E	E(T)	E(S)(T)	ET	E	E	E	E		E	E	E(T)	ET	
Participant 16	1	Old	66	M		41	E	T		E	T(E)	T(E)	S(T)(E)	E		T5E	E	E	E	E		E	E	E	E
Participant 17	1	Old	69	F		49	E	SE	E	S(E)	S(E)	S(E)	E		SE	E	E	E	E		E	E	E	E	E
Participant 18	1	Old	65	F		46	T	T	T(E)	E(M)(T)	E	E	E(T)	E(T)(M)	E	E(T)	E(T)	E(T)	E		NA	E	E	E(T)	E
Participant 19	1	Mid	43	F		11	E	E	E	E(S)(T)	E(S)	E(S)(T)	E(T)		ETS	E(S)	E(T)	E	E		E	E	E	NA	E
Participant 20	1.5	Y	30	F		20	T	T	T	T	T	E(T)	E(T)	T		E(T)	NA	E	E	E(T)		E	E	NA	E
Participant 21	1	Old	60	M	23	7	T	T	T	T	T	T	T		T(E)(D)	T(D)(E)	TE	E(T)	E		ET	T	T	T	T
Participant 22	1	Mid	59	F	18	12	T	T	T	T	T	T	T		T(E)	T	TE	E(T)	T		ET	T	T	T	T
Participant 23	1	Mid	51	F	9	21	T	T	T	T	T	T	T		T	E(T)	TE	TE	E		T	NA	NA	T	
Participant 24	1	Old	61	F	20	11	T	T	T	T	T	T	T		T	TE	T(E)	T	E		T	T	NA	T	
Participant 25	1	Mid	50	F	15	7	T	T	T	T	T	T	T		T	T(E)	T(E)	NA	E		E	T	T	NA	T
Participant 26	1	Mid	49	F	12	10	T	T	T	T	T	T	T		T(E)	TE	T(F)(E)		ET		E	T	T	NA	T
Participant 27	1	Mid	49	F	16	11	T	T	T	T	T	T	T		T(E)(F)	TFE	T	E(F)(T)	FET		T	T	NA	T	
Participant 28	1	Old	62	M	25	6	T	T	T	T	T	T	T		T(E)	TG	TE	E(T)	T		E	T	T	NA	T
Participant 29	1	Mid	52	F	10	6	T	T	T	T(E)	T(E)	T(E)	T(G)	T	T(E)	E(T)	E	E	E		ET	E	ET	NA	ET
Participant 30	2	Y	30	M	28	2	T	T	T	T	T(D)	DE	E(T)(D)	TD	DE	NA	E	E	ED		E(T)(D)	DE	D	NA	D
Participant 31	2	Y	19	F	18	1	T	T	T	T	T	SG	NA	T/SG/G	TESG	NA	E	SG/G	SG		ESGT(G)	E	SG	NA	SG(T)(E)
Participant 32	2	Y	19	F	10	9	T	T	T	T(E)	T(F)	E(T)	NA	TF	E	NA	E(T)	E(F)	E		E(T)	E	E	NA	TF
Participant 33	2	Y	26	M	7	19	EG	T	T(G)(E)	T		G	E	G	E	NA	E	E	EG		GE(T)	E	E	NA	G(E)
Participant 34	2	Y	19	M	12	7	T		TE	T(E)	T(E)	E	NA	FT	T(E)	NA	TE	E	E		ET(F)	E	TE	NA	E
Participant 35	2	Y	20	F		20	T	T	T	T(E)	T(E)	NA	ET		T(E)	NA	T	ET	E		T(E)	E	ET	NA	ET
Participant 36	2	Y	23	F		23	T	T	T	T	T	E(T)	NA		ET	NA	E(T)	E	E		E(T)	E	E	NA	E
Participant 37	2	Y	19	M		19	T	T	T	T(E)	T(E)	E(T)	NA		E(T)	NA	E(T)	E	E		E(T)	E	E	NA	E
Participant 38	2	Y	22	M		22	T			T(E)	T(E)	TE	NA		T	NA	E	E	E		E(T)	E	ET	NA	TE
Participant 39	2	Y	25	F		25	T	TE	E(T)	E(T)	E(T)	E	NA		E	TE	E(T)	E	E		E(T)	E	E	NA	E
Participant 40	2	Y	26	M		25	E	E(T)	E(T)	E(T)	E	E	E(T)	E(T)	E(T)(P)	NA	E(T)	E(T)	E		E(T)	E	E	NA	E(T)
Participant 41	2	Y	24	M		24	E(T)	E(T)	E(T)	E(T)	E	E	E	E(T)	E	NA	NA	E	E		E	E(T)	NA	E	
Participant 42	2	Mid	40	M		40	E	E	E	E	E	E	E		E	E	E	E	E		E	E	NA	E	

Those who came to Europe as adults were considered Gen 1, whereas those who arrived as children below the age of five or who were born in Europe were counted as Gen 2. One participant was Gen 1.5, as she was born in Sri Lanka but migrated with her mother to the UK when she was ten years old. As before, the table indicates a range of contexts of use and language choices for each, with Tamil 'T' and English 'E' use being the primary languages. Where onward migration took place from EU countries, a few other languages such as French (G), German (G), Swiss-German (SG) and Danish (D), are indicated. Gen 1 SLTs who grew up in Sri Lanka occasionally reported Sinhalese (S) use. Gen 2 SLTs who have multi-ethnic friendship networks report occasional limited use of Panjabi (P).

As with the Panjabi data, Table 5.3 shows, unsurprisingly, that Gen 1 participants opt for exclusive use of Tamil in more contexts than Gen 2 in their daily lives, but also that they are actively bilingual in both Tamil and English. Those from the EU use a mix of language resources learnt when on the continent in particular situations. Gen 2 SLTs show more bilingual or multilingual practices but still have instances of exclusive situation-based Tamil use, e.g. at the temple, with older people, and with their mothers. Crucially, even though the amount of Tamil use is lower and more mixed among Gen 2 than Gen 1, there is still robust maintenance of Tamil in the second generation.

Some interesting mixing practices amongst Gen 2 SLTs involve drawing on Tamil cinema as a resource for interaction, where they quote Tamil film dialogue from 'Kollywood',[1] the Indian Tamil film industry (Sankaran 2021, 2022). The example below is from Participant 32 (Gen 2, female, 19 years), talking about some of her friends' language practices using Tamil.

> (2) I do hear my friends have it yeah um.. it's just things like from movies and they would just like repeat like some dialogues...
> ... they would say something and then they would- I think that- that dialogue was in a movie and they would just kind of continue with it and they just have banter.. they are really up-to-date with recent movies. (Participant 32)

Other Gen 2 participants reported similar practices, corroborating Canagarajah's (2019: 34) claim that the South Indian dialect spoken in Tamil movies influences the Tamil spoken by younger SLTs in the diaspora. The South Indian dialect is typically considered more colloquial and features more English borrowings, with slightly different lexical words and a distinct pronunciation (Canagarajah 2019: 35). Below is an example taken from a conversation with Participant 30 (D) and Participant 20 (A) which illustrates this.

> (3)
> D: I feel like I've learnt a lot of Tamil and I actually speak better than my friends, but. I speak- because I learnt through the elder generation, my Tamil is different from my friends' Tamil.
> LS: Huh that's so interesting. How is it different?
> D: It's very like, their's is much more like [a mix of English] and Tamil=
> A: [swag]
> D: =and with swag as well yeah.

Language in the South Asian Diaspora in Britain

LS: s- with with what?
A: [Slang- or slang]
D: [Swag.. slang]
LS: °slang°.. [°ok°]
D: [yeah] where they kind of use it more as a jokey.. kind of Tamil.
LS: Jokey.. [ok].
D: [em::] so I struggle to do that now. [Cos when I speak]
LS: [What kind of- can you give me] that jokey.. w- you mustn't be familiar with that.. Is it-
A: - I don't know, it's more like movie quotes. [whatever]
LS: [quotes]
D: [yeah] it's a lot of quotes they kind of bring in and they repeat and they.. put on like an English.. take on it.

In these ways, heritage language use among Gen 2 SLTs is evolving, adopting elements of South Indian Tamil dialects through exposure to Tamil popular culture, streamed from Tamil Nadu, South India.

An interesting detail in Table 5.3 is the presence of a communicative context in which Gen 2 participants' use of Tamil far exceeds that of Gen 1, namely in 'new media (writing)'. The younger generation claim more expertise in manipulating different language resources in this particular context. Gen 1, by contrast, tend to use more limited language resources in this domain preferring to use mostly English. Interview data provided more insight into this practice. One participant, Participant 31 (Gen 2, female, 19 years) referred to as 'S' in (4) spoke about how she uses 'so many different [languages]' when texting that she has removed the predictive text feature on her phone as it slows down communication. She claims to use German, Swiss-German, English and Tamil when texting, often mixing them together. When employing Tamil, she previously employed the Tamil script, but then switched to transliterating Tamil using the English alphabet (Sankaran 2021).

(4)
LS: When you use new media-chats-, so you've- I know you were talking about using er Swiss-German, using Swiss-German font. You'd use Tamil using Tamil font sometimes but mostly when you use Tamil.. is it English?
S: oh no I write it in English
LS: But with the one friend you use Tamil letters?
S: yeah. But like I only did that because I thought it was really cool to use that.
LS: Do you still do it?
S: uh no because it takes so much time {laughs}. It's so much easier to actually write it in English.
LS: What about Swiss-German? Does that also take as much time or?
S: It takes a bit longer. You know we have this um
LS: yeah. [predictive texts]
S: [yeah so I] always have to go up and I hate that. but, yeah it takes a bit longer but I'm used to it because I always do it.
LS: Okay and you have the ones that are most popular, most common uses that- does that come in the fore-font? How does that work? I mean-

S: um.. well.. I guess you have to [set it up]
LS: [like predictive texts?]
S: yeah but the thing is like- um because Swiss German is like- you don't really have any rule for the writing. It doesn't- I write in so many different ways, it doesn't really..
LS: really?
S: yeah. Because you don't have any like.. grammar rules for Swiss-German.. so like I can decide if I wanna use two 'a' or one 'a'. But, it doesn't come up. And um I think most of them are like language based, so I don't want to set up a language because I use so many different ones and then it would like predict a different language and then you would like mix it up.
LS: ah so you've taken off the predictive text
S: yeah

Similarly, Participant 33 (Gen 2, male, 26 years) claims to mix German, English and Tamil when communicating with his family, as described in (5).

(5) If you- If you- If you see at home, I speak Tamil to my mum.. German to my dad.. and in English to my brother and sister... and if we're all having conversations we.. we tend to change languages all the time. (Participant 33)

A longer example of this is given in the appendix to this chapter. These findings accord with Canagarajah's (2019) observation that 'it is such mixed languages that might be considered the heritage language for diaspora participants' (2019: 28), where conversational interactions involve more than the use of one language (i.e. using a mix of both English and Tamil, particularly influenced by cross-diaspora contact with South Indian Tamil). This view of heritage language is shared by Garcia (2011) and Blommaert (2010). Onward or 'double' migration can have other effects too. In the case of Tamil, the non-English EU context[2] often led to greater maintenance of Tamil. So when Tamil speakers migrate from the EU to the UK, they often bring with them active Tamil repertoires that can galvanise Tamil use within the UK context (Sankaran 2021).

Comparison to other communities and contexts

The usage and change outlined for the above two communities can be observed elsewhere too. In a recent study, Mesoudi et al. (2016) conducted research on generational changes in thinking style between first- and second-generation individuals in the London Bangladeshi community in East London. Among the external factors documented, the team adopted a simple version of the approach used in Sharma and Sankaran (2011), asking for languages regularly spoken as an indication of the maintenance of Bengali/Sylheti in the community. The study used survey methods rather than the semi-ethnographic approach in the two cases discussed earlier, and had a larger sample of 286 participants. The study found that almost all of the first-generation Bangladeshi heritage respondents reported themselves as Bengali dominant bilinguals or in some cases even only reported

Bengali, just as in the Panjabi community of Southall. Among the second generation, the study found that the majority (approx. 80 per cent) reported use of both languages, but 60 per cent of these listed English as their first language rather than Bengali. Although these self-reported language details are much simpler than those presented earlier for the Panjabi and Tamil communities, the generational pattern of language maintenance but with a shift in dominance and intensity of use is observed here too.

It is worth noting that Fox (2015), in her research with British Bangladeshi teenagers in a youth club, observed informally that the young people reported limited ability in Bengali. Fox (2015) and Cheshire et al. (2011) documented a major shift to the new dialect of Multicultural London English in this community, particularly driven by multi-ethnic friendship groups in public housing estates and local schools. Fox and Sharma (2017) argue that very subtle differences in the social class of the Asian community play a vital role in these language and dialect outcomes, in large part because working-class communities often live in multi-ethnic housing estates whereas lower middle-class communities can rent or buy housing close to other community members. We thus see a widespread shift to a multi-ethnic English dialect among working-class Bangladeshi youth in East London, in contrast to a more mono-ethnic, stable bilingualism in the lower middle-class Gujarati community of Wembley and the Panjabi community of Southall. This is then an additional factor in the degree of language use and language mixing that arises within British diaspora.

Conclusions

This overview of Indian diaspora contexts in Britain, with a focus on London, has offered impressions of the social contexts of Indian language use in the United Kingdom. We have seen that socio-demographic factors such as community size, 'onward' migration, social class and language ideologies directly affect community language use and maintenance.

The more detailed examination of Panjabi and Tamil communities revealed some regularities in multilingual repertoires across generations. Gen 2 Panjabis and Gen 2 Sri Lankan Tamils were all found to be English dominant in their bilingual/multilingual practices, but still with demonstrable maintenance of Panjabi and Tamil. Another similarity across the two communities is the slight decline in balanced bilingualism as we move from Gen 1 to Gen 2, part of an inevitable shift from South Asian language dominance to English dominant bilingualism.

Differences between the two main case studies were also observable. The smaller size of the Tamil community revealed a slightly greater tendency for Gen 1 individuals to find themselves with no Tamil-speaking contexts (Participants 17 and 19 in the Tamil data); this was not observed in the Panjabi data. There also seems to be marginally more mixed code usage in the Panjabi community, whereas the use of Tamil is more context-based, with a tendency to use Tamil exclusively in particular situations, e.g. with the grandparents' generation, with older people, and with mothers.

Finally, a particular feature of the Sri Lankan Tamil case is the influence of double or onward migration, introducing additional languages into hybrid diasporic styles, and in some cases fostering revitalisation of Tamil use in Britain, by boosting the overall number of Tamils in the UK as well as the numbers of migrants who maintained their language in the absence of English in the EU (Sankaran 2021).

Looking towards future research, one area that we have not been able to comment on in detail is the specific linguistic structures found in these heritage languages. This is due to a long-standing lack of research in this area. Informally, the authors have observed ongoing processes of koineisation and change when Hindi is used as a lingua franca among South Asians from different native language backgrounds, e.g. in grocery stores or delivery services. These unique processes of contact and change are occurring daily across the United Kingdom, offering a rich context for further investigation of these under-studied processes within large and diverse South Asian communities.

Appendix

Extract from Participant 27 – Vasuki (pseudonym) – (Gen 1, female, 49 years)

Ammaa inga thaan irunthaanga. EnguuDa thaan iruppaanga. Six month-*kku orukkaa anga poy* visa-*vai eduthuTTu varuvaanga... engalukku thaan* [French] citizen. *Avangalukku* French- refugee passport *ammaa, appo avangalukku* six month *thaan inge* stay *pannalaam... thiruppi poy* visa *eduthuTTu thiruppi varuvaanga. Appadi thaan ippo oru* nine years-*aa irunthaanga. Inga thaan irunthaanga, enguDa... intha viiTTile thaan. Ippo avangalukku konja kaal ellaam nadakkamaaTTaanga... eyilaameirunthuTTu. Appo antha* government-*antha* passport *thaanemaa, appo ange irukkiruaanga. Enga therinja oru* family *viiTTille irukkiraanga. Avanga paarthikkuraanga. Poona vaaram- appaDi naa-vaaram vaaram poovom...* husband *orukkaa poovaaru,* brother *poovar. Poona vaaram* cousin-*da mahallukku* registration. *Approm ellaarum poy vanthom.* Next week *naan pooven-maa. Ivangallukku* holiday *vanthavuDane naan poy-Duven. Approm* two- two days, three days *appaDi poyTTu poy ammaavai paarthuTTu varen.*

[**Gloss:** 'Mother stayed here [with her in London] only. She would stay with us only. Every six months she would go there [France], get the visa and return... Only we are French citizens. Mother has a French refugee passport, which means she can only stay with us for six months... Again she would go, get her visa and come back again. That's how she has been for the past nine years. She used to stay only here, with me... in this house only. Now her legs are [bad]... she doesn't walk. She doesn't feel well. Since she belongs to that government and has their passport, she stays there now. She is living in a house belonging to a family known to us. They are looking after her. Last week- we go regularly every week... my husband goes sometimes, my brother goes. Last week was my cousin's daughter's registration. So, we all went and came back. I'll be going next week. As soon as they [her children] begin their holidays I will be going. Then I will go for two or three days, see my mother and return.']

Annotation of the first three sentences from above:

Ammaa   inga   thaan   irunthaanga.
Mother   here   only   stay-past.
Mother stayed here only [*only* is more of a focus marker than a limiting adverb].

EnguuDa   thaan   iruppaanga.
us-with   only   stay-would.
She would stay with us only [*only* – as above].

Six month-*kku*   *orukkaa anga   poy* visa-*vai   eduthuTTu varuvaanga...*
Six months (DAT.)   every   there   go   visa (ACC.)   get   return
Every six months she would go there [France], get the visa and return.

Notes

1. This refers to the Tamil film industry based in the Kodambakkam neighbourhood in Chennai, Tamil Nadu. 'Kollywood' is a colloquial term used to describe this industry, the word being a portmanteau of Kodambakkam and Hollywood (https://en.wikipedia.org/wiki/Tamil_cinema).
2. Since parents living in EU countries did not have similar levels of proficiency in the respective national language/s as their children, and because parents and children often did not have proficiency in English, Tamil became the default lingua franca in family interactions.

References

Agnihotri, R. K. 1987. *Crisis of Identity: The Sikhs in England.* New Delhi: Bahri Publications.
Baker, C. 1995. *Foundations of Bilingual Education and Bilingualism.* Buffalo, NY: Multilingual Matters.
Blommaert, J. 2010. *The Sociolinguistics of Globalization.* Cambridge: Cambridge University Press.
Britain, David. 2016. Sedentarism and nomadism in the sociolinguistics of dialect. In Nikolas Coupland (ed.), *Sociolinguistics: Theoretical Debates.* Cambridge: Cambridge University Press, pp. 217–41.
Calvet, Louis-Jean. 1987. *La Guerre des Langues et les Politiques Linguistiques.* Paris: Payot.
Canagarajah, S. 2019. Changing orientations to heritage language: The practice-based ideology of Sri Lankan Tamil diaspora families. *International Journal of the Sociology of Language*, 255: 9–44.
Canagarajah, S. and S. Silberstein. 2012. Diaspora identities and language. *Journal of Language, Identity, & Education*, 11: 81–4.
CARF, Campaign against Racism and Fascism (1981). *Southall: The Birth of a Black Community.* London: Institute of Race Relations.
Cheshire, Jenny, Paul Kerswill, Susan Fox and Eivind Torgersen. 2011. Contact, the feature pool and the speech community: The emergence of Multicultural London English. *Journal of Sociolinguistics*, 15 (2): 151–96.

Choudhry, A. and M. Verma. 1994. The Gujaratis in England: Language maintenance and shift. Paper presented at Sociolinguistics Symposium 10, Lancaster University.

Dave, J. 1991. The Gujarati speech community. In S. Alladina and V. Edwards (eds), *Multilingualism in the British Isles, Volume 2: Africa, the Middle East and Asia*. London: Longman, pp. 88–102.

David, A. R. 2012. Embodied migration: Performance practices of diasporic Sri Lankan Tamil communities in London. *Journal of Intercultural Studies*, 33 (4): 375–94.

Ealing JSNA. 2010. Joint Strategic Needs Assessment report. Available at: http://www.ealingpct.nhs.uk/Publications/needs-assessment.asp (accessed 3 November 2010).

Extra, Guus and Kutlay Yağmur. 2004. *Urban Multilingualism in Europe: Immigrant Minority Languages at Home and School*. Clevedon: Multilingual Matters.

Fox, Susan. 2015. *The New Cockney: New Ethnicities and Adolescent Speech in the Traditional East End of London*. Basingstoke: Palgrave Macmillan.

Fox, S. and D. Sharma. 2017. The language of London and Londoners. In D. Smakman and P. Heinrich (eds), *Urban Sociolinguistics: The City as a Linguistic Process and Experience*. London: Routledge.

Ganesh, K. 2018. The call of home and violence of belonging: Diasporic Hinduism and Tamils in exile. In E. Hermann and A. Fuhse (eds), *India Beyond India: Dilemmas of Belonging*. Göttingen: University of Göttingen Press.

Garcia, Ofelia. 2011. From language garden to sustainable languaging: Bilingual education in a global world. *Perspective: A Publication of the National Association for Bilingual Education*, September/October: 5–10.

He, A. 2010. The heart of heritage: Sociocultural dimensions of heritage language learning. *Annual Review of Applied Linguistics*, 30: 66–82.

Husain, J. 1991. The Bengali speech community. In S. Alladina and V. Edwards (eds), *Multilingualism in the British Isles, Volume 2: Africa, the Middle East and Asia*. London: Longman, pp. 75–87.

JCQ, Joint Council for Qualifications. 2021. GCSE Other Modern Foreign Language Entries, Summer 2021. https://www.jcq.org.uk/wp-content/uploads/2021/08/GCSE-Other-MFL-Entries-Summer-2021.pdf.

Jones, Demelza. 2013. *Diversity and Diaspora: Everyday Identifications of Tamil Migrants in the UK*. PhD thesis, University of Bristol.

Jones, Demelza. 2020. *Superdiverse Diaspora: Everyday Identifications of Tamil Migrants in Britain*. Basingstoke: Palgrave Macmillan.

Lawson, Sarah and Itesh Sachdev. 2004. Identity, language use, and attitudes: Some Sylheti-Bangladeshi data from London, UK. *Journal of Language and Social Psychology*, 23 (1): 49–69.

Lindley, A. and N. Van Hear. 2007. New Europeans on the move: A preliminary review of the secondary migration of refugees within the European Union. *Working Paper No. 57*. Oxford: Centre on Migration, Policy and Society.

McCarthy, K. M., B. G. Evans and M. Mahon. 2013. Acquiring a second language in an immigrant community: The production of Sylheti and English stops and vowels by London-Bengali speakers. *Journal of Phonetics*, 41 (5): 344–58.

Mahandru, V. K. 1991. The Panjabi speech community. In S. Alladina and V. Edwards (eds), *Multilingualism in the British Isles, Volume 2: Africa, the Middle East and Asia*. London: Longman, pp. 115–27.

Mesoudi Alex, Kesson Magid and Delwar Hussain. 2016. How do people become W.E.I.R.D.? Migration reveals the cultural transmission mechanisms underlying variation in psychological processes. *PLoS ONE*, 11 (1).

Oates, Jonathan. 2002. *Southall and Hanwell*. London: The History Press Ltd.

ONS, Office for National Statistics. 2011. *2011 Census: Ethnic Group, Local Authorities in England and Wales (Table KS201EW)*. Retrieved 21 December 2012 from: http://www.ons.gov.uk/ons/publications/re-referencetables.html?edition=tcm%3A77-286262.

Pirouet, L. 2001. *Whatever Happened to Asylum in Britain?* Oxford: Berghahn.

Rampton, B. 2015–18. Leverhulme Trust Ref: RPG-2015-279. Adult language socialisation in the Sri Lankan Tamil diaspora in London.

Rosa, J. and S. Trivedi. 2017. Diaspora and language. In Suresh Canagarajah (ed.), *The Routledge Handbook of Migration and Language*. London: Routledge, pp. 330–46.

Sankaran, Lavanya. 2021. 'Talk in Tamil!' – Does Sri Lankan Tamil onward migration from Europe influence Tamil language maintenance in the UK? *International Journal of the Sociology of Language*, 269: 123–49.

Sankaran, Lavanya. 2022. Sri Lankan Tamil experiences of the home-land and host-land: The interaction between language and diasporic identity. *Language in Society*, 51 (1): 143–66.

Saxena, Mukul. 1995. *A Sociolinguistic Study of Panjabi Hindus in Southall: Language Maintenance and Shift*. Unpublished PhD dissertation, University of York.

Sevinç, Yeşim. 2016. Language maintenance and shift under pressure: Three generations of the Turkish immigrant community in the Netherlands. *International Journal of the Sociology of Language*, 242: 81–117.

Sharma, Devyani. 2011. Style repertoire and social change in British Asian English. *Journal of Sociolinguistics*, 15 (4): 464–92.

Sharma, Devyani and Ben Rampton. 2015. Lectal focusing in interaction: A new methodology for the study of style variation. *Journal of English Linguistics*, 43 (1): 3–35.

Sharma, Devyani and Lavanya Sankaran. 2011. Cognitive and social forces in dialect shift: Gradual change in London Asian speech. *Language Variation and Change*, 23: 399–428.

Sharma, Devyani and Jessica Wormald. Forthcoming. South Asian Language in Britain. In S. Fox (ed.), *Languages of the British Isles*. Cambridge: Cambridge University Press (2nd edition).

Sharma, Devyani, Ben Rampton and Roxy Harris. 2008–10. ESRC Standard Grant RES-062-23-0604. Dialect development and style in a diasporic community.

Sneddon, R. 2000. Language and literacy practices in Gujarati Muslim families. In M. Martin-Jones and K. Jones (eds), *Multilingual Literacies*. Amsterdam: John Benjamins, pp. 103–25.

Stuart-Smith, Jane and M. Cortina-Borja. 2012. A law unto themselves? An acoustic phonetic study of tonal consonants in Panjabi. In A. Willi and R. Probert (eds), *Laws and Rules in Indo-European*. Oxford: Oxford University Press, pp. 61–82.

Tan, E. K. 2017. A rhizomatic account of heritage language. In Suresh Canagarajah (ed.), *The Routledge Handbook of Migration and Language*. London: Routledge, pp. 468–85.

Velamati, M. 2009. Sri Lankan Tamil migration and citizenship: Time for reconsideration. *India Quarterly: A Journal of International Affairs*, 65 (3): 271–94.

Verma, M., A. Mukherjee, A. Khanna and R. K. Agnihotri. 2001. The Sylhetis in Leeds: An attempt at a sociolinguistic profile. *Journal of Social Issues*, 91: 38–58.

Vidal Rodeiro, Carmen L. 2009. Some issues on the uptake of Modern Foreign Languages at GCSE. Statistics Report Series No. 10. Cambridge: Cambridge Assessment.

Visram, Rozina. 2015. *Ayahs, Lascars and Princes: The Story of Indians in Britain 1700–1947*. London: Routledge.

Zunzer, W. 2004. Diaspora communities and civil conflict transformation. Berghof Occasional Paper 26. Berlin: Berghof Research Centre for Constructive Conflict Management.

CHAPTER 6

Symbolic Value as a Catalyst for Language Maintenance: Sanskrit in the US Diaspora

Rajeshwari V. Pandharipande

1. Introduction

Research on the languages of transnational immigrant communities has primarily focused on their maintenance, shift and/or loss in diasporic contexts and the sociolinguistic determinants of these phenomena (Fishman 1991, Haugen 1953, Manosuthikit 2018, Pauwels 2016, among others). However, there is paucity of research on languages of multilingual communities in diaspora. Current research in sociolinguistics on language maintenance and shift has not adequately discussed the following questions in diasporic context:

1. Which sociolinguistic factors allow/promote maintenance of a language without the presence of the community to which it originally belonged in its native land?
2. Why are some languages in the multilingual diaspora maintained while others are not?
3. Do motivations for and patterns of maintenance of a language vary across diverse sociolinguistic contexts in diaspora?
4. How does the migrated language adapt to the new linguistic and cultural landscape and impact the new context?
5. Are there universal factors which can predict maintenance of languages in the diasporic contexts.

In the context of these questions, this chapter focuses on the maintenance of Sanskrit in the US diaspora. In particular, the chapter will examine four 'incarnations' of Sanskrit in four different contexts and demonstrate that the structure and function of Sanskrit vary significantly in these contexts. It will be shown that the symbolic value of Sanskrit's 'capital', Bourdieu's (1982: 14) term for 'accumulated prestige and honor' as the language of Hinduism *par excellence*, has been influential in determining the patterns of its maintenance. The significant point to note is that the primary symbolic value of Sanskrit is 'converted' into different 'capitals' in the four contexts. The four contexts under focus in the US are (1) the nineteenth-century Transcendentalist community, (2) post 1965 including the present Hindu immigrants' religious practices in the US, (3) digital religion in the contemporary US, and (4) the secular American context of Yoga (where Yoga practitioners express two mutually exclusive views on the symbolic value of Sanskrit). In particular, the motivations for the maintenance of Sanskrit and its function in each context will be discussed. The mutual impact of the interaction of Sanskrit and the new sociolinguistic and cultural context in the US will also be examined.

The following discussion is divided into six sections (2–7) to show how the symbolic value of the Sanskrit language becomes a catalyst for its maintenance in the US diaspora in various socio-cultural and linguistic contexts at different points in time including the present. The major point is that the major/primary value of Sanskrit as the symbol of Hinduism *par excellence*, is 'converted' into diverse symbolic values in different contexts. While its primary value is consistently maintained, it further acquires additional symbolic values in different contexts, which become the motivations for its maintenance. The second section focuses on the nineteenth-century socio-cultural context of the US, when the 'Boston philosopher-thinkers' disillusioned with the inequality in their society, found the ideology of unity and equality of all existences in the Hindu scriptures (in Sanskrit). Sanskrit functioned as 'the path to the eastern mind' and consequently, the study of Sanskrit was adopted and encouraged. The third section, 'Sanskrit as a symbol of Hindu identity', presents discussion on the post-1965 Hindu community in the US (which is multilingual, multicultural and of multinational origin) that chooses Sanskrit as the symbol of the pan-Hindu identity. The fourth section, 'Structure of Sanskrit in Hindu rituals in the US', illustrates the structure and function of Sanskrit in the Hindu rituals (in the US), where it is now mixed with English (and other languages) in the ritual discourse. For the Hindus, Sanskrit in rituals symbolises 'authenticity' of the Hindu ritual. However, the discussion points out that the patterns of the 'hybrid Sanskrit' discourse vary according to the context (Hindu temple vs. home), participants' ethnicity (Hindu vs. American or mixed), as well the type of ritual (wedding vs. house-warming ceremony). The fifth section, 'Sanskrit in the digital media: blurring the line between the secular and the sacred', examines the role of Sanskrit in the digital media. It covers the maintenance and revival of Sanskrit in the US diaspora and raises further questions about the authenticity/efficacy of the digital/online rituals and the religious experience mediated through the digital media. The sixth section, 'Sanskrit in Yoga practice in the US: appropriation or adoption of the immigrant tradition?', presents the issue of inclusion/maintenance or exclusion of the use of Sanskrit in the Yoga practices in the US and points out that the value of Sanskrit as a symbol of Hinduism becomes the catalyst for its inclusion in the Yoga practices of those who accept the connection of Yoga with Hinduism while the same symbolic value becomes the cause of its exclusion from the Yoga practices of those who want to dissociate Yoga from Hinduism. The seventh and concluding section reviews the themes of this chapter, including the symbolic values of Sanskrit across contexts of time and the socio-cultural spaces.

2. Sanskrit as the 'path to the eastern/Indian mind': the nineteenth-century arrival of Sanskrit in the US

This section focuses on the first question, i.e.: which sociolinguistic situation (s) motivate maintenance of a language in a diasporic context without the presence of the community to which the language belongs in its native homeland? Unlike other Indian languages (for example, the regional languages of India), which primarily arrived in the US with the speech community, Sanskrit has a different history. It first arrived in the US in the form of the Hindu religious scriptures without the Indian/Hindu speech community. Sanskrit texts, the *Bhagavadgītā*, the *Upaniṣads*, the *Vedas*, *Purāṇas* and *Manusmriti*, arrived in the US during the period (nineteenth century) of the transcendentalists on the east coast, in the state of Massachusetts (Eck 2001, Goldberg 2010). The earliest English translations of the Hindu texts in Sanskrit by Charles Wilkins, Max Muller and William Jones were brought to the US via Germany. It was a period in the US when the 'Boston philosopher-thinkers', Emerson, Thoreau, Whitman and Alcott among others, were disillusioned with the materialistic and commercial workings of their religion amidst slavery and social injustice and unequal rights in the contemporary America. They were searching for the ideology which would provide a vision of the unity of diverse forms, physical and ideological, and thereby transform the consciousness of the people. Their idealistic quest for such an ideology of the unity and equality of all found its answers in the Hindu scriptures. They found resonances in the Hindu scriptures, especially the *Bhagavadgītā*, the *Vedas*, *Upaniṣads* and *Purāṇas*, which presented the system of thought in which all forms of existence were viewed as diverse expressions of the one Divine Being, *Brahman*. The Hindu philosophy presented in the scriptures of underlying unity, equality and divinity of all, the power of one's own actions (the laws of *karma*), the cosmic justice through reincarnation of all forms, heavily influenced the transcendentalists' vision of religion, society and humanity at large. They found a reflection of the Unitarian religion in America in the Hindu scriptures. The realisation of one's divine nature was viewed in the Hindu scriptures as the fulfilment of life and the only obstacle was believed to be ignorance about the divine nature of all including oneself. Unmediated connection with the Divine was the other most attractive vision for the transcendentalists, who were not happy with the Church-controlled and -mediated religion (Christianity). They found answers to their questions related to the individual social and spiritual life in the Hindu scriptures. As Eck (2001: 95) in her influential study, *A New Religious America*, remarks, 'In Emerson himself the perspectives of the ancient India, Upaniṣads and the nineteenth century transcendentalists came together, directing our human vision toward the oneness of spirit underlying the whole universe.'

Thus, Sanskrit arrived in the nineteenth century, as a path, an intellectually convincing voice of wisdom, which satisfied the religious and spiritual needs of the elite and influential thinkers in America. This was the motivation for the reception of Sanskrit, which became a powerful symbol of Eastern thought in the US. Sanskrit played an important role in turning the consciousness of American intelligentsia towards the Eastern Indian vision of the world, and its relevance to the important questions of religion, society and individuals. Sanskrit in this context becomes a representation and a symbol of the Hindu or Eastern vision of the world and humanity and their interaction. This value of Sanskrit was the reason for its introduction, and maintenance, in the academic landscape of America in the nineteenth century. The primarily Hindu vision of the world (presented in the Hindu scriptures) was perceived as the 'eastern' vision of the world, and Sanskrit was viewed as the path to access that vision.

The impact of this is seen in the introduction of the study of Sanskrit and Oriental Studies at Yale University. Sinha (2013: 75) points out that William Dwight Whitney played a major role in the development of 'a public understanding' of Sanskrit in America: 'Through Whiney, Sanskrit became an aspect of the popular consciousness of contemporary culture, which was vitally affected by Victorian debate on language, race, religion and identity.'

Sanskrit became part of the curricula of the American university system. In this way, it became instrumental in establishing a connection between America and India. Sinha (2013: 75) points out that this is the beginning of 'American engagement with the orient'. While the transcendentalists provided the major cultural and religious impetus for the beginning of the study of Sanskrit, Whitney and Bopp focused on the study of the grammar of Sanskrit within the comparative philological and literary framework. Whitney's grammar (1879) and Lanmann's *Sanskrit Reader* (1889) established the American tradition of the study of Sanskrit, which was based on the Western rather than the Indian grammatical tradition. For example, Whitney's grammar reads like a grammar of Latin in focusing primarily on phonology and morphology. There is no section on syntax in the grammar. Sanskrit is transliterated into the English script instead of using the traditional Devanagari script. The Western/Latin format is clear if we contrast Whitney's grammar with later grammars of Sanskrit such as the grammar by Macdonell, *A Sanskrit Grammar for Students* (1916) and M. R. Kale's *A Higher Sanskrit Grammar* (1961), which are closer to the Sanskrit grammatical tradition. The point in focus is that the primary motivation for the study of Sanskrit was to understand the 'Oriental view' of the world of humanity, individuals, their underlying unity, and the implications of the view of the unity for equality, and social justice in the US. Thus, the symbolic value of Sanskrit as the representation of the Indian/Eastern perception of reality motivated its promotion in the early US context. Since the goal of the study of Sanskrit was to access the Oriental ideology, the emphasis was not on the study of grammar and its framework. Sanskrit was a tool to access the Hindu scriptures for understanding the Hindu perspective on the world and of human beings and their interaction in relation to philosophical and transcendental concerns of American intellectuals of the time.

Since this inception of an academic home for the study of Sanskrit in the US, there has been a tradition of teaching Sanskrit at the university level as a classical language with a large range of writing covering Indian religion, culture, history, creative literature, linguistics, law and philosophy. Currently, Sanskrit is taught at twenty-six major universities from the introductory to the advanced levels in various departments such as Linguistics, Indian/South Asian Studies, Comparative Literature, India Studies, South Asian Languages and Cultures, and Religion. Students in diverse academic disciplines are currently studying Sanskrit to accomplish various career goals. Additionally, Sanskrit University of America, Hindu University and Maharshi University are other institutions where Sanskrit is taught. In addition to the established universities, Sanskrit is taught in many Hindu temples in the US (as discussed in the following section). Thus, the uptake of Sanskrit in the new academic and religious context expanded the influence of Hindu scriptures there. In the process, the function of Sanskrit and its grammatical tradition was somewhat changed in the new landscape (as discussed further in section 4).

3. Sanskrit as a symbol of Hindu identity in the US

This section focuses on the maintenance of Sanskrit as the symbol of the Hindu identity of immigrants. In particular, the discussion will examine the structure and function of Sanskrit in the religious context of the immigrant community in the US.

Although migration from India to the US dates to the nineteenth century, large-scale migration is only seen after 1965, which continues to today. Inspired by the civil rights revolution in American society, the 1965 Immigration Act explicitly abolished the discriminatory national origins quotas that had regulated entrance into the country since the 1920s. According to the data from the America Census Bureau, the Indian immigrant population in the US in 2015 was 3.982 million and over 50 per cent of Indian immigrants are Hindus. According to the 2016 Public Religion Research Institute data, 1 per cent of the US population is Hindu. Although a large proportion of the Hindu immigrants came from different parts of India, many groups of Hindus have also arrived from other countries such as Canada, Sri Lanka, Singapore, Malaysia, South Africa, Kenya, Uganda, and so on. Thus, the Hindu community in the US is culturally and linguistically diverse.

A large body of research on Hindu immigrants (Eck 2001, Goldberg 2010, Fenton 1998, Narayanan 1996, Pandharipande 2001a, 2001b, 2010, Williams 1996) has already discussed the Hindu immigrants' choice of religion as their identity marker in the US. When immigrants arrive in the new homeland, they bring cultural patterns of ethnicity, which provide them with a sense of security and a framework to establish an identity for themselves in the new homeland and try to transfer their identity to the next generation. Reconstructing or remaking their cultural identity in the new homeland is the strategy, which the immigrants utilise to repair their fractured or disturbed grammar of culture. This changing identity and culture constitutes three interdependent components: (1) cognition of the world (a philosophical component), (2) expression of the worldview through social patterns of behaviour such as language, art, language etiquette, and so on (a social component), and (3) goals, aspirations and desires (an ideational component (see Pandharipande (2001a: 235)). As Geertz (1973: 89) points out, culture is 'a system of inherited conceptions expressed in symbolic forms by means of which men communicate, perpetuate, and develop their knowledge about and attitudes toward life'.

It is observed that the immigrants overwhelmingly choose to maintain their religion in a new homeland (see especially the case of Jewish immigrants in the US, and Israel, and Muslim immigrants in different parts of the world). Religion provides them with a distinctive group identity in a new space and the constitution of the US allows religious freedom to its residents. Geertz (1973: 123) points out that, 'The importance of religion lies in its capacity to serve, for an individual or a group, as a source of general, yet distinctive conceptions of the world, the self, and the relation between them ... .' Thus, religion can provide a distinctive identity to a group of immigrants. Additionally, religion provides them with a platform from which they can articulate, negotiate and adapt their inherited framework of identity to the new space, at a physical, social and psychological level.

Temples in the US provide the major platform for expressing and experiencing the Hindu identity in the US. Wikipedia lists 900 Hindu temples/Hindu centres in the US. The Hindu centres dedicated to Hindu saints are growing in numbers, e.g.: Chinmaya Mission centres, Dayananda Saraswati's institution, Arsha Vidya Gurukulam, Mata Amritanandamyi's centres across the US, Ramakrishna Mission centres, Vivekananda Vedanta societies, Sai Baba centres, the Divine Life Society. Additionally, Hindu student organisations and local Hindu associations are actively contributing to the ongoing study and maintenance of Hinduism. The temples and centres differ in the sects of Hinduism and methods of practising the religion. However, they converge in one major aspect of their practices, the prominent use of Sanskrit as opposed to regional languages of India. Thus, Sanskrit is perceived by the Hindu community as the linguistic and cultural symbol of their identity.

Hindu rituals in public spaces such as Hindu temples, religious centres or wedding halls, as well as in homes (house-warming ceremonies, rituals related to death), are primarily performed in Sanskrit as opposed to regional Indian languages. Hindu priests who perform rituals are generally from India, where they are trained in Sanskrit language in general as well as in methods of recitation and performance of rituals in Sanskrit. The level of the priests' understanding of the Sanskrit scriptures varies considerably. Of the five priests I interviewed, two had undergone the study of scriptures before being trained in the performance of the rituals, while three were trained in preforming the rituals but had never studied the scriptures. It is interesting to note here that Sanskrit is not understood by the majority of Hindus in the US. It is –expectedly – even less understood by the second-generation Hindus. (While Sanskrit is not understood by the majority of Hindus in India, most of them are closely familiar with Sanskrit vocabulary commonly shared with their native languages. Moreover, the frequency of their exposure to Sanskrit in the religious context is significantly higher in India, where more rituals are celebrated together and temples are visited more frequently in which they hear Sanskrit prayers and recitation of Hindu scriptures more regularly.) Nevertheless, in the fifteen weddings I attended in the US, and the five weddings I performed, both the first- and the second-generation Hindus chose Sanskrit as opposed to their own regional language for their respective wedding rituals. In other Hindu rituals in the US, including *Ganeśachaturthi, Śivarātrī, Vijayādaśamī, Dīpāvalī, Durgāpūjā* and other life-cycle rituals (for example, *Upanayana*), the priest presides over the worship rituals, which include the recitation/singing of Hindu scriptures in Sanskrit. Although the participants in the rituals do not speak and only marginally understand Sanskrit, the Hindu community overwhelmingly supports the use of Sanskrit over regional languages. However, the local regional worship rituals of the family deities, new year celebrations (which vary across regions in India), may be performed in Sanskrit when the priest is invited or in regional languages as deemed convenient. Similarly, some Hindu groups such as Satya Sai Baba's followers use a mixture of many languages including Sanskrit, regional languages (Tamil, Hindi, etc.) and English.

There are three major reasons for favouring Sanskrit in the US. The first is that Sanskrit is the language of Hinduism since the time of its inception and has continued to enjoy its status as *Devavāṇi* (gods' language) through the entire history of Hinduism. Sanskrit has authority as the language of Hindu philosophy, theology, sociology, linguistics and literature. It has been authenticated; that is, its authority has been sanctioned by the Hindu saints and mystics of the past and present who have the highest authority to sanction linguistic codes and rituals in Hinduism. While regional languages have also produced Hindu scriptures, (for example, *Jnāneśvarī* in

Marathi and *Rāmacritamānas* in Awadhi) and are accepted as legitimate languages of Hinduism, they do not wield the same prestige and power as Sanskrit.

The second reason is that, unlike Sanskrit, the modern languages represent 'regional' and not' 'pan-Hindu' identity. In the diaspora of the US, immigrant Hindus form a linguistically, culturally and nationally diverse community. Thus, to unify the diverse community under a 'pan-Hindu' identity, the choice of Sanskrit as opposed to regional languages has been the most appropriate.

The third reason is that Sanskrit is considered the most powerful signifier of Hinduism throughout its history. We may pose the question, 'Why is Sanskrit chosen as the most powerful signifier of Hinduism or Hindu identity when other Indian languages also have been used to express Hinduism and therefore equally qualify as markers of Hinduism or Hindu identity?' The answer to this question is provided in Pandharipande (2006, 2010) where I have argued that Sanskrit is more 'transparent' in its function of symbolising Hinduism compared to other Indian languages. I have claimed that a language is considered 'transparent' in its function when there is an invariable/inalienable connection between the two. There is an invariable connection between Sanskrit and Hinduism, i.e. Sanskrit invariably and exclusively symbolises Hinduism (and no other religion). In contrast to this, other Indian languages have a 'less transparent' or 'opaque' connection with Hinduism – i.e. they do not unambiguously symbolise Hinduism since they are used to express religions other than Hinduism as well. Examples of this multifunctionality include Hindi-Urdu (for Islam), Pāli, Prākrit, Marathi (Buddhism), Malayālam, Hindi, Marathi, Tamil, etc. (Christianity), Punjabi (Sikhism), and Gujarati, Marathi, Hindi, etc. (Jainism). Though used for Jainism and Buddhism in the earlier stage of their inception, Sanskrit did not acquire the distinctive symbolic value as a 'signifier' of these religions. Therefore, it is viewed as the most powerful symbol of Hinduism within and outside the Hindu community and, to provide a distinctive identity to the Hindus in the US, Sanskrit is chosen as the preferred language of Hinduism in Hindu practices. The regional languages are used in many rituals, which the Hindus perform at home. One such ritual is worship of *Ganesha* at home. For example, the Hindu community from the state of Maharashtra may choose to sing *Aratī*, a devotional song, in Marathi, a regional language of Maharashtra. However, when the Hindu community collectively celebrates major religious festivals and rituals, Sanskrit is preferred. The Hindu temples consciously choose Sanskrit over the regional languages in order to allow the entire group of Hindu devotees with diverse nationalities, languages and cultures to gather in the temples and relate to or participate in the Hindu rituals through Sanskrit.

Recent research supports the claim that the inalienable/'transparent' connection with a particular religion helps maintenance of immigrants' language in diaspora such as the Brazilian Portuguese in London (Souza (2019)) and Standard Arabic in Israel (Amara (2019)). Additional evidence (Pandharipande 2006: 158) for the ' transparent' connection of Sanskrit with Hinduism is seen in the failure of the nineteenth-century British Baptist missionaries (mentioned in Young 1981: 33–65,William Carey 1808, Mill 1831, Muir 1844, Ballantyne 1855, among others) who tried to use a Sanskrit translation of the Bible (*Dharmapustaka*) for promoting Christianity among Hindus (specially Brahmins). As Young (1981: 61) points out, the readers were 'hard pressed' to understand and accept it because of the Christian (as opposed to Hindu) semantics of Sanskrit used in the Bible translation! It was difficult for the readers to dissociate Sanskrit from its connection with Hinduism and associate it with Christianity. As young explains, 'One can see why readers were hard pressed to understand Muir (one of the Baptist missionary who translated the Bible into Sanskrit). His vocabulary (in the Sanskrit translation of the Bible) was borrowed from Hindu sources, but its meaning was galvanized within a Christian context ... Each tersely worded *śloka* carried the burden of a particular theological doctrine on one or more words appropriated from Hindu philosophy and religion.' Young (1981: 46, 63) claims that despite Mill's defensive claim that he had taken only 'the material language (Sanskrit) and measure, in which ... Christian sentiments might be expressed', 'a Sanskrit treatise on the Evidences of Christianity, with a refutation of Hinduism, is a desideratum ...'. Young (1981: 62) discusses Carey's difficulty of finding the Sanskrit equivalents of the words in the Bible such as God, salvation, atonement, etc., since their respective Sanskrit equivalents *dev, mukti* and *prāyaschitta* could not match their Christian semantics. The 'Hindu meaning' of the borrowed Sanskrit words could not be readily replaced by their Christian counterparts. As a result, the Sanskrit Bible never gained credibility among Hindus (for further discussion, see Young 1981: 42, 45, 60–6) and Ballantyne's intention of 'making every educated Hindu a Christian' could not succeed. Thereafter, the missionaries switched to the use of the regional languages for the translation of the Bible and successfully used it for their missionary work. At present, Christian churches in India use the Bible translated in regional languages.

4. Structure of Sanskrit in Hindu rituals in the US

Hindu rituals provide the most significant context in which Sanskrit is maintained in the US. The term 'Hindu ritual' is used here to refer to Hindu practices/activities such as prayers, recitation of the Hindu scriptures, singing devotional songs (Bhajan), practices related to the life-cycle events of childbirth (Janma), initiation into the phase of education of the child (Upanayana), weddings (Vivāha), deaths (Antyeṣṭi), and many more. However, unlike in India, English is used alongside Sanskrit when it is used in the rituals. Leach (1968: 524), in his well-known article 'Ritual', defines rituals as 'culturally defined sets of behavior'. It assumed here that all religious rituals are authenticated and governed by the rules of their performance prescribed by the particular religious traditions. However, they vary in terms of the flexibility of the rules, i.e. the rules of the recitation of scriptures and wedding are more stringent compared to those of singing devotional songs and prayers.

In the US, unlike in India, English is used alongside Sanskrit when it is used in the rituals. In particular, in a Hindu wedding ritual, the priest recites the text/scriptural injunctions in Sanskrit (only) and explains those in English for the participants such as the bride and the groom, their parents, and the larger audience which includes Indians as well as Americans. In this case, the priest does not necessarily provide a literal translation of the text but explains the overall meaning of the text and its role in the ritual. For example, the Hindu wedding ritual begins with the fire ritual where the priest offers worship to the fire-god (*agni-devatā*) and requests him to take the prayers of the participants to the gods in the heaven and bring back their blessings to the participants including the bride and the groom. Fire (*agni*) is believed to be the *purohita*, the priest who acts on behalf of the performers of the ritual. The priest recites the following verse in the Vedic Sanskrit:

agnimīḷe purohitaṃ yajnasya devaṃ ṛtvijaṃ hotāraṃ ratnadhātamam (Ṛgveda 1.1)

[Literal translation: 'Agni we worship, the priest, the deity of our sacrificial ritual, the invoker, the highest source of the treasure.']

The priest briefly explains, 'Now we worship the fire god and ask for his blessings at the beginning of the ritual.'

The pattern of using Sanskrit together with English in the ritual discourse is the most common pattern in Hindu rituals in the US. The pattern of using Sanskrit with English varies across contexts. If a bride and the groom prefer to repeat the Sanskrit ritual text after the priest (as is often the case if they can pronounce the Sanskrit), then the discourse pattern changes. Both the priest and the couple use Sanskrit exclusively for the performance of the ritual and the priest uses English to communicate the meaning of the ritual to the audience. Hindus of the second generation show a great deal of variation in their patterns of language preference and use. Despite being brought up in the US with English as their first language, their preference is for Sanskrit in the wedding ritual. For example, in a wedding which I performed in 2000, the couple repeated after me the wedding vows of commitment and duty to each other in Sanskrit. They believed that the vows had to be in Sanskrit. They both said that the efficacy of the ritual would be lowered if they were to use an English translation of the vows. They practised the Sanskrit text ahead of the time. I translated the text orally in English for the audience. Thus, I recited the vows in Sanskrit for the bride and the groom and then they each repeated those.

Note the following example:

dharme ca arthe ca kāme ca nāticarāmi.

'In the pursuit of righteous life, prosperity and love, I will always be with you.'
[Literally: I will not transgress (the scriptural/traditional injunctions for the pursuit of duty, material prosperity and love.]

At some Hindu weddings, the couples choose to use exclusively an English translation of Sanskrit texts for the ritual as they are not confident about their pronunciation of the Sanskrit text.

Another reason for switching between Sanskrit and other languages is that inter-religious/intercultural marriages are becoming more common. I have performed a marriage (in 2017) where the groom was Hindu and the bride was Zoroastrian, and in another wedding in (2010) the groom was Hindu and the bride was Christian.

Since most of the Sanskrit texts used in the Hindu rituals are ancient Hindu scriptures, the structure of Sanskrit is not changed when it is used in the rituals. The excerpts taken from the *Vedas, Upaniṣads, Purāṇas* and *Stotras* do not undergo any structural changes. It is the discourse pattern which undergoes a significant change with the admittance of a fair amount of code-switching, not only into English but other classical languages too. For example, in a wedding where the groom was Hindu and the bride was Zoroastrian, and two Zoroastrian priests and one Hindu (designated) priest were called upon to officiate the wedding, the Hindu ritual of the worship of the god *Gaṇeśa* was followed by the Zoroastrian ritual of *Ashirwad*. While the Hindu ritual was performed with the prayer to *Gaṇeśa* in Sanskrit, the Zoroastrian ritual was performed in the ancient Persian language of *Avesta*. The Sanskrit prayer to *Gaṇeśa* was as follows:

vakratuṇḍa mahākāya sūryakoṭisamaprabha |
nirvighnam kuru me deva sarvakāryeṣu sarvadā||

'O god with curved trunk and large body, whose brilliance is equal to a million suns, may you be kind to me and always make all my undertakings free of obstacles.'

The ancient ceremony of Ashirwad begins with a prayer, which the Zoroastrian priest recites in Old Persian: *Har do tan ramashni awazun bad* ('May mighty God bestow upon you both joy and prosperity').

The structure of the Sanskrit text is not changed in the religious rituals performed in the temple by the priests. Hindus believe that the efficacy of the ritual depends on the use of flawless language, i.e. one that is unchanged in grammar and pronunciation down the ages. The priests in the Hindu temples in the US are generally trained in India. Therefore, Sanskrit metres, the prosody and the pronunciation of Sanskrit are meticulously preserved. The purity of language is emphasised in the rituals performed in the temples. There is more flexibility in the choice of language (Sanskrit versus modern Indian languages) and scriptures in the rituals performed at home. Hindu temples also host rituals in which the congregation participates. These include recitation of Sanskrit devotional songs (which involve praise of gods) and scriptural passages. Generally, the recitation is led by the priest, who is trained in Sanskrit. However, those who repeat after the priest are usually not similarly trained. It is no surprise that their pronunciation of Sanskrit is not always flawless, but is tinged with regional pronunciation of Indian languages or of US English.

In India, juxtaposing Sanskrit with English (which wields high prestige in the secular context) is traditionally not acceptable in the Hindu wedding ritual since English has been viewed as 'impure' and not worthy of being used in the sacred/religious rituals. However, in present-day India, in a context in which both bride and groom or one of the two is a foreigner, or a non-Hindu, code-alteration between Sanskrit with English is also noticed. Moreover, Hindu weddings across diverse linguistic communities currently are on the rise. In India, where the groom and the bride do not belong to the same linguistic community (i.e., do not speak the same regional language), the priest chooses to alternate Sanskrit with either Hindi or English as directive languages (if he is competent in them) or restricts himself to Sanskrit. Additionally, use of a regional language to explain ritual actions is also noticed in the context where the couple share a common regional language.

5. Sanskrit in the digital media: blurring the line between the secular and the sacred

This section focuses on the role of digital media in the maintenance of Sanskrit in the modern globalising world in general and in the US in particular. It also focuses on the impact of this 'new digital incarnation' of Sanskrit and on the perception of its authenticity and validity as a religious symbol. One of the major revolutionary changes from the late twentieth century onward is in the world of technology and digital media. These have proven instrumental in the maintenance of Sanskrit in the US. Major Sanskrit scriptures and literary texts have been and are currently being digitised and made available online. Additionally, Hindu discourses of the Hindu mystics' and saints' religious *ācāryas* (teachers) are being made accessible to devotees and people across the world. Due to the enhanced connectivity worldwide, Hindus in the US can connect with the saints and mystics in India, visit Hindu temples and attend Hindu rituals in India through virtual meetings. Students and immigrants in the US attend rituals at their respective homes in India. Within the US, priests perform online worship in Sanskrit and people can attend from anywhere in the world (Pandharipande 2018, Scheifiner 2013). YouTube, Zoom meetings or online religious discourses, and performance of Hindu rituals in virtual temples are the most common spaces for the preservation and revival of Sanskrit in the US (as well as in India and elsewhere). Most of the Hindu scriptures including the *Vedas*, *Upaniṣads*, *Purāṇas* and the *Bhagavadgītā* are easily accessible to devotees as well as to those who want to study them. The most common Hindu rituals involving reciting scriptures and listening to their recitation are now possible online. Recordings of scriptures are made by priests or devotees who have been trained in the art of flawless recitation of these scriptures. For example, in many gatherings devotees silently listen to the recitation of the Sanskrit epic, the Rāmāyana on YouTube. Digital media also provide religious music online. *Bhajan* 'devotional songs', which are sung individually or collectively, are also available online. Devotees sing along with the online recordings of prayers or devotional songs and excerpts from the scriptures or listen to them in a group. In India, such *Bhajan* are generally sung in regional languages. In the US, in the temples as well as in private gatherings, the devotees listen to the online pre-recorded devotional songs in Sanskrit and sing together as a group It is significant that the need to invite the Pandit/Pujari is thus being reduced. Hindus in India now also make use of technology for ritual practice. A friend in India routinely asks her daughter in the UK to join them in their Zoom meeting for the worship of the Hindu goddess Durga. Also, such international prayers were offered via Zoom meetings in the COVID-19 era for lost family members.

The efficacy of the rituals performed online or with the help of digital media is sometimes questioned and/or debated (see Pandharipande 2018). For example, the online ritual of *Gurūpūjā* (worship of Guru) is performed in Sanskrit not necessarily by the priest but by a person who knows the Sanskrit text (https://www.youtube.com/watch?v=_tbzXrMn4fE). The devotees recite or listen to the recorded tapes of the *stotras* (texts recited/sung for the gods/goddesses) on YouTube (https://www.youtube.com/watch?v=MWK9-Ztl5j8). The assumption is that by reciting or listening to the *stotras*, the devotees perform the worship ritual. The online rituals are conducted either entirely in Sanskrit or in alternate codes (Sanskrit–English). While the texts of *stotras* are also available online in modern Indian languages, Hindu devotees prefer use of *stotras* in Sanskrit in temples and homes.

Two major questions are raised by this online-mediated religious practice: (1) are these legitimate/authentic Hindu practices? and (2) does the Sanskrit of those who are not priests or saints have the same authority/efficacy as the Sanskrit used by the priests? More generally, the concern is whether online-mediated Sanskrit produces the same religious experience for devotees as the offline Sanskrit of priests and saints.

In Pandharipande (2018: 203–4) I have argued that media provide a different space (virtual space) and different method for the religious practices. The online deities and recorded language are new signifiers of religious meaning. Authenticity of digital religious practice is sanctioned by the saints and mystics since they themselves use these symbols (virtual images of deities as well as recorded texts of the scriptures) in their religious practices. This virtual space does not cancel or dismiss the offline space but, rather, it provides an alternative space. This virtual space particularly benefits the diasporic Hindu community because devotees can connect with their counterparts in India and other countries. I have also argued (Pandharipande 2018) that the signifiers of religious meaning and the method of religious practice have gone through many changes in the history of Hinduism. For example, metal or clay statues of deities were not present at the time of the *Vedas*; they were introduced later in later Hindu practices (Salmond 2004). Similarly, the original oral tradition of reciting scriptures was later supplemented by reading of the written scriptures. This shows that the relationship between signifier and signified religious meaning has not been static. Contemporary media/virtual space, virtual images of deities, recorded Sanskrit speech are new signifiers of the religious meaning. As the use of virtual space increases, the relationship between the new signifiers and the signified meaning will become established.

Another question raised in this context has been the expertise of the web masters, and censorship of the information and practices on the websites. Unless there is provision for a committee to critically examine web-based material, the latter is open to charges of being misleading. Cheong (2013: 79) mentions the example of orthodox Jews in Israel who use technology for the dissemination of their teachings and who also supervise and control the online information provided. The Hindu community in the US treats the online ritual practices conducted in Sanskrit as a complementary resource available to the community. Since these practices are relatively recent (belonging to the new millennium) they are neither standardised nor scrutinised for their linguistic and theological accuracy. It has been argued by Cheong (2013) and Turner (2007) that the virtual practices undermine the traditions, conventions and particularly the authority of priests and religious leaders, since the web-based practices are accessible to all and bypass the need for the presence of the religious leader/priest. These authors (Turner 2007: 20, cited in Cheong 2013: 76) argue that these are democratising practices. A very important theological question is raised regarding the efficacy of these practices. Does the sound of the Sanskrit language in the orally based scriptures itself have the power to create the religious experience regardless of who recites them?

Thus online digital Hindu practices including use of Sanskrit configure the cultural/religious meaning via new tools. Whether the meaning is the same as its counterpart in offline practices remains to be investigated.

6. Sanskrit in Yoga practice in the US: appropriation or adoption of the immigrant tradition?

This section discusses the role of Sanskrit in the practice of Yoga in the US. Immigrants' cultures continue to contribute to the construction of America in the new millennium. We are witnessing a revival of interest in the study of Sanskrit via the practice of Yoga in the US. According to the *Yoga Journal*, there are 6,000 Yoga studios in the US. And 36 million Americans practise Yoga today. The classical Yoga of Patanjali's *Yoga sutras* (a collection of aphorisms in Sanskrit), a second-century BCE text, was primarily a treatise on the path to attain union with the Divine through the control of mind. Physical training was viewed as the prelude to the mental discipline and meditation to attain the spiritual goal. Yoga has gone through many incarnations in the US. After Emerson's mid-nineteenth century emphasis on spiritual Yoga, numerous Yoga proponents of Indian origin in the late nineteenth and the twentieth centuries focused on diverse aspects of the classical Yoga in the US. These included Swami Shivananda's disciple Satchidananda, Swami Vivekananda, Yogananda, Vishnudevananda, Pattabhi Jois, B. K. S Iyengar and Jiddu Krishnamurti. While Emerson and Swami Vivekananda, among others, emphasised the spiritual goal of Yoga practice, Swami Satchidananda treated physical exercises as the training to achieve the mind control essential for the realisation of the spiritual unity and divine nature of all creation. Many influential Yoga masters including Pattabhi Jois and B. K. S. Iyengar, who popularised Yoga in the US after the late 1960s, emphasised physical training and exercises for mind-body wellness.

Notable works include Vivekananda's lectures in the late nineteenth century, compiled in the book *The Complete Book on Yoga*, Mircea Eliade's *Yoga: Immortality and Freedom* (1970), Swami Vishnu Devananda's *The Complete Illustrated Book of Yoga* (1960) and Iyengar's *Light on Yoga* (1966). These books clearly exemplify the diverse emphases of the authors and Yoga practitioners. While the early Yoga masters studied the original Sanskrit text of Patanjali, the later Yoga centres use their own training courses designed by the 'Yoga master' who does not necessarily know Sanskrit.

My pilot project in 2020 examined the extent to which Sanskrit was present in Yoga centres in the US, finding that there is increased emphasis on the knowledge of Sanskrit in the teacher's training in those centres. Regardless of their emphasis (exclusively physical wellness, or inclusion of philosophical/spiritual knowledge of Yoga), Yoga centres in general are actively promoting the study of Sanskrit at various levels. The reasons for this emphasis on the study of Sanskrit are various, and the motivations of two representative centres are presented below. These represent other centres' perspective as well. The Aura Wellness Center of Yoga in Attelboro, Massachusetts provides the following reasons (https://www.yoga-teacher-training.org/2011/03/29/the-importance-of-sanskrit-in-yogaclasses/). Sanskrit provides the subtlety and precision needed to practise perfectly. Since Sanskrit is considered to be a tool for understanding and practising Yogic methodology and philosophy, most Yoga teacher training courses cover a fair number of Sanskrit terms from Patanjali's Yoga text, which facilitates communication across Yoga teachers in diverse Yoga centres. The nationally known *Yoga Journal* claims that basic knowledge of Sanskrit provides confidence to the practitioners, an understanding of the roots of common names of yoga poses, philosophical terms, and demystifies and deepens understanding of the entire yoga practice. For example, the root word of *āsana* – which we usually translate as posture or seat – is *ās*, which means to be present, to sit quietly, to celebrate, to continue to do anything without interruption.

In order to understand the Yoga teacher's perspective on the role of Sanskrit in the teaching of Yoga, I sent a questionnaire to Dr Lois Steinberg, director of a major Yoga institute in Champaign-Urbana, Illinois. I gave talks on the *Bhagavadgītā* at Steinberg's Yoga institute for the Yoga teachers from various parts of the world. They were interested in understanding the philosophical, religious and social moorings of the Yoga practices in the Hindu scriptures. Dr Steinberg studied Hatha Yoga in Pune, India, for more than thirty-five years with B. K. S. Iyengar, a world-renowned Yoga practitioner and teacher. She wrote back to me that it is essential to thoroughly understand the *Yoga sutras* of Patanjali. She further claims,

> Only when I chanted them with guidance and wrote the sutras out in Sanskrit and then committed them to memory, did I begin to understand their meaning. I continue to study one sutra a week using all three commentaries [...] One is not a Yoga *Sadhaka* ('practitioner') unless all the limbs of yoga are undertaken. That is, *Yama, Niyama, Asana, Prāṇāyāma, Pratyāhāra, Dhāraṇā, Dhyāna,* and *Samādhi.* If one is only practicing the physical postures, that is not yoga. Yoga is systematic intelligence of the body, mind, breath, soul, and spirit.

In Dr Steinberg's view, the knowledge of Sanskrit is very helpful in order to have a wholistic understanding of Yoga. However, she does not insist that all her students must learn Sanskrit. The eight limbs of Yoga aim at integrating the different aspects of life: ethical – *yama* (abstinences), *niyama* (observances); physical – *āsana* (yoga postures), *prāṇāyāma* (breath control); and spiritual – *pratyāhāra* (withdrawal of the senses), *dhāraṇā* (concentration), *dhyāna* (meditation) and *samādhi* (absorption).

Adil Palkhivala and Savitri jointly teach Yoga in their Yoga centre and claim that Yoga should not be taught merely as physical training for wellness of the body. 'Humility is the key and foundation of yoga. It must be beyond the mat and in everything you're doing. It eventually opens the doorway to love and to respect.' Savitri said she believed that the focus on the *āsana* 'physical postures/exercises' in popular culture – without any humility – is a big part of the problem. 'The physical body is where the ego is created, so if you don't teach physical humility, you're never going to be able to reach your soul, you're never going to be able to train your mind, and you'll never evolve your physical form of all your attachments and *karma*.'

While a large number of Yoga centres include varying levels of teaching of Sanskrit in their curriculum, there are many Yoga practitioners who do not approve of including Sanskrit in their curriculum. They prefer their Yoga training to be completely dissociated from its roots and treat Yoga as purely physical training. The book *No Om Zone: A No-Chanting, No-Granola, No-Sanskrit Practical Guide to Yoga* by Kimberly Fowler articulates the contrary perspective on Yoga. According to some other centres, Yoga should be treated as an independent training of body wellness. Yoga, within this perspective, should not be connected with Hinduism or Indian culture, and all elements such as chanting Om and the Sanskrit language should be eliminated from Yoga practice. Rina Deshpande, a Yoga teacher from New York, and

Dr Shreena Gandhi, a Religious Studies professor, call this cultural appropriation, where Yoga is cut off from its Hindu roots and thereby its essential meaning (https://www.yogajournal.com/yoga-101/yoga-cultural-appropriation-appreciation). These two perspectives on Yoga reinforce a crucial dimension of Sanskrit in the US; namely, its symbolic meaning, its almost inalienable connection with Hinduism and Hindu identity. Inclusion of Sanskrit in the teaching of Yoga symbolises acceptance of the Hindu/Indian roots of Yoga and provides authenticity to its practice while its exclusion marks the dissociation of Yoga from Hinduism.

7. Conclusion

This discussion shows that the symbolic value of Sanskrit as the language of Hinduism is the major catalyst for its maintenance in the US. However, contextual factors such as the US Constitution (which allows religious freedom to immigrants and citizens), the need of the multicultural, multilingual Hindu community to unify under the umbrella of one identity marker (religion), and technology (which facilitates access to Sanskrit texts, etc.) also facilitate maintenance of Sanskrit in the US. The discussion demonstrates that the symbolic capital of Sanskrit as a language of Hinduism 'converts' (Bourdieu 1982: 14) into other 'capitals' in different contexts. In the nineteenth-century US it functioned as the path to the Indian thought. In the context of the twentieth century it functions as the symbol of pan-Hindu identity of the immigrant Hindu community. In the context of the digital representation Sanskrit is instrumental in configuring a virtual reality. Although the use of other regional Indian languages (Tamil, Marathi, Hindi, etc.) in such online Hindu practices is also observed in Hindu immigrant communities from specific regions of India, the use of Sanskrit is preferred in multilingual and multinational Hindu communities. This is especially the case in large cities like New York and Chicago, etc., as well as in pan-Hindu practices of weddings and funerals, etc. Despite their diverse cultural, linguistic and national backgrounds, the Hindu immigrants accept Sanskrit as the language of their Hindu identity. Finally, Sanskrit functions as the pointer to the cultural and religious moorings of Yoga. The value of Sanskrit as the dominant symbol of Hinduism as well as of the identity of the Hindu community serves as a catalyst for its maintenance beyond the migrating generations.

In a multilingual community of immigrants, the language which is transparent to its symbolic value and function has more power in the religious sphere compared to other languages. Furthermore, the embedding of Sanskrit in diverse contexts in the US influences the function and discourse structure of Sanskrit, especially in rituals, which have become more multilingual. In other words, the process of converting symbolic capital into another capital (for example, for Sanskrit the symbol of the 'path to the Indian/eastern mind', 'identity of the Hindu community', 'digital icon of devotional practice', and, finally, 'the symbol of authenticity of Yoga') depends on the perception of the American as well as the perception of the Hindu community. Overall, we see an extension of the symbolic capital of Sanskrit (for example, as the symbol of the 'path to the Indian/eastern mind' and 'a symbol of the authenticity of Yoga') as well as a conversion into other forms of capital (for example, 'identity of the Hindu community' and 'digital icon of devotional practice'). These conversions depend on the perception and practices of the American as well as the Hindu community.

This chapter has also dwelt on the transparency of Sanskrit as a religious medium in the Indian and, more so, the US context. Although other Indian languages are also used to express Hinduism, the invariable connection with Hinduism makes Sanskrit the most powerful symbol of the identity of the Hindu community in the US.

Finally, the discussion in this chapter shows the utility of the interdisciplinary framework which combined the insights of sociolinguistics, religious studies, media studies and history to better understand the phenomena of maintenance of Sanskrit in the US. Further research across languages in diasporas in the world is needed to compare the determinants of language maintenance and the role of symbolic 'capital' of languages in their maintenance or loss.

References

Amara, M. (2019), The role of Islamic movement in maintaining Standard Arabic in Israel. In R. V. Pandharipande, M. Khemlani and M. Eisenstein Ebsworth (eds), *Language Maintenance Revival, and Shift in the Sociology of Religion*. Bristol: Multilingual Matters, pp. 138–47.

Bourdieu, P. (1982), *Language and Symbolic Power*. Cambridge, MA: Harvard University Press.

Carey, W. (1808), *Dharmapustaka*. Serampore: Missionary Press.

Cheong, P. H. (2013), Authority. In *Digital Religion: Understanding Religious Practice in New Media Worlds*. London: Routledge, pp. 72–87.

Eck, D. (2001), *A New Religious America: How A 'Christian Country' has now Become the World's Most Religiously Diverse Nation*. San Francisco, CA: Harper.

Eliade, M. (1970), *Yoga: Immortality and Freedom*. Bolligen Series, Vol. LVI (2nd edition).

Fenton, J. Y. (1998), *Transplanting Religious Traditions: Asian Indians in America*. Praeger.

Fishman, J. A. (1991), *Reversing Language Shift: Theoretical and Empirical Foundations of Assistance to Threatened Languages*. Clevedon: Multilingual Matters.

Fowler, K. (2010), *No-Om Zone: A No-Chanting, No-Granola, No-Sanskrit Practical Guide to Yoga*. New York: Rodale.

Geertz, C. (1973), *The Interpretation of Cultures*. New York: Basic Books.

Goldberg, P. (2010), *American Veda*. New York: Harmony Books.

Haugen, E. (1953), *The Nowegian Language in America: A Study in Bilingual Behavior*. Vol. 1. Bloomington: University of Indiana Press. Vol. 2. Philadelphia: University of Pennsylvania Press.

Iyengar, B. K. S. (1966), *Light on Yoga*. London: Allen and Unwin Ltd.

Kale, M. R. (1961), *A Higher Sanskrit Grammar*. Delhi: Motilal Banarasidass.

Lanman, C. R. (1889), *A Sanskrit Reader*. Boston, MA: Ginn and Company.

Leach, E. R. (1968), Ritual. In David L. Sills (ed.), *International Encyclopedia of the Social Sciences* (vol. 13). New York.

Macdonell, A. A. (1916), *Sanskrit Grammar for Students*. Oxford: Oxford University Press.

Manosuthikit, A. (2018), A critical review of theoretical perspectives: From language maintenance and shift to postmodern/post structuralist bi/multilingualism. *KEMANUSIAA.N' the Asian Journal of Humanities*, 25: 141–62. https://doi.org/10.21315/kajh2018.25.1.

Narayanan, V. (1996), Creating South Asian experience in the United States. In R. B. Williams (ed.), *A sacred Thread: Modern Transmission of Hindu Traditions in India and Abroad*. New York: Columbia University Press, pp. 147–76.

Pandharipande, R. V. (2001a), Constructing religious discourse in diaspora. In B. B. Kachru and C. Nelson (eds), *Diaspora, Identity, and Language Community*. Special Issue of *Studies in the Linguistic Sciences*, 31 (1). University of Illinois: Department of Linguistics, pp. 231–52.

Pandharipande, R. V. (2001b), Mixing as method: English translation of the Sanskrit text. In E. Thumbu (ed.), *Three Circles of English: Language Specialists Talk about the English Language*. Singapore: The Center for Arts, The National University of Singapore, pp. 301–16.

Pandharipande, R. V. (2006), Ideology, authority, and language choice: Language of religion in South Asia. In T. Omoniyi and J. Fishman (eds), *Explorations in the Sociology of Language of Religion*. Amsterdam: John Benjamins Publishing Company, pp. 141–64.

Pandharipande, R. V. (2010), Authenticating a tradition in transition: Language of Hinduism in the US. In T. Omoniyi (ed.), *The Sociology of Language of Religion: Change Conflict and Accommodation*. Basingstoke: Palgrave Macmillan, pp. 58–83.

Pandharipande, R. V. (2018), Online Satsang and online Puja: Faith and language in the era of globalization. In A. Rosowsky (ed.), *Faith and Language Practices in Digital Spaces*. Bristol: Multilingual Matters, pp. 185–208.

Pauwels, A. (2016), *Language Maintenance and Shift*. Key Topics in Linguistics. Cambridge: Cambridge University Press.

Salmond, N. (2004), *Hindu Iconoclasts*. Waterloo, ON: Wilfrid Laurier University Press.

Scheifiner, H. (2013), Hindu worship online and offline. In H. Campbell (ed.), *Digital Religion: Understanding Religious Practice in New Media Worlds*. London: Routledge, pp. 121–7.

Sinha, M. (2013), Orienting America: Sanskrit and modern scholarship in the United States, 1836–1894. In A. Bernard, Ziad El-Marsafy and David Atwell (eds.), *Debating Orientalism*. Basingstoke: Palgrave Macmillan, pp. 73–93.

Souza, A. (2019), Faith and language: Brazilian Christian settings in London. In R. V. Pandharipande, M. Khemlani and M. Eisenstein Ebsworth (eds), *Language Maintenance Revival, and Shift in the Sociology of Religion*. Bristol: Multilingual Matters, pp. 81–97.

Swami Nikhilananda (1984), *Vivekananda: The Yogas and Other Works*. New York: Ramakrishna-Vivekananda Center.

Swami Vishnu Devananda (1960), *The Complete Illustrated Book of Yoga*. New York: Three Rivers Press.

Turner, B. S. (2007), Religious authority and new media. *Theory, Culture and Society*, 24 (2): pp. 117–34.

Whitney, W. D. (1879), *A Sanskrit Grammar: Including Both the Classical and the Older Dialects of the Veda and Brahmana*. Leipzig: Breitkopf and Hartel.

Williams, R. B. (1996), Sacred threads of several textures: Strategies of adaptation in the United States. In R. B. Williams (ed.), *A Sacred Thread: Modern Transmission of Hindu Traditions in India and Abroad*. New York: Columbia University Press, pp. 1–6.

Young, R. F. (1981), *Resistant Hinduism: Sanskrit Sources on Anti-Christian Apologetics in Early Nineteenth-century India*. Vienna: E. J. Brill.

CHAPTER 7

Indian Languages in Singapore

Ritu Jain and Rajesh Rai

1. Introduction

Discussions around languages of overseas Indian communities have revolved around focal periods defined by types of emigration. Moag (2003) categorises these into post-indenture communities (in the nineteenth and early twentieth centuries) and the non-returned Indians from around the 1950s. In contrast, Mesthrie (2008) lists these as occurring broadly in three waves. The first diaspora (until the 12th century) resulted from mostly mercantile or religious impetus to places such as Asia, Africa and Europe. The languages of these were either South Indian languages or classical ones such as Sanskrit and Prakrit and little is known about their trajectories of survival.

The second diaspora, formed from the eighteenth century to approximately the middle of the twentieth century, involved semi-forced or forced migration to British, Dutch and French colonies such as Cape Town and Mauritius (Mesthrie 2008, Moag 2003, Oonk 2007) as well as Asia. Sociolinguistically the most interesting, the languages of this diaspora were chiefly varieties of Hindi, Tamil, Telugu, Urdu and Marathi (Mesthrie 2008). Among the linguistically diverse people on many settlements (e.g. Fiji, Burma), variants of simplified Hindi, or Bazaar Hindustani, served as the lingua franca (Siegel 1988, Verma 1991). The focus of various studies of these languages has mainly been varieties of Hindi (the dominant community languages in Fiji, Guyana, Mauritius, Surinam and Trinidad) and Tamil (predominantly in Malaysia, Singapore, Natal, South Africa and Reunion).

In comparison, the 'third diaspora' constitutes the voluntary movements of individuals after 1947 to countries such as the United Kingdom, United States, Canada, Australia, etc. Often professionally qualified and from urban areas, these Indian (or more appropriately, South Asian) migrants have been seen as non-assimilatory and lacking in the cohesion and homogeneity that marked the second diaspora. They have also remained 'temporary migrants' often with the potential to either move elsewhere or return home one day. Among others, studies highlight the languages of these communities in the US, the UK and Canada (Mahandru 1991, Oonk 2007, van der Avoird 2001, Verma 1991) with some attention to minority Indian communities in Malaysia (Mukherjee and David 2011, Mukherjee 2003) and Hong Kong (Detaramani and Lock 2003). Mesthrie (2021) has more recently added a fourth diaspora that refers to the globally oriented migrants, often with advanced computer-related or business interests – a description that fits some of our transmobile populations described in this chapter.

Scholars have pointed out that much of the commentary, particularly around varieties of Hindi, has remained largely descriptive with little in the way of analysis (Moag 2003). In a bid to address this, Moag (2003) offers a 'feature-factor matrix' of thirty-one socially operative factors (grouped into four categories of demographic, political, socio-cultural and sociolinguistic (see Appendix Table A7.1)) that constitute a framework for evaluating the health of a language and predicting the likelihood of its maintenance within a specific community. Moag has also highlighted that binaries such as the presence/absence of individual factors (e.g. critical mass of native speakers (1), positive attitude towards preserving the language (31)) are severely limiting, but scalar designations (indicating the degrees to which they are present/absent) may help provide a better picture in the absence of more precise data. Therefore, this framework has proved more robust for assessing maintenance/shift of languages in previously stable post-indenture societies (e.g. Fiji, Guyana) rather than in sites with both settled and transnationally mobile populations (or what Moag terms as NRIs – non-resident Indians) such as in the UK and the USA. In the latter countries, with ongoing migration and heterogenous 'communities', the framework remains a useful rubric for characterising and assessing language health among multilingual, mobile communities. Even though some factors – assuming a homogeneous community with a shared language – fail to apply, the broad demographic, political, socio-cultural and sociolinguistic categories serve as a useful guide.

Therefore, using Moag's feature-factor matrix to guide the discussion, this chapter offers an assessment of Singapore's Indian community and their languages in pre-colonial years until 1965 and then beyond to contemporary times. It begins with a historical background on the establishment and demographic shifts among the Indian community as well as of the national language policy before 1965; next, it details the impact of political decisions (particularly the implementation of government language policies) on the Indian community in the newly established nation; it then highlights socio-cultural factors that forced a reconsideration of the language education policy; finally, the chapter concludes with a description and discussion of the contemporary sociolinguistic situation and associated challenges. The chapter draws on archival records, census data and community school enrolment figures, as well as data from a large-scale survey and interviews with twenty-nine families of diverse Indian language backgrounds.

2. The making of the South Asian diaspora in Singapore

The South Asian diaspora in Singapore is the product of myriad trajectories of migration extending over two centuries. Forged initially in the context of what Mesthrie describes as the second diaspora which followed the advent of British colonial control, that movement was embedded in a region where the first diaspora had already left a profound legacy on the local religious culture and language. Even more, the last three decades have seen the South Asian presence in Singapore embellished by the emergence of a third diaspora – comprising migrant professionals and entrepreneurs from the subcontinent – who, in the second decade of the twenty-first century, are nearly equal in number to the more settled descendants of the second diaspora. Alongside the complex multi-layered character of the diaspora that is the product of multiple trajectories of migration and settlement, the diaspora's distinctiveness is punctuated by her position in what was once a colonial port city – as different from a plantation colony – and which today is a global alpha city, marked by tremendous ethno-cultural diversity, mobility and, notwithstanding the presence of a strong state, a certain porousness to global political, economic and socio-cultural currents. What follows in this segment is an unpacking of the making of the South Asian diaspora in Singapore during the colonial period – with layers of ethno-cultural and socio-economic diversity between waves of migrants, sojourners and settlers. That façade paves the way for an understanding of the South Asian diaspora's complex language landscape on the island, and the transformations evident from the late twentieth century onwards, with the emergence of the third diaspora.

A recent decryption of an ancient Kawi inscription suggests the possibility of the Chola empire's direct connection with the island dating back a millennium (Sinclair 2019) – thus confirming a 'first diaspora' presence. That interpretation of the engraving on the 'Singapore stone' adds to the already existing body of evidence in the Sejarah Melayu, and in archaeological findings that reveal ties between the port and the subcontinent centuries before the European arrival. Be that as it may, when the British established an outpost in Singapore in 1819 there was no known South Asian presence in what was then a thinly-populated settlement comprising only a few Malay fishing villages and Chinese farms. The constitution of the island changed rapidly following the British arrival. Under the umbrella of the empire, the free port positioned at the centre of the India-China and the intra-archipelago trade bourgeoned expeditiously. Thousands flocked annually from China, India and other parts of Asia. By the turn of the twentieth century, the island's population exceeded 220,000, of whom Indians – a category utilised in Singapore for all South Asians – numbered approximately 18,000 (Yeoh 2003). Their number swelled exponentially in the first half of the twentieth century, so that by the 1957 Census, the last conducted prior to Singapore's independence in 1965, the Indian number had increased to just under 125, 000 in a total population of approximately 1.45 million (Han 2010).

Several factors underpinned why Indian immigration to the island grew rapidly following the establishment of the British outpost. The search for profit drew traders and businessmen from the subcontinent. Tamil Muslims from the Coromandel Coast, who had long established an ubiquitous presence in the region, were the earliest Indian commercial group to arrive in large numbers. Other commercial groups arriving from southern India in the first half of the nineteenth century included the prominent Nattukottai Chettiars, a tightly knit, caste-based community from 'Chettinad' – an area that today straddles Ramanathapuram and Pudukottai districts of Tamil Nadu (Evers and Pavadarayan 1993). They emerged as powerful financiers in the British colonies in Southeast Asia. The number of Indian commercial groups in the region increased further in the second half of the nineteenth century. Amongst the new entrants during this period included Sindhi, Gujarati and Punjabi businessmen engaged in a wide range of business activities, including the textile and spice trade, retail and the provision of services.

Beyond Singapore's centrality as a trading outpost and the commercial opportunities it offered, the growth of the Indian diaspora was catalysed by the fact that for nearly five decades after the establishment of the colony, Singapore, as part of the Straits Settlements, was governed directly by British India. Consequently, Indians constituted the mainstay of the security personnel defending the colony and a significant segment of the lower rung of the administration. Until the early twentieth century, military personnel drawn variously from the Bengal, Madras and Bombay armies comprised the mainstay of the garrison here. Often tied to the militia were the quarters for followers including domestic servants, chaiwallahs, dairy farmers, grooms and dhobis, some of whom chose to remain on the island rather than return. Even after the Straits Settlements ceased to be a part of British India in 1867, the trajectory ensured that imperial auxiliaries continued to be frequently recruited from the subcontinent. Notably, Sikhs were utilised for the police force from 1881, and English-educated personnel were recruited from the Jaffna Peninsula and Kerala to work as clerks, surveyors, engineers, teachers and administrators in the colonial government (Rai 2014). Concomitantly, immigrants from the subcontinent who were not directly part of the colonial administration were engaged as educated personnel and security guards in the private sector.

The initial administrative connection with British India, along with the critical shortage of labour for public works in the budding colony, also facilitated the transfer of large numbers of convicts from the subcontinent. From 1825 to 1860, approximately 15,000 convicts from British India were transported to the Straits Settlements, with the largest penal settlement for Indian convicts in the region based in Singapore. The prisoners represented a cross-section of Indian society, with diverse religious, caste, linguistic and socio-economic backgrounds. They provided much needed labour for public works, clearing the jungle frontier, building roads, and contributing to the making of some of the most iconic edifices of nineteenth-century Singapore (McNair 1899). Often rejected by their kinsmen when they sought to return to the 'homeland', the overwhelming majority of these transported convicts remained in the colony after their release.

Transported convicts, however, provided only part of colonial Singapore's incessant demand for labour. Indian labourers in the plantation sector were initially recruited through the indenture system, but from the late nineteenth century mainly through the kangani system[1] and as 'free' labourers (Rai 2014). They were also utilised for public works, in the construction industry, and as harbour workers. These labour migrants were overwhelmingly recruited from the Madras Presidency, due to restrictions put in place by the British Indian government which sought to delimit the region from which the Straits Settlements and Malaya could recruit Indian labour.

In sum, the movement of commercial emigrants, imperial auxiliaries and labourers provided the basis for the formation of a diaspora that was an ethno-cultural, linguistic and socio-economic mosaic. It is true that even at the port city, labourers comprised the largest segment of the second diaspora ushered by colonial rule, but it was different from some plantation colonies in that it also included sizeable numbers who were from the higher echelons, engaged in business or in service, as educated or security personnel. This had implications not only in terms of their mobility, but also on the ability to support cultural production in the host land. Secondly, the diaspora was located in a region that was proximate to the subcontinent, and in the context of growing transportation links enabled sojourning patterns in a wide section of the diaspora who tended to travel to and from the 'homeland' frequently. In this sense it differed from diaspora in many far-flung plantation colonies, whose experience was marked by a distinct break from the homeland. The proximity and the tendency to circulate in turn made them conscious of social, cultural and political currents emanating from the homeland. Thirdly, the fact that they were positioned in an urban environment also had a deep bearing. For one, the number of South Asian women was miniscule. This was partly due to cultural norms that frowned on the emigration of women but also was due to the limited economic opportunities available for women in that environment. Suitable housing for families especially in the lower strata was also an issue. Consequently, even in 1921, South Asian women comprised less than one-fifth of the total South Asian population. This exacerbated tendencies towards maintaining sojourning patterns and also ensured that children comprised only a small proportion of the diaspora even in the early decades of the twentieth century. Finally, as evident from the discussion above, the Indian diaspora at the port was clearly ethno-culturally heterogeneous internally. While Tamil speakers comprised the majority, a variety of Indian languages were spoken including Hindustani/Hindi, Urdu, Punjabi, Telugu and Malayalam. In this context, while language was a powerful source of unity amongst some, it could also become the basis for binaries at the intra-Indian level. Collectively, these factors played an important role in shaping the Indian language landscape in colonial Singapore, which will be discussed in the section that follows.

3. Indian languages in colonial Singapore

Singapore was a multilingual labyrinth very soon after her establishment as a British colony. Within a decade, the spectrum included an array of languages from China, South Asia and beyond, alongside Malay – the language of the indigenous inhabitants – and English. To 'manage' the different ethnic groupings, British administrators had initially introduced a policy of demarcating settlements on the basis of 'race'. This initial British policy to some extent acted as a boundary to inter-ethnic communication, but that position was quite untenable in the context of a rapidly expanding population. In this context, Bahasa Pasar (literally the language of the market), a creole based on erstwhile Malay pidgin, emerged as the main language of communication across ethnic lines.

Given that emigrants from the Tamil country comprised the majority of Indians, the Tamil language held a dominant position amongst them. It was certainly commonplace in the South Asian enclave in the Chinatown area at the Singapore River in the nineteenth century, and would later have a strong presence in Serangoon Road as the South Asian population there increased. Tamil presses publishing newspapers and books functioned intermittently from the 1860s, and more regularly from the 1930s (Rai 2014). That said, in the context of an ethnically diverse diaspora, Tamil did not displace other Indian languages in the budding colony. For example, at the prison for transported convicts drawn from various parts of subcontinent, Superintendent McNair informs us that 'the Hindustani language … was spoken by the bulk of the convicts in the jail' (McNair 1899). Likewise, Punjabi held sway at the quarters marked for the Sikh police contingent from the final decades of the nineteenth century and Malayalam was commonly spoken at the naval base in the north of the island as the concentration of Malayalis working there increased in the 1930s.

Unlike other British colonies, no creolised Indian pidgin developed for communication between South Asian groups of different ethnic backgrounds. Instead, existing languages were utilised. For example, in communications amongst emigrants from southern India, Tamil was the lingua franca, with most Telugus, and a significant proportion of the Malayalis, having a hold of the language. Likewise Hindustani (or Hindi),[2] was commonly used for communications amongst emigrants from northern India. In inter-ethnic communications across broader regional lines, i.e. northern and southern Indians, Bahasa Pasar was usually spoken, except perhaps for the English-educated higher classes from the late nineteenth and early twentieth centuries who instead preferred to use the colonial language.

Notwithstanding the diversity of languages, or perhaps because of it, nineteenth-century Singapore saw very little in the way of Indian vernacular language education. Tamil language classes were introduced in 1834 but were terminated soon after due to a lack of support, teaching materials and students (Rai 2014). Indeed, little headway was made in the nineteenth century in part because of the predilection of erstwhile South Asians immigrants who saw their stay on the island as temporary. The inordinate gender disparity did not help, and with few families, concern over children not being literate in their vernacular languages was not a central concern. There were some exceptions, for example the Methodist Girls' School established in 1887, which provided Tamil language education for girls from Tamil homes.

A more consistent trajectory in South Asian language education was evident in the inter-war period. As the number of families increased, concerns amongst 'the older people ... [of] the growth of a generation which could not read or write its ... vernacular' became more pressing. With little support from the colonial government, this was left to the communities to organise. In the mid-1920s, two schools, alongside a small number of 'village' institutions provided Tamil language education to about 130 children from working-class families. Tamil classes were bolstered by the spread of the Tamil Reform Movement in the 1930s, which alongside its reformist ideals strongly advocated Tamil language learning through its mouthpiece the Dravida Murasu [later Tamil Murasu] and its theatrical productions. In 1932, the Vivekananda Boys School and later the Saradamani Girls School would also run Tamil language classes. In the late 1930s a Tamil School was also established near the crowded harbour, catering to children of Tamil Muslim families mainly from Kadyanallur and Tenkasi. While middle-class Tamils tended to send their children to English-medium schools, some enrolled their children in Tamil [language] classes after regular school hours. Collectively, these efforts ensured that prior to the Second World War, there were some 1,000 pupils studying Tamil in '4 Mission Tamil Schools [and] 14 private schools' (Rai 2014).

The study of other South Asian languages also increased in the early decades of the twentieth century. However, interest vacillated because these students tended to come from bourgeois families who in time favoured English-medium education alongside part-time 'mother tongue' studies. Classes were therefore typically conducted at home or at the premises of associations or religious institutions. By the 1920s, some Singapore-based students trained by private tutors had succeeded in the Cambridge Hindi exams. The Arya Samaj was the first association to organise Hindi classes, and by 1932 it had an enrolment of eighty students. Two years later the organisation established the D. A. V. Hindi School, which offered free Hindi and English lessons. Reflecting political trajectories in India, the study of the Hindi language was not limited just to children from Hindi-speaking families but also to others perhaps because the spread of Indian nationalism had ushered in the possibility that Hindi 'stood all chances of being adopted as the future lingua franca of [independent] India' (Rai 2014). By 1939, Hindi classes were also being organised at the premises of the Indian nationalist-orientated Indian Youth League (IYL) and at the naval base.

In the early decades of the twentieth century Punjabi language education in Singapore was largely imparted in gurdwaras. This role would later also be taken up by the Singapore Khalsa Association, a sports and social organisation established in 1931. Less is known about the development of the other South Asian languages, most of which, if studied, would have largely been the result of home schooling. While no record of institutions teaching Malayalam exists, Malayali associations were nevertheless active in promoting vernacular literary and theatrical activities during this period, particularly in the naval base area.

The general pre-war trajectory of South Asian vernacular education was disrupted when Japanese forces took control of the island from 1942 to 1945. The new regime's support for Indian nationalism, which included the formation of the famed Indian National Army in Singapore, saw a tilt in favour of Hindustani language education. Consequently, Tamil schools and the Tamil Reform Association, which were deemed as potentially 'divisive', were suspended (Rai 2014). Instead, South Asian children were encouraged to enrol in Indian national schools established in Singapore, where learning Hindustani was made compulsory. This interlude, however, was an anomaly, and the British return in 1945 quickly saw a restoration of the pre-war educational trajectory, albeit in different circumstances.

In the post-war years, Tamil cultural production and language education expanded exponentially. Several factors informed this trajectory. Most important was the rise of the Dravidian politics in Tamil Nadu (India), which emphasised Tamil pride and staunchly opposed the primacy of Hindi in independent India. Advocates of the movement in Singapore emphasised the need for Tamils, who comprised the mainstay of the South Asian population, to take charge of Indian organisations. They also sought to unify different segments of Tamil society under the umbrella of the Tamil Representatives Council, which acted as a lobby of Tamil interests vis-à-vis the colonial government and emerging political parties. In the mid-1950s, these groups, through their mouthpiece the Tamil Murasu, also drew segments of the hitherto aloof, albeit influential, Sri Lankan Tamil community into their ranks by highlighting concerns over the spread of Sinhalese majoritarianism in Sri Lanka. The outcome of these efforts took the form of growing support by the colonial government for Tamil vernacular education, and growing recognition for Tamil as the representative language for Indians in Singapore. Tamil programmes were introduced on Singapore radio and there was a flowering of Tamil literature and theatre during this period. On the other hand, the position of Hindi/Hindustani diminished considerably in the post-war years. Bereft of the support that had been rendered during the Japanese Occupation, Hindi language education was limited to two community-run organisations, the DAV School run by the Arya Samaj, and the Netaji Hindi High School. Likewise Punjabi education continued via the Khalsa Association, while most of the other smaller Indian languages either disappeared completely or were sustained mainly through home schooling.

4. 1965: entrenchment of official/community identities in independent Singapore

In post-independence Singapore, the process of nation-building and consolidation of an ethnically diverse population was founded on the pillars of racial classification. The nation's social policies initiated the Chinese-Malay-Indian-Others (CMIO) racial classification that, in turn, served to establish official/administrative definitions of community identities and equations with cultural attributes such as language. The CMIO classification was the foundation for all social policies including parliamentary representation and allocation of public housing (in order to discourage ethnic enclaves). Through this system, people of South Asian origin came to be officially identified as Indians and to be symbolically represented by the numerically dominant Tamil language and culture (Rai 2009, Solomon 2012). Notwithstanding the institutional flattening of the community identity, various sub-groups, defined along lines of region of origin, continued to endure over the years (Table 7.1). However, in official records, the diversity has been gradually reduced and the latest 2020 Census captures only four groups.

The CMIO category was also foundational in the design of the bilingual education policy of Singapore in 1965. The three ethnic languages/community mother tongues (Mandarin for the Chinese, Malay for the Malays, and Tamil for the Indians) and

Table 7.1 *Census data on Indians by ethnic group, 1957–2010*

Ethnic group	1957 (%)	1970 (%)	1980 (%)	1990 (%)	2000 (%)	2010 (%)	2020 (%)
Tamil	60.40	66.26	63.88	63.94	58.26	54.17	54.8
Malayali	16.82	11.97	8.05	8.56	8.43	7.57	7.4
Punjabi	5.99	8.36	7.78	1.21	1.83	1.63	-
Ceylonese	3.12	3.72	-	-	-	-	-
Sikh	2.63	-	-	6.67	5.12	3.72	3.5
Bengali	1.86	0.75	-	-	-	-	-
Sinhalese	1.06	-	-	1.04	0.94	0.90	-
Gujarati	0.70	1.00	1.05	1.05	1.26	1.18	-
Telugu	0.45	0.35	-	-	-	-	-
Pathan	0.24	-	-	-	-	-	-
Hindustani	-	-	-	2.02	1.96	1.38	-
Sindhi	-	-	-	1.49	1.56	1.14	-
Urdu	-	-	-	1.15	1.16	1.37	-
Hindi	-	-	-	0.60	1.54	3.76	5.1
'Indians' and 'Pakistanis'	2.37	-	-	-	-	-	-
Others	4.34	7.60	19.25	12.29	17.94	23.17	29.2
Total		129,510	145,169	154,632	190,907	257,791	348,119

Source: Jain (2021), Singapore Department of Statistics (2021).

English were given the status of official languages mandated as languages in education (Moag's factors 9 and 10). Ironically, as Kuo (1980) highlights, over 80 per cent of schoolchildren used languages other than the official languages at home in 1965. While Malay was spoken by 85 per cent of the Malays, Tamil was spoken by 60 per cent of Indians and Mandarin by 0.1 per cent of the Chinese (Jain and Wee 2019b). Further, demographic factors such as ongoing immigration and the lack of ethnic enclaves impeded language use beyond the immediate family and discouraged societal multilingualism.

Against this context, the bilingual policy (mandating the ethnic languages as subjects in education for students from the associated communities) became instrumental in consolidating ethnic identities along official identity categories. Census data over the years indicates the relative success of the policy for the Chinese and, to a lesser degree, for the Malay community (Table 7.2). Despite the overall shift towards English, Mandarin has become the predominant household language of 48 per cent of the Chinese while Malay has retained its hold on 83 per cent of the Malays. In contrast, the linguistic diversity within the South Asian community posed a greater challenge to the simplified 'Indian' category. As Solomon (2012: 258) points out, 'the collapsing of the heterogeneity contained within these simple [CMIO] racial taxonomies has resulted in a gulf between the self-definitions of ethnicity… and the wider official definitions …'. This is illustrated by the changes within the Indian community, within which the proportion of Tamils has declined to 54 per cent (Table 7.1) and the community language, Tamil, now used by only 37 per cent, has gradually lost ground to English (the main household language of 42 per cent of the Indians) and other languages (14 per cent).

The following section details the reasons for the language shift within the Indian community, the challenges of language diversity, and a series of policy reactions and responses to the shifting community demographics and needs.

5. 1965–90: diversity-related challenges to language education policy

Even though the political choice of Tamil as the representative language served to establish its official position with the community, it failed to consolidate the

Table 7.2 *Census data on predominant household languages by ethnic groups, 1980–2010*

Ethnic group	Language	1980	1990	2000	2010	2020
Chinese	English	10.2	21.4	23.9	32.6	47.6
	Mandarin	13.1	30.0	45.1	47.7	40.2
	Chinese dialects	76.2	48.2	30.7	19.2	11.8
Malays	English	2.3	5.7	7.9	17.0	39.0
	Malay	96.7	94.1	91.6	82.7	60.7
Indians	English	24.3	34.3	35.6	41.6	59.2
	Tamil	52.2	43.5	42.9	36.7	27.4
	Malay	8.6	14.1	11.6	7.9	6.0
	Other Indian languages	14.9	8.1	9.9	13.8	7.1

Source: Jain (2021), Singapore Department of Statistics (2021).

community linguistically in the manner of Mandarin for the Chinese and Malay for the Malays. A primary impediment was the linguistic diversity among the 40 per cent of the population (Table 7.1) who identified with non-official languages. The option of Tamil as the official mother tongue for all school-going children of Indian ethnicity was sounder in principle than in practice. Compared to students from Dravidian language backgrounds (Malayalam, Telugu and Kannada speakers), those from Indo-European language backgrounds (e.g. Punjabi, Gujarati) found Tamil arduous to learn. Such awareness led the government to offer an exceptional latitude (denied to those from the Chinese and Malay communities) of choice among the three official mother tongues to Indian students. Therefore, those from Indian backgrounds could opt to study either Tamil or Mandarin/Malay in lieu. By Moag's factor 13, while Tamil speakers were 'insulated from pressure to adopt out-group language', the lack of restrictions on non-Tamil Indian speakers impeded the linguistic cohesion of the community. As Rai (2009) points out, many from Indo-European language backgrounds preferred Malay for its Romanised script 'or Mandarin, which was considered economically more useful than either Tamil or Malay' (p. 148). Therefore, while Tamil acquired the status of an official language (Moag's factor 26), it could not compete with other high-status languages such as English and could not attract too many out-group members to learn and use the language (factor 30). Interestingly, as Kuo (1980) highlights, Malay was not only the lingua franca of two-thirds of the total population but also the most understood language among the Indians. Illustrating the extraordinary position of Malay within the Indian community, an interview participant (third-generation Singaporean Indian who identifies as Bhojpuri) in the author's (Jain) ongoing research recounts:

> My father was born here and studied English and Malay at school. My mother came from India but she didn't know any English. My Dad doesn't speak Bhojpuri well – horribly as me – so they communicated in broken Bhojpuri until she learnt Malay language ... and cooking and all ... and now they speak a *rojak* of Malay and Bhojpuri. She can now understand English perfectly and even speaks a little.

Notwithstanding the flexibility of choice of language in education, students from the northern regions of India continued to struggle academically due to the burden of learning what was essentially a foreign language. Jain (2021), citing a news report, highlights that only 55 per cent of Indian students opted to study Tamil as the second language in 1979 while the rest studied Mandarin or Malay.

These sociolinguistic dynamics and prevalent linguistic diversity further hampered the establishment of Tamil as the pan-Indian linguistic and cultural identity. The academic difficulties of Indian students were further aggravated by a nationwide language reform to boost academic standards in the early 1980s. Performance in language subjects was given greater weight by the new measures and ultimately resulted in greater attrition and failure to enter university. Such policy-related challenges had a direct impact on the community demographics.

The 1980s witnessed a rapid out-migration of Indians (Moag's factor 5) with their numbers falling to a historic low of slightly above 6 per cent of the total population. Among other reasons, dissatisfaction with the educational underperformance and related insecurity of future opportunities for their children was considered a significant impetus. The government's response to the population shortfall was twofold: a concerted recruitment drive to attract qualified professionals from various parts of India, and systemic policy reforms to promote the educational performance of Indian children.

6. 1990 and beyond: shifting demographics, changing policies

The 1990s marked a turning point in the demographic profile as well as the language policy for the Indian community. The government's talent hunt from the Indian subcontinent had begun to have a positive impact on the immigration of qualified professions from various parts of India. Commenting on the government's drive, Sinha notes that the inflow of Indian professionals 'would reconfigure both Indian community demography and socio-cultural dynamics in irreversible modes' (Sinha 2015: 42–3). As a result, while the overall population of ethnic Indians grew, the influx comprised both Tamils and what Moag terms 'out-group members' (factor 6). These demographic shifts also had a corresponding impact in reconfiguring the ethno-linguistic make-up of the Indian community with an increase in the linguistic heterogeneity that was more representative of the complex linguistic landscape of India.

At around the same time, conceding to the recommendations of the expert committee (Singapore Action Committee on Indian Education) set up to study the educational underperformance of the Indian students, the government took certain focused measures. Steps were taken to enhance exposure and support for certain key subjects (Mathematics, Tamil) in which performance had been below the national average. In addition, action was taken to reduce the burden of studying Tamil, Mandarin or Malay as a second language for students of non-Tamil backgrounds.

Most pertinent among these was the nod to expanding language options from the previous three official language to five other non-official languages: Bengali, Gujarati, Hindi, Punjabi, and Urdu. Justified on the grounds of their availability in O Level (year 10 of school) examinations conducted by the Cambridge Local Examinations syndicate, the five languages offered hope to those from North Indian language backgrounds. Noticeably, none of the more commonly spoken Dravidian languages (e.g. Malayalam) was included to – as Rai (2009) hypothesises – allay the insecurity of the Tamil leaders who were anxious to avoid weakening the position of Tamil in Singapore.

The 'refreshed' language policy for the Indians meant that Indian students, regardless of language background, could request permission to study any of the seven languages in lieu of Tamil if they had no prior familiarity with the latter/ official language. In principle, this facility boosted the possibility of maintenance and transmission of the various Indian languages. However, in practice, the provision of and institutional support for the languages did not result in the envisaged uptake as the following discussion illustrates.

In design and delivery, the 'model' of what have come to be known as Non-Tamil Indian Languages or NTILs differs greatly from that for the official languages. The various aspects of language management (including standardised curriculum design, resource development, teacher training, language instruction, and assessments) are managed by the Board for the Teaching and Testing of South Asian Languages (BTTSAL), comprising representatives from the five associated communities. Under its oversight, the various language organisations operate independently. Other than a variable government grant approximating SGD1.5 million (Shah and Jain 2017) to subsidise tuition for the five languages, the cost of language learning is borne by parents.

In this model, the languages are weighted as full subjects in the school curriculum. The classes for these community languages are held after school hours (on Saturdays) within the premises of public schools. However, the Singapore model has made a unique departure from the normative Saturday school design in the years following its rollout. Faced with large numbers of non-Tamil Indian students (mainly enrolled in Hindi schools) who needed to be managed during the mother tongue period, certain public schools requested and acquired approval for the conduct of the language lessons during curriculum time. With this exception, community schools have the option of arranging for teachers to teach within the school premises during school hours provided parents are willing to bear the extra costs. As a result, these in-school languages are relatively on a par with the official mother tongues while those taught in Saturday schools suffer some disadvantage of intensive language learning across four hours (Jain (2021) offers a more detailed comparison).

Language interest in the community is evident in both the engagement of the communities as well as student enrolment in the five languages. As Table 7.3 indicates, among the five languages, Bengali and Hindi are both offered by two community organisations, and Gujarati, Punjabi and Urdu by a single organisation each. The popularity of Hindi is evident in the number of venues that are required to serve those opting for the language through both Saturday schools (18) and in-school classes (122 schools).

Such institutional support has offered an impetus to the various minority languages within the Indian community. Community school enrolment data from 2010–18 (embargoed after 2018)[3] indicates an overall robust growth in student numbers over the years (Table 7.4).

Despite the declining number of students for Gujarati, Punjabi and Urdu, both Bengali and Hindi have continued to flourish. However, recent research (Jain and Wee 2018, 2019a) has also demonstrated that much of the growth in the non-Tamil languages has come from Hindi, which accounts for 80 per cent of the total enrolment. Analysis of data from Jain's recent research has indicated that Hindi is preferred not only by students whose mother tongues are not available as school

Table 7.3 *Number of venues for community schools in 2021*

	Saturday schools	In-school venues
Bengali	4	0
Gujarati	1	0
Punjabi	1	1
Urdu	1	0
Hindi	18	122

Source: Board for the Teaching and Testing of South Asian Languages website, https://bttsal.com/.

Indian Languages in Singapore

Table 7.4 *Student enrolment for non-Tamil Indian languages, 2010–18*

	Bengali	Gujarati	Hindi	Punjabi	Urdu	Total
2010	629	154	3581	1111	311	5786
2013	820	124	4826	857	317	6944
2015	995	108	6475	744	322	8644
2018	906	77	7629	605	264	9481

Source: Board for the Teaching and Testing of South Asian Languages website, https://bttsal.com/.

subjects but also by those whose languages (i.e. Bengali, Gujarati, Punjabi, Urdu, and even Tamil) are.

Therefore, as the foregoing discussion has demonstrated, changes in the demographic make-up of the community have required responses from language policy which, in turn, have further reconfigured the linguistic landscape. As the next section illustrates, these continual negotiations between policies and communities have directly impacted the various community languages.

7. Outcomes and implications of demographic and policy shifts

The Indian community in Singapore stands out from the other ethnic groups for the singular flexibility and advantages its languages have received from facilitative policy measures. For the 54 per cent from a Tamil background, the status of Tamil as an official language has greatly enhanced the possibility of language learning, maintenance and transmission. Tamil is not only used in government communication, education and in the media (factors 21–3, 26), it also retains its majority and is popular among local-born Indians from Dravidian language backgrounds. In addition, the use of government machinery, via the Tamil Language Council and other bodies, aims to foster the use of Tamil among the Indians. Other than social initiatives such as the annual Tamil Language Festival, the government also invests in the teaching and learning of the language in schools. However, despite such government support, Tamil has suffered a gradual decline over the years. Jain and Wee (2019b: 282) attribute the weakening of Tamil to two main reasons: 'the diglossic nature of the Tamil language and the increasing linguistic heterogeneity of the Indian community resulting from large-scale immigration'.

The former characteristic, of Tamil diglossia, has been aggravated by education initiatives such as language standardisation considered necessary for the maintenance and promotion of the 'acceptable' form of official languages. This has seen the adoption of Literary Tamil (LT), traditionally used by the educated, as the language of education at the expense of Spoken Tamil (ST), a variety looked down upon but popular within the community. Discussing this divergence, Schiffman (2003: 106) deplores the institutional choice of the literary, formal variety in education that bears little communicative value, and the disregard of the popular, spoken variety as corrupted and 'ungrammatical'. Further, given that many students of Tamil come from Telugu or Malayalam language backgrounds, the insistence on the literary form in education and the media further deters informal use of Tamil within the community.

Similarly, while the recent immigration of Indians from various parts of South Asia has led to a greater linguistic diversity, their languages have not fared too well in the face of competition from languages (English, and to some extent, Hindi) of higher status at the international level (Moag's factor 27). This is evident in the census data (Table 7.2) illustrating the preference for English as the most commonly used language among 42 per cent of Indians. Discussing this, Jain and Wee (2015: 75) highlight the following:

> While Malay served as the common language in the past (Kuo 1980, 51), the immigration of educated and upwardly mobile Indians has led to a shift to English as the lingua franca. Among the newer diaspora, Tamil holds neither an instrumental value (that Mandarin does among the Chinese) nor serves an integrative function (served by Malay among the Malay people).

Beyond the official languages, Hindi is gradually emerging as an attractive alternative, especially among the relatively recent arrivals and transmobile families who remain unsure of their long-term plans. Demonstrating that the popularity of Hindi is directly related to the shifting demographics among the Indian community, Jain (2021: 77) highlights that only 22 per cent of the students studying Hindi are citizens of Singapore, while 78 per cent are either permanent residents or foreigners. Further, among the more recent immigrants, parental decisions around languages in education are shaped by previous language experiences and the anticipated future education and professional needs of their children. The tendency to view languages as subjects in education rather than as aspects of one's familial identity reflects the increasingly pragmatic attitude of the more recent Indian immigrants. Increasingly, the preference for languages (e.g. English, Mandarin, Hindi) that are evaluated as being more economically advantageous takes a toll on the home languages. Anecdotal evidence (and Jain's ongoing research) suggests that Tamil may not be the default choice of the recent Tamil immigrants.

The shifting linguistic landscape as well as the diminishing popularity of Tamil among the Indian community has exacerbated underlying sensitivities. Many among the Tamil community have long held that all Indians should study Tamil in the manner that all Chinese are required to study Mandarin, and all Malays to study Malay. Despite the government's reassurance that Tamil would remain protected and continue to enjoy its official status, such sensitivities have remained and find expression every now and then. Jain (forthcoming) highlights a few examples such as the mistaken use of Hindi in lieu of Tamil in a flyer announcing the relocation of a market. This *faux pas* required the government to calm the situation. Public comments on forums and social media further underscore the language insecurities that will have to be managed as the profile of the Indian community evolves and shifts through migration over time.

8. Conclusion

This discussion has demonstrated that Singapore's Indian community is uniquely positioned within the global Indian diaspora. Not only does its representative language, Tamil, enjoy an equal status as those of the majority groups but its minority languages also find institutional support. However, these advantages may not be enough to secure the future of these languages for future generations. In Moag's feature-factor matrix, despite positive demographic factors (e.g. critical mass of speakers, ongoing influx of immigrants), no singular language can remain predominant due to the absence of aspects such as 'living in cohesive enclaves', and the 'greater security accorded to competing groups'. Similarly, even as Tamil enjoys the support of political factors (9–11) as well as of many among the local born Tamils, certain socio-cultural factors (17–20) threaten to erode its social position. The adoption of the purist variety in education, lack of a linguistically homogeneous society, and migration patterns work against Tamil and in favour of alternate languages. Similarly, despite sociolinguistic factors (21–31) such as the use of Tamil in government activities, education and media, the language is facing a decline within the home and community.

Simultaneously, initiatives of the non-Tamil Indian language communities and support from the government has invigorated alternate Indian languages. Therefore, despite the attraction of English, various Indian languages are likely to thrive in Singapore. While the stature of Hindi is likely to grow more than the alternate non-Tamil Indian languages (i.e. Bengali, Gujarati, Punjabi and Urdu) the latter will retain their position as languages in education and serve the associated communities.[4]

Finally, although government policies will remain the crucial elements for the survival and vitality of the Indian languages, community and family initiatives will remain the bastions of language maintenance in Singapore. Looking ahead, we envisage that community-state dialogues will prove critical in managing the expectations and needs of the various sub-groups within the Indian community. At the same time, the community itself would benefit from celebrating diversity, appreciating sensitivities and differences, and co-existing in harmony.

Acknowledgement

This work was supported by the Ministry of Education Academic Research Fund Tier 1 research grant (RG70/17 (NS)).

Appendix

Table A7.1 *Moag's typology of factors supporting language maintenance*

Categories	Factors
Demographic	
	1. Critical mass of native speakers
	2. Rural habitat
	3. Living in cohesive enclaves
	4. Ongoing influx of new immigrants
	5. Minimal out-migration
	6. Minimal influx of out-group members

Table A7.1 *(continued)*

Categories	Factors
	7. Short time in new country
	8. Competing group(s) enjoy greater security
Political factors	
	9. Official status for language
	10. Government policy to encourage language
	11. Lobbying efforts on behalf of the language
	12. External threat to the group as a whole
Socio-cultural factors	
	13. Position on social scale insulating group from pressure to adopt out-group language
	14. Primary linguistic reference group internal to speech community
	15. Ongoing contacts with speakers in homeland
	16. Perceived great tradition with which language is identified
	17. Endogamous marriage pattern
	18. Joint family living pattern
	19. Work mainly with other L1 speakers
	20. Social activities mainly with L1 speakers
Sociolinguistic factors	
	21. Language used in governmental activities
	22. Language used in education
	23. Language used in media (print/broadcasting)
	24. Language used in religious observances
	25. Stable language-use patterns
	26. Language enjoys high status at national level
	27. Low international prestige for competing languages
	28. Healthy percentage of monolingual speakers
	29. Language passed on to next generation
	30. Out-group members learn and use the language
	31. Positive attitude towards preserving the language supported by action

Source: Moag (2003: 35).

Notes

1. The kangani system was a labour system akin to indenture, in which a Tamil foreman was involved in the recruitment and management of labourers.
2. The terms, Hindi and Hindustani are used interchangeably here and reflect the preferred choice through the years. Colonial censuses predominantly used 'Hindustani' but recent censuses have elected to use 'Hindi'.
3. Sources of information are limited as data on community school enrolment is classified. Further, the national census does not capture any data on non-official language use.
4. The settled Gujarati and Punjabi communities prefer their languages as subjects in education for maintenance of culture and community identity. Bengali is preferred primarily by those from Bangladesh while Urdu is studied by students from Pakistan.

References

Detaramani, C. and G. Lock (2003). Multilingualism in decline: Language repertoire, use and shift in two Hong Kong Indian communities. *Journal of Multilingual and Multicultural Development*, 24 (4): 249–73.

Evers, Hans-Dieter and Jayarani Pavadarayan (1993). Religious fervour and economic success: The Chettiars of Singapore. In K. S. Sandhu and A. Mani (eds), *Indian Communities in Southeast Asia*. Singapore: ISEAS, pp. 847–65.

Han, Lim Peng (2010). The history of an emerging multilingual public library system and the role of mobile libraries in post-colonial Singapore, 1956–1991. *Malaysian Journal of Library & Information Science*, 15 (2): 85–108.

Jain, R. (2021). The other mother tongues of Singaporean Indians. In R. Jain (ed.), *Multilingual Singapore: Language Policies, Linguistic Realities*. Abingdon: Routledge, pp. 65–84.

Jain, R. (Forthcoming). Contentious consensus: Challenges of diversity to identity-based language policies. In A. Ghosh (ed.), *Language, Communication and Conflict in South and Southeast Asia*. Kolkata: Asiatic Society.

Jain, R. and Wee, L. (2015). Multilingual education in Singapore: Beyond language communities? in Yiakoumetti, A. (Ed.) *Multilingualism and Language in Education: Sociolinguistic and Pedagogical Perspectives from Commonwealth Countries*. Pp 67-85. Cambridge: Cambridge University Press.

Jain, R. and L. Wee (2018). Cartographic mismatches and language policy: The case of Hindi in Singapore. *Language Policy*, 17: 99–118.

Jain, R. and L. Wee (2019a). Diversity management and the presumptive universality of categories: The case of the Indians in Singapore. *Current Issues in Language Planning*, 20: 16–32.

Jain, R. and L. Wee (2019b). Language education policy, Singapore. In A. Kirkpatrick and T. Liddicoat (eds), *The Routledge Handbook on Language Education Policy in Asia*. Routledge, pp. 272–85.

Kuo, E. C. Y. (1980). The sociolinguistic situation in Singapore: Unity in diversity. In E. A. Afendras and E. C. Y. Kuo (eds), *Language and Society in Singapore*. Singapore: Singapore University Press, pp. 39–62.

McNair, J. F. A. (1899). *Prisoners their own warders: A record of the convict prison at Singapore in the Straits Settlements, established 1825, discontinued 1873, together with a cursory history of the convict establishments at Bencoolen, Penang and Malacca from the year*. Westminster: A. Constable.

Mahandru, V. K. (1991). The Panjabi speech community. In S. Alladina and V. Edwards (eds), *Multilingualism in the British Isles Africa, the Middle East and Asia*. Longman, pp. 115–27.

Mesthrie, R. (2008). South Asian languages in the second diaspora. In B. B. Kachru and S. N. Sridhar (eds), *Language in South Asia*. Cambridge: Cambridge University Press, pp. 497–514.

Mesthrie, R. (2021). Contacts and contexts: Varying diasporic interactions and koineisation outcomes for Indian languages in South Africa. *Journal of Sociolinguistics*, 25 (5): 703–19.

Moag, R. F. (2003). Language loss versus language maintenance in overseas Indian communities. In R. Sharma and E. Annamalai (eds), *Indian Diaspora in Search of Identity*. Mysore: Central Institute of Indian Languages, pp. 1–39).

Mukherjee, D. (2003). Role of women in language maintenance and language shift: Focus on the Bengali community inMalaysia. *International Journal of the Sociology of Language*, 161: 103–20.

Mukherjee, D. and M. David (2011). *National Language Planning and Language Shifts in Malaysian Minority Communities*. Amsterdam: Amsterdam University Press. https://doi.org/10.1515/9789048513383.

Oonk, G. (2007). *Global Indian Siasporas: Exploring Trajectories of Migration and Theory*. Amsterdam: Amsterdam University Press.

Rai, R. (2009). The attrition and survival of minor South Asian languages in Singapore. In R. Rai and P. Reeves (eds), *The South Asian Diaspora: Transnational Networks and Changing Identities*. London and New York: Routledge, pp. 143–59.

Rai, R. (2014). *Indians in Singapore, 1819–1945: Diaspora in the Colonial Port-city*. New Delhi: Oxford University Press.

Schiffman, H. (2003) Tongue-tied in Singapore: A language policy of Tamil? *Journal of Language, Identity and Education*, 2 (2): 105–25.

Shah, S. and R. Jain (2017). Gujarati in Singapore. In C. Seals and S. Shah (eds), *Heritage Language Policies around the World*. Abingdon and New York: Routledge, pp. 199–217.

Siegel, J. (1988). Language contact in a plantation environment. *English World-Wide*, 9 (1): 129.

Sinclair, Iain. (2019) Traces of the Cholas in Old Singapura. In A. Mahizhnan and N. Gopal (eds), *From Sojourners to Settlers: Tamils in South-East Asia and Singapore*. Singapore: Indian Heritage Centre.

Singapore Department of Statistics (2021). *Singapore Census of Population 2020, Statistical Release 1: Demographic Characteristics, Education, Language and Religion*. Singapore: Department of Statistics. Retrieved from: https://www.singstat.gov.sg/-/media/files/publications/cop2020/sr1/cop2020sr1.ashx.

Sinha, V. (2015). *Singapore Chronicles, Indians*. Singapore: Straits Times Press.

Solomon, J. (2012). The decline of pan-Indian identity and the development of Tamil cultural separatism in Singapore, 1856–1965. *South Asia: Journal of South Asia Studies*, 35: 257–81.

van der Avoird, T. (2001). *Determining Language Vitality: The Language Use of Hindu Communities in the Netherlands and the United Kingdom*. Dissertation, Tilburg University.

Verma, M. K. (1991). The Hindi speech community. In S. Alladina and V. Edwards (eds), *Multilingualism in the British Isles Africa, the Middle East and Asia*. Longman, pp. 103–114.

Yeoh, Brenda S. A. (2003). *Contesting Space in Colonial Singapore: Power Relations and the Urban Built Environment*. Singapore: NUS Press.

CHAPTER 8

East Indian Languages in the Caribbean Diaspora

Surendra Gambhir

1. Introduction

All diasporas live between two worlds, at least in the first few generations. They accept and adapt the essential elements of the host culture while trying to retain some distinctive features of their home culture. Thus, the transmigration of any community or of groups of people who become a community in diaspora is a long-lasting tale of cultural change and cultural preservation. The predominant concern of sociolinguists is the community's heritage language, amidst a changing repertoire. In an English-dominated environment, we have seen immigrants' language being most vulnerable to shift. In non-English dominant countries, however, the maintenance of immigrants' languages often has a different trajectory.[1] This chapter focuses on the heritage language experience of East Indians in the Caribbean area amidst the new multilingual environment there. Our path of enquiry will be a combination of historical, theoretical, empirical and data-driven information.

Besides its islands, the Caribbean area may also include countries on the border. In this study, I include Guyana and Suriname, south of the Caribbean Sea and lying on South America's northern edge. The Caribbean area is multi-ethnic with diverse languages and religions. Despite diversity, most nations connect through English and a vague Caribbean identity. However, such an implicit unity does not suggest that inter-ethnic competitiveness, conflicts, prejudices and discriminations are non-existent.

2. South Asian presence

At least sixteen nations in the Caribbean area have an identifiable segment of people of Indian origin, ranging from a minimal number to several hundred thousand. The end of African slavery was the beginning of the importation of cheap labourers from India. A massive contractual labour force came under the Coolie Trade of the nineteenth century to replenish the void created by freed African slaves in 1834.[2] These indentured labourers, numbering 463,923, came directly into eight Caribbean colonies – British Guiana, Trinidad and Tobago, Jamaica, Suriname, Saint Lucia, Grenada, Saint Vincent and Saint Kitts – during 1838 and 1917. Most of them were from the North Indian areas of Bihar and the United Provinces (later Uttar Pradesh), and a significant minority was from India's southern regions. Out of the sixteen nations, three French islands – Martinique, Guadeloupe and French Guiana – received South Indian labourers directly from the Karaikal port located in the current Union Territory of Puducherry (earlier Pondicherry) in South India.

While many Indo-Caribbeans continued in the agricultural field, their upwardly mobile descendants today are in various professions as lawyers, doctors, professors, teachers, politicians, and intellectuals or writers of acclaim. The current population of Indian origin in the Caribbean area is close to 1.2 million, which includes a small number of free passengers who migrated there for business, through marriage or via a job offer. These free passengers mainly include Sindhis, Gujaratis and Panjabis. Approximately half a million Indo-Caribbeans have migrated out to other countries like Canada, the United States, the United Kingdom and the Netherlands for prospects of a better life.

Table 8.1 presents relevant information about the East Indian communities in sixteen Caribbean nations.

Ethnic population numbers can vary depending on the source we use and because of population mixing. The population figures in the above table are mainly based on UNO's country-wise population for the year 2020. I have explored the internet to determine if there is an Indian restaurant, a Hindu temple, an Indian cultural centre, and if the people of Indian origin celebrate *Indian Arrival Day* in these territories. This information is included in column 1 of Table 8.1 and may help detect survival elements of Indian ethnicity in these territories for which other information is currently unavailable. Three noteworthy points can be inferred from Table 8.1.

1. The first three countries, Guyana, Trinidad and Suriname, have a significant percentage of the Indic population, all others range between 10 and 0.1 percent.
2. Eleven of the sixteen in the area use English and an English-based creole. Five regions are non-English speaking: Martinique, Guadeloupe and French Guiana are foreign territories of France where people use French and French-based creole; Suriname has Dutch and Dutch-based creole, and Puerto Rico's principal language is Spanish.
3. Hindustani or a Bhojpuri-based lingua franca has been the most widespread in eleven of the sixteen regions.

In this study, nations are grouped together based on their shared migration history, resettlement patterns, multi-dialectalism and emergence of a lingua franca from multiple dialects. Regarding the current research situation, three countries – Guyana, Trinidad and Suriname – which have the lion's share of research in the Caribbean area will be the focus of this chapter. Several scholars have contributed essential insights into the historical and synchronic status of the Indic languages in these countries during past decades. For Trinidad, the key works are Durban (1973), Mohan (1978), Mohan and Zador (1986), Bhatia (1983, 1988), Bhimull (2019). Suriname studies abound in Roseval (1977), Bosch (1978), Huiskamp (1978, 1980), Kishna (1981), Damsteegt (1983, 1988), Marhe (1985), Gautam (1999, 2017), Yakpo (2017) and Bajnath (2019). For Guyana, Ramdat (1978), Gambhir (1981, 1983a, 1983b, 1988) and Satyanath (2003) are the main sources.

Table 8.1 *Indian diaspora in the Caribbean area*

Country/Island name	Migration period	Official/dominant language(s)	Country's total current populations* (approx.)	Current Indian ethnic group population (approx.)	Percentage of the total population (approx.)	Main incoming heritage languages	Indic languages widely used, currently (Sp)oken, (U)nderstood but not spoken, (I)conic
Guyana R T C	1838–1917	English Creole	787,000	317,000	40.3	Bhojpuri, Avadhi, Tamil, Telugu	I
Trinidad and Tobago R T C	1845–1917	English Creole	1,400,000	470,376	33.6	Bhojpuri, Avadhi, Tamil, Telugu	I
Suriname R T C	1873–1915	Dutch/English Creole	587,000	161,000	27.4	Bhojpuri, Avadhi, Tamil	Sarnami (Hindustani) Sp U I
Martinique R	1853–83	French Creole	315,000+	40,000	10	Tamil	I
Guadeloupe R T	1861–83	French/Creole	400,000+	36,000	9	Tamil	I
St Vincent R A	1861–80	English Creole	111,000	5,900	5.3	Hindustani	I
Jamaica R T C A	1845–1917	English Creole	3,000,000	36,000	1.2	Bhojpuri, Sindhi, Gujarati, Kutchi, Punjabi, Tamil, Telugu, Bengali	I
French Guiana R?	1862–83	French Creole	298,000+	12,000	4.1	Tamil, Guyanese, Bhojpuri, Sarnami	I
British Virgin Islands R	?	English Creole	30,000+	1,100	3.7	Hindustani	I
Grenada R	1857–90	English Creole	112,500+	3,900	3.5	Hindustani	I
St Kitts and Nevis R	1861–74	English Creole	53,000	500	0.9	Hindustani	I
St Lucia R A	1859–93	English Creole	183,000+	5,200	2.8	Hindustani	I

Table 8.1 (continued)

Country/Island name	Migration period	Official/dominant language(s)	Country's total current populations* (approx.)	Current Indian ethnic group population (approx.)	Percentage of the total population (approx.)	Main incoming heritage languages	Indic languages widely used, currently (Sp)oken, (U)nderstood but not spoken, (I)conic
Belize R T	1880s–	English Creole	400,000	12,452	3.9	Hindustani	I
Barbados R	1913–free-passengers	English Creole	287,000	4,000	1.4	Hindustani, Bengali, Gujarati, Urdu, Tamil, Sindhi	Hindustani Sp U I
U.S. Virgin Islands +R	1863–70	English Creole	104,000+	1,000	1	Sindhi, Hindustani	Sp
Puerto Rico +R	?	Spanish English	2,860,000+	4,100	0.1	Hindustani	I

Key: A – Arrival day celebration; C – Indian cultural organization; I = Iconic; R – Indian restaurant; Sp – Spoken; T – Hindu temple; U – Understood.

People in the Caribbean area acquired the vernacular Bhojpuri effortlessly at home during their childhood and expanded their proficiency through informal interactions with East Indians outside the home. Examples of informal domains included domestic chat, interaction with relatives, and friends. The acquisition of Standard Hindi/Urdu was possible through formal education in a school setting, where children could learn literacy skills, some formal vocabulary, very basic grammatical understanding of sentence formation, and basic discourse-level speech patterns. Since the imported Hindi soap operas were (and still are) extensively watched on television, I assume that passive exposure to various external sources such as Hindi movies and TV soap operas also reinforced some of these features. Regarding their communicative proficiency in the heritage language, my extensive personal connections and observations in Guyana suggest that apart from Hindu priests, it is rare for someone to develop a proficiency beyond a basic level (roughly equivalent to the Intermediate Mid on the ACTFL scale[3]). My impression is that the situation in Trinidad was not different from Guyana. The story of Suriname is certainly different, as discussed later in this chapter.

3. Indentured labour migration

Slavery ended legally in British colonies after the British Parliament passed the Abolition of Slavery Act of 1833. For French colonies, slavery ended fifteen years later in 1848, and for the Dutch colony of Suriname after another fifteen years in 1863. A further period of four to ten years stipulated as transition from slavery to freedom can be added to these dates. The slave workers were then free to leave the sugar plantations to assert their autonomy and pursue their independent livelihood. Cheap labour from multiple countries, mainly from India, filled the void caused by the loss of African labour. At that time, the British rulers of India helped sugar plantation owners to recruit labourers in large numbers. Indian labourers came under a five-year agreement mainly from the northern regions of the then Oudh, United Provinces, Bihar, and the southern province of Madras Presidency. These indentured labourers were known as *girmityas* among labourers themselves. The Bhojpuri expression *girmiTyaa* derived from the English word *agreement* became current among recruits of local Bihari dialects in India. The labourers were taken to far-flung colonies to work in sugar plantations. The colonies were Mauritius and La Reunion in the Indian Ocean, several in the Caribbean area, Fiji in the Pacific Ocean, and Natal (South Africa). The first shipload of indentured labourers arrived in British Guiana (now Guyana) in the Caribbean on 5 May 1838. The process of importing labourers from India to different regions in the Caribbean area continued unabated until 1917. In this chapter, I will focus on Indian labourers' heritage languages, in diachronic and synchronic perspectives.

4. Multi-dialectalism and dialect-levelling

Most of the indentured labourers from the eastern United Provinces and Bihar spoke various typologically related dialects and languages, which formed a linguistic continuum in India's Hindi belt. In the new colonies, many migrants speaking different dialects were forced to live together and interact daily. In due course, contact between the various dialects gave rise to a common lingua franca in every colony. The gradual development of a common form of communication passed through four stages: mixing, levelling, simplification, and selection, as explained in Gambhir (1981). Demographic preponderance also played a very important role in the selection process. Later the works of Siegel (1985), Trudgill (1986), Mesthrie (1992), Britain and Trudgill (1999), Yakpo (2017) and Kerswill and Williams (2000) have contributed many more studies in the field of indenture and koineisation.

Britain and Trudgill (1999: 254) brought further clarity to the concept when they state that 'linguistic outcomes of dialect contact are not haphazard but tend to follow a relatively limited range of possibilities'. Trudgill (1986) also came up with a new category of *reallocation*, where competing variants in a dialect-mix survive and adopt new communicative roles as social or geographical variants. The category of reallocation is not frequent in koine studies, but is, nevertheless, a useful one for data analysis. In Guyanese Bhojpuri, I had explained the merger of dental and retroflex sounds into alveolars, which was distinctly visible in the younger generation (Gambhir 1981: 57–9). The alveolarisation of dental and retroflex sounds in Guyana was a case of phonological reallocation. The examples of /okar/ and /uske/ and /gaya/ and /gawa/ in Fiji Hindi are claimed in Britain and Trudgill (1999: 250) as cases of reallocation, but in my opinion, they are not. These examples do not fit into Trudgill's own definition of reallocation, which, according to him, refers to situations 'where the ingredient forms to the dialect-mix take on different roles'. According to him, original forms in the dialect-mix are refunctionalised. In the above case of /okar/ and /uske/ and /gaya/ and /gawa/ in Fiji Hindi, the distinct forms as well as their different roles in both the cases were not different from the Bhojpuri area in India, where Bhojpuri and Standard Hindi are used together in a unified communication complex.

Since most labourers were broadly from the Bhojpuri speaking area, the emergent lingua franca in all the British colonies of the Caribbean area was based on demographic preponderance, which was Bhojpuri, a variety spoken in eastern Uttar Pradesh (UP) and western Bihar in modern India.[4] Although all the emergent vernaculars in different territories were mutually intelligible, some minor differences occurred among them. The emerging lingua franca assimilated linguistic elements from the participating regional languages by certain selection processes. Linguistic features widely shared by the participating varieties had the best chance of survival in the emergent koine.

One point that could be a source of confusion is whether the koineisation process is a type of linguistic convergence. Convergence is more properly reserved for the gradual structural adaptations shown by languages in prolonged contact, which nevertheless may remain outwardly distinct. As opposed to this, the term *koine* reflects both linguistic unification and social integration, the latter possibly being the motivating factor for the former.

Four fundamentals characterise a koine:

1. It is primarily based on a language continuum, rather than vastly different languages.

2. It absorbs most structural elements from related varieties within the continuum.
3. It shows structural simplification over the previous linguistic systems.
4. Its users perceive in the koine a structural continuity with their own regional language varieties.

As part of the socialisation among migrants, speakers needed to smoothen communication across their dialect diversity. Via face-to-face accommodation and subconscious trial and error, they gradually converged upon a common set of norms. Such an attempt towards linguistic selection facilitated better communication among speakers from different backgrounds and promoted an imagined coherence within the larger community. Both linguistic unification and social integration forged a common ethnic identity. Other factors like journeying together, living together, inter-caste marriages, and creation of alternative models of religious practices were major contributors to adjustments and assimilation processes of the times. Linguistic integration and a common lingua franca indeed turned out to be the most crucial uniting factor.

4.1 Development of koineised features

While analysing my field data from Guyana (Gambhir 1981), I found a widely used element in the verb category, which I called *stem + -e*. This grammatical form was highly ambiguous and was used in the sense of present indicative, past indicative, past habitual, and occasionally in future tense and subjunctive. Of course, we were able to disambiguate the usages in appropriate contexts.

Tracing this form's historical relationship to India's source, I realised during my fieldwork in India that Indian Bhojpuri did not use this form as much. However, the Bhojpuri speakers understood its use in appropriate contexts. Moving to the Hindi belt's regions to the west, I found in my data that speakers of western dialects used the feature quite heavily. Map 8.1 is the graphic representation of its usage in India's source regions in the Hindi belt area.

Later, browsing through studies of Indian Bhojpuri, it became clear that Grierson (1903: 52) is the only one who took cognizance of this form in his *Linguistic Survey of India*. Grierson described the form as an alternate in the present tense second and third persons used with conditional clauses, such as 'if you see'[5]. On the other hand, Tiwari (1960) traces the use of this form in some proverbs and songs but otherwise mentions it as obsolete in modern-day Bhojpuri. In sum, the Indian Bhojpuri speakers do not actively use this form themselves but do understand its meaning when used by others. Opposed to the Bhojpuri situation, the use of the form *stem + -e* was widespread in western Hindi dialects. It led us to a reasonable conclusion that Guyanese Bhojpuri (GB) assimilated the active use of the *stem + -e* form from western Hindi dialects. In the variety that emerged in Guyana, we see the predominant use of *stem + -e* form in the present tense second and third persons (the same as in western dialects) while the present tense first person has retained the predominant use of *la-* form (same as in IB). Such a combination is indeed a hallmark of an emergent koine.

We turn to another example that illustrates an outcome of the koineisation process. On the Indian subcontinent, Hindi dialect area has four different morphological

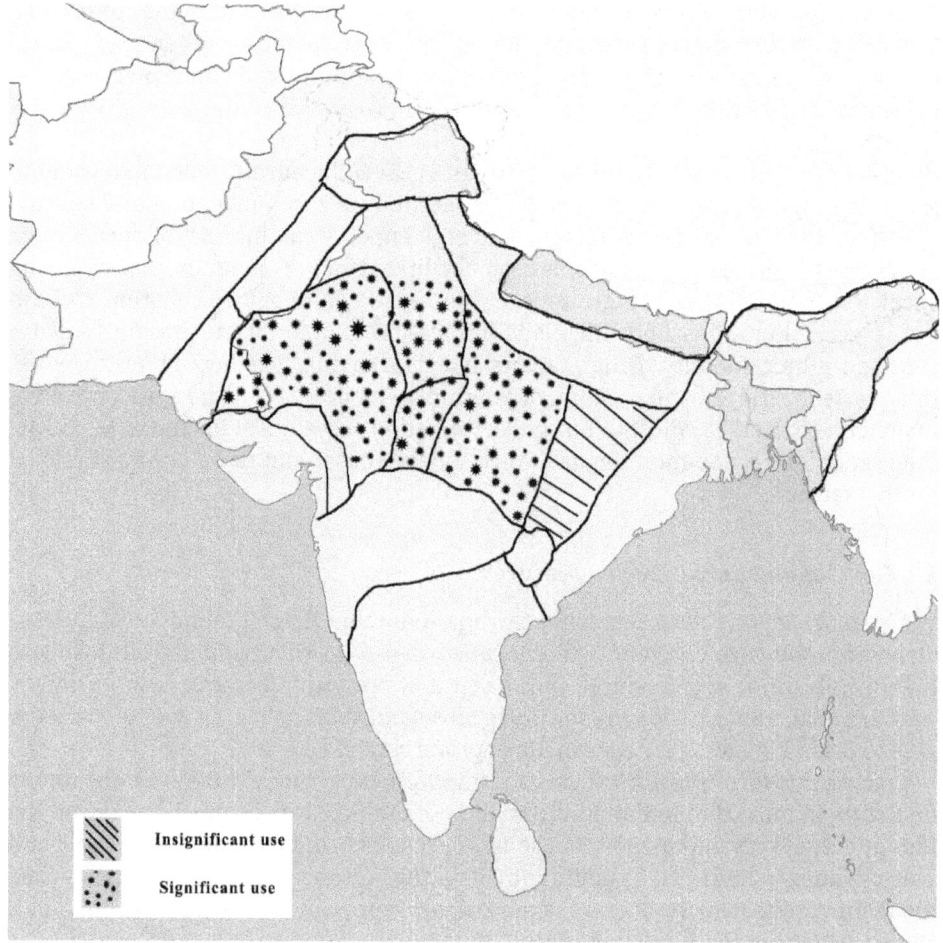

Map 8.1 *Sketch map of regional use of stem + -e verb forms in the North Indian continuum by frequency of usage*

endings for the future tense. Map 8.2 shows the graphic presentation of these four elements.

In GB, the future tense paradigm consists of a *b*-future in the first person and a *h*-future in the second and third persons. The selection process for this feature has materialised differently in different colonies, even though they have similar historical profiles. Table 8.2 gives a summary of the future tense verb endings.

GB has a *b*-future in the first person and the *h*-future in second and third persons. The third-person future *i*-ending is historically derived from the *h*-future (Hoernle 1880: 356, Tiwari 1960: 190), and therefore subsumed under it for the current analysis. When we compare the GB set of future tense endings with the corresponding endings in IB, we do not find a complete set of the same forms in any variety of IB. Further comparison with other Indian varieties shows that GB inherited its *h*-future in the second person from a source other than IB. My study of the western dialects of Hindi shows that in the second person, the *h*-future is the norm in western and

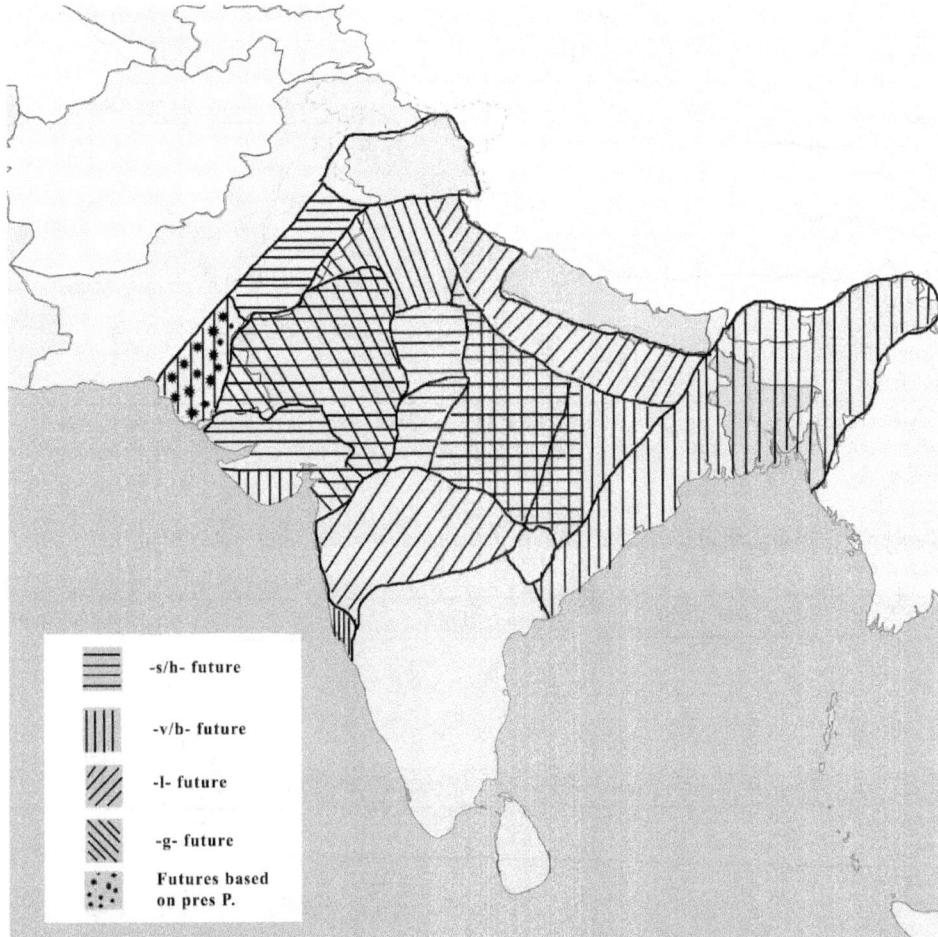

Map 8.2 Sketch map of distribution of future endings in modern Indo-Aryan
Source: based on Southworth (1968).

eastern Hindi varieties – Kannauji, Braj, Bundeli, Western Avadhi and Central Avadhi. The future tense endings in Guyanese Bhojpuri are therefore an amalgam from different sources (Bhojpuri, W. Hindi and E. Hindi), which is a clear case of koineisation. This is summarised in Table 8.3.

The framework I have provided here should apply, by and large, to the emergence of a lingua franca in all similar situations. The koineisation process in Sarnami, for example, must have been very similar, as confirmed by Yakpo (2017): 'Sarnami shows characteristic effects of koineization that have been documented in the literature, namely mixing, leveling, simplification, and reallocation.' As mentioned above, I have reservations about what has been claimed to be reallocation.

In the context of the colonies under discussion, one interesting and unexpected feature was that Standard Hindi or Urdu did not contribute to the homogenisation process that produced a koine. Gambhir (1981) concluded that Standard Hindi or Urdu speech was not actively involved in the everyday colloquial interactions, which

Language in the Indian Diaspora

Table 8.2 Variation in the future endings in different transplanted varieties

Variety	SINGULAR			PLURAL		
	First person	Second person	Third person	First person	Second person	Third person
Guyanese Bhojpuri	-b	-he	-i	-b	-ho	-i
		-ha	-ihe		-he	-ihe
			-iha			-iha
Trinidad Bhojpuri	-b	-be	-i	-b	-be	-i
Surinam Bhojpuri	-b(e)	-he	-gaa	-b(e)	-he	-gaa
Mauritian Bhojpuri	-b	-be	-i	-bas	-baa(s)	-an sa
				-b ja(s)		
Fiji Hindi	-egaa	-egaa	-ii	-egaa	-egaa	-ii
South African Bhojpuri	-b	-be	-i	-b (ja)	-be (ja)	-i (ja)

Source: adapted from Gambhir (1981). Other sources: Guyana (Gambhir 1981: 222); Trinidad (Mohan 1978: 158); Surinam (Huiskamp 1978: 210); Mauritius (Domingue 1971 and personal communication); Fiji (Moag 1977: 207); South Africa (Mesthrie 1992: 42).

Table 8.3 Comparison of the b- and h-future in Guyanese Bhojpuri and India's regional varieties in India

	Western Hindi				Eastern Hindi			Bihari			Guyanese Bhojpuri
	Hindi	Kannauji	Braj	Bundeli	Western Avadhi	Central Avadhi	Eastern Avadhi	Indian Bhojpuri	Magahi	Maithili	
Singular	-	-	-	-	+	+	+	+	+		-b
Plural	-	-	-	-	+	+	+	+	+	+	-b
Singular	-	+	+	+	+	+	-	-	-	-	-h
Plural	-	+	+	+	+	+	-	-	-	-	-h
Singular	-	-	-	-	+	+	+	+	-	-	-i
	-	+	+	+	-	-	-	+	-	+	-h
Plural	-	+	+	+	+	+	+	+	+	+	-h
	-	-	-	-	-	-	-	+	-	-	-i

Source: based on Gambhir (1988: 86).

produced the GB koine. Their role was confined to formal and religious domains. The same should be true of the other colonies.

5. Nomenclature

The main generic names for the spoken variety in the Caribbean plantation nations were *Hindustani, Hindustaniyaa* or *Hindi*, even though these linguistic varieties had little to do structurally with Hindustani or Hindi in the sense in which they are used in India. However, when speakers needed to differentiate between their regional variety and Standard Hindi, they described the former, for lack of a better name, as *Puraniya Hindi* (old Hindi) or *TuuTal bhaakhaa* (broken language). The name *Bhojpuri* was not available to these diasporic communities as it is a recent innovation from the academic world. On the other hand, speakers of Bhojpuri in India never called their regional dialect *Puraniya Hindi* or *TuuTal bhaakhaa*. For them, their localised variety has been Bhojpuri or simply *Hindi*.

For Muslims, the situation was not much different. They used the same words to name their regional variety, but more often Hindustani rather than Hindi. In the sense of the standard language, most used the term Urdu, where Hindus would say Hindi. In academic writings, the name of the koine in each country is often qualified as *Mauritian Bhojpuri, Guyanese Bhojpuri, Trinidad Bhojpuri, South African Bhojpuri*. In Fiji, however, the appellation *Fiji baat* or *Fiji Hindi* is more common. In Suriname, most people call their language by its Dutch name '*hindoestaans*'. Adhin (1964) introduced the term *Sarnami Hindustani* for the language, which was later simplified to just *Sarnami*. The latter denotes the language of *Sarnam*, the Indian pronunciation of the country's name Suriname. The term *Surinami Bhojpuri* is not used, even though it would also have been appropriate.[6]

6. Relationship between the vernacular and Standard Hindi/Urdu

On the cognitive level, the distinction between colloquial dialect and the standard written variety has been inadequately appreciated among the general public. Some people interviewed in Guyana described their vernacular as having no grammar. Although in linguistics this is an established conclusion that every language or dialect is governed by a set of rules (as also illustrated in the close grammatical analysis of GB in Gambhir 1981), such an understanding has not seeped down to the folk culture.

However, in terms of language use, the situation is different as people clearly comprehend subconsciously where the two varieties belong. Such a sociolinguistic relationship between the regional vernacular of Bihar and Standard Hindi/Urdu goes back many centuries and has become more expressive and expansive over time. In the Indian context, the relationship was so profound that it seeped down to the lowest echelon of India's speech communities and later even travelled with them to distant lands. This orientation led to the acceptance of Standard Hindi/Urdu for literacy, literature and formal use in India. This is how in areas of the United Provinces and Bihar, varieties like Bhojpuri and Hindi gradually became two parts of a unified communication matrix. Bhojpuri had thus bypassed languages with earlier literary traditions – Maithili, Avadhi and Braj – while allying itself with Standard Hindi/Urdu, the dominant languages of political India. It was Standard Hindi for Hindus and Standard Urdu for most Muslims. The affinity between Bhojpuri and Hindi grew so deep that their phrase structure rules and transformational rules do not differ significantly from the viewpoint of generative syntax (cf. Govind 1980). Even in more surface-oriented analyses, differences between the western extremity (Khari Boli) and the eastern extremity (Bhojpuri) are, for the most part, of the nature of one-to-one substitution. (A major exception is the use of ergative marking in the past tense in the western areas.) In genetically related languages 'insofar as conversions are regular, they diminish the inter-dialectal gap and simplify the problem of the bilingual' (Weinreich 1974: 2). It is because of this lack of significant difference between the two systems that the acquisition of Standard Hindi has been within the reach of Bhojpuri speakers. Both varieties have continued to feed into each other and have been inseparably unified into one communicative scheme. While Hindi/Urdu is the principal lexifier for learned lexis, the regional variety has strengthened Standard Hindi/Urdu with localised cultural content and its associated vocabulary.

In the current diasporic contexts, the hierarchical relationship between the local koineised variety and Standard Hindi/Urdu has also continued uninterrupted. For most members of the transplanted varieties, acquisition of Standard Hindi has been largely limited to passive competence. In my survey in Guyana, almost everyone who claimed to understand GB also claimed to understand Standard Hindi (Gambhir 1981: 294). In Suriname, however, where the language is still relatively active, the hierarchical relation between the two varieties continues to serve both the active and passive competence of speakers there.

In the Caribbean colonies, opportunities to use Standard Hindi/Urdu have been extremely limited. Since Hindi and Urdu have not been a part of the curriculum in state-sponsored schools, some parents encouraged their children to attend evening or weekend classes organised by community volunteers. Without an incentive to learn Standard Hindi or Urdu for lack of their use in any economically or socially advantageous domain, learners in these community schools remain at the elementary proficiency level in all four language skills. Despite deep interest in the imported Hindi media, there is no evidence of any increase in using the language interactively. The presence of English or Dutch subtitles in Hindi movies triggers little need to learn the language of dialogues in the soap operas or movies on television. As far as media entertainment is concerned, the need to use the language is very limited. I have observed some young people of the post-shift generation in Guyana write down songs from Hindi movies in Roman script in notebooks as a basis to practise singing them. During my interactions with them, I found that except for a word or two they did not generally know the meaning of the lines. This has in no way diminished their enjoyment of singing Hindi songs. Despite the deficit in understanding Hindi language, the Hindi media looks all set to continue to entertain Indo-Caribbeans into the future.

7. Emergence of an intermediate variety

Earlier in Guyana and Trinidad and even now in Suriname, a natural offspring originated from the continuum between the koineised variety and Standard Hindi, and it produced a kind of 'mesolect' (intermediate variety) for those who had some proficiency in the latter. In such a mix, we see a blend of both varieties, though far less animated when compared to the Creole-English continuum in the Caribbean. Effortless mingling of the two varieties without psychological impediment, which some speakers (mostly priests) perceive expedient and which they see within their competence, occurs in two ways. First is the use of the 'lower' variety with occasional interference from Standard Hindi/Urdu, and the second is the use of Standard Hindi/Urdu with frequent interference from the 'lower' variety. In both cases, the use of the high end of the continuum, Standard Hindi, is motivated by its prestige but is also often marked by insufficient control in its usage. Hashami (2016) has documented a similar situation in Bihar itself today, where a contact variety of Hindi has emerged,

East Indian Languages in the Caribbean Diaspora

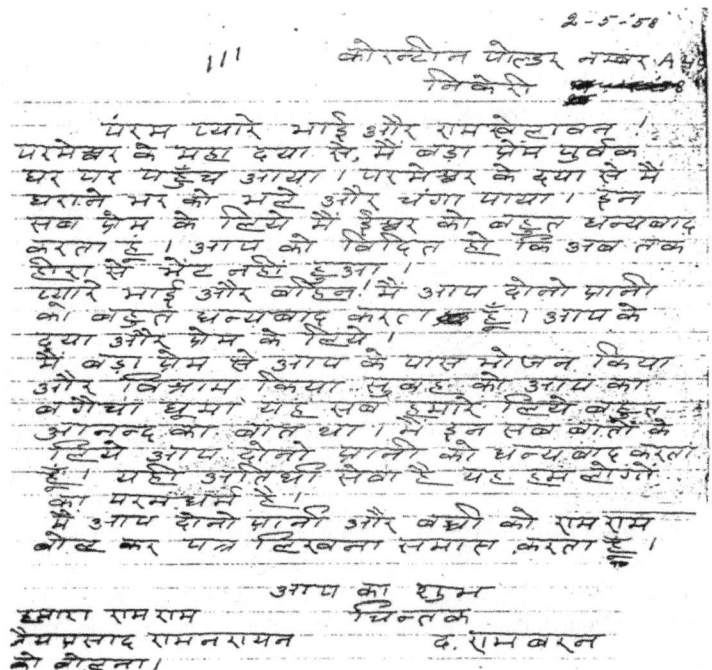

Figure 8.1 *Letter written in Hindi showing influence of Sarnami*

much influenced by Bhojpuri. Mesthrie and Hashami (2021) raise the question whether this is best described as a variety of Hindi influenced by Bhojpuri substrate, or a variety of Bhojpuri influenced by Hindi superstrate.

In all the three communities, priests have managed to acquire and maintain Standard Hindi to some extent. They needed this 'classical' touch to their language to assert their religious authority. Their performance, however, shows considerable influence from below (from their koineised variety). Figure 8.1 is an example of a letter dated 2 May 1958 from a priest in the Nickerie district of Suriname to a priest friend in Crabwood Creek in Guyana.[7] A transliteration and translation are provided below the figure.

Transliteration

May 2, 2058 Corentyn Polder Number A Nickerie
param pyaare bhaaii aur raam khelaavan, parmeshvar **ke** mahaa dayaa se, main baRaa prem **purvak** ghar par pahuNch aayaa.
parmeshvar **ke** dayaa se **maiN** gharaane bhar ko **bhale** aur changaa paayaa.
in sab prem ke liye maiN iishvar ko bahut dhanyavaad kartaa huuN.

Translation

May 2, 2058 Corentyn Polder Number A Nickerie
My dear brother and Ram Khilavan, with the great grace of God, I reached home with good feelings of affection.

With the great grace of God, I found all my extended family members hale and hearty. For all these feelings of love and affection, I thank God a lot.

aap ko vidit ho ki ab tak heeraa se bheNT nahiiN **huaa**.	For your information, I have not met with Heera as of now.
pyaare bhaaii aur bahin, main aap donoN **praanii** *ko* bahut dhanyavaad kartaa huuN. aap **ke** dayaa aur prem ke liye.	Dear brother and sister, I profusely thank both of you for your kindness and affection.
<u>**maiN**</u> baRaa prem se aap ke saath bhojan kiyaa aur vishraam kiyaa. subah *ko* aapkaa **bagaichaa** X ghuumaa.	I ate with you with great cordiality, I took rest; I strolled in your garden during morning hours.
yah sab hamaare liye bahut aanand **kaa** baat **thaa**.	All of this was a matter of great joy for me.
maiN in sab batoN ke liye aap donoN praanii *ko* dhanyavaad kartaa huuN.	I thank both of you for all these things.
yahii **atithii** sevaa hai. yah ham logoN kaa param dharm hai.	This is the hospitality shown to a guest, and this is our great culture.
main aap donoN **praanii** aur bachchoN ko raam raam bol kar patr likhnaa smaapt kartaa huuN.	After greeting both of you and the children, I will stop writing this letter.
aapkaa shubh chintak d. raam baran.	Your well-wisher D. Ram Baran.
hamaaraa raam raam jaiy prasaad raam naraayan ko bolnaa.	Convey my greetings to Jai Prasad Ram Narain.

Key: **Bold** words indicate deviations from gender, number, or spelling of Standard Hindi. **Bold and underlined** words indicate Bihari usage of a subject without the ergative marker *ne*. X denotes a missing postposition. *Italicised* words indicate non-standard use of the postposition).

The above letter is predominantly in Standard Hindi as letter-writing is often considered a formal task. One learns the script while learning Standard Hindi in school. However, variation in gender agreement, verb agreement, ergative subject-marking and spelling variants reflect an imperfect control of the standard variety. One would expect even more variation in the spoken form of such a compromise variety, given that it is produced in real time without the possibility of planning or editing.

8. Relationship between heritage language and culture

A widely believed idea is that if the heritage language is vulnerable, the culture will be lost. However, the empirical evidence from diasporic communities is not in line with this view. Within Indian communities in the Caribbean and in other Western countries, people have been able to preserve significant aspects of their culture through Creole, English, French and Dutch, etc. These Western languages have proved reasonably good vehicles for transmitting religious, philosophical and most socio-cultural practices of their culture. Religious centres in all these countries often use English or another Western language. In homes also, most parents of the diasporic communities lay more emphasis, to the extent possible for them, on passing on their cultural and religious values to the next generation through a Western language, rather than emphasising the use of their heritage language. Among all the components of culture, religion is best preserved in almost all diasporic communities (cf. Rauf 1974, Gambhir 1981). If the young people do not understand the heritage language well, it makes sense to use another language comprehensible to them. Some aspects of material culture in people's day-to-day lives undergo changes no matter what, but the reason for those changes cannot be ascribed to an 'outside' language. These changes are a part of the natural cycle of the times. Some people who wish to dive deeper into religious and philosophical concepts also resort to Western languages for their study. It seems that diasporic communities do strike a balance at the fundamental level between the two cultures they live in – one that provides material gains and the other that maintains their religious and cultural identity, all through a single vehicle of the dominant language of their new homeland.

For most people, language is simply an instrument of oral communication. For many others, language can be a passionate subject to talk about. However, we see ample evidence even among such people who let their heritage language go eventually when they realise that it is not accruing practical benefits for them. My extended interaction with members of the Caribbean communities in Guyana, Trinidad and in the United States has allowed me to detect very closely the fact that the language loss for most people is a comfortable and dispassionate transition to a new reality of life. Even for those who value their heritage language central to cultural maintenance, the loss is not severe. In the above-mentioned nations, people have successfully used English to pass on their cultural principles to younger generations. Most proceedings in Hindu temples, cultural centres, socio-cultural activities and family celebrations are almost exclusively in English or another Western language.

9. Heritage language recession

At the turn of the twentieth century, there was no more linguistic reinforcement from fresh waves of immigration from India after 1917. At this juncture, people finally realised that they belonged to the soil where they had lived for many years, and thus their hopes became entwined with Creole, English or Dutch, which weakened their alignment with the ancestral language(s) from India. Furthermore, the upward mobility in the African-origin population was becoming a reference point for Indian communities in Guyana and Trinidad. At around the 1920s, people recognised the value of education to compete with other sections of the society and of sending their children to school. As the schoolgoing children brought English to their home environment, it further reinforced the language shift.

Language shift in most diasporic communities is a reality that happens sooner or later. The concept of language shift refers to the language shift at the community level, and not to isolated individuals, who may continue to have varying levels of proficiency for personal reasons. Language shift also implies a significant change in patterns of interpersonal communication at the community level and goes much beyond the use of selected words or formulaic expressions retained from the heritage language.

If we look at the social processes of language shift, the socio-economically advanced middle-class group typically leads the change. In diasporic contexts, the decline of a language starts in urban centres with children. The younger generation thus becomes the agent of change when they start bringing home from school the language and culture of their peers. A result of this practice is the gradual changeover of the ethnic language environment at home affecting to some extent the usage of adult members of the families. The inter-generational difference in spoken patterns eventually becomes a warning signal for the future. The language shift spreads gradually from cities to towns and then to villages. Guyanese Bhojpuri's data suggest that it was given up in the capital city of Georgetown at least a generation before it started losing ground in the other areas (Gambhir 1981).

The survival of immigrants' language in a multilingual environment depends on its practical use in real-life contexts. Its usefulness depends on economic advantages accruable from it. The ethnic pride in the language starts to take a back seat in relation to another dominant language like Creole or English, which are perceived to be more advantageous or even prestigious.

My first visit to Guyana and Trinidad was in late 1970s when I found that only the oldest generation of those over fifty-five was able to speak in their heritage language GB, which they did only when they needed to speak in it (for example, with people like me). In their day-to-day interaction, their default language was the local creole, which they used interactively with each other like everyone else in the community. With a little more experience in the community, I was able to see that the younger adults understood the heritage language when spoken to, but could not sustain a conversation in it. The youngest generation neither understood nor had any ability to speak in it, except for a few formulaic phrases and culturally significant words, which they had retained due to their frequency or because of their cultural significance. The inter-generational recession was a clear sign of the language decline.

However, a receding language does not vanish suddenly. When it ceases to be a creative means of interpersonal communication, its fragments, especially in domains of cultural significance, continue to survive. Such domains include food, kinship, religion, social festivals, folk songs, wedding rituals, dresses, and ornaments. Many Indian names have also survived with spellings adapted to the Roman script and pronunciation as understood by English men at the time of original recruitment. The pronunciation and spellings of many of these names are accordingly different from their written version in Standard Hindi. Some examples of male names are *Ramnarine* (for *Ramnarain*), *Ragoonath* (for *Raghunath*), *Jaggernauth* (for *Jagan Nath*), *Seecharan* (for *Shiv Charan*), *Avi Nash* (for *Avinash*). Additonally, many pejorative terms from the original rustic culture have also survived. Both Guyanese Bhojpuri (see Ramdat 1978, Gambhir 1981) and Trinidad Bhojpuri (see Baksh-Soodeen 1995) attest to such usages by both men and women. Evidence from videos on YouTube suggests that such terms are also in use in many circles in Suriname. Most of these usages in all the three countries are related to women and their sexuality. However, as the male domination of these societies is progressively changing, and women are emerging prominently in different professional and powerful roles, many sexually explicit and derogatory words are gradually losing their significance.

Despite the loss of language as a means of communication, the heritage language has lived on in the Caribbean as an icon for political or social purposes. An emotional image of the language is projected finding expression in political or cultural speeches. People continue to retain an emotional identity with the language for a few generations. A few words in the heritage language used strategically in a political speech can be electrifying in triggering ethnic solidarity. Such examples include *jahaajee bhaaii* ('ship brothers' – referring to those who came on ships and lived in their new land together, jettisoning their caste and regional differences), *bhaiiyo aur bahno* ('brothers and sisters'), occasionally mildly abusive words like *namak-haraam* ('disloyal'), or *poohar* ('inexperienced, one deprived of vitality') used sarcastically to publicly criticise someone.[8] Another example of iconic or symbolic use of the language over functionality is available from political demands in 1976 for teaching Hindi in Guyanese schools. The government consented to the community demand and introduced the language in some schools during the 1980s, but unfortunately there were few or no takers. Obviously, people's demand was out of reverence for the language, but they saw no practical value in it when confronted with the option to study it in real life.

10. Survival of Sarnami

In Suriname, maintenance of the heritage language Sarnami has a better history, which is used there up to this day. While the loss of immigrant languages within two or three generations has been the norm in many Western nations, Suriname is a beacon of success in upholding Indo-Surinamese traditional speech. Even after about 150 years, Sarnami is still a spoken language in many sections of everyday life. In contrast, while Indo-Surinamese have been able to keep their heritage language alive, the use of the heritage language in Guyana and Trinidad began declining around the 1920s. How do we explain this important difference in two adjacent countries with a similar history of labour importation from India and Western imperialism ruling their lives in their new homelands?

The Dutch government made primary education mandatory for all children between the ages of seven and twelve years and introduced Hindi as a subject in schools (Adhin 1973). In Suriname, the Christian missionaries – the Moravian Church, the Roman Catholic Church, and the Summer Institute of Linguistics (recently renamed SIL International) – had strategies that favoured the immigrant language maintenance. All of them recognised Indian needs, which they believed was an easier path for them to achieve their evangelical goals. In particular, the Moravian Church took the teaching of Hindi very seriously (see Damsteegt 1988 for details). The first two groups incorporated Hindi in the school curriculum to encourage Indian parents to send their children to schools. The McNeil Chimman Lal report of 1914 confirms this when it states that the teaching of Hindustani helped increased attendance in schools. The missionaries did not see the teaching of Hindi as contradictory to their mission to expose children to Christian doctrines through stories and songs in learners' heritage languages. At a later stage, the Moravians decided to teach Sarnami to women and children, and Hindi to men, which they thought was more in line with the hierarchical culture of Indians. Thus, the missionaries were very sensitive to Indian needs and made different experiments with language teaching, without compromising, of course, their own religious aspirations.

The third evangelical group, the Summer Institute of Linguistics, was also language-oriented in Suriname. The group published a series of books in Sarnami that contained Biblical stories. The Moravian Church's and the Roman Catholic Church's success prompted the Summer Institute of Linguistics to go a step further. During the 1970s the Institute published seven booklets with Biblical stories written in Sarnami in Roman script. The eighth book consisted of useful expressions in Sarnami, with translation into Dutch, English and the local creole Sranan Tongo. The first seven publications are as follows:

1. *Jiesoe Masie e marne aure oethal ke kahanie* ('Jesus Christ Death and Resurrection story')
2. *Estar ke kahaanie* ('Easter story')
3. *Jisoe Masie ke djaanam dien ke kahaanie* ('Jesus Christ birthday story')
4. *Joona ke kahanie* ('The story of Jonah')
5. *Das djanaawar ke khiesa* ('Ten animals story')
6. *India ke tien khiesa* ('Three stories from India')
7. *Daaniejel ke aur okar sanghatian ke kahanie* ('The story of Daniel and his friends')

Barz (1988) also mentions a few later SIL publications, which were not related to the gospel but contained secular animal stories. Below is an excerpt from a Sarnami biblical story reproduced from *Jiesoe Masie ke marne aur Oethal ke kahanie* ('Jesus Christ Death and Resurrection story'), one of the seven books mentioned above:

> Jiesoe pahaar par raha – Ek dien Jissoe Peetras ke aur Joehanas ke aur Jakoobas ke leegail ekgo oetja pahaar par. Oe hoewa par praatna kare gail. Okar tien tjilaalogan bahoet thak gail raha aur soete lagal. tab djab Jiesoe praatna karat raha tab okar tjehera aur okar kapra soeroe bhail tjhamke. Aur okar tien tjilaalogan djaagail aur dekhies kie doei aadmielog ail raha. [...]

> ['Jesus was on the mountain. One day Jesus took Peter and Johannes and James up on a high mountain. He went there to pray. His three friends were very tired and started falling asleep. While Jesus was praying, his face and clothes began to shine. His three friends woke up and saw that two men had come. [...]')

Since most Indo-Surinamese and their children understood Dutch reasonably well by this time, one could ask why the missionaries chose Sarnami and not Dutch for their biblical mission. The answer lies in the Evangelists' own perception of the situation. In their view, their publications in Sarnami created a gregarious meeting point between them and the Indian community. Evangelists wanted to further the convivial feeling with Indians by publishing secular animal stories as part of their meticulous strategy to suggest to the Indian mind that their focus was educational, and not religious.

For Indo-Surinamese parents, the use of their heritage language and the linguistic input provided in schools came from a respected and educated source. The Indian parents must have been happy to see a formal platform for their heritage language in the written form. It seems that these publications helped Indo-Surinamese to perceive their hitherto non-prestigious language (in their own eyes) in more positive light. The SIL publications also inspired a series of creative writings in Sarnami in later years (see Barz 1988 for details).

Two more factors bolstered the reinforcement of Sarnami. One was the upsurge of Sarnami writings after the pro-Sarnami movement in the Netherlands, where many Suriname Indians had migrated in 1975. These writings included collections of poems, novelettes, stories, plays and general articles. A Sarnami grammar was also produced, along with two language courses in Sarnami (see Damsteegt 1988 for details). The second factor was the extensive exposure to Sarnami and Hindi on television, on radio, in Bollywood movies, in plays, in literary writings,[9] in the enactment of the Ramayana epic story, in magazines, in Bible translations, in court summons, etc. (Bajnath 2019). All these factors contributed to substantially strengthen the ongoing use of Sarnami and Hindi in Suriname. The publication of Sarnami grammar certainly enhanced the prestige of Sarnami, albeit in the eyes of a small section of the speech community members who were aware of it.

In contrast, Guyana and Trinidad's administrative environment treated Indians like slaves (cf. Tinker 1974). Their focus was to entice Indian labourers to stay in the colonies for the work for which they were brought there. Although Canadian Presbyterian missionaries, who worked in Trinidad and Guyana, also taught Hindi in schools for Indians, governmental policies showed minimum interest in the emotional and cultural needs of Indians. Thus, unlike in Suriname there was little significance attached to the heritage languages of East Indians in Guyana and Trinidad.

In the light of a positive history of Sarnami and Hindi in Suriname, and a differential one in the use of Dutch and English, we arrive at the following reasons why the Indic languages survived in Suriname better than in the other two countries. The reasons are a combination of endogenous and exogenous factors.

10.1 Endogenous factors

(a) Dutch could not have been as overpowering for Indo-Surinamese as English had proved for Indo-Guyanese and Indo-Trinidadians. Indo-Surinamese people also had come from British-dominated colonial India, and they must have held the English language in high esteem. Even during their journey to Suriname, they dealt with English-speaking officers on their ships. In sum, the differential between the supremacy of English and Dutch did not influence Indian minds equally.

(b) Many indentured labourers who had come to Suriname were unsure about their long-term stay in the country. About 12,000 labourers, which was approximately one-third of the total Indian workforce in Suriname, did return to India after completing their contractual period. They certainly wanted to maintain their culture, including their language, while in Suriname, as was confirmed in the McNeil Chimman Lal Report[10] of 1914. Witnessing the successful return to India of large numbers of migrants possibly also had a positive impact on their minds about their self-image and their culture.

10.2 Exogenous factors

(a) As mentioned above, the Dutch rulers' policy regarding Indians' education and culture was more sympathetic than that of the British.

(b) The strategies of evangelical groups in Dutch Suriname were more in line with Indians' linguistic needs than in the other two British colonies.
(c) Exposure through movies, media, Hindi education, Indian cultural activities, etc., was extensive in the three Caribbean countries since 1962 (cf. Hosein 1976). Combined with the other exclusive factors in Suriname, the media presumably made greater positive impact while their heritage language was alive.

Although Sarnami and Hindi in Suriname have thus far managed to survive, unfortunately it is also true that there are now signs of incipient shift. Their erosion, not perceptible to the uninitiated, has been in progress for more than fifty years. The Hagoort and Schotel study of 1982 (quoted in Damsteegt 1988) found that Hindustani children in Paramaribo schools had the following patterns of use of Sarnami.

1. 100 per cent claimed to use it with their grandparents.
2. 64.8 per cent claimed to use it with their parents
3. 49.1 per cent claimed to use it with their own generation

The study clearly showed a gradual generational decline in the use of Sarnami within the community. Even though the schoolchildren in Paramaribo were still using Sarnami to a considerable extent in communication across the three generations, the figures do show lesser use amongst themselves. My ongoing work in this regard based on online questionnaires suggests that the language shift has advanced considerably since then (Gambhir in preparation). Nevertheless, attitudes among older people remain positive towards Indian languages and culture. Most Indo-Surinamese consider Sarnami and Hindi important languages for their religious services, cultural survival, entertainment needs and social interaction. A slight majority of respondents considered Sarnami and Hindi more important than Dutch and English for their entertainment needs on television (Gambhir in preparation). Many Indo-Surinamese also claimed using Hindi (70.2 per cent), Sarnami (27.7 per cent) and Sanskrit (2.1 per cent) in their written invitation cards for social events. The current president of Suriname, Mr Chan Santokhi, who is of Indian origin, took his oath of office in Sanskrit in 2020. Some efforts are also being made in promoting the use of Sarnami and Hindi in the Netherlands, where about 200,000 Indo-Surinamese currently live. However, although some groups there are active in language preservation and promotion, many Indo-Surinamese there also now communicate with each other in Dutch, even in social and cultural domains.

More worryingly, in a recent online panel discussion organised by the Indo-Caribbean Cultural Centre on the status of traditional Indian languages, a linguist-panelist from Suriname, Wanita Ramnath, mentioned that 'if you speak with the younger generation, they are ashamed of speaking in Sarnami'.[11] Such negative attitudes are a warning signal for language endangerment in a not-too-distant future. It is hoped that the cultural eminence of the heritage languages in Suriname will contribute to language maintenance, despite the signs of actual shift.

11. Conclusion

Historically, the emergent koines of the Caribbean were primarily based on the demographic preponderance of their speakers among the multitude of related varieties. These speakers became a reference group for later arrivals. The Indian koines, which emerged in the different forms of Bhojpuri in the Caribbean, had their heyday for almost eighty years in Guyana and Trinidad. Eventually they were unable to resist the pressure of English, whose prominence had grown in homes. Although Sarnami in Suriname continues to be used to this day, it is also beginning to show distinct signs of receding under the influence of Dutch and to some extent of English. However, linguistic activism as a socio-cultural activity carried out by community members can turn this around, if it manages to recreate real-life needs for the use of the heritage language in socio-cultural domains. The case of Guyana and Trinidad revival may require Herculean efforts but in the case of Suriname, the ongoing language loss can still be reversed with systematic planning.

Notes

1. See Gambhir (2022) for details on this aspect of language maintenance and language loss.
2. The Slavery Abolition Act 1833 was an act of the British Parliament to abolish slavery in most British colonies. It received Royal assent on 28 August1833 and became effective on 1 August 1834.
3. ACTFL stands for the American Council on the Teaching of Foreign Languages – see https://www.actfl.org/sites/default/files/guidelines/ACTFLProficiencyGuidelines2012.pdf.
4. This observation is not changed by subsequent further subdivisions of these territories, since not many migrants had emanated from what became the newer territories of Jharkhand and Uttarakhand, carved out of Bihar and UP respectively in 2000 CE.
5. Grierson provided alternate forms of *dekhe* in simple present and present conditional. His example was in the first person, which I have changed to second person, but Grierson did not provide its usage in a sentence.
6. Mesthrie (1992) mentions that a generation ago the colloquial in-group label in South Africa was *Kalkatiyaa baat* 'language of those who had come via Calcutta port', with *Hindi* as the official out-group term. A few families knew the term *Bhojpuri*. The people themselves were referred to as *Kalkatiyaa loNg*, or *Hindustani*, the latter mainly as an out-group term.
7. Used with family permission, to whom my gratitude is hereby expressed.
8. I acknowledge help from Raviji of Trinidad and Dr Maurits Hassankhan of Suriname for providing these examples.
9. Some examples are *gyaan prakaash* (1952), *dohaa shikshaavalii* ((1953) by Munshi Rahman Khan (1874–1972)); *chandra muktaavali* (1985) by Chandra Mohan Singh; *is ghaaT ko chhoR us ghaaT gaye* (2020) by Sharmila Ramratan.
10. McNeill and Chimman Lal mention in 1914 that teaching 'Hindustani' has 'gratifying results as regards the attendance at the schools', adding that parents 'who

have not finally decided to settle in the Colony naturally regard Dutch as an even less attractive medium of instruction than English'.
11. https://www.youtube.com/watch?v=Hb3GUilVtsA (time counter 37.0 into 1:29 minute video).

References

Adhin, J. H. 1964. *Geromaniseerde spelling van het Sarnami Hindustani*. Paramaribo: Bureau Volkeslectuur.

Adhin, J. H. 1973. Honderd Jaar Onderwijsontwikkeling in Vogelvlucht. In J. H. Adhin (ed.), *100 Jaar Surinam e*. Paramaribo: Nationale Stichting H indostaanse Immigratie, pp. 85–111.

Bajnath, K. 2019. Survival of the Indian language of origin in Suriname. In A. Murugaiyan (ed.), *Langues de l'Inde en Diasporas*. Paris: Scitep Éditions, pp. 323–42.

Baksh-Soodeen, Rawwida. 1995. *A Historical Perspective on the Lexicon of Trinidadian English*. PhD dissertation, St Augustine, Trinidad and Tobago, University of the West Indies.

Barz, R. 1988. Language maintenance and literary use: The case of Mauritian Bhojpuri, Sarnami and Fiji Hindi. In R. K. Barz and J. Siegel (eds), *Language Transplanted*. Wiesbaden: Otto Harrassowitz, pp. 197–220.

Bhatia, T. 1983. Trinidad Hindi: Three generations of a transplanted variety. *Studies in the Linguistic Sciences*, 11 (2): 135–50.

Bhatia, T. 1988. Trinidad Hindi: Its genesis and a generational profile. In R. K. Barz and J. Siegel (eds), *Language Transplanted*. Wiesbaden: Otto Harrassowitz, pp. 179–96.

Bhimull, V. 2019. The misunderstood language of Caribbean Hindustani. In A. Murugaiyan (ed.), *Langues de l'Inde en Diasporas*. Paris: Scitep Éditions, pp. 343–60.

Bosch, T. 1978. Margenes de citas en el dialect hindostan de Suriname. In S. H. Levinsohn (ed.), *Lenguasde Panama*, vol. 5, Laestructura de dialogo en el discurso narrative. Panama: Instituto Nacional de Cultura.

Britain, D. and P. Trudgill. 1999. Migration, new dialect formation and sociolinguistic refunctionalisation: Reallocation as an outcome of dialect contact. *Transactions of the Philological Society*, 97 (2): 245–56.

Damsteegt, T. 1983. De basis van het Sarnami. *Lalla Rookh*, 6 (8): 10–16.

Damsteegt, T. 1988. Sarnami: A living language. In R. K. Barz and J. Siegel (eds), *Language Transplanted*. Wiesbaden: Otto Harrassowitz, pp. 95–120.

Domingue, N. 1971. *Bhojpuri and Creole in Mauritius: A Study of Linguistic Interference and its Consequences in Regard to Synchronic Variation and Language Change*. Doctoral dissertation, University of Texas.

Durban, M. 1973. Formal changes in Trinidad Hindi as a result of language adaptation. *American Anthropologist*, 75 (5): 1290–1304.

Gambhir, S. 1981. *The East Indian Speech Community in Guyana: A Sociolinguistic Study with Special Reference to Koine Formation*. Doctoral dissertation in Linguistics, University of Pennsylvania.

Gambhir, S. 1983a. Diglossia in dying languages: A case of Guyanese Bhojpuri and Standard Hindi. *Anthropological Linguistics*, 25 (1): 28–38.

Gambhir, S. 1983b. Two koines compared: Guyanese Bhojpuri and Calcutta Bazar Hindustani. *International Journal of Dravidian Linguistics*, pp. 471–80.

Gambhir, S. 1988. The modern Indian diaspora and language. In Peter Gaeffke and David Utz (eds), *The Countries of South Asia: Boundaries, Extensions, and Interrelations*. Philadelphia, PA: Department of South Asia Regional Studies, pp. 147–57.

Gambhir, S. 2022. The Indian diaspora: Language maintenance and loss. In *The Cambridge Handbook of Language Contact Vol. 2: Multilingualism and Population Structure* ed. by Salikoko S. Mufwene and Anna Maria Cambridge U.K.: Cambridge University Press.

Gautam, M. 1999. The construction of the Indian image in Suriname: Deconstructing colonial derogatory notions and reconstructing Indian identity. In M. Gosine and Dhanpal Narine (eds), *Sojourners to Settlers: Indian Immigrants in the Caribbean and the Americas*. New York: Windsor Press.

Gautam, M. 2017. *surinaam meN hindii bhaashaa kaa itihaas*. In Gambhir (1917): 71–87.

Govind, R. 1980. *Some Basic Transformations in Bhojpuri*. MPhil dissertation, University of Delhi.

Grierson, G. A. 1903. *Linguistic Survey of India, Vol. V Part II*. Delhi: Motilal Banarsidas (reprint 1963).

Hashami, Sabiha. 2016. *Contact Hindi in Bihar and Jharkhand: Structure and Use*. Unpublished PhD thesis, Jawaharlal Nehru University.

Hoernle, A. F. 1880. *Gaudian Languages with Special Reference to Eastern Hindi*. London: Trubner & Co.

Hosein, E. N. 1976. The problem of imported television content in the Commonwealth Caribbean. *Journal of Caribbean Culture*, 22 (4).

Huiskamp, A. B. 1978. *Languages of the Guianas*, Vol. 2. Suriname: Summer Institute of Linguistics.

Huiskamp, A. B. 1980. SOEROE SE SOEROE KAR 2 (An audio-visual course in Sarnami Hindustani for beginners [Part 2]/Een audio-visuele cursus Sarnami Hindoestani voor beginners [Deel 2]). In *Languages of the Guianas*, Vol. 4. Suriname: Summer Institute of Linguistics.

Kerswill, P. and A. Williams. 2000. Creating a new town koine: Children and language change in Milton Keynes. *Language in Society*, 29: 65–115.

Kishna, S. 1981. The recipient state construction in Sarnami. In T. Hoekstra et al. (eds), *Perspectives on Functional Grammar*. Dordrecht: Foris Publications, pp. 135–56.

Marhe, R. M. 1985. *Sarnami Byakaran: een elementaire grammatica van het Sarnami*. Leidschendam: Stitching voor Surinamers.

Mesthrie, R. 1992. *Language in Indenture: A Sociolinguistic History of Bhojpuri in South Africa*. London: Routledge.

Mesthrie, Rajend and Sabiha Hashami. 2021. Connecting the contact Hindi of Bihar with the Bhojpuri-Hindi diaspora. In Tariq Khan (ed.), *Alternative Horizons in Linguistics: A Festschrift in Honour of Prof. Panchanan Mohanty*. Munich: Lincom (Lincom Studies in Linguistics and Culture 01), pp. 150–8.

Moag, R. 1977. *Fiji Hindi: A Basic Course and Reference Grammar*. Canberra: Australian National University Press.

Mohan, P. 1978. *Trinidad Bhojpuri: A Morphological Study*. PhD dissertation. Ann Arbor: University of Michigan.

Mohan, P. and P. Zador. 1986. Discontinuity in a life cycle: The death of Trinidad Bhojpuri. *Language*, 62 (2): 291–319.

Murugaiyan, A. 2019. *Langues de l'Inde en Diasporas*. Paris: Scitep Éditions.

Ramdat, K. 1978. Some areas of Indic influence in the creolized English of East Indians in Guyana. Paper presented at the Society for Caribbean Linguistics at Barbados.

Rauf, M. A. 1974. *Indian Village in Guyana*. Leiden: E. J. Brill.

Rickford, John (ed.). 1978. *A Festival of Guyanese Words*. Georgetown: University of Guyana.

Roseval, H. 1977. *Sarnami Hindi:eenvoudige handleiding*. Utrecht: Stitching Landelijke Federatie van Welzijnsstichtingen.

Satyanath, S. 2003. On the maintenance of transplanted Indian languages overseas. In Rekha Sharma and E. Annamalai (eds), *Indian Diaspora: In Search of Identity*. Mysore: Central Institute of Indian Languages, pp. 85–104.

Siegel, J. 1985. Koines and koineization. *Language in Society*, 14: 357–78.

Southworth, F. 1968. Grierson revisited: The inner and outer groups of Indo Aryan. Paper presented at the 10th International Conference of Anthropology at New Delhi.

Tinker, H. 1974. *A New System of Slavery: The Export of Indian Labor Overseas 1830–1920*. Oxford: Oxford University Press.

Tiwari, U. 1960. *The Origin and Development of Bhojpuri*. Calcutta: The Asiatic Society.

Trudgill, P. 1986. *Dialects in Contact*. Oxford: Basil Blackwell.

Weinreich, U. 1974. *Language in Contact: Findings and Problems*. The Hague: Mouton.

Yakpo, K. 2017. Out of India: Contact-induced change in Caribbean Hindustani. In Kofi Yakpo et al. (eds), *Boundaries and Bridges: Language Contact in Multilingual Ecologies*. Berlin: Gruyter Mouton, pp. 129–49.

CHAPTER 9

A Sociolinguistic Investigation of the Retention of Ancestral Dialect Features in Kokni Spoken in Cape Town

Ruta Paradkar

1. Introduction

In this chapter, the retention of some ancestral dialect features in the language of a diaspora of the Kokni Muslims in the South African city of Cape Town will be examined. This retention is fairly remarkable since the diaspora of the Koknis of Cape Town (henceforth, KCT) dates back to well over a hundred years. The focus of this chapter will be the examination of the specific regional features from the areas of origin in India and their retention in the Kokni speech by the KCT community in Cape Town. The features examined in the chapter are taken from the samples of the KCT Kokni collected in various data-collection visits made to Cape Town over a period of three years. With the help of the earlier literature on this Kokni language variety in India as well as contemporary data, these features that mark the region-based varieties in Cape Town will be compared with the specific areas of origin in India.

The maintenance of at least some grammatical features that index to specific Indian regions (villages, in the case of KCT) for over a century, thereby inhibiting the development of a fully homogenous Cape Town Kokni variety, is striking and calls for an examination of the possible causes for the maintenance of variation. In the case of KCT Kokni, the likely reasons can be inferred from the migration history and the social structure of the KCT community. The place of Kokni in Cape Town in comparison with the other Indian languages in diaspora in South Africa (Bhojpuri, Tamil, Telugu and Gujarati), both in terms of the migration history and linguistic development after migration, has been assessed in Mesthrie (2021, and in this volume). After discussing each diaspora situation, Mesthrie notes that with varying degrees of initial dialect input, Bhojpuri and Telugu in South Africa emerged as koines, while Tamil and Cape Town Gujarati were dominated by one prominent dialect. He observes that Kokni in comparison has moderate initial regional diversity; moderate internal contact; and differential persistence of village features (ibid.). The discussions in this chapter are centred around the context of the migration that contributed to the initial diversity in input varieties, the status of Kokni in Cape Town today based on the domains of language use of the KCT community, and the grammatical features from the ancestral villages retained in KCT Kokni today.

2. Kokni migration to Cape Town

The migration of the Koknis to Cape Town began towards the end of the nineteenth century from the Konkan region of the state of Maharashtra in India. Among the Indian diaspora in South Africa, the Kokni community has resided and worked in the city of Cape Town for over 140 years. They were historically classified as 'passenger Indians' in the literature, as distinct from the contract-bound indentured migrants. Starting with menial jobs, the early migrants worked hard to establish businesses like grocery stores, butchery shops, etc. (Dhupelia-Mesthrie 2009). Mesthrie (2008) identifies three periods of movements out of India, out of which the migration from the Konkan coast to Cape Town can be classified among the 'second diaspora' that took place in the era of European imperialism.

The coastal belt in the state of Maharashtra in India that lies between the western ghats and the Arabian Sea is broadly referred to as the Konkan region. Among various other communities, it is home to the Konkani Muslim settlements that form pockets (of entire villages or parts of villages) scattered across the region. The ancestral villages reported by the KCTs in Cape Town are located in two districts in the Konkan region – Raigad and Ratnagiri. The subdivisions of these two districts (administrative units referred to as *talukas*) that include the ancestral villages reported in the database are Murud, Mangaon, Mahad, Mhasla, Shrivardhan (five out of the total fifteen talukas) in the Raigad district, and Khed, Chiplun, Sangameshwar and Mandangad (four out of the nine talukas) in the Ratnagiri district. Map 9.1 shows the location of the sending areas in India in the Raigad and Ratnagiri districts of the state of Maharashtra in India.

The Konkan region is mostly comprised of rural or semi-urban areas. Many of the villages that were visited in the course of fieldwork are situated in remote locations even today. The region of out-migration indicated in Map 9.1 expands over a small territory in the two districts mentioned above. Out-migration in search of better opportunities from the Konkan region is fairly common among all communities, but the migration to South Africa was limited to the Konkani Muslim community. The Konkani Muslim migration to South Africa out of the villages in Ratnagiri was noted as early as 1920 and 1929 in the land records in the Sangameshwar and Khed talukas (Yamin 1991). Gogate (1991) notes the historical links of trade of the Konkani Muslims from Ratnagiri with the African nations in her study of the recent migration of the same community to the Gulf countries.

The Kokni Muslims migrated to South Africa to improve the economic conditions of their families in India. The Konkani migration pattern was of 'chain migration' in which young male members of the family followed the elder male members who had already migrated. In the early years, the migrants preferred not to establish families in South Africa as it increased their living costs. The migration was also 'circular', with the migrants typically working in South Africa for two or three years and returning to the village to rest and recuperate for a similar duration. In this way, they divided their working years between India and South Africa and maintained a strong attachment with their villages in India. The goal of the early migrants was to permanently return to India after retirement, after ensuring that their son was settled in the business in Cape Town. This became more and more difficult with the introduction of new immigration laws,

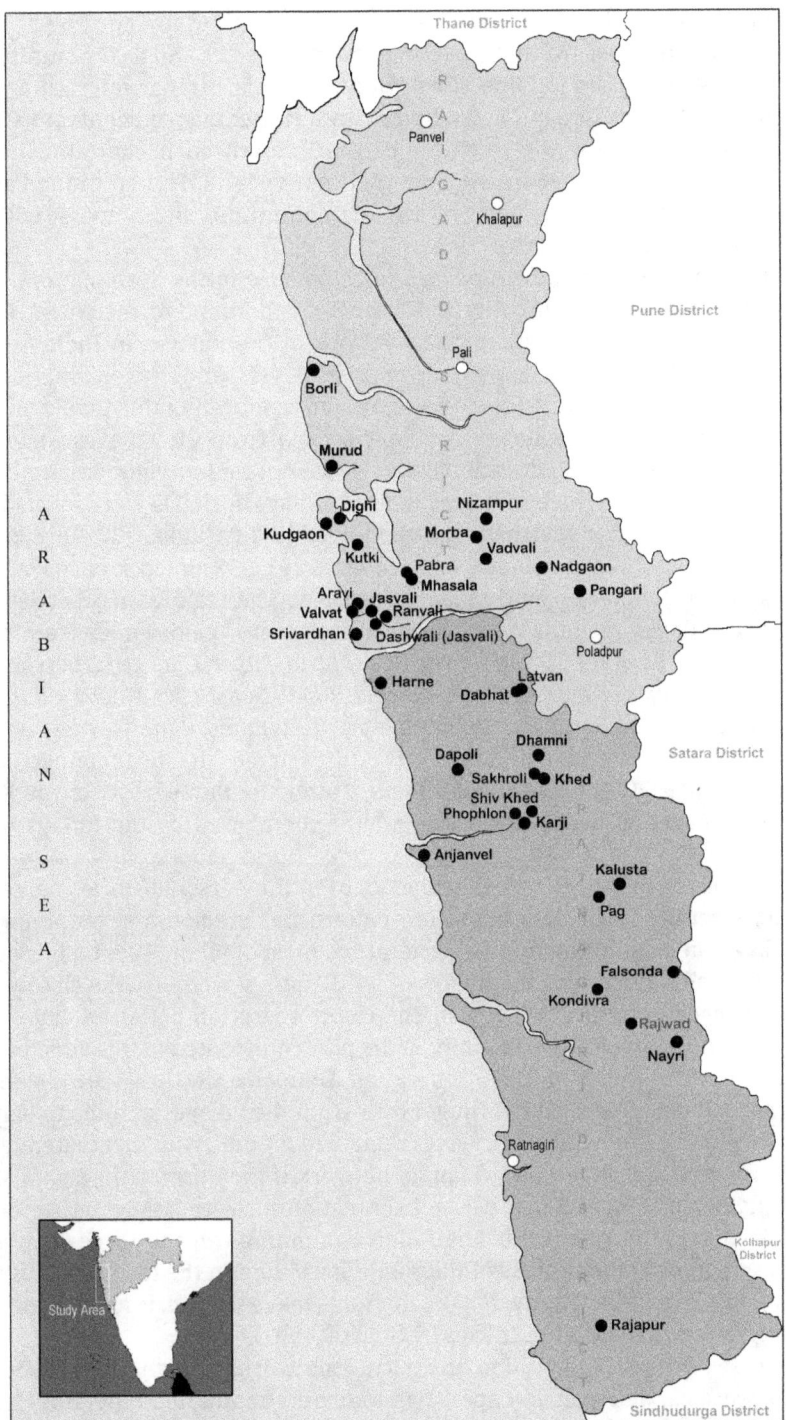

Map 9.1 *Sending areas in the Kokan, Maharashtra State, India*
Source: Kulkarni-Joshi, Mesthrie and Pradhan (2021).

and slowly the Kokni Muslims started establishing families in Cape Town. The circular migration pattern gradually declined over the years and a community of the Kokni migrants emerged in Cape Town. However, this circular migration pattern meant that the Koknis in Cape Town had maintained continued contact with their villages of origin, unlike the migrants of the indentured background in South Africa, who were largely separated from their native land. This continued association is reflected in various aspects of the KCT community life, some of which are briefly stated below.

The KCT community members played an active role in the development of their ancestral villages while improving the financial conditions of their own families since the early days of migration. Charity work in the villages in India – such as construction of hospitals, schools and mosques – was undertaken by the village societies formed in Cape Town and the signs commemorating this involvement are easily noticeable in these villages. A village society from the villages Kalusta and Karji named 'Kalusta Karji Educational Society' celebrated its eightieth anniversary in Cape Town in 2010, which indicates that the village societies were formed in the early years of migration. Mesthrie, Kulkarni-Joshi and Paradkar (2017) report on a cricket tournament held in Rylands, Cape Town in 2012–13 aimed at encouraging the young people of Kokni descent to play more sport. The team names corresponded to ancestral villages in India, coupled with prominent team names from the IPL (Indian Premier League). These were the *Kalusta Super Chargers, Latvan Lions, Sangameshwar Super Kings, Habsani Royals, Khed Badshahs, Morba Challengers, Karji Night Riders* and *Furus Phantoms*. Signage in Rylands, Cape Town, where most of the KCT community resides, quite often features names that bear connection with the Indian villages, (e.g. shops named *Janjira*, after the famous fort in the Konkan coast). The villages of origin are thus visibly remembered by the Koknis of Cape Town.

The attachment to the villages is also evident in the personal stories narrated by the interviewees. The circular migration pattern has created a strong impression of the villages at least for today's old generation, most of whom spent a few years in India in their childhood. The family ties of a KCT family were usually closely linked with the villages of origin in the past. The chain migration pattern along with the marriage norms in the KCT community in the past contributed to this attachment. In her study on the archives of Indian migration, Dhupelia-Mesthrie (2014) elaborates on how sons and nephews were brought over from the villages in India to help with the growing businesses while their wives remained in India with their extended families. Marriage within the extended family network is the norm in the Kokni Muslim community, which resulted in the establishment of intricate family networks in the villages in India. The reliance of the Kokni community on the three-generational family set-up in both the process of migration itself, and in the facilitation of migration by taking care of the family that the migrants leave behind, is noted in her study on the migration to the Gulf countries by Gogate (1991).

In the case of the KCT migration, these same networks of high significance to the migrants were carried over to Cape Town and were maintained there. As a result, a potential spouse in an arranged marriage even in Cape Town was usually chosen from the family network with shared roots in the Indian villages. A special term *bhargavtso* (meaning 'belonging to an outside village' in Kokni) for a spouse who did not belong to the same village roots was reported by some interviewees. This term was not mentioned by interviewees in the short fieldwork trips to the ancestral villages in the Konkan region in India. However, it was said there that arranging marriages in far-off villages was a rare phenomenon among the Konkan villages. It is likely that arranging marriages within the close proximity of villages is merely a matter of convenience in the Konkan. However, the dependence of migrants on the networks established through these locally arranged marriages has likely led to the rise of taboos such as *'bhargavtso'* in the post-migration transnational community. This strong attachment with the villages influenced Kokni speech in Cape Town to some extent as shown in the rest of this chapter.

3. Kokni situation in Cape Town today

An initial overview of Kokni speech in Cape Town is provided in Mesthrie, Kulkarni-Joshi and Paradkar (2017). They note that the survival of the Kokni language is remarkable for well over a century, despite it being restricted to a considerably smaller community in Cape Town. However, they also note that long-term maintenance of Kokni is a significant challenge.

Figure 9.1 represents the average KCT Kokni use in the family domain. An elaborate list of eighteen interlocutors in the family domain was prepared and the respondents in all age groups were asked to report the frequency of their Kokni language use with each of these eighteen interlocutors. The list was further grouped according to the generations to which they belong: grandparents' generation (father's mother, father's father, mother's mother, mother's father, grandparents-in-law); parents' generation (father, mother, father's sister, father's brother, mother's sister, mother's brother, mother-in-law, father-in-law); same age generation (sister, brother and spouse); and children's generation (son and daughter). A clear pattern of inter-generational decline in the KCT Kokni usage can be observed in Figure 9.1.

It can be observed in Figure 9.2 that Kokni is sparsely used in various social domains in Cape Town by all three generations of the KCT community, and that Afrikaans and English have taken over.

In section 2, the continued contact of the KCT community members with their ancestral villages was noted. With the help of Figures 9.1 and 9.2, it can be established that the usage of Kokni was mainly restricted to the family domain, and that it has declined inter-generationally. Both these serve as the factors that possibly contributed to the retention of a few region-based distinctions in the KCT Kokni that is discussed in this chapter.

Based on these region-based distinctions, three broad groups of villages out of which the distinct features originate in the Kokni spoken in Cape Town have been identified. These groups are referred to as the KALUSTA-variety, LATVAN-variety and HABSAN variety (where the upper-case terms KALUSTA, LATVAN and HABSAN refer to ancestral origin in these and the surrounding group of villages in India where social linkages are the strongest). The SANGAMESHWAR-variety from the southernmost region in Map 9.1 will also be briefly referred to in the discussion in section 6.3.

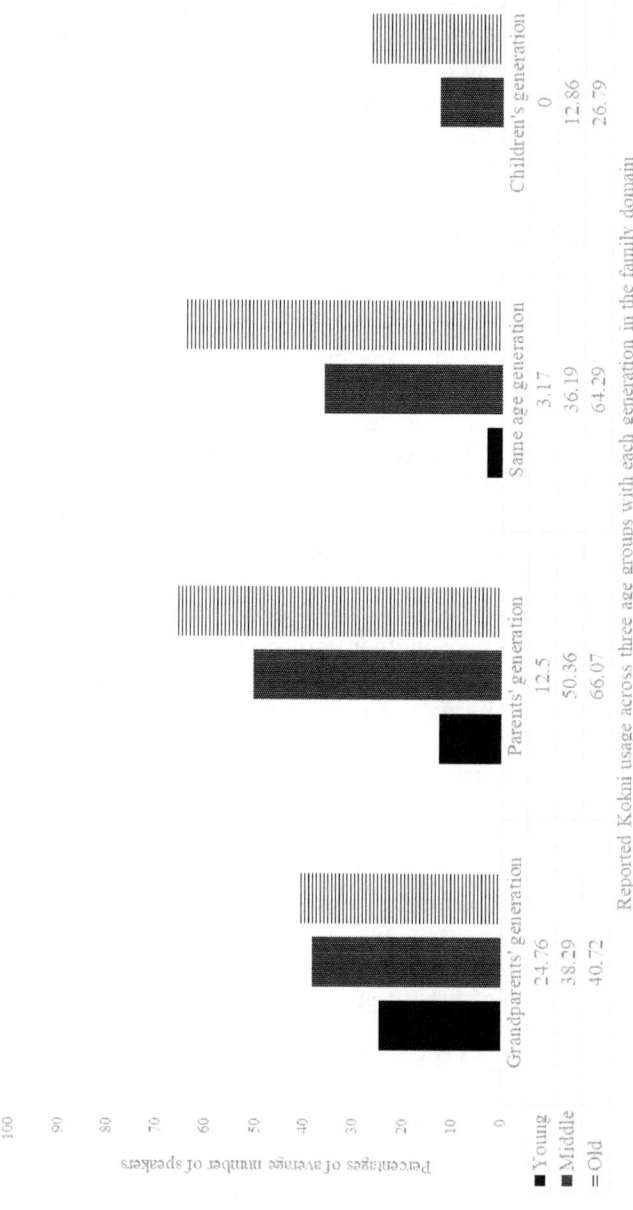

Figure 9.1 *Average Kokni use in the family domain across young, middle and old age groups*

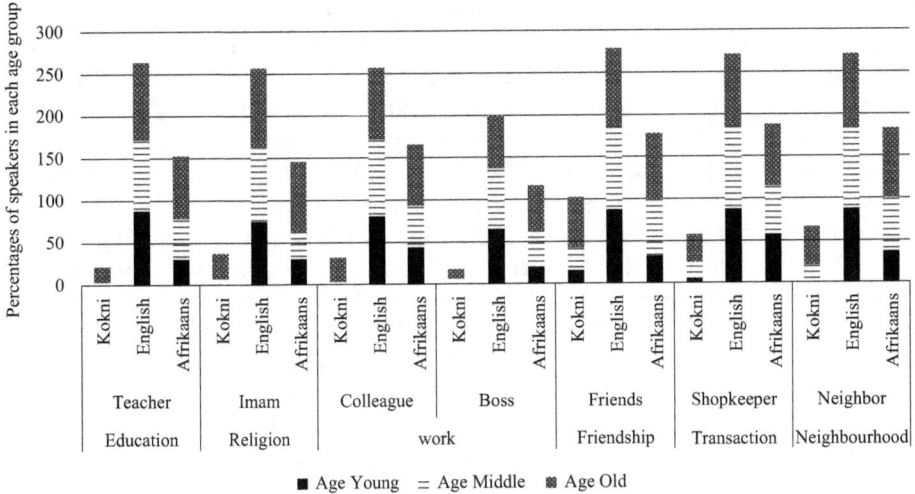

Figure 9.2 *Kokni, English and Afrikaans usage in various social domains among the young, middle and old age groups. The domain of language use and an interlocutor are represented on the x-axis*

4. Previous sources on the language varieties of the Konkan

The Linguistic Survey of India edited by Grierson is the earliest and the most wide-ranging documentation of the language varieties spoken in the area of outmigration in the Konkan. In volume VII of the *LSI*, Grierson (1905) described the varieties spoken in the Konkan region as the 'Konkan standard of Marathi'. He defined this standard as 'the form of speech intermediary between that dialect (Konkani) and the Standard form of Marathi current in the Dekhan' (1905: 61) to avoid confusion with either Konkani (language of the southern Konkan) or Marathi of the Deccan. Grierson remarks that the varieties under the Konkan standard partly denote locality and partly caste or occupation. Most of the area denoted in Map 9.1 falls under the region where the Konkan standard varieties are spoken, except some varieties in the Ratnagiri district which are classified under Konkani or Marathi.

For the sake of this chapter, those specimens from the *LSI* which belong to the regions which can be loosely mapped onto the areas of origin of the KCT Koknis will be considered, irrespective of occupation or caste. Since specimens of the Kokni Muslims from Raigad and Ratnagiri districts are not given in the *LSI*, this will give a general idea as to the regional characteristics of these varieties in 1905.

Grierson is a valuable resource since it is contemporaneous with the period when migration started. Though the samples are highly helpful in understanding the Konkan standard speech, a discussion regarding the samples and their relevance to the KCT study is necessary. Though the criteria for choosing the speech samples is not clearly specified, it seems that those samples are chosen which represent the identified characteristics of the Konkan standard speech, with variations and other points of interest noted wherever necessary. Grierson concludes that the differences are minimal among the dialects grouped as the Konkan standard, irrespective of the caste or occupation or sub-region of the speakers. Looking at the range of the caste-/religion-based varieties reported in the *LSI*, it is possible to imagine the diversity of the population in the Konkan. It is likely that in the absence of any peculiar features of interest, many of the samples representing the entire range of this diversity were omitted. Apart from the Konkani Muslim speech from Thana, a district outside the out-migration area indicated in Map 9.1, samples of the Kokni Muslim speech from other regions are not accessible in the *LSI*.

A quick look at the specimens reveals that many of the samples classified under the Konkan standard in the *LSI* are restricted to the Janjira state and Kolaba district (which constitute today's Raigad district). These loosely correspond to the HABSAN-variety area in the KCT sample. The grouping is made up of mainly caste-based varieties from the region: Koli, Kunbi, Dhangari, Daldi and Bhandari from the Janjira state, and Agri, Thakri and Kathodi from the Kolaba district. The Kokni Muslim variety from Raigad is not sampled in the *LSI*. However, these samples of other caste-based varieties from the region are useful for tracing back the HABSAN-variety speech in the region where the HABSAN-variety is spoken by Kokni Muslims.

Three samples which appear to be definitely collected from the Ratnagiri district based on the demographic information stated under them are available in the *LSI*. These are Bankoti from Mandangad in Ratnagiri and Chitpavani and Kudali from Ratnagiri. Among these, Bankot and Kudal represent geographical regions, whereas Chitpavani is a caste-based variety spoken in the Ratnagiri district. Unlike the HABSAN-group, the other two village groups (LATVAN and KALUSTA) belong to the Ratnagiri district. The features associated with these two groups will be examined with the help of these three samples from the *LSI*.

A note on the Sangameshwari sample in Grierson's *LSI* should be made here. The sample is taken not from Sangameshwar in the Ratnagiri district, which is the southernmost area of the KCT migration, but from Bombay Town (present day Mumbai), which is further north of the area. Grierson remarks that the samples received from Ratnagiri among others 'have proved to be ordinary specimens of the common Marathi of the Deccan' and the only sample that corresponds to the Konkan standard variety collected from Bombay Town is included. Kazi (2019) in her work on Sangameshwari notes that the sample is collected from Bombay Town, and thus raises doubt on the credibility of the sample listed as Sangameshwari in the *LSI*. She also notes that Grierson's account of Bankoti shares some features with the Kokni spoken by Muslims in Sangameshwar today. Since the *LSI* data for the Sangameshwari variety is insufficient, Kazi's (2019) contemporary account of Sangameshwari will be referred to for the discussion regarding Sangameshwari in the concluding section.

5. Data collection and methodology

The data collection for this study was conducted by the author mainly in three visits to Cape Town in September 2016, November 2017 and July 2018, and in a team visit to three villages in the Raigad and Ratnagiri districts in the Konkan in December and January 2016–17. The first visit to Cape Town in September 2016 aimed to gather a preliminary knowledge of the Kokni language spoken in Cape Town, and the social history of the Kokni migration. The fieldwork involved interviews with forty speakers. The sample was subdivided into three age groups which were identified on the bases of their current degrees of Kokni language usage: over 60 (n = 24), 40–60 (n = 10) and under 40 (n = 6). Each sub-group was balanced for gender. A questionnaire was used to collect basic language usage information. Data from word lists and sentence lists were collected from the three most fluent old speakers. The interviews focused on free narratives.

Based on the data collected in this fieldwork, the major centres of migrations out of the Konkan were identified. These were the villages of Karji, Mhasla, Janjira, Shrivardhan, Kalusta, Khed, Morba, Murud and Latvan. After the primary analysis of the Cape Town data, some linguistic features of interest were identified. A working hypothesis for the future analysis of the data at this point was that for the most part people appear to maintain their original village variety, rather than converging towards a Cape Town variety of Kokni. Three villages from among the twenty-one villages reported by Cape Town speakers were identified as representatives of the original input varieties. The second phase of data collection was carried out in a team consisting of the author, her PhD supervisor and co-supervisor in two villages of Konkan out of these three – Morba (in Raigad district) and Latvan (Ratnagiri district) in Konkan. Kalusta, which was another major centre of migration in Ratnagiri, was visited in January 2017. Based on the preliminary transcription and analysis of the data gathered in the earlier fieldworks in September 2016, another trip to Cape Town to fill the gaps identified in the data was undertaken in November 2017. Some of the data collected by the author's PhD supervisor in her visit to Cape Town in May 2017 were also utilised. The primary aim of the data collection was collecting samples of Kokni from fluent speakers. It was difficult to access many middle-aged or young-age fluent speakers of Kokni in the short duration of the fieldwork, and thus the number of such samples is limited. However, the data collected give a good idea of the linguistic characteristics of the KCT Kokni.

6. Retention of the ancestral village-based grammatical features in KCT Kokni

A total number of five lexical, phonological and morphological features indexing with the ancestral villages are identified from the available data. Each of these features will be discussed in the next section, with the help of data collected in Cape Town, and the other sources discussed in section 4. Three of these features gathered from the primary analysis of data were reported in Mesthrie, Kulkarni-Joshi and Paradkar (2017), which included the lexical variants for the distal adverbs of place 'there' in all three groups, and two features that mark the LATVAN-variety speakers. The reported lexical variants are *tite* in the LATVAN-variety, *tʰətə* in KALUSTA-variety, and *tʰəvər* in the HABSAN-variety. The markers of the LATVAN-variety are the purposive dative marking *-kala* (as against the *-la* marker in the speech of KALUSTA-variety and HABSAN-variety speakers), and the first-person singular marking *dzatav* 'I go' (as against *dzatu/dzataj* in the other two groups) (Mesthrie, Kulkarni-Joshi and Paradkar 2017: 91). The markers of the HABSAN-variety speakers identified later

Table 9.1 Differential features in the ancestral village-based varieties in KCT Kokni

		HABSAN-variety	LATVAN-variety	KALUSTA-variety
Lexical	Lexical variants for adverbs of place	həvər/həja tʰəvər/tʰəja	hite/tite	hətə/tʰətə
Phonological	Masculine gender marking	-a	-o	-o
Morphological	Number distinction in the first-person marking on imperfective verbs	-av, -a, -aj (Singular)	-av, -u, -a, -aj (Singular)	-av, -u, -a, -aj (Singular)
		-av, -u, -a, -aj (Plural)	-u, -a (Plural)	-av, -u, -a (Plural)
	Non-finite + dative construction to mark purpose	-ej/-ja+la	-u+ka/kala	-ja+la
Morpho-syntactic	Overt ergative case-marking on the subject NP in transitive perfective construction	First and second person may be overtly case-marked Third person is only rarely not case-marked.	First and second person never overtly case-marked Unmarked third person also acceptable	First and second person never overtly case-marked Unmarked third person also acceptable

are the masculine gender marking ending in -*a* (as against the -*o* ending masculine nouns in the other two groups), and the agentive suffix -*ni* attached to the first-person (*mini*) and the second-person (*tuni*) pronouns (*mi* and *tu* in the speech of the other two groups).

Table 9.1 summarises all the five features, which will be examined in detail in the following section.

6.1 Lexical variants for adverbs of place

This was the feature that was identified widely by the KCT speakers as a marker of ancestral village based linguistic differences. The HABSAN-variety speakers use *həvər/həja* and *tʰəvər/tʰəja*, LATVAN-variety speakers use *hite/tite* and the KALUSTA-variety speakers use *hətə/tʰətə* as the proximal and distal adverbs of place.

Examples of lexical variants for adverbs of place:

HABSAN-variety
1. mi   dʒəja   pəida   dʒəj-la   **tʰəja**   velingtən-la   **tʰəja**   khas
   I   where   born   be-PERF.1S there   Wellington-LOC there   specially
   mansa   bol-ət   hotə   afrikans
   people   speak-IMPV were   Afrikaans
   'Where I was born, there, in Wellington, people specially spoke Afrikaans'.

LATVAN-variety
2. ata   **tite**   ekuts   rʰej-l-et   an   **hite**   ek   fuidʒis
   Now   there   one-EMPH   remain-PERF-3P   and   here   one   aunt
   'Now only one relative lives there and one aunt (lives) here.'

KALUSTA-variety
3. ami   boltu   hətə tʰətə,   ti   rimoʈ   hətə tʰeʊ
   we   talk.IMPV.1PL   here there   that.3SN remote   here keep.IMP
   tʰətə tʰev
   there keep.IMP
   'We say hətə-tʰətə. Keep that remote here, keep it there.'

No specific pattern could be observed for the distal adverbs of place tokens in the *LSI*. However, this is the ancestral village-indexed feature most widely reported by the KCT speakers. In fact, in example (3), a young speaker aged forty reports this same feature by using the term *ami* 'we' to indicate the KALUSTA-variety of her village group. The frequent reporting of these variants by the KCT Kokni speakers indicates the consciousness of village-based differences among the KCT community.

6.2 Masculine nouns endings -o and -a

In the KCT Kokni, nouns ending in -o are characteristically masculine in the KALUSTA-variety and LATVAN-variety. In the HABSAN-variety, the same masculine nouns end in -a. Examples of the masculine nouns in each variety are marked in bold below.

KALUSTA-variety
4. tjantso   irado   naj   hoto   ki   ami hətə kep ʈəʊn-la
   3P.POSS.3SM   intention   not   be.PAST.3SM   that we   here Cape Town-LOC
   pərmənənʈli setəl   ʊʰava
   permanently settle   be.SUB
   'They did not intend to permanently settle down here in Cape Town.'
   Masculine nouns ending in -o: LATVAN-variety

5. hite   rəsto   həj
   Here   road   be.PRES
   'Here there is a road.'
   Masculine noun ending in -a : HABSAN-variety

6. ek   an**a**   əs-la   hja an**a**   haf   ʊʰə-il
   one anna   be-PERF-3MS   this anna   half   become-FUT
   adʰa tumtsa   adʰa madza
   half yours   half mine.
   'If you have one anna (1/16th part of a rupee), then half anna will be yours and half will be mine.'

In the LSI samples, the -o ending masculine nouns are reported in Chitpavani and Kudali in the Ratnagiri district. It is however absent from the Bankoti dialect sample. In the samples collected from the Kolaba district, except Koli and Daldi in Janjira, -a ending masculine nouns can be observed in all other samples. Based on the *LSI* samples, it is possible to loosely correlate the -o ending masculine nouns with the varieties hailing from the Ratnagiri district (the LATVAN-variety and

KALUSTA-variety) and the -*a* ending masculine noun to the variety belonging to the Raigad district (the HABSAN-variety).

6.3 The non-finite + dative construction to mark purpose

In the KCT Kokni, the purposive dative -*ka* or -*kala* form was observed in two ancestral village groups. The interviewees who noted the distinctness mostly identified it with the LATVAN-group speakers, but the feature was also observed in the SANGAMESHWAR-variety samples in the data. Two distinct village groups – corresponding to the among LATVAN-variety and SANGAMESHWAR-variety speakers – could be identified. They were relatively distinct because of separate marriage alliances and preferences (until the recent present), as recounted by older women during interviews. This separateness can be seen from the persistence of two ancestral village societies – the 'Sangameshwar Muslim Society' and the 'Cape Latvan Society'. Thus, their social connections do not overlap much in Cape Town. Examples from each group are given below.

HABSAN-variety
7. basna   dhoʋ-**aj-la**,   sink udzl-**ej-la**,   saf   kər-**ej-la**
   Clothes wash- **INF-DAT** sink polish- **INF-DAT** clean do- **INF-DAT**
   '(He helps me) to wash clothes, to wash the sink and with overall cleaning.'

KALUSTA-variety
8. por-a-la   pən ami traj kər-taʋ   ʃikəʋ-**ja-la**
   kid-OBL-DAT also we   try   do-HAB.1.PL teach-**INF-DAT**
   'We try to teach our kids too.'

LATVAN-variety
9. məla   sʈədi   kər-**u-ka-la**   dza-**u-ka-la**   həʋa   hota
   1.DAT   study   do-**INF-DAT-DAT** go-**INF-DAT-DAT** want   be.PST
   'I wanted to go to study.'

SANGAMESHWAR-variety
10. pəjljan ami   mop   fir-**u-ka**   dzaʋ   ani
    earlier we.EXCL a lot roam-**INF-DAT** go-PST.HAB and
    turisʈ   dzagi   bəg-**ka**
    tourist places see-**DAT**
    'Earlier, we used to travel a lot and would visit tourist places.'

In the LSI, the -*ka* dative is exhibited by the southernmost varieties in the Konkan standard group. As noted above, the Sangameshwari speech sample in the *LSI* was not collected from Sangameshwar. Kulkarni-Joshi and Kelkar (2020) trace the development of the dative forms and functions in Marathi, in which they note the -*ka* dative in the Sangameshwar speech in their samples, which is absent in the *LSI* Sangameshwari sample.

Kazi (2019) observes that the dative suffix -*la* in Sangameshwari Kokni marks nouns, while -*ka* marks purpose. In one of her samples, the -*kala* marker can also

Ancestral Dialect Features in Cape Town Kokni

be observed. In the data collected in the Latvan village the same distribution is observed. Since no previous samples that note the occurrence of the *-ka* form in these two varieties are accessible, it can only be remarked based on the contemporary data that this dative marker is at least observed today in these two varieties to mark the purpose.

Geographically, the LATVAN-variety and the SANGAMESHWAR-variety village groups are separated in Konkan by the ancestral villages of the KALUSTA-variety speakers in between. However, anecdotal evidence for an earlier internal migration of Koknis from Sangameshwar to Latvan in Konkan was provided by both an elder speaker in Cape Town and another one in Latvan. The internal migration of Kokni Muslims from the Sangameshwar group of villages to Latvan and surrounding villages could be a probable explanation for the occurrence of this feature in both village groups.

However, the LATVAN-variety identity and SANGAMESHWAR-variety identity are quite distinct in Cape Town, for the social reasons noted above. Based on the available data, it is interesting to note that the two groups maintain a relatively distinct identity, even though they share a marked feature, which was often pointed by other KCT speakers as being a LATVAN-group marker (only).

6.4 Number distinctions in the first-person imperfective verb forms

The set of four markers that mark the number distinctions in the first-person imperfective verb forms are given in Table 9.1. Out of these, the marker *-aʋ* exclusively marks the singular forms in the LATVAN-variety in the first person. This form marks plural in both first- and second-person forms in the other two varieties – KALUSTA-variety and HABSAN-variety in the KCT speech. The LATVAN-variety has retained this use only in the second person.

LATVAN-variety

11. mi   ti-la   hajər   post   de-t-**aʋ**
    I   3.F-DAT   higher post   give-IMPV-AUX. **1.SG**
    'I am giving her a higher post.'

12. ami   bʱeʈ-l-o   mitrə   mʱəndʒɛ   kokni   pən   bol-t-**aʋ**
    we   meet-PERF-1M   friends   then   kokni   also   speak-IMPV-AUX.1.Pl
    ani English   pən   bol-t-**aʋ**
    and English   also   speak- IMPV-AUX.1.PL
    'When we friends meet, we speak Kokni as well as English.'

KALUSTA-variety and HABSAN-variety

13. mi   kokni   bol-t-**aj**
    I   Kokni   say-IMPV-AUX.**1.SG**
    'I speak Kokni.'

14. ami   dʒa-t-**aʋ**   ghəra
    We   go- IMPV-AUX.**1.PL**   home.LOC
    'We go home.'

6.5 Ergative marking on the first- and second-person pronouns and agreement in the transitive perfective construction

In the HABSAN-variety in KCT Kokni, the first- and the second-person subjects are variably marked with the ergative case marker *-ni*. The first- and the second-person subjects are not overtly marked in the KALUSTA-variety and LATVAN-variety.

In the *LSI* samples, the ergative case marked on the first person can be observed in the Koli and Bhandari samples from the Janjira state. Among the Ratnagiri varieties, it was not observed in the Chitpavani variety and no tokens were available in the Bankoti and Kudali varieties. The third-person subjects are overtly marked with the ergative *-ni* in all three KCT varieties. However, the usage of non-case-marked subjects in the third person in a transitive perfective construction is acceptable in the LATVAN- and KALUSTA-varieties. No such tokens of non-case-marked third-person subjects were obtained in the *LSI* and in Kazi's (2019) data.

Deo and Sharma (2006) discuss loss of overt case-marking on subjects in transitive perfective constructions across various varieties in Marathi. They interpret it as 'markedness reduction'. Kulkarni-Joshi (2016) observes loss of overt case-marking on subjects among the varieties of Marathi in contact with Kannada. Both these studies suggest that the absence of overt case-marking on subjects in transitive perfective constructions indicates language change in the varieties of Marathi. Thus, such non-case-marked subjects demonstrate a possible instance of language attrition in the KCT Kokni speech.

HABSAN-variety
15. **tu-ni**   likʰ-lə-la   buk   **mi-ni**   pər-l-a
    2S-ERG write- PERF.PART -3NS book 1S-ERG   read-PERF-3NS
    'I read the book that you had written.'

KALUSTA-variety and LATVAN-variety
16. **tu**   likʰ-lə-la   buk   **mi**   ʋats-l-a
    2S   write- PERF.PART-3NS book 1S   read- PERF-3NS
    'I read the book that you had written.'
    Example of a non-case-marked subject (observed among the KALUSTA- and LATVAN-variety speakers):

17. amtʃi   ma   bap   hətə dzago   ghet-l-in
    our   mother father here land.3MS   take-PERF-3P
    'Our mother and father bought land here.'

The data were analysed to examine the association between the ergative marking and verbal agreement in the transitive perfective constructions. Agreement with the object is observed throughout the *LSI* varieties in the Raigad and Ratnagiri districts. Kulkarni-Joshi (forthcoming) reports variability in verbal agreement in the Sangameshwar villages based on Kazi's (2019) data. The verb agrees with the second-person plural and third-person (sg. or pl.) subjects; elsewhere the verb agrees with the nominative object (Kazi 2019).

Ancestral Dialect Features in Cape Town Kokni

In all three varieties of KCT Kokni, the verb in the transitive perfective clauses was observed to agree most commonly with the subject in person and number, and sometimes also in gender. Examples (17) and (18) demonstrate agreement with a third-person plural subject, and a first-person singular subject respectively. Though this was the preferred pattern, object agreement was also attested.

18. mi bəg-l-u naj tja lokan-la
    I see-PERF-1MS NEG those people-ACC
    'I did not see those people.'

7. Summary of the connections between Cape Town and the Konkan

The persistence of even a few features that index to the villages of origin in India is of particular interest in the case of KCT Kokni, especially when compared with the other languages of Indian origin in South Africa. The context of circular migration and the family structure intricately linked with the villages of origin are the factors that need to be taken into consideration to understand this retention. The family networks of the Kokni Muslims are clustered together in small pockets in the Konkan, creating an extended family network in the closest villages. The Koknis migrating to Cape Town were highly dependent on the family networks, a pattern that is still observed in the migration to the Gulf countries in Gogate's study (1991). The circular migration pattern meant that the villages of origin were as permanently important for the Kokni migrants as the country in which they earned their livelihood.

An analysis of the domains of language use of the KCT community in Cape Town (Paradkar 2022) shows that the use of Kokni has weakened in the social circles even in today's older generation. Instead, social interaction within the community is dominated by Afrikaans and English. It is likely that the KCTs have continued speaking Kokni only in the social circles sharing the same roots. This would have included their family network in Cape Town as well as in India.

Table 9.2 *Variants in the KCT Kokni attested in the LSI samples from Raigad and Ratnagiri districts*

		Masculine -o ending	Masculine -a ending	Purposive dative –kala/-ka	Ergative marking on the first person
LSI Ratnagiri varieties	Bankoti	-	+	-	*
	Chitpavani	+	-	-	-
	Kudali	+	-	+	-
LSI Raigad varieties	Koli	-	+	-	+
	Kunbi	-	+	-	*
	Dhangari	-	+	-	*
	Bhandari	-	+	-	+
	Thakri	-	+	-	*
	Kathodi	-	+	-	-
	Daldi	+	-	-	*
	Agri	-	+	-	*
	Ghati	-	+	-	-

(+ indicates presence, - indicates absence and * indicates unavailability of the data in the specimen)

Based on the discussion in section 6, at least three of the five features can be traced back to Grierson's *LSI*. The LATVAN-variety seems closest to the Kudali specimen collected in Ratnagiri in the *LSI* with -*o* ending masculine nouns and the dative -*ka*. The KALUSTA-variety appears closest to the Chitpavani sample from Ratnagiri with -*o* ending masculine nouns. Based on the demographic information, both samples appear to be collected from the southern part of the district. The -o ending nouns are absent in the Bankoti sample collected at Mandangad, which is on the northern border of Ratnagiri while moving towards Raigad. That the Kokni spoken in Latvan in India is more similar to Kudali in the south than to Bankoti in Mandangad which is geographically much closer to it is perhaps the result of the internal migration as reported by the older speakers in Latvan and the LATVAN-variety speakers in Cape Town. Its similarity with the SANGAMESHWARI-variety also indicates the same possibility.

The HABSAN-variety appears similar to the Koli and Bhandari varieties in the Raigad district. Masculine nouns ending in -a seem to be the general feature of the area, which the HABSAN-variety speakers have maintained in their KCT speech.

A summary of these observations is given in Table 9.2.

8. Discussion and conclusions

The observations presented in this chapter suggest that KCT is not a homogenous variety. Though all the varieties maintained in the KCT Kokni are mutually intelligible, they are differentiable by a few linguistic features which are observable even today. Some of these features can be traced back to the broad regions of origin in India, and can be attested in the contemporary speech of specific villages there.

Though the data from the *LSI* is divided into Ratnagiri and Raigad districts for the analysis in this article, the varieties demarcated by the five linguistic features observed in Cape Town are identified on the basis of the specific villages of origin. The main reason for this is the strong village consciousness maintained by the KCT speakers. Also, among the Ratnagiri varieties, LATVAN-variety and KALUSTA-variety share two distinct features (non-finite + dative construction to mark purpose and number distinction in the first-person marking on imperfective verbs).

Two among the five features (lexical variants for adverbs of place and non-finite + dative construction to mark purpose) are associated with specific village groups by the KCT Kokni speakers as gathered in the interviews. A point that should be noted here is that these features acquired a specific village-based reference in Cape Town, where these village groups came into contact with each other. In the informal discussions in the Indian villages during fieldwork in the Konkan, the villagers said that Kokni Muslims from other regions speak differently, but did not point to specific features. In contrast, many interviewees from the KCT community pointed out at least two features that denoted separate village of origin varieties. The village groups in India appear to have maintained the same social networks as before. The networks established through these village groups were useful to the new migrants coming from India to Cape Town. However, contact between the social networks belonging to specific geographical areas in India was facilitated more easily in

Cape Town after migration. Thus, it was in the diaspora that the village identities developed in relation to each other. The consciousness of the distinctness of the village groups is stronger in Cape Town. The grammatical features discussed here are a reflection of this consciousness of slightly separate identities that emerged in a distant land.

There must have been some amount of dialect levelling in the KCT Kokni due to the contact among various input varieties. Since no specimens of both KCT Kokni and the specific Indian village varieties from the past are available, it is difficult to definitively determine the features that underwent levelling. However, the five features discussed in this chapter appear to be definitely maintained based on the KCT database. If Kokni had continued to be spoken in the social circles in Cape Town, these observed distinctions could possibly have blurred. However, the analysis of the domains of language use – even of older speakers – indicates that Kokni was sparingly used in social domains. It remained more-or-less a family language. The family was highly important in the migration scenario – first as the unit of migration and second in the marriage patterns. The principal argument in this chapter is that family networks in the KCT community, networks that had extended from the Indian villages of origin, were instrumental in the retention of the distinct grammatical features. The family network still remains strong, though the Kokni language use itself has declined to a large extent now.

Going back to Mesthrie's (2021) observations noted in the section 1, the initial diversity in input varieties is ascertained in this chapter with the help of Grierson's *LSI* in comparison with Tamil and Cape Town Gujarati migration, each of which appear to be dominated by a single input variety. At least a moderate maintenance of these input varieties in comparison with Bhojpuri or Telugu which largely converged towards a single koine is also established. In the case of KCT Kokni, the circular pattern of migration and the significance of village-based social networks resulted in only a moderate level of internal linguistic contact in Cape Town, thus limiting the convergence towards the formation of a homogenous KCT variety. On the basis of his knowledge of South African Englishes and Afrikaans, Mesthrie (personal communication, July 2021) remarks that convergence within the KCT community overall is saliently provided by the other languages of its repertoire today, viz. Afrikaans and English with a Cape Town flavour.

In conclusion, KCT presents an interesting and unusual case among the Indian diaspora language varieties in South Africa. Kokni in Cape Town is likely to survive only as the heritage language of the KCT community in the future. However, the analysis of the Kokni more than a century later since it first reached Cape Town has demonstrated some intriguing patterns in the context of dialect contact in diaspora.

Appendix

Sample text: The Prodigal Son story from a KALUSTA-variety speaker (an excerpt)

ek saʊkaratsə don porgə hotə. pəjlo mop mehnəti hoto. həmeʃa babatsas əikət əsə. ani mop bes manus hoto. dusrjatʃi adət mop nirali hoti. alʃi hoto. babatsa ʃetatljan kam naj kərja magət hoto. ani tjantʃi bat əikət nəsə. tjala adzad dzindəgi hoʋi hoti.

[Gloss: 'A very rich person had two sons. The first son was hard working. He always obeyed his father. He was a very good and a nice person. The second son was totally different from the first son. He was lazy. He did not work in his father's field. He was disobedient to his father. He wanted to lead a gay and free life.']

Annotated gloss of first four sentences

1. ek   dʰulkhuprja   porgja-tʃi   mat
   one   prodigal   son-OBL-GEN.3FS   story
2. ek   saʋkara-tsə   don   porgə
   one   rich man-OBL-GEN.3SM   two   boys
3. hotə   pəjlo   mop   mehnəti
   be.PST.3P first   very   hardworking
4. hoto   həmeʃa   baba-tsas   əik-ət
   be.PST.3S always   father-GEN.3SM   listen-IMPV

Acknowledgements

Funding for this project comes from a joint project awarded to Prof. Rajend Mesthrie (UCT, South Africa) and Prof. Sonal Kulkarni-Joshi (Deccan College, Pune) by the National Institute for the Humanities and Social Sciences (NIHSS, South Africa) as well as the Indian Council for Social Science Research (ICSSR), as part of a BRICS initiative, Reference number NIHSS/ICSSR 201514. The research was also facilitated by R. Mesthrie's NRF research chair (Migration, Language and Social Change) grant number 64805.

References

Deo, A. and Sharma, D. (2006). Typological variation in the ergative morphology of Indo-Aryan languages. *Linguistic Typology*, 10 (3): 369–418.

Dhupelia-Mesthrie, Uma. (2009). The Passenger Indian as worker: Indian immigrants in Cape Town in the early twentieth century. *African Studies*, 68 (1): 111–34.

Dhupelia-Mesthrie, Uma. (2014). Split-households: Indian wives, Cape Town husbands and immigration Laws, 1900s to 1940s. *South African Historical Journal*, 66 (4): 635–55.

Fishman, J. A. (1965). Who speaks what language to whom and when? *La linguistique*, 1 (Fasc. 2): 67–88.

Gogate, S. (1991). Impact of migration to the Middle East on rural Ratnagiri. In M. Rao, C. Bhat and L. N. Kadekar (eds), *A Reader in Urban Sociology*. Hyderabad: Orient Longman, pp. 371–88.

Grierson, G. A. (1905). *Linguistic Survey of India VII: Indo-Aryan Family, Southern Group (Marathi)*, vol. 7. Delhi: Motilal Banarsidass.

Kazi, S. (2019). *A Grammatical Sketch and Texts of the Speech Variety of Sangameshwar*. Unpublished master's thesis, Deccan College Post-Graduate and Research Institute, Pune.

Kulkarni-Joshi, S. (2016). Forty years of language contact and change in Kupwar: A critical assessment of the intertranslatability model. *Journal of South Asian Languages and Linguistics*, 3 (2): 147–74.

Kulkarni-Joshi, S. (Forthcoming). Variation and change in dialects of Marathi: A socio-dialectal approach. In P. Chandra (ed.), *Variation in South Asian Languages: From Macro to Micro Differences*. Springer Nature.

Kulkarni-Joshi, S. and M. Kelkar. (2020). Synchronic variation and diachronic change in dialects of Marathi: The case of dative marking. In T. Khan et al. (eds), *Alternative Horizons in Linguistics. A Festschrift in Honour of Prof. Panchanan Mohanty*. Munich: Lincom Europa.

Kulkarni-Joshi, S., R. Mesthrie and S. Pradhan. (2021). The sending areas in the Kokan in the state of Maharashtra in India. [Map].

Mesthrie, R. (2008). South Asian language in the Indian diaspora. In B. B. Kachru, Y. Kachru and S. N. Sridhar (eds), *Language in South Asia*. Cambridge: Cambridge University Press.

Mesthrie, R. (2021). Contacts and contexts: Varying diasporic interactions and koineisation outcomes for Indian languages in South Africa. *Journal of Sociolinguistics*, 25: 703–19. https://doi.org/10.1111/josl.12529.

Mesthrie, R., S. Kulkarni-Joshi and R. Paradkar. (2017). Kokni in Cape Town and the sociolinguistics of transnationalism. *Language Matters*, 48 (3): 73–97.

Paradkar, R. (2022). *Language and Transnational Identity: A Sociolinguistic Account of the Kokni Diaspora in Cape Town*. Unpublished PhD thesis, Deccan College Post-Graduate and Research Institute, Pune.

Yamin, G. M. (1991). *The Causes and Processes of Rural–Urban Migration in 19th and Early 20th Century India: The Case of Ratnagiri District*. Unpublished PhD thesis, University of Salford.

CHAPTER 10

The Dialect Roots of Varieties of Gujarati in South Africa

Rajend Mesthrie and Vinu Chavda

1. Introduction – historical background

1.1 Gujarat and the Indian diaspora

The Indian diaspora has proved a rich topic of investigation within the sociology of migration, as evidenced by works such as Oonk (2007), Vertovec (2003), Mawani and Mukadam (2014) and Lal (2006). There is much to investigate and ponder over, given the complexities of the history of migration. Oonk (2007: 9) observes that '... many South Asians living overseas tend to reproduce their Indian culture, values, language, and religion as much as possible'. What is missing in this characterisation is that South Asians have been able to adapt in positive ways and contribute immensely to their new home territories. Oonk's statement should be modified to reflect 'reproduction with modification'.

Bhojpuri-Hindi diasporas in the context of indenture have been quite well-studied in terms of their linguistic outcomes as well as from the perspectives of language maintenance and shift – see e.g. Barz and Siegel (1988), Siegel (1987) and chapters by Gambhir and Auckle in this volume. We know rather less about languages outside this group of migrants. To this end our current work aims to unearth a linguistic and sociolinguistic account of Gujarati in South Africa (see parallel work on Kokni in Cape Town by Paradkar, in this volume). At the very least we would like to document exactly what kinds of spoken Gujarati were brought to South Africa, their relations with Standard Gujarati, interactions between different varieties spoken by Gujarati migrants, and influences from local languages that they came in contact with. While this was initially conceived of as heritage research, an unexpected spin-off has been that we were also able to contribute to a socio-historical dialectology of Gujarat itself.

Gujarat remains an important 'sending area' for emigrants, wishing to gain a better economic foothold than possible by remaining in the home village or district. However, as for the Konkan area described by Paradkar in this volume, those who remained in India played an equally important role in providing the family stability amidst immense hardship that enabled the frequently lone migrant to venture abroad. For Gujarati studies, important work of a sociological and anthropological nature by Mario Rutten gives a detailed account of the presence of the diaspora in village Gujarat (see e.g. Upadhya and Rutten 2012). A popular account based on extensive research and personal experience is the book *Leaving India*, with the subtitle *My Family's Journey from Five Villages to Five Continents* written by Gujarati-American journalist Minal Hajratwala (2009). As discussed in the introduction to this volume, the book is a highly recommended read for anyone wishing to come to terms with the Gujarati diaspora from within. The panoramic account in *Leaving India* reminds us that the linguistic account of diaspora – technical as it must be with its focus on language change – exists within the complex human stories behind it. However, the technical linguistic story is equally interesting.

1.2 Background to Gujarati in South Africa

Gujarati is spoken in many countries within Africa, as the language of diaspora par excellence for the Indian communities in especially in east and southern Africa in countries such as Kenya, Tanzania, Malawi, Mozambique, Zambia, Zimbabwe and South Africa. Most of these communities fit the description of transnational citizens well, since they have a sense of home in both Africa and India. However, by the third generation within families there is no doubt of the new territory having become home. In our experience, recent 'double diasporic' Gujarati migrants of South African background in Australia are as much nostalgic for South Africa as for India.[1] Work on Gujarati in Africa includes accounts by Oonk (2007) on language loss among Kenyan Gujaratis and Sheena Shah (2018) on influences from Kiswahili in East Africa and of the survival of this variety in London, among East African Indian migrants. Lodhi (2008) provides a comprehensive account of languages like Kacchi, Hindi and Gujarati in East Africa. Shah discusses how older speakers find positive value in maintaining the features of East African Gujarati, notably loanwords from Kiswahili, despite being immersed among speakers from India in the UK. Her work reinforces the duality of the concept of ancestral home in these circumstances.

Gujarati was not the main Indian language in South Africa, as the system of indenture between 1860 and 1911 brought in many more speakers of Tamil and Bhojpuri-Hindi.[2] Yet given its stronger transnational role, it has survived better – proportionally speaking – than the languages of indenture. However, it must be acknowledged that even Gujarati is little spoken today among the younger members into the fourth or later generation. Attachment to it as a language of heritage remains strong. The Gujarati community is found in the major cities but is also notable for its spread into small towns and country districts, where a lone Gujarati store could always be expected. Thanks to the work of Usha Desai, we have a good sense of literary production in South African Gujarati, whose most famous writer was M. K. Gandhi himself – see also the survey by Mrunal Chavda and Mesthrie in this volume. Desai (1997) and Desai and Ramsay-Brijbal (2004) focus on historical background, language maintenance, shift and pedagogy, with some preliminary observations about sporadic variation in South Africa. The present authors have therefore started a project recording and analysing Gujarati in four cities: Cape Town, Durban, Johannesburg, and Port Elizabeth. The bulk of this work was based in Cape Town, despite the smaller presence of Gujarati there. In this chapter we report on the main features of spoken Gujarati in Cape Town from the viewpoint of a diasporic dialectology. We then compare it briefly with the features found among older speakers in Durban and Port Elizabeth, leaving the analysis of our Johannesburg data for the future. Our interest is both linguistic in ascertaining the degree of variation and dialect retention in South Africa, but also sociolinguistic in terms of illuminating diasporic differences and syntheses in the different cities.

Indentured immigration followed closely upon the abolition of slavery in the British Empire (1834), and indentured workers were shipped to the colonies right away to keep the plantations from bankruptcy. The first indentured immigrations were to Mauritius in 1834 and Guyana in 1839. Gujaratis did not travel to the colonies as indentured workers but tended to follow a decade or two later paying their own passage (hence the historical term 'passenger Indians', which has nothing of the pejoration of this phrase in everyday terminology of someone not pulling their weight). Gujaratis usually took up menial positions on arrival at the docks, in factories and the like, and moved up as petty traders. Only a few had arrived as large-scale traders (Dhupelia-Mesthrie 2009, Swan 1985, Vahed 2010). They had representatives from several castes (and not just the Vaishya/Vania castes as the often-derogatory out-group term *banya* tended to imply). In South Africa there were as many Muslim as Hindu migrants from Gujarat. Fatima Meer (1969: 16) describes the diversity among the earliest of these passenger Indians in Durban as follows:

> Abubaker's [Abubakr Jhavari, 'a young Mehmon'] success attracted other traders from India, mainly from Gujarat – Mehmons from Kathiawad and Kutch, Sunni Vohras from Surat, and Hindu clerks from both districts. Though most *passenger Indians* spoke Gujarati, there were also among them Urdu-speaking Muslims – Mian Bhais, Sayeds, Shaiks, Khans, and Pathans – some of them coming from the United Provinces and embarking at the port of Calcutta. There were also a few Marathi-speaking, Kokinee Muslims, and some South Indians from the South and East coasts.

An important consideration for sociolinguistic research is the place of family origins in India. Bhana and Brain (1990) carried out a historical survey of the origins of Gujarati migrants born in India before 1911 – when Indian immigration to South Africa was officially, but not quite, terminated. They found that half the migrants emanated from Surat and Valsad districts, citing the major towns of Surat, Rander, Kholvad, Kathor, Bardoli, Baroda and Navsari. Map 10.1 shows the main districts of Gujarat today. Clustered together on the Gulf of Khambhat are the four districts from which most of Cape Town's migrants emanated (and which are subsumed under a 'Surti' identity, discussed further below): Bharuch, Surat, Navsari, and Valsad. Another major source of migrants to South Africa was Kathiawad district, which included many Muslims who spoke Meman (Kacchi) and Gujarati. As Kathiawad is a large peninsula across the bay from Surat, we might say there was a gulf between the two regions – literally and metaphorically. Thus, the interaction between Kathiawadi and Surti dialects and their relation to the standard is a relevant theme for a dialectology of South African Gujarati – and presumably internationally too. These two dialects are part of a broader regional identity in South Africa, with cities like Durban and Johannesburg having long-standing Surti and Kathiawadi societies or associations. They also have Patidar associations, which are more caste or socially rather than regionally based (Patidar being the adjective derived from the caste title and ubiquitous surname Patel, denoting a landowner and/or village headman). For a long

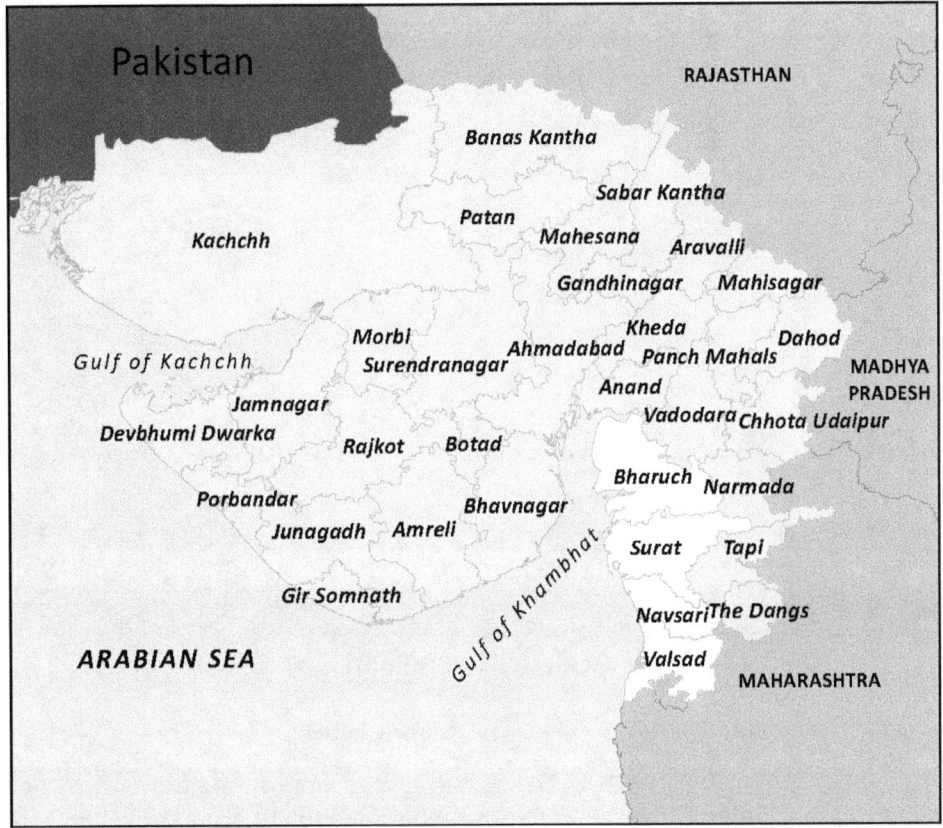

Map 10.1 *The main districts of Gujarat today*

time, members of these three groups did not socialise freely nor intermarry, though there were exceptions. Kalpana Hiralal, a historian confirms (personal communication April 2021) that it was rare in her upbringing in the 1960s and 1970s for families of Surti descent in Durban to socialise with the other Gujarati groups, let alone other Indians or South Africans. Goolam Vahed (2010: 618) writes that 'Kathiawadis [of Durban] were smaller in number but economically powerful'. Surtis of Muslim and Hindu background had cordial social and business relationships, but intermarriage was and still is rare. While Muslims seeking brides or grooms in Gujarat would initially look close to their ancestral villages, in time they would settle for potential sons – or daughters-in-law – from the wider Surat district (Vahed 2010: 622). Usha Desai, a Gujarati lecturer of considerable experience proferred the view in an interview with Vahed (2010: 618) that in Durban 'the Kathiawadi dialect is a bit more "polished" than Surti's, Gandhian style I would say ...'.

Internal social segregation among Indians was considerably weakened with a Western-oriented education in the rapidly improving schools of the 1960s onwards, and the formation of the University College for Indians, later the University of Durban-Westville which catered almost entirely under apartheid regulations for Indian students between 1961 and the mid-1980s.[3] The role of education in

Map 10.2 *Four fieldwork sites for Gujarati in South Africa (in bold)*

dissolving old Gujarati-internal barriers among the young around the 1980s is again captured by Desai:

> In the old days parents took their children to India to get married. If you were Kathiawadi, you married Kathiawadi, Surti married Surti. Not only that, if you were a Patel, you married Patel; if you were a Brahmin, you married Brahmin ... Change was brought about by the children going to university. Once they were at university and the children were from whichever group or class, it didn't matter, rich class or poor class, higher caste or lower caste, but being Gujarati was still important. First, Surtis married other Surtis and Kathiawadis married Kathiawadis, slowly they were breaking the caste system and then slowly the Kathiawadis and Surtis also started mixing. (Usha Desai, interview with Goolam Vahed 2010: 622)

This view of the unfolding changes in community orientations in diaspora among Kathiawadis is confirmed in Bhana (2011).

1.3 Fieldwork, sample and transcription details

In this chapter we proceed as follows: we identify three clusters of features (totalling twenty-one) that were reported as varying socially and regionally in Gujarati by Grierson (1908). These clusters are (1) interchanges between retroflex and dental consonants, (2) a consonantal sound shift involving /k kʰ c cʰ s ś h ɦ ø /, (3) miscellaneous other consonant and vowel changes. Our main discussion is on the extent to which these are characteristic of the Cape Town data, which forms the main part of our empirical work, followed by brief comparisons with Gujarati in Durban and Port Elizabeth.

All speakers reported on this study are of the older generation, who had been born and/or brought up in South Africa. Of necessity they were aged above fifty years and in many cases well above sixty years. Community members younger than this are not very fluent and have difficulties in extended conversation. All of the thirty-two speakers interviewed and analysed for the initial and main Cape Town study emanated from the southeastern parts of Gujarat. The majority of interviewees were of the second generation in South Africa and had ancestral ties with the districts of Navsari ($n = 17$) and Surat ($n = 11$), with the remaining three from the neighbouring districts of Valsad, Bharuch and Bardoli ($n = 1$ each) – see Map 10.1. These are all areas in which the Surti dialect is spoken (Grierson 1908), with speakers from these districts accepting the appellation Surti as a term for their regional identity.

Of the nineteen Durban speakers interviewed, eleven were analysed for this study (as the rest tended to speak much more in English). Their ancestral districts were Surat ($n = 4$), Navsari ($n = 3$) and Rajkot ($n = 4$).[4] The first two of these are part of the Surti dialect area, the last is a district of Kathiawad. The Cape Town and Durban interviews were conducted in Gujarati by Vinu Chavda, a speaker of the standard variety of Ahmedabad, the major city of Gujarat. In contrast, our Port Elizabeth sample is a small one comprising four speakers, interviewed in English by Rajend Mesthrie, using a Gujarati word list with extended discussion, devised on the experience of the Cape Town research. Surat ($n = 3$) and Valsad ($n = 1$) were the relevant ancestral areas, and it was confirmed by community members that such a background from Surat and neighbouring districts was typical of the small Port Elizabeth Gujarati community. The Cape Town and Durban interviews were summarised by Chavda and selected portions were transcribed when the interviewee was speaking freely in (mostly) Gujarati. The Cape Town data were subjected to a variationist analysis utilising a five-minute sample of speech of each of the thirty-two speakers (reported in Mesthrie and Chavda 2020). This sample yielded a high number of relevant consonant and vowel tokens (e.g. a total of 2,329 for retroflex–dental variation of / ṭ / / ḍ / / t / / d / and their aspirates).

As far as transcription and transliteration is concerned, we use IPA symbols where necessary for phonetic accuracy. Since our work is more socio-historical, we also use a Romanised Oriental transliteration for citation forms, in the hope of intelligibility to a wider audience. Thus, while the reader should expect to see symbols like [ḍ ḍʰ ṭ ṭʰ ṇ ḷ] in a phonetic transcription, in citation forms where the phonetics are not at stake we use equivalent symbols like < d dh ṭ ṭh ṇ ḷ > respectively. Finally, we prefer square brackets as much as possible when describing the phonetic correspondences across dialects; and we avoid phonemic slashed brackets, unless we are certain of change at the phonemic level.

2. Dental–retroflex interchanges

In this section we first focus in some detail on the Cape Town findings pertaining to changes to dentals and retroflexes, before offering briefer comparisons with Durban and Port Elizabeth. Table 10.1 provides a summary of the four features that apply within this set, in relation to Cape Town on the extreme right and the four main dialects of Gujarati in India. (The Pattani and Charotari dialects are included here for the sake of completeness, even though they do not have a significant presence in South Africa.)[5]

2.1 Retroflex realisations of standard dentals

Features 1 and 2 in Table 10.1 concern large numbers of words for which some Gujarati dialects of India have retroflex consonants in place of a standard dental.[6] Conversely there is also the use of dentals where the standard has retroflexes (Grierson 1908). This dual interchange leads Grierson (1908: 382) to remark that 'cerebral and dental letters are absolutely interchangeable' in Surti. In Mesthrie and Chavda (2020) we undertook a quantitative analysis of our Cape Town data, calculating percentage occurrences of retroflex realisations [ʈ ʈʰ ɖ ɖʰ] in words which have the following realisations in the standard: [t̪ t̪ʰ d̪ d̪ʰ]. We called this phenomenon 'retroflex boosting', since the reverse correspondence of dialect dentals for standard retroflexes was much less common (as we describe below). The high proportion of retroflex 'boosting' can be gauged from the following:

(a) All four sounds are affected by this dialect characteristic.
(b) Retroflex boosting occurs in all three positions (initial, medial and final).
(c) The phenomenon is variable rather than categorical: a word may show retroflex or dental realisations in apparent free variation.
(d) Proportions of standard dental tokens realised as retroflexes in Cape Town Gujarati range from 8.5 per cent (n = 47) for [d̪ʰ] > [ɖʰ] to 61.6 per cent (n = 138) for [d̪] > [ɖ].
(e) The proportion of words affected by the phenomenon, showing some retroflex realisations ranges from 20 per cent (for [d̪ʰ] > [ɖʰ] in initial position (n = 15) to 70 per cent (for [d̪] > [ɖ] in initial position (n = 50).

Table 10.1 *Variable dental–retroflex interchanges in colloquial nineteenth-century Gujarati and present-day Cape Town that differ from the standard*

	Surti	Kath-iawadi	Charo-tari	Pattani	Cape Town
Cluster I: Dental–retroflex interchanges					
1. Retroflex [ʈ ʈʰ ɖ ɖʰ] for std dentals	+	−	−	+	+
2. Dental [t̪ t̪ʰ d̪ d̪ʰ] for std retroflexes	+	−	−	+	+R
3. [r] for std retroflex [ɖ]	+	+	+R	+	+
4. [n̪ l̪] for std [ɳ ɭ]	+	−	−	+	+

Key: R – rare.
Source: based on Grierson (1908: 326, 382) and Mesthrie and Chavda (2020).

Table 10.2 *The most common tokens that show some retroflex for dental realisations in Cape Town Gujarati by consonant type and environment*

	[t̪] > [ʈ]	Gloss	No. of retroflex tokens	%	Total
Initially	ṭo	'so, then'	77	26.7	288
Medially	gujarāṭī	'Gujarati'	49	38.0	129
Finally	vāṭ	'tale, talk'	7	16.3	43
	[t̪ʰ] > [ʈʰ]				
Initially	ṭhai	'happened'	15	71.4	21
Medially	sāṭhe	'together'	15	35.7	42
Finally	–	–	–	–	–
	[d̪] > [ḍ]				
Initially	ḍāḍa	'grandfather'	10	47.7	21
Medially	āḍar	'in, inside'	13	65.0	20
Finally	yāḍ	'recall, remember'	1	16.7	6
	[d̪ʰ] > ḍʰ]				
Initially	–	–	–	–	–
Medially	baḍhu	'everything'	21	41.2	51
Finally	–	–	–	–	–

Source: adapted from Mesthrie and Chavda (2020).

Some of the most common tokens of Cape Town Gujarati forms showing retroflex boosting are given in Table 10.2. All of the retroflexes in the table correspond to a dental in the standard form (with all other phonological features like aspiration and voice being preserved). However, since not all speakers show retroflex boosting and those that do evince it variably, Table 10.2 also supplies the percentage occurrences of the retroflex realisation of the standard dentals for each word.

The paucity of examples in final position in Table 10.2 is a consequence of Gujarati morphophonology, since most words end in a vowel, usually marking details of verb or noun morphology. In all other instances the proportion of non-standard variability is high, if we recall how proportions as low as 5–10 per cent can have a salient effect in marking local or dialect speech. That this is likely to be free variation rather than structurally conditioned is suggested by lack of conditioning by environment, especially of following vowel (for further discussion see Mesthrie and Chavda 2020: 10–11). It remains to consider how frequent retroflex boosting is per speaker. All but two of the thirty-two speakers show some retroflex boosting within the excerpts analysed. And, conversely, all but one make some use of standard dentals.[7] Thus, as far as retroflex boosting is concerned, no one in the Cape Town sample is a standard speaker or entirely a non-standard user. The phenomenon does not appear to be subject to style shifting, as in our observation community members who make public speeches retain some use of retroflexes for standard dentals. The feature is also prominent in the very name of the language and culture (with Cape Town speakers showing 38 per cent of retroflexion of the /t̪/ in *Gujarati* as per row 2 of Table 10.1). It also occurs in other words of religious and cultural significance such as *prasad* ([prəsɑːḍ]), *Diwali* (possible variant [ɖivɑːɽiː]) and *namaste* ([nəmesʈeː]) . Even proper names like *Praneet* may show a weak retroflex rather than dental for the final consonant (i.e. [prəniːʈ]).

2.2 Dental realisations of standard retroflexes

Feature 2 in Table 10.1 covers the converse process – having dentals for standard retroflexes, which is again a feature of Surti, but not Kathiawadi in Gujarat. This reverse feature is much less common in Cape Town (and goes against the full certainty of Grierson's dictum of absolute interchangeability cited above for Surti). Only seven words were found in our sample: *motā* 'elder', *chutā* 'change', *māte* 'for' (std *moṭā, chuṭā, māṭe*); *angutho* 'large toe', *kāthiāwādi* 'from Kathiawad', *āth* 'eight' (std *anguṭho, kāṭhiāwaḍi, āṭh*) and *dabbo* 'container' (std *ḍabbo*). Again, these are variable, rather than categorical, realisations of the words.

2.3 Other changes to retroflexes

The third feature of this cluster concerns other changes to retroflexes, especially to /ḍ/, /ḷ/ and /ṇ/.

(a) Firstly, Grierson (1908: 329) notes that /ḍ/ and /ḍh/ in the colloquial dialects (but not the standard) have the tapped medial allophones [ɾ] and [ɾʰ] (as do several other Indo-Aryan languages). Furthermore, in the northern Gujarati dialects '*ḍ, ḍh,* and *ḷ* generally become *r*', the latter being described by Grierson (1908: 28–9) as a 'pure *r*'. The Cape Town data gives evidence of a (weak) trilled [r] as the (variable) equivalent of medial retroflex [ḍ] of the standard. Thus, for standard /ḍ/ we have the following Cape Town equivalent forms:

Cape Town variant	Std form	Gloss
terā	teḍā	'invite'
payrũ	paḍyũ	'fallen'
lākru	lākḍu	'piece of wood'
kaprā	kapḍā	'clothes'
rareli	raḍeli	'she cried'
morā	moḍā	'late'
pare	paḍe	'fall, occur'

There is only one occurrence in final position in our data: *papar* 'papadam' where Std Gu has a final *ḍ*. We must ask whether this medial retroflexion is a Surti feature somehow missed by Grierson, whether it is a natural change in diaspora, or whether it is a northern form that somehow seeped into Surti in diaspora. The last option seems unlikely, since no one makes any mention of Gujaratis in South Africa emanating from the northern area.[8] The second possibility – that of a natural change – seems the most likely.

(b) Secondly, there are changes to /ḷ/ – a retroflex phoneme that is frequent in the standard, though restricted to non-initial position (Cardona and Suthar 2003: 663). In the Cape Town data standard /ḷ/ may be variably realised as [l], or [r]. The following (variable) correspondences show a weak trilled [r] in the Cape Town database:

Cape Town variant	Std form	Gloss
bārako	bāḷako	'children'
vepārvārā	vepārvāḷā	'business persons'

ḍhori	ḍhoḷi	'spill'
thāri	thāḷi	'plate'
nihār	niśāḷ	'school'
mer	meḷ	'setting'

The correspondence of [r] to standard /ḷ/ is mentioned by Grierson only in connection with Kathiawadi. On the other hand, Sampat's (1973: 51) study of three Gujarati dialects suggests the opposite, putting Kathiawadi in the standard camp for this feature with Surti (and Charotari) having [r] instead.

(c) Surti – especially – shows a further correspondence of retroflex /ṇ/ of the standard to dental [n̪]. Again, our data are variable, with the dental variant being quite frequent.

Cape Town variant	Std form	Gloss
pan	paṇ	'but'
ghanā	ghaṇā	'many'
bārpan	bālpaṇ	'childhood'
kāran	kāraṇ	'reason'
bhanvu	bhaṇvu	'learn'

Grierson (1908: 382) notes that 'cerebral ṇ and ḷ are rare' in Surti, supplying an example of standard /ṇ/ becoming [n̪]. We may conclude that this is the source of the change in CPT Gujarati.

Thus overall – despite some uncertainties of dialect description in Gujarat – we may say that Cape Town Gujarati shows strong evidence of retaining changes to retroflexes that occur in the dialects of Gujarat, especially of Surti.

2.4 Comparisons with Durban and Port Elizabeth

We now turn briefly to Durban and Port Elizabeth in respect of these retroflexion features, being able to report on the first two of these four features. In our Durban sample retroflex–dental interchanges are exceedingly rare. The substitution of [t̪] for [ṭ] is close to zero: of the eleven speakers only one speaker used this substitution, and only once at that (overall percentage 0.2 per cent, $n = 496$). The use of [d̪] for [ḍ] was also infrequent. This time two speakers were involved (overall percentage 2.9 per cent, $n = 105$). The other five Durban speakers with Surat ancestry would appear to have accommodated to the Kathiawadi variety here, or to have been influenced by the standard.

The Port Elizabeth data are similar to Cape Town insofar as dentals turn up as postalveolar stops quite frequently, while retroflex stops of the standard turn up as dentals only occasionally. One informant who was from a Kathiawadi-background family expressed an awareness of gradual changes in her lifespan, after marrying into a Surti-background family in Port Elizabeth. In her words, this change of speech was 'not an issue, but an adjustment'.

3. The chain shift in colloquial Gujarati

This section concerns the chain shift of consonants in Gujarati dialects of India, which has – rather surprisingly – not been studied before, prior to Mesthrie (2022), who labels it the 's-shift'. One reason for this omission is that analysts have tended to focus on standard Gujarati, whose unshifted norms are similar to those of languages like Hindi. However, the dialects evince a series that can in an idealised form be characterised as *k, kh → c, ch → s, ś → ḥ* and *ɦ → ø*. (The arrow notation in chain shift studies indicates that one sound impinges on the space of another without necessarily displacing it.) In expanded form this formula can be fleshed out as follows: earlier *k* and *kh* become *c* and *ch* before front vowels; earlier *c* and *ch* become *s* (and sometimes *ś*); earlier *s* becomes voiceless *ḥ*; and earlier voiced *ɦ* becomes zero (often with murmur on the accompanying vowel – hence the notation *hV → øV̤* in Table 10.4 below). From Grierson's (1908) lists of features of early twentieth-century Gujarati, it is clear that the dialects do not participate equally in the shift. Mesthrie (2022) provides a handy bird's-eye view of the differential uptake of the shift in the four main dialects of Gujarat, repeated here as Table 10.3, with his accompanying notes.

Mesthrie (2022) provides loanword evidence from the fourteenth CE to argue that this is a chain shift of long duration. As with all chain shifts, matters are more variable and complex on the ground than allowed for in the idealised form, by virtue of other sound changes, dialect borrowings, and influence from the standard forms. Moreover, as Table 10.3 shows, not all parts of the chain shift apply to all dialects equally. For example, earlier *ɦ* in initial position is not dropped in Kathiawadi; and related to this is the fact that earlier *s* in this dialect becomes aspirated [s^h] not *ḥ*. There are parallels among the voiced consonants showing shifts of *g, gh → j* and *j, jh → z*. The chain shift thus provides a useful diagnostic to assess the extent of dialect survivals in South African Gujarati. Table 10.4 repeats the information for Surti and Kathiawadi in a tabular form and summarises the findings for Cape Town Gujarati in the rightmost column.

3.1 *ɦ → ø*

Feature (1) in the above list of Table 10.4 concerns the (variable) deletion of /ɦ/, which is well attested in the Cape Town data.

Table 10.3 *A skeletal summary of the s-shift in four Gujarati dialects and the standard*

Surti:	*ch → s → ḥ; h → ø*
Charotari:	*k, kh → c, ch → s → ḥ; hV → øV̤*
Kathiawadi:	*k, kh → c, ch → s → ḥ; h → ø*
North/Pattani:	*k, kh → c, ch → s → ḥ; h → ø*
Std Gujarati:	*hV → øV̤* (variably)

Notes:
k → c applies only before front vowels.
kh → ch applies only before front vowels. Double shifts to *s* occur variably in Charotari, and to *ś* in Kathiawadi.
ś is a regular co-variant of 'derived *s*' before front vowels in Kathiawadi.
ch → s is highly variable in initial position in Charotari, with variants *ch, ćh, s.*
c → s is highly variable in initial and medial position in Charotari with variants *c, ć, s.*
s → ḥ does not apply in sC clusters. *s^h* is a major initial reflex in Kathiawadi. Final *s* shows double shifts to *ø* with numerals.
h → ø does not apply initially in Kathiawadi.

The Dialect Roots of Varieties of Gujarati in South Africa

Table 10.4 *The s-shift in Surti and Kathiawadi dialects and its uptake in Cape Town*

	Surti	Kathiawadi	Cape Town
Cluster II: Chain shifting in consonants			
1. Earlier [ɦ] variably deleted	+	+	+R
2. Earlier [s] > voiceless [h]	+	+	+
3. Earlier [s] > [sʰ] initially	−	+	−
4. Std [ʃ] > [s] or [h] (or [ʃ])	+	−	+
5. Earlier [cʃʰ] > [s]	+	+	+
6. Earlier [cʃ] > [s]	−	+	−
7. Earlier [k kʰ] > [cʃ cʃʰ]	−	+	−
8. Earlier [dʒ] and [dʒʰ] > [z]	−	+	−
9. Earlier [gh] > [dʒ] before front vowels	−	−	−
10. Earlier [g] > [dʒ] before front vowels	−	−	−

Cape Town variant	Std form	Gloss
utu	hatū	'was'
oy	hoy	'have'
ohe	haśe	'might, can be'
reṭā	rahetā	'lived'
revā dem	rahevā daũ	'I'll leave it'
kiyũ	kahyũ	'told'

The loss of medial /ɦ/ in the above set (for *rahetā*, *rahevā* and *kahyũ*) is associated with syllable loss of /ah/ and in the case of *kahyũ* – insertion of /i/ before /y/ to keep a bisyllabic structure.

3.2 s → ḥ

Under (2) in Table 10.4 we consider the change of [s] to [h], which is well attested in the Cape Town data. The following examples are from the Cape Town database:

Cape Town variant	Std form	Gloss
hāru	sāru	'good'
hāthe	sāthe	'together'
paihā	paisā	'money'
behe	bese	'sit'

3.3 c, ch → s

Under (5), we note the correspondence of Cape Town [s] to std [cʃʰ].

Cape Town variant	Std form	Gloss
oso	ocho	'less'
vắcu su	vắcu chũ	'I am reading'
pusavānu	puchavānu	'to ask'
pasi	pachi	'after'

We have not come across [s] corresponding to unaspirated [cʃ] forms. This is a confirmation of the Surti character of CPT Gujarati, since all other dialects in Table 10.4 show both c and ch → s.

3.4 ś → s

Feature (4) involves dialect [s] or even [h] corresponding to std [ʃ] is well attested in the Cape Town variety:

Cape Town variant	Std form	Gloss
sakaṭu	śakatū	'should be done'
des	deś	'homeland'
suḍh	śuddh	'pure'
su	śū	'what'
sikhelā	śikhelā	'learned'
nihār	niśāḷ	'school'
ohe	haśe	'might, can be'
hikhavtā	śikhavatā	'were teaching'

However, there is considerable variation by speaker, with ś forms also found fairly commonly. Turning to other segments of the shift (feature 7 in Table 10.4), we find no examples of k, kh → c, ch in the Cape Town data. Once again this conforms to the summary in Table 10.4 for the dialects of Gujarat.

3.5 Voiced segments

There are also no examples involving shifts within the voiced set of consonants (features 8–10).[9] Changes of the sort g, gh → j or of j, jh → z are not part of the Cape Town data. Thus, Cape Town Gujarati exactly parallels Surti point by point for the segments of the shift. We stress that the correspondence of standard [ʃ] to [s] or even [h] is variable, with both [s] or [ʃ] occurring with roughly the same frequency among the six speakers studied.

3.6 Comparison with Durban and Port Elizabeth

We again turn briefly to our data from Durban and then Port Elizabeth. We might ask whether Surti descendants in Durban show evidence of the shift as robustly as in Cape Town. We also ask how Kathiawadi descendants of Durban fare in this regard, and finally ask if there is evidence of some degree of convergence between the two dialects in Durban with respect to features associated with the chain shift.

For s → ɦ the figure for the total number of tokens in the five-minute sample is 28/191 (or 14.7 per cent). Although this is a feature of both Surti and Kathiawadi dialects in India (see Table 10.4), the correlation in Durban is stronger with speakers of Surti ancestry. Three of five speakers of Surti ancestry in the sample used this feature – with occurrences of 11/13 (84.6 per cent), 14/23 (60.9 per cent) and 2/11 (18.2 per cent) respectively. In contrast, one of four speakers of Kathiawad ancestry used this feature – with a rate of occurrence of 28/191 (14.7 per cent). Kathiawadi speakers thus use the more standard forms, in keeping with the general impression of Usha Desai, cited in section 1.2.

Likewise for ɦ → ø there appears to be a degree of convergence in our sample, rather than a clear differentiation between the two dialects. In word-initial position there are no tokens with ɦ → ø in the way we report for Cape Town above. However, some speakers in Durban do show loss of an initial syllable containing /ɦ/ + vowel. This would appear to be a fast speech feature (for speakers of either dialect), involving past forms of the verb 'to be': *to, ti, ta* for *hato, hati* and *hata* (n = 4 tokens among three speakers). Thus *gayā hatā* 'had gone' may become *gyātā* in fast speech. Apart from this fast speech effect, Kathiawadi descendants do not show any loss of [ɦ] in initial position, in keeping with what is reported for India (Grierson 1908). Medially, both dialects are reported to show /ɦ/ loss in Gujarat. This is also the case in Durban (Kathiawadis 25/47 = 53.2 per cent of tokens; Surtis 6/7 = 85.7 per cent).

In final position we have too few tokens for reliable analysis, but for sake of completeness will record that of the three instances, all were used by speakers of Kathiawadi ancestry.

There is a high uptake of ś → s among Surti speakers in Durban, as in Cape Town. Whereas the Durban data has five tokens of ś → s used by a single Kathiawadi, there are fifteen tokens among four different Surti descendants. Again, the suggestion of greater use of standard forms among speakers from Kathiawad appears to hold, though the one speaker would appear to show accommodation to Surti speakers, since this feature is not reported in the Kathiawad area of Gujarat.

k → c: in Gujarat this change occurs before front vowels in all dialects except Surti, though even in Kathiawadi this is a lesser variant. The Durban data shows no signs of this change at all (0 per cent; n = 33 before front vowels).

The related change of /j/ > [z] does not occur in the Durban data (0 per cent, n = 284).

As far as Port Elizabeth is concerned, the following changes were in evidence. s → ḥ; ś → s. Other segments of the shift were not evident in the cited forms, nor did they not seem familiar to interviewees. Port Elizabeth thus gives evidence of some Surti features, but not as strongly as Cape Town.

4. Miscellaneous changes

We now turn to the set of miscellaneous changes in the dialect literature.

4.1 Miscellaneous consonantal features

Table 10.5 gives a short list of further consonantal features of the dialects of Gujarat, with a summary of their appearance in Cape Town in the rightmost column.

Under (1) in Table 10.5, we do find instances in our Cape Town data of the doubling of medial consonants compared to the standard.

Cape Town variant	Std form	Gloss
tājjā	tājā	'fresh'
rammat gammat	ramat gamat	'sport'

Table 10.5 *Miscellaneous consonant features in dialects of Gujarat*

	Surti	Kathiawadi	Charotari	Pattani	Cape Town
Cluster III: Misc. consonant features					
1. Medial consonants may be doubled	+	–	–	–	+
2. Earlier C + [j] > [j] + C	+	–	–	–	+
3. [n] covaries with [l] in some words	+	–	–	–	+

Whereas the above examples of doubling are 'spontaneous', other instances are a result of miscellaneous phonological processes like apocope or assimilation:

Cape Town variant	Std form	Gloss
addhi	aḍadhi	'half'
pelli	paheli	'first'
pannelo	parṇelo	'he is married'

Addhi above shows the loss of medial [ə] and assimilation of [ḍ] to the following [dh]. *Pelli* shows the loss of medial /ah/ noted above, but this time with doubling of the following consonant. *Pannelo* shows loss of pre-consonantal [r] before [ṇ], with compensatory doubling. The retroflex standard [ṇ] appears as a dental, which undergoes doubling. The loss of pre-consonantal [r] is not widespread, this being the only example in our database.

In the Durban data we do get some spontaneous doubling, mostly among those of Surti background. However, one speaker of Kathiawadi background also produced doubling in *baddhā* 'obstruction, restriction' (Std Gu *bādhā*). This would appear to be under the influence of Surti speakers in Durban, since this word so pronounced occurred twice in the Surti data. Other examples are *ummare* 'at that age' and *ākkhi* 'whole (f)'. Doubling resulting from apocope is fairly common among the Durban Gujarati speakers irrespective of ancestral background: *pellā* 'first' (from *pahelā*) being of particular frequency and used by five speakers (two of Kathiawadi and three of Surti background).

Feature (2) in Table 10.5 is a Surti characteristic of metathesis showing /aɪ/ + C + V > C + /y/ + V and is quite prominent in Cape Town Gujarati, especially with verbs, since /y/ + V may carry past participle meaning:[10]

Cape Town variant	Std form	Gloss
bhaiṇā	bhaṇyā	'learned'
boilā	bolyā	'said'
bainu	banyu	'occurred'
lāigo	lāgyo	'began'
kāiḍho	kāḍhyo	'removed'

Again, the Durban data provide evidence of a small degree of convergence in the direction of Surti. Of twenty-one tokens of this feature, eighteen occurred among Kathiawadi descendants, three among Surti descendants. This feature therefore shows possible dialect diffusion in Durban, since Grierson and Sampat give no indication of this feature for Kathiawadi in Gujarat.

The Dialect Roots of Varieties of Gujarati in South Africa

Feature (3) in Table 10.5 is one associated with Surti (Grierson 1908: 382) that is also found in Cape Town, viz. the correspondence of std [ṇ] with dialect [l̤]. Hence *nāllo* is a form found in the Cape Town data, together with Std *nāno* 'little'. In the Durban data this feature does not occur within our sample, though the authors have heard the standard/Kathiwadi form in Durban, rather than *nallo*. Summarising cluster III, we see that Cape Town Gujarati matches Surti in the three features that set it apart from the other three dialects of Gujarati in India. Durban speakers show the influence of the Surti characteristics over Kathiawadi speakers. We have no data from Port Elizabeth on these forms.

4.2 Miscellaneous vowel features

There are two vowel features that vary across the dialects of Gujarat (Grierson 1908), as reflected in Table 10.6. These two features concern *i ~ e* in words like *nĕche* for *nĭche* 'below' and [aː] ~ [ɔː] in *pani* versus *poni* 'water'. These features are rare in our overall data. Feature (1) does occur in the set phrase *e loko* 'these people' among some speakers in Durban. Feature (2) is absent in Surti and in Cape Town Gujarati, nor did we come across any such forms in Durban and Port Elizabeth.

5. Conclusion

We began this study of Gujarati in Cape Town as an effort in heritage linguistics, to document what we could about a language that had first arrived over 140 years ago and had been spoken continuously since. We had been expecting a fair amount of change under language contact in a multilingual situation where speakers are additionally fluent in English and Afrikaans. We had not anticipated the degree to which dialect loyalty was prevalent in Cape Town, with Surti characteristics alive and well after 140 years. In comparison, the influence of language contact is not as strong, nor is the influence of the standard which is introduced in part-time Gujarati schools and used in formal speech making and at religious functions. Vinu Chavda who undertook the Gujarati interviews notes that influences via borrowings from English and code-switching seem less prominent than in present-day Gujarat. She also notes the paucity of loanwords from Afrikaans, though this may have been minimised by interviewees' being aware of her lack of knowledge of this language.

Two further unanticipated discoveries awaited us in this research. The first was the antiquity of many of the features described in this chapter. Retroflex variation may well go back to a pre-Sanskritic phase. Beames (1871: 222–32) provided copious examples of Sanskrit words with a dental turning up differentially and

Table 10.6 *Miscellaneous vowel features in dialects of Gujarat*

	Surti	Kathiawadi	Charotari	Pattani	Cape Town
Cluster IV: Misc. vowel features					
1. [i] covaries with [e]	–	+	+	+	–
2. [ɑː] covaries with [ɒː][11]	–	–	+	+	–

unsystematically across Indo-Aryan languages, with a retroflex in some and a dental in others. Whereas standard Gujarati appears to side with languages such as Hindi in respect of the use of retroflexes, its dialects appear to side with Rajasthani-aligned varieties such as Marwari and Mewati.

Likewise, the *s*-shift shows a bifurcation between Standard Gujarati and the dialects that goes back centuries (see the evidence for the operation of the shift in loanwords from the fifteenth CE on in Mesthrie 2022). The dialects of Gujarati side with the Rajasthani-aligned varieties, as well as Marathi, Assamese and Bengali with regards to *c, ch* → *s* and *s* → *ḥ*, while taking the shift to an extreme in having murmured or even zero realisations of earlier *h*. Standard Gujarati sides with Central Indo-Aryan, especially Hindi in respect of the shift. It gives us some satisfaction to have uncovered deep historic-phonological variation via initial investigations of a humble, receding dialect spoken in diaspora.

Appendix

Sample of Cape Town Gujarati (showing some typical Surti features). Speaker JP (female, aged 67 years).

māy madhar ṭo pahelā jyāre shāḍi karine āyvā tyāre tabiyat brābar hati. to baddhā ahīyā gāmamā ene jāri ketā. jāri ketā pan eno sabhāv to bahu j naram. ekḍam naram haṭo. mārā bāpuji key tem karyā karatā, ne pachi ḍukān rākhi eṭle ḍukhānmā ākho ḍivas bhizi. baḍhā poyrā ek bijā, ek pachi ek baḍhā born thiyā te badhā dukānmā j ame moṭā thayelā. pan māy madhar amne baddhu shikhavelu che/she? rā̃dhavānu shikhavelū che/she. ame skule jatā skulethi āyavā pachi amāre bas rasorāmā javānū eṭale javānū j. masṭ rā̃dhvā hikhavānū j. amāre hivānū kām karavānū, naṭī̃gnū kām karavānū eṭale gūṭhavānū kām karavānū. e baddhu ame hikhelā che. evu k, evu ek ben evū ni male ke nathi hikhli.

[**Gloss:** When my mother first came after her marriage, her health was good. People, here, called her fatty. Despite being called fatty, she was congenial. Very polite. She followed my father's instructions and when we bought a shop, she became busy. We, the children, were born one after the other and were raised in the shop only. But my mother taught us everything. Taught us cooking. After returning from the school, we had to enter the kitchen and it was mandatory to learn cooking. We had to learn sewing. We had to learn knitting. We have learnt all that. There is nothing that I have not learnt – household chores and managing the shop.]

Annotated gloss of first three sentences:

my madhar   ṭo   pahelā   jyāre shāḍi   karine   āyvā
my mother   TOPIC   first   when marriage   do.PAST   come.PAST

tyāre tabiyat brābar ha-ti.
then health FOCUS be-PAST

to	baddhā	ahīyā	gāma-mā̃	ene	jāri ketā.
then	all	here	village.in	her	fat call.PAST

jāri ketā	pan	eno sabhāv to	bahu j naram.
fat call.PAST	though	she always TOPIC	very polite

ekḍam	naram	ha-ṭo.
extremely	polite	be.PAST

Notes

1. Reasons given for their relocation to Australia include the growing uncertainty in South Africa over crime and increasing rather than decreasing hostility towards Indians in KZN province in the post-apartheid era.
2. Bhojpuri-Hindi must be taken as a convenient label to refer to varieties from the vast continuum of languages and dialects from the old Bengal presidency and neighbouring districts: it could even be labelled a Bhojpuri-Magahi-Awadhi-Hindi-Urdu continuum in full, with Bhojpuri and Awadhi forming the most influential components.
3. The university began as the University College for Indians in 1961. By the mid-1980s it had become more racially integrated and with the collapse of apartheid it more or less dissolved to become part of the amalgamated University of KwaZulu-Natal.
4. The figures include one person of joint Surat and Navsari origin.
5. Desai (1997) mentions one prominent family in Durban of migrants from the Charotar district, which forms an exception to the Surti-Kathiawadi-Kacchi nexus in South Africa. Work on Kacchi (Memani) in South Africa has yet to be undertaken.
6. The retroflex realisation is also typical of cognate forms in other languages such as Hindi.
7. The exceptional speaker showed a general paucity of tokens but did produce some standard forms in other parts of the interview.
8. In contrast, there is mention of one prominent family emanating from the Charotari dialect area (Desai 1997).
9. Apart from voiced ɦ which we have already treated under the shifting of voiceless consonants.
10. An additional example, *poyrā* for standard *poriyā* 'children' retains Parsi influence in Indian Surti and thence in Cape Town Gujarati.
11. Grierson's (1908: 329) symbol is 'broad o' or ô.

References

Barz, Richard and Jeff Siegel. 1988. *Language Transplanted: The Development of Overseas Hindi*. Wiesbaden: Otto Harrassowitz.

Beames, John. 1970 [1871]. *A Comparative Grammar of the Modern Aryan Languages of India*. New Delhi: Munshiram Manoharlal (reprint of original three volumes).

Bhana, Surendra. 2011. The dynamics of preserving cultural heritage: The case of Durban's Kathiawad Hindu Seva Samaj, 1943–1960 and beyond. *South Asian Diaspora*, 3 (1): 15–36.

Bhana, Surendra and Joy Brain. 1990. *Setting Down Roots: Indian Migrants in South Africa, 1860–1911*. Johannesburg: Witwatersrand University Press.

Cardona, George and Babu Suthar. 2003. Gujarati. In George Cardona and Dinesh Jain (eds), *The Indo-Aryan Languages*. London: Routledge, pp. 659–97.

Desai, Usha. 1997. *Investigation of Factors Influencing Maintenance and Shift of the Gujarati Language in South Africa*. PhD dissertation, University of Durban–Westville.

Desai, Usha and Malini Ramsay-Brijball. 2004. Tracing Gujarati language development philologically and sociolinguistically. *Alternation*, 11 (2): 308–324.

Dhupelia-Mesthrie, U. 2009. The Passenger Indian as worker: Indian immigrants in Cape Town in the early twentieth century. *African Studies*, 68 (1): 111–34. https://doi.org/10.1080/00020180902827498.

Grierson, Sir George A. 1908. *Linguistic Survey of India*. Vol. IX, Part II: *Indo-Aryan Family, Central Group – Rajasthani and Gujarati*. Delhi: Motilal Banarsidas.

Hajratwala, Minal. 2009. *Leaving India: My Family's Journey from Five Villages to Five Continents*. Milton, FL: Houghton Mifflin Harcourt.

Lal, Brij. 2006. *Encyclopedia of the Indian Diaspora*. Singapore: Éditions Didier Meillets.

Lodhi, Abdulaziz. 2008. Indians and Indic languages in Eastern Africa: The status of South Asian languages in Eastern Africa. Paper given at workshop on language planning and language policies, 4–6 March 2008, Central Institute of Indian Languages (CIIL), Mysore, India.

Mawani, Sharmina and Anjoom Mukadam (eds). 2014. *Globalisation, Diaspora and Belonging: Exploring Transnationalism and Gujarati Identity*. Jaipur: Rawat Publications.

Meer, Fatima. 1969. *Portrait of Indian South Africans*. Durban: Avon House.

Mesthrie, Rajend. 2022. A chain shift in Indo-Aryan with special reference to Gujarati dialects. *Language Dynamics & Change*, 12 (1): 124–54.

Mesthrie, Rajend and Vinu Chavda. 2020. Cape Town Gujarati and its relation to Gujarati dialectology: A study of retroflex boosting. *Journal of South Asian Languages and Linguistics*. https://doi.org/10.1515/jsall-2020-2022.

Oonk, Gijsbert (ed.). 2007. *Global Indian Diasporas: Exploring Trajectories of Migration and Theory*. Amsterdam: Amsterdam University Press.

Sampat, Madhu. 1973. *Comparative Study of Three Gujarati Dialects (Surti, Charotari, and Kathiyawadi)*. PhD dissertation, Deccan College, Poona.

Shah, Sheena. 2018. The use of Kiswahili loanwords in London Gujarati. Paper presented at the International Congress of Linguists, Cape Town, July.

Siegel, Jeff. 1987. *Language Contact in a Plantation Environment*. Cambridge: Cambridge University Press.

Swan, Maureen. 1985. *Gandhi – The South African Experience*. Johannesburg: Ravan Press.

Upadhya, Carol and Mario Rutten. 2012. Migration, transnational flows and development in India – A regional perspective. *Economic and Political Weekly*, 47 (19): 54–62. LP_SA_CarolUpadhyay23April2012_PC-2.indd (nias.res.in) (accessed 3 October 2021).

Vahed, Goolam. 2010. An 'imagined community' in diaspora: Gujaratis in South Africa. *South Asian History and Culture*, 1 (4): 615–29.

Vertovec, Steve. 2003. *The Hindu Diaspora: Comparative Patterns*. London: Routledge.

CHAPTER 11

South African Gujarati Literature: An Inventory and Critical Commentary

Mrunal Chavda and Rajend Mesthrie

1. Introduction

South Africa offers a unique political, religious and cultural diversity, including a complex body of language and literature in many languages. Indian literature in English (including writers of Indian origins born or living abroad) has been well studied. In contrast, literature produced in Indian languages in the diaspora does not appear on the radar of many literary scholars. Yet P. S. Joshi (1949: 612), whose work is discussed below, had argued seventy years ago in a survey on South African Indian writing that their 'abundant Indian literature' required an 'exhaustive investigation'. Similarly, in his study on Urdu as an African language, Nile Green (2012: 174) suggests that the Gujarati corpus in East Africa is still 'waiting to be discovered'.

Building on Usha Desai's (1997, 2000) work on South African Gujarati language and literature, this chapter aims to produce a critical inventory of South African Gujarati literature and commentary on the genres created in South Africa from 1920 onwards. The chapter first traces the early history of Gujarati migrants from Gujarat to South Africa. Secondly, it examines how Gandhi's protest writing in South Africa metamorphosed into an annual writing tradition and gradually receded after the 1990s. Thirdly, it engages with Gujarati literary history by emphasising contributions made by South African Gujaratis to Gujarati literature. Finally, it questions why such an active literary culture has not been adequately acknowledged in the mainstream histories of Gujarati. Hence, this chapter cautions against the erasure of a once vibrant literary culture within South Africa. This chapter focuses on themes of cultural identities, transnational places and local spaces to characterise the literature produced by South African writers in Gujarati poems, short stories and essays.

A full assessment of South African Gujarati literature has not been made, though essential contributions have been made by Joshi (1949) and Usha Desai (1997) in her chapter on 'Gujarati literature in South Africa' as part of a larger PhD thesis on language maintenance and shift. This literature is a collaborative one – a composite of Gujarati tradition, British education and South African concerns. These religious and secular confluences form a new sense of Gujaratiness in the diaspora.

2. Gujarati literary history: a brief overview

Majeed (2005) points to a vexed conflict between historical and literary studies in South Asia. Quoting S. Mehta, Majeed argues that the complex polyglot nature of literature emanating from Indian languages multiplies regional literary histories and creates a conglomeration inside South Asian geopolitical boundaries that leaves no space for others. Where India and its regional mainstream literary histories are concerned, this 'other' is South African Gujarati literature. Majeed's reading of Pollock's 'reconstruction' of South Asian literary cultures extends to considering how languages were not necessarily tied to any specific regional territories in pre-modern South Asia. For Majeed (2005: 8), the question of 'space' occupied by specific languages and literary cultures also needs to be rethought. In this sense, South African Gujarati traverses Gujarat's territorial and linguistic boundaries to create new literary locations.

Gujarati is one of the constitutional languages of India and the official language of Gujarat state. Around six crore Gujaratis in India have it as their first language, and the language has additional speakers worldwide, including in Africa, Asia and the Americas.[1] Gujarati has nearly 700 years of literary history, from the twelfth century onward. Table 11.1 illustrates this history briefly.

This chapter considers Gujarati literary history post-1900 (i.e. the fourth phase in Table 11.1) and its literary corpus produced in South Africa. Yashwant Shukla (1977) outlined three significant features of this era: (1) Goverdhanram Tripathi's four-volume novel *Sarasvatichandra* (1887–1901), (2) Gandhi's arrival from South Africa in 1914, and (3) the establishment of Gujarat Vidyapeeth in 1920. In Shukla's words (1977: 69), Gujarati literature witnessed 'a panorama of literature' between 1887 and 1930. Gandhi extended the range of this literature to include South African Gujarati. Born in India, Gandhi was 'made' in South Africa through politics and writing in Gujarati. Gandhi's immense influence is recognised by literary historians' naming two significant periods after him, *Gandhi Yug* (1915–45) and *Anu-Gandhi Yug* (1940–55) ['Gandhian era and post-Gandhian era']. The features Shukla identified above tended to eclipse Gujarati literary traditions outside the geopolitical boundaries of the state. Even literary histories that embraced a broad view of Gujarati and Indian literature, like Sisir Kumar Das (1995), Amaresh Datta, Natarajan and Nelson (1996) and Sujit Mukherjee (1998), have contributed to this neglect. This chapter focuses on Gujarati literature produced in South Africa by writers other than Gandhi. The reason for this is that Gandhi's writings are well known in both Gujarati as well as English originals or translations. The vernacular writing of other Gujaratis is contrarily hardly known and hence subject to an archaeology of its own.

Table 11.1 *Phases of Gujarati literary history*

Phase	Description	Time
First	Old Gujarati	6th–11th centuries
Second	Early Gujarati	11th–mid-14th centuries
Third	Middle Gujarati	Mid-14th–mid-17th centuries
Fourth	Modern	Mid-17th century to 1925
Fifth	Contemporary	1926 onwards

Source: adapted from Gujarati literature (http://gujaratonline.com)

The South African Gujarati community contributed to Gujarati literature in a community magazine entitled *Hitechchu* ['Well-Wisher'], which was published and consumed by Gujaratis in Surat (Gujarat). This tradition remains isolated from mainstream Gujarati literary histories.

3. Gujaratis in South Africa

The Slavery Abolition Act of 1833 in Britain necessitated a new indentured labour policy in colonies such as South Africa, Australia and the Caribbean (Lal 2014: 1146). Enslaved Indians had been taken to Cape Town in the Dutch period from the 1650s onwards. The first batch of Indian labourers arrived on the ship *Truro* in 1860 (Du Bois [1860] 2010: 12). Kalpana Hiralal (2008: 27) discussed the terms 'indentured labour' and 'free or passenger' Indians and stresses that both were 'subjects of the British Empire' in the late 1890s. Redefining this 'free passenger Indian' concept away from preconceptions of privilege, historian Uma Dhupelia-Mesthrie (1985, 2010) identified the trades, occupations and menial work carried out by Indians of such background.

The Gujarati community, with their trade and economic abilities, competed with the white traders, albeit on unequal terms. Legal measures to disadvantage Gujarati (and other Indian) traders led Gandhi, then a lawyer, to stay on in South Africa and enter politics in the 1890s. Gandhi witnessed the injustice to non-whites and turned the legal battle into a socio-political movement. Gandhi started a weekly newspaper, *Indian Opinion*, to spread political, social and literary awareness among South African Indians. This newspaper was published in four languages (Hindi, Gujarati, Tamil and English) and remained 'an excellent asset for those interested in learning more about the cultural practices of South African Indians in the early decades of the twentieth century' (G. Desai 2011: ix). Contributions to this newspaper constructed a socio-political platform and created a kind of sub-genre of Gujarati writings in South Africa.

South Africa witnessed many political upheavals between Gandhi's departure in 1914 and 1961, the year of the last issue of *Indian Opinion*. One of the most significant laws, the Group Areas Act (1950), segregated Africans, coloureds, Indians and whites. This legal measure aimed to change the South Africans' social geography and weaken Indian competitiveness in trade. It forced Indian families to live in designated areas and re-established their lives almost from scratch, as with Gujaratis and other Indians in Rylands, Cape Town. The entire process was hostile and a cause of agony to its targets.

The subsequent relocation to a specifically Indian area brought further modifications of a socio-religious, cultural and educational nature, often shaped by caste, class and religion (Vahed and Waetjen 2010). In Cape Town, caste considerations saw a community split into *Mochis* (shoemakers) versus the rest of the Gujarati community. Two associations which emerged from the split, the Cape Hindu Cultural Society (CHCS henceforth) and the Cape Town Hindu Samaj Seva Centre (CTHSSC henceforth), also known as *Kshatriya Hindu Mitra Mandal*, have a bearing on Cape Town's literary productions.

During these forty years of apartheid, the Hindu Gujarati community in South Africa continued to invest in its language, literature, religion and culture.

Muslim Gujaratis, likewise, were highly conscious of their Indian cultural roots while adhering to Islam. Some of this literary output has resurfaced in the works of historians such as Bhana and Hunt (1989), Bhana and Shukla-Bhatt (2011) and the sociolinguist Usha Desai (2000). Dhupelia-Mesthrie studied *Daan-Daataa Granth* (1995) for historical records of the shoemaker community, names of donors and family histories in Gujarat and South Africa. This *Granth* contains a poem, an editorial and an essay (in English) by Babar Chavda. Similarly, citing a short story from *Indian Opinion* based on migrant families' experiences, Hiralal (2014: 75) explores historical and literary sources with the aim of unearthing' female migration experiences and challenge traditional historiography, which viewed women as 'independent categories of analysis'.

4. South African Gujarati literature

Usha Desai (2000) cites the following genres in periodicals, magazines and special editions in South Africa: political literature, religious-cultural literature, fiction, drama, poetry, and short stories. She points to writers' 'urge' and 'inspiration' (Desai 2000: 24) to compose in their first language and preserve the Gujarati language in South Africa. She observes that rather than being 'literary masterpieces', these writings express 'concerns about socio-political issues', frequently giving vent to their emotions on various topics (Desai 2000: 71). While this may also be said of some of the writings surveyed in this chapter, this view does not do justice to the literary qualities of Gandhi's writings and a few others from the South African Gujarati community discussed below.

Mansukhlal Hiralal Nazar's letters in Gujarati written during 1902–3 (ed. with translations by Surendra Bhana and James Hunt 1989) fall squarely into the political genre. These sixty-one letters are personal exchanges between Gandhi and Nazar concerning daily operations editing the *Indian Opinion*. The writings give insight into Nazar's role as editor of *Indian Opinion* and Gandhi's support of individuals in the South African struggle. Published at Phoenix Settlement (Durban), this weekly newspaper informed a large audience of the status of the *Satyagraha* movement in South Africa. Gandhi's interaction with his readership helped build a literary culture, as seen from the poems, short stories and essays published in the newspaper. The poems were collected in the publication *A Fire that Blazed in the Ocean*, carrying the subtitle *Gandhi and the Poems of Satyagraha in South Africa 1909–1911*, edited by Bhana and Shukla-Bhatt (2011). In their introduction, they cite the development and evolution of a literary culture led by Gandhi and followed by Indians in South Africa. Like Desai (cited above), the editors acknowledge that the poems often 'lack the sophistication of fine literary works with some exceptions' (Bhana and Shukla-Bhatt 2011: 14). It is unlikely, however, that Gandhi was expecting this literary culture to reflect the Gujarati Literature of the *Pandit Yug* ['scholar era'], as those who were contributing at that point of history in South Africa were traders and not literary specialists. Instead, Gandhi generated public conversations through the newspaper, with readers espousing the ideals and values of the Satyagraha movement. Their writings had 'virtually remained unknown' (Bhana and Shukla-Bhatt 2011: 14), previously untranslated from the Gujarati medium.

These poems convey personal pain and hardship at one level, but at another level they reflect the gradual evolution of Gandhi's political ideology. The *Indian Opinion* merged political, social and literary consciousness in its addresses to readers, urging them to join Gandhi's *Satyagraha*. For example, Sheik Mehtab articulated the sacrifice expected of the *Satyagrahi*: *If you are ready to give up / Delicious meals, luxuries, and loved ones, / Then, readily put on handcuffs; / Otherwise, the path is straight* (ll.14–17, transl. Bhana and Shukla-Bhatt (2011: 120)). The resolve implied in these lines evokes a sense of the early Indian struggle led by Gandhi in South Africa without much poetic embellishment. This intent to organise and unite against political discrimination is confirmed in S. H. L. Alipurwala's poem 'Oh, What Times Have Come'. Similar to Mehtab's efforts, this poem pledges to end social and racial discrimination through Gandhi's *Satyagraha*. Interestingly, this poem by Alipurwala appeared in the *Indian Opinion* as a *Poem for Struggle* in Gujarati script. However, a careful reading of the poem indicates that the language of the text is, in fact, Urdu.

Political prose writers made parallel contributions to South African Gujarati Literature. One such writer is Pranshankar Someshwar Joshi, better known as P. S. Joshi. He was born on 20 February 1897 in Jetpur, Rajkot. Joshi studied in Junagadh at Bahauddin College, affiliated with Bombay University. Joshi came to South Africa in 1920, taking up an appointment at the Government Indian School in Newtown, Johannesburg. An active contributor to literature, politics and translations, he was the president of *Shri Satsadhak Samaj* (Truth Seeker Society) and vice president of *Transvaal Hindu Seva Samaj* (Transvaal Hindu Service Centre). He was active in international organisations such as the International Club, the Indo-European Joint Council, and the I.I.O. German Academy (Bramdaw 1939). He represented India at a South African Spiritualist Conference in Germiston in 1928. In addition, he lectured on Hindu religion and philosophy, Indian art, culture, and history at scholarly bodies such as the Mystic Quest Fellowship, the Spiritual Association, and Kindred Philosophies. In 1943, he became the first non-European member of the writers' organisation, PEN.

Joshi's best-known work is *the Tyranny of Colour* (1942), an English translation of the Gujarati version published in 1937 as *Rangdvesh no Durga* (Joshi 1942: preface). This work makes him – together with Gandhi – a pioneer of political writing in Gujarati Literature. His other writings include *Verdict on South Africa* (1945), *Apartheid in South Africa* (1950), the *Struggle for Equality* (1951), *Resurgent India* (1953), *Unrest in South Africa* (1958) and *Mahatma Gandhi in South Africa* (1980). His other Gujarati works include *British Shahivad ni Janjiro* (Shackles of British Monarchy), *Dakshin Africani Rangbhumi* (South Africa: A Racial Laboratory) and *Smruti Prasango* (1958) (What I Recall). Joshi also translated into Gujarati works such as C. F. Andrew's *Claim for Independence* as *Svatantrata no Davo* and Harindranath Chattopadhyay's *The Sleeper Awakened* as *Ungh ane Jagruti*. In his review of the book in the *Journal of Negro History*, Holmes (1944) writes that Joshi remained 'loyal and thorough' in his historical perspective about the conditions faced by Indians, blacks and coloureds within the South African white supremacist philosophy. Such confrontation with the South African authorities during apartheid led to his being put under house arrest and subsequent deportation in 1957. Desai (1997: 199) notes, 'The Censor Board of South Africa placed a ban on *Tyranny of Colour*, and some 200 copies were confiscated and burned.' It is evident from Joshi's writing that his knowledge of historical, cultural and economic ties between South Africa and India remains at par with any other during his time. This acumen is further exposed in his *Smruti Prasango* (1958) (What I Recall), published after one year of his deportation.[2] Writing in the first person, Joshi offered convincing political and legal accounts of the Apartheid times:

> e navaa kanunthi parinitaa vayani ane bhavishyani hindi prajaane, khaasa karine jeonu gnyaati ke lagna karavanu vartuL vishaL naa hoy temane khaasso phaTako laagyo. teone aa deshamaan akudarati patni vihin jivan gaLavun athavaa to desh choDi javo te sambandhe antim nirnay karavaano samay aavyo. 1956ni sharuaata thai ane svadesaman rahelan kuTumbo dakshin aphrika aavavaa lagyan. 10 phebruaarini amangaL tithie je stri chokaran naa aavi shakya teono daksin aphrikaana vasavaaTano hak sadaane mate calyo gayo. aavo hak khonaara kuTumbo sarvaanshe Gujaraati hataa. teman ek marun hatun. (Joshi, *Smruti Prasango* (What I Recall): 255–6)

> [This new law affected eligible Indians with narrow social caste circles for marriages. Such Indians have to decide now between leaving this country or remaining here without a natural wife. At the beginning of 1956, families started to return to South Africa from their hometowns. Those who could not enter on the inauspicious day of 10th February had to forgo their right to live in South Africa. As a result, many families lost their rights. My family was one of them.]

Joshi paints a vivid picture of the law's psychological and legal implications on Indians, including himself. The simplicity of language enables the readers to visualise concrete images of personal experiences. Under the shadow of Gandhi's political writings, Joshi's contribution to political journalism, in both English and Gujarati, remained largely unnoticed in India. Moreover, under the shadow of apartheid censorship, this state of affairs is slightly different in South Africa.

South African Gujarati literature faced competition not only from English but from Urdu as well. Buzme Adab, a literary organisation, was founded in 1932 and currently promotes mainly Urdu literary activities in South Africa (Tayob 1995, Mesthrie 2010). Mesthrie (2015: 135) describes Buzme Adab as 'a Muslim cultural organization devoted to supporting Urdu and has promoted this language in poetry, religion, and writing. There are also individuals who wrote poetry in Gujarati and Hindi … .' The group initially functioned as an 'Eastern cultural' association, representing Indians of different backgrounds in South Africa. Harishchandra Arya, one of the secretaries of the organisation, stressed this in an editorial to a Bazme Adab publication of 1967:

> We came to this country with our Eastern cultural background and found ourselves contacting African and Western cultures. In the process, we have continued to lose and gain. We are standing today on the threshold of a new cultural development manifesting itself from intermingling different cultures. We strongly feel, however, that there are certain features of our Eastern cultures – specifically in the field of artistic, linguistic and philosophical expressions – that we must retain at all costs if we are to contribute our share in

the enrichment of the emerging common culture in our country – South Africa. Here, the work of an organization such as the Buzme Adab (Transvaal) comes in. Through its activities, it contributes to preserving our language, literature, music, and arts. Thereby the organization promotes and satisfies our people's and our country's cultural needs.

The excerpt stresses both the value of traditional Indian cultures and the need to contribute to the cultures of South Africa. Bhabha's (2002) tenet that 'identity is never an *a priori*, nor a finished product' holds valid for indentured and passenger Indians in the diaspora. While Yusuf Sheikhji's (1967) 'Ode to 1967 Kavi Sammelan' is overtly a celebration of the gathering of poets in Natal, it also reminds us that traditional Indian culture did not always embrace religious unity:[3]

I that behold Buzme Adab's Kavi Sammelan in Natal
[...] Hindu-Muslim Unity dream I saw realized
Zeal to serve culture through literature arrived
Dipak and Sheikhji poet participants here I saw
Love and hugs to all poets from Transvaal I saw.

Many other poems reiterate the new communal harmony that Arya projected. He promotes the maintenance of Indian identity without religious compartmentalisation among South African Indians in the 1960s. The organisation promoted this culture through literary activities and celebrating festivals such as Eid and Diwali with *Mushairaya* and *Kavi Sammelan*. *Mushairaya* and *Kavi Sammelan* refer to a poetic symposium, a tradition where poets gather and recite their work, especially in the regions where ghazals (short poems composed in Gujarati, Hindi or Urdu) predominate. The issues of the *Diwali* magazine (published in Cape Town, Johannesburg, and Durban and with contributions from other parts of South Africa) from 1967, 1968 and 1971 invited artists, musicians and poets from India. These include D. S. Maharaj, Natwar Bhimji, Rekha Devi, Hassan and Asim Randeri (a Gujarati poet born in Surat, 1904–2009). This sense of, or at least intention towards, unity among Gujaratis in South Africa, articulated by Arya and Sheikhji, is perhaps less strong today in an era of different class dynamics and the dominance of English. On the inevitability of 'a radical historicization' arising from a constant 'process of change and transformation' in all diasporas, see Stuart Hall (2002: 17). In the Gauteng region, Umiyashankar Jokhakar, who was a Gujarati teacher and secretary of Buzme Adab (writing under the pen name *Dipak* meaning 'light'), produced, edited and cyclostyled a handwritten annual publication of *Kavya Guccha* in his garage in Lenasia, based on written submissions from poets (Jokhakar-Vaidya 2017).[4]

Like Jokhakar, Kanti Mehta came to South Africa as a Gujarati teacher serving in the *Shree Bharat Sharda Mandir* (temple) in Fordsburg (Johannesburg). He composed his poems under two pen names – *Raktashru* (Tears of blood) and *Ashlesh* (Embrace). His poetical works comprise *Zankar* (1993) (Sounds of Anklets), *Gujarat Na Gungaan* (Praises of Gujarat), *Baharo Phul Barsavo* (Nature's Shower of Flowers) and *Mehaki Uthi Suvas* (Smelling the Fragrance). He co-authored poetical works such as *Ankur* (Bud) and *Lagan ma Jarak Dokiyu* (A Glimpse into a Marriage) with

Karasandas Prajapati. His poem *Viday Vele* (On Farewell) expresses his mental agony in leaving his homeland:

> Embarking for South Africa
> On a moment of farewell
> The *Vayu*[5] god sanctified
> Flying fragments of my motherland
> Bidding me farewell
> Deposited them on my forehead
> Preserving them all, I
> In my tiny heart's treasure!

The theme of longing for Gujarat and the Gujarati language recurs among South African Gujarati poets. Mehta employs personification and supernatural imagery, demonstrating a highly skilled command of the language. He also emphasises the proximity of the two locations (South Africa as 'host' and Gujarat as 'home') in his heart. Jokhakar (1967) wrote an appreciation of Mehta's ability as a poet and his employment of Gujarati meters in his works. A Gujarati poet Natwarlal Pandya (1967), also known as *Ushnas*, commented that Mehta's poems reflect his love for nature, the Gujarati language, and a strong desire for his 'homeland' of Gujarat. Pandya's remarks on Mehta's work signal an awareness of South African Gujarati literature in India.

These poets not only expressed their love for the motherland and feelings of Indian nationalism in their poems but often articulated a spirituality rooted in Indian philosophy. Dineshchandra Bhatt's pen name *Kailash* is testimony to this, since it references a Himalayan mountain where Lord Shiva resides according to ancient mythology. Bhatt, from Louis Trichardt, a town in Limpopo province in South Africa, had published numerous poems in *Kavya Guccha* (Bouquet of Poems). His poem 'Imprisoned I' registers the enchained existence of human beings. The poet yearns for spiritual attainment, which his worldly attachments prevent him from achieving, keeping him 'Entrapped in circumstances / Fastened by love chains':

> I am a prisoner without chains
> Captured in worldly attachments
> [...] Such a prisoner I am bound in life and death
> I am a prisoner without a chain. (D. Bhatt 1967: 19)

However, the desire to attain moksha (salvation) has not progressed to fruition, as the poet cannot detach himself from the world around him. The direct references to symbols from the *Bhagavad Gita*, such as the bird with clipped wings, love chains and souls as prisoners, connect strongly with Indian philosophy. Contemporary human life is portrayed as an internal psychological turmoil conjoined with physical discomfort.

Despite the efforts of several Hindu organisations and individuals, Gujarati's written output gradually subsided in South Africa. Buzme Adab is primarily associated with the Urdu language and literature in the absence of a generation of Gujarati writers. The swing towards Urdu also reflects a fracture of Gujarati identity into Hindu Gujaratis and Muslims against the earlier aspirations to 'Indian' identity in general. Furthermore, it can be argued that in time the necessity changed from literary productivity to a concern for maintaining religion, culture and language in the face of increasing access to Western education and the professions.

5. Diwali and annual magazine writing culture: genres and themes

As Standing (2014) and Ettlinger (2007) discuss in connection with diasporas generally, South African Gujarati writers emerged from 'a distanced underclass' to create micro-social and cultural spaces for themselves. An important part of this assertion came from periodicals in the form of annual publications. Gujaratis in South Africa capped the Diwali festival with an annual magazine. Organisations produced their magazines for the annual festival. The magazines such as Diwali, *Yuvak*, *Pathik* and *Adarsh* used a bilingual medium (Gujarati and English) to publish their creative outputs.

Since these magazines were annual publications, their titles did not change. The aims of these magazines were manifold: to educate the next generation, to motivate the community to read and write in Gujarati, to express their identity through the means of literature, and to create and represent a sense of belonging to South Africa. Subscribers across South Africa received their copies by post. The publication committees of these magazines followed the Gandhian model of *Indian Opinion* in inviting community members to contribute pieces in English or Gujarati. The magazines typically consisted of an editorial, a president's message, a short story, prose (with essays on education, religion and the importance of the Gujarati language), poems, a children's section and a recipe section. Community business advertisements were interspersed throughout, asserting a commercial and family identity. Because of the lack of printing technology, these annuals were handwritten. Amanuenses (scribes) ensured that mistakes were corrected, crossing out of words avoided, and diacritics were used appropriately. Much creative imagination was exercised in the absence of modern word-processing facilities.

Among the prominent themes in the magazines is that concerning travel and heritage sites in India. Mohanlal Bulsara was a regular correspondent on this theme. He had arrived in South Africa in 1926 at the age of thirteen and settled in Port Elizabeth. His short articles give a vivid picture of religious, historical and archaeological sites on subsequent visits to India. These appear to have involved an extensive tour and shorter visits from the 1950s onward. For example, he describes Hindu sites (such as Haridwar, Kashi and Jagganathpuri), Mount Abu as a Jain site, and Buddhist places such as Sanchi, Sarnath and Bodh Gaya. In these writings, he presents one of the earliest critiques of the commercialisation of religious tourist places. While he attracts his readers to religious pilgrimages, he also warns against their commodification. His writings stress their transformation from places of faith to places of religious consumption. He invites readers to recall general historical, mythical and prevalent social thoughts among Hindus, Jains and Buddhists. Bulsara (1982: 53) writes that 'correct readings on these heritage sites would allow one to relish their historical, cultural and social significance'. He criticises locals and visitors for performing religious activities like baths and other rituals, believing them to display 'superstition' that such rituals can remove sins.

Moreover, these acts had, in his view, become commercialised. Bulsara suggests a devaluation of religious and spiritual values in these places, along similar lines that Gandhi (1938: 40–1) had attributed to the railways in Hind Swaraj. Bulsara (1982: 57) writes in no uncertain terms, 'With the decline of these spiritual spaces, I am disgusted to see those who become instruments in this moral fall. This *nandanvan* [Holy Land] has become a desert, and similar is the heart of human beings.' The metaphor of the desert speaks for itself in terms of spiritual decay coupled with hardship and suffering. Bulsara's outspokenness is meant to relate to South African Gujaratis and the Hindu population of India and worldwide. His writing thus draws on a new spatio-temporal concept of identity for his times. At the same time, his diasporic idealism contrasts with the ongoing flow of religious tourism in the Indian homeland.

Hindus in South Africa have contributed to their faith physically (through temple constructions) and spiritually (by producing religious literature). Kalpana Hiralal (2018) explored the roles of the South African Hindu Maha Sabha, religious leaders like Pandit Nardev Vedalankar and temple committees in South Africa. This discussion misses the creation of a small body of South African Gujarati religious literature. This literature comprises bhajans, hymns and commentaries upon Vedas, Upanishads and the Bhagavad-Gita. These are available in the form of translations into Gujarati, paraphrases of the original and summaries. Amongst such writers and translators, Lallu Hari's contribution is enormous.

Lallu Hari (1897–1973), educated to a primary school level in Billimora near Surat, is dominant among religious writers in South Africa. His *Laharivandana* (In Praise of Lahari) is a notable collection of forty poems and articles published previously in a Gujarati magazine called *Hitechchu* ('Well-Wisher') from Surat. His works have been published in different magazines in Navasari, Bilimora, Ahmedabad and Surat. He started a press in 1929 in East London, South Africa, to publish and distribute his books.[6] His translations of Hindu scriptures from Sanskrit to Gujarati accompanied his interpretation and discussion in short essays. His works include *Jivan Sudharas* (Nectar of Life), *Pragati Na Panthe* (On a Progressive Path), *Sansar Ma Sachu Ghar* (True Bliss in Worldly Affairs), and many more. Readers acknowledged his contributions to religious literature by labelling him the *Narsinh Mehta* of South Africa after Gujarati's founding poet (born in Gujarat in the early fifteenth century). South African Gujarati literature, especially in the *bhakti* literature that L. Harry was writing, suggests a rivalry between the Sanatan Dharma and Arya Samaj Movement (Hindu Reformists) in South Africa. Western education, the need for social reform and incomplete access to Hindu scriptures are challenges addressed in Babar Chavda's poetry.

Babar Chavda (1907–91) was a popular social and cultural leader who had migrated to Cape Town as a young boy with his father in 1921. He became an official of the Kshatriya Hindu Mitra Mandal (previously known as the Cape Town Mochi Mandal) and later became founding president of the South African Kshatriya Mahasabha (Dhupelia-Mesthrie 2012b: 178). This institute was to work for the upliftment of the shoemaker community through education and religion in South Africa. A collected book of poems, unpublished and published essays, and other poems assert his high literary position among South African Gujarati writers. He was influenced by the Arya Samaj Movement, South African contemporaries such as Mohanlal Bulsara, L. Harry and Jokhakar, and Indian leaders such as Gandhi and Sarojini Naidu. Chavda lampoons a Hindu priest of the Sanatan Dharma in his poem *Khar Nakal* (Stupid Imitator) thus:

વેદ શાસ્તરનો ભારો લઇને, એક ગધેડો આવે છે,
જ્ઞાન ખજાનો ખાધે રાખી, પંડતિમાં પરખાવે છે,
શાંત ભર્યો એ ચાલે ધીરૂ, સંત બન્યો સમજાવે છે,
માથું નીચું જુલતું રાખી, ધ્યાન ધરે બતલાવે છે,
લોકો જાણે મહાન શાસ્તરી, પરચાર કરવા આવે છે,
ભૂંકવાનું જો શરી થાય તો, જાત ખરી પરખાવે છે.

The pretence of being loaded with Vedic Knowledge
Arrives a stupid imitator
Hump fills with wisdom
Admits self among Pundits
Silent walks justify his Sainthood
Drooping and swinging head beneath exhibits his meditation
Folks call him 'the great sage', propagates religion
His braying reveals his actual being. (Chavda 1991: 14)

Chavda employs the timeless or habitual present tense of the verb 'to be' (*che*) effectively to indicate his criticism of the detachment of the holy visitor. This provocative characterisation is intended to sway the traditional Hindu sect towards the *Arya Samaj* reformist movement that the poet prefers.

Particularly pertinent to the history and maintenance of Gujarati in South Africa are the genres of autobiography and history. These writings reflect their emotional connection to their homeland, linguistic identity and local community spaces within the emerging Gujarati identity in South Africa. Thus, Babar Chavda, cited above, writes in his poem *Parichay* (Introduction):[7]

Gadat village is my home,
Navasari is the region
[...] In the Chavda clan and Christian year nineteen hundred-seven,
Seventeenth of December Tuesday at eight. (Chavda 1991: 2)

This autobiographical beginning introduces the poet, his family history and his 'home' in India and gives crucial historical snippets on Gujarati migration to South Africa. The biography of Bhulabhai Chita, a man who went from hawking fruit and vegetables in Johannesburg to creating the Golden Era Group, is documented by Naresh Bhatt (2002) in English and Gujarati. This biography entitled *Sanskari Vyakti* (Cultured Man) details Chita's commitment to the Indian, Gujarati and Patidar communities in South Africa.

In addition to this biography, Bhatt (2002) wrote on the history of the Patidar community in South Africa, one of the Indian communities that supported Gandhi's work in the country. Gandhi was pivotal in establishing the Transvaal United

Patidar Society (TUPS) in 1912. Bhatt describes endeavours like the erection and maintenance of community halls, temples and schools. The society published an annual magazine called *TUPS*, aiming to appeal to young authors and strengthen 'communal' unity while promoting the Gujarati language and culture (Bhatt 2002, 2003).

Similar community history echoes in *Daan-Data Granth* (A Book of Donors) (1995), as mentioned earlier regarding the Mochi Samaj (Shoemaker Community) in South Africa. The editors write that the shoemaker community is descended from warrior clans whose ancestors migrated from Afghanistan and the Sindh region (now in Pakistan) in the thirteenth century. This migration was caused by Muslim invasions, which forced people to take refuge with Harijans, known as untouchables, in regions such as Central Gujarat, Saurashtra and Southern Gujarat via Kutch. These Harijans collected dead animal skins for various household purposes. According to the *Daan-Data Granth* (Bulsara 1995: 216), the new migrants living adjacent to Harijans took to making *mojadis* (footwear) from animal skins and, therefore, came to be known as 'Mochi' (Shoemaker). Identical narratives occur among the Rajput-Dhobi community in South Africa (Hiralal 2013). Since such accounts are – to our knowledge – unheard of in India, this editorial claim is of much interest, though whether as history or myth is difficult to say.

These histories in the Gujarati and English languages attempt to rebuild aspects of a Hindu cultural identity in the newly created local spaces in South Africa. The editors and contributors of this *Granth* had had their primary schooling in India, with minimal economic prospects, causing them to migrate to South Africa. Despite the limited educational opportunities, these first-generation authors show a level of writing commensurate with adult native-speaker levels in Gujarat. For example, Mohanlal Bulsara, the editor of the *Granth*, demonstrates an accomplished prose style similar to that of an educated person:[8]

> aa saahityne aapaNaan gnyaati samaajanaa ītihaasaanu svarup apaayun che. Ek drashTie prakaashanamaa vilamb laabhadaai banyaa che. Pahelaani yojanaa ek naanaa ank rupe chaapavaani hati [...] Varsho pahelaa jyaare e saahityanu sankalananu kaary naaaa paayaa par hastagat thayelu tyaare 'hitecchu' ek khaassa ank rupe prasiddha thaay te vicradhaaraa hati, kaaraN ke te samaye daana-daataani sankhyaa ochi hati ane chabi paricay saahitya e samayanaa TrasTnaa pramukh tarikeekalaa haathe khubaja patra vyavahaar karine pu (pujy). Sant shri laharie saghaLun saahitya meLavi lidhelun ane te saathe e sarveno jivan paricay lakhavaama sahakaar samarpelo. (Bulsara 1995: 'Editorial' 221)

[This literature embodies the history of our caste. According to one view, the delay in publication has benefited it. Earlier, a decision was to publish this literature as a particular issue. Before some years, when compiling and editing for this literature began, 'Hitechhu' was a target as a particular issue. The smaller-scale approach was due to the availability of only a few donors to this venture. As the President of the Trust, Rev. Lahari contributed by collecting these literary and picture-biographical details through extensive correspondence].

The language of this text suggests a comprehensive reading and writing culture within some community members. This culture combines the experiences of South African Gujaratis with forms of storytelling that produce a distinctly South African Gujarati literary discourse. This endeavour reflects a desire to continue Gandhi's literary tradition in Gujarati.

Our ongoing inventory of South African Gujarati literature includes thirty-six short stories, three-full-length plays, and a novel. In addition, other short pieces exist in annual Diwali magazines published between 1989 and 1992, in newspapers such as *Indian Opinion* and *Indian Views*, and unpublished writings in the latter part of the twentieth century. In this section, we offer an overview of these works and then examine a short story by Gulab Patel, who emerged as a significant short story writer and novelist.

Major themes of the South African Gujarati writings are love (Gulab Patel's *Andharyu Milan* (Unexpected Union)),[9] family (Ghelaji Rathod's *Umda Kutumbbhavana* (Noble Family Matters)[10] and *Ekbijana Sahakare* (Cooperative Ventures))[11] and death (Gulab Patel's *Sansanatibharya Samachar* (Sensational News)). Such works are rooted in the community's historical, cultural, social and political circumstances.[12] The Cape Hindu Cultural Society (CHCS) has published these stories in its annual Diwali magazines. Community magazines such as *Adarsh* (published by *Shree Adarsh Yuvak Mandal*, Johannesburg),[13] *Yuvak* and *Pathik* (published from Uitenhage, Eastern Cape) also published short stories related to the influence of the Western lifestyle on the community there. These short stories include Karsandas Prajapati Chakradhari's *Be Sabdachitra* (Two Character Portraits),[14] 'Shree Magna's *Choru Kachoru Thay Pan* (Children Can be Irresponsible)[15] and Laxmiben Dullabh Patel's *Ashruvan Ek Ma* (A Mother's Plight).[16] In addition, *Pathik* magazine published a novel titled *Sadhana* (Meditation) in serial form written by Gulab Patel.

Gulab Patel's short story, *Vachanpalan* (Promises are to be Kept), written in Gujarati in the magazine *Diwali* is a historical romance that stands apart from community-internal identity themes. It deals with the plight of a young African *ayah* (nursemaid), Makenna, portrayed as a heroine who embraced death to keep a promise to her Dutch employer during the African-Dutch wars. Patel sets the plot of the story within the Dutch-Khoikhoi War in the vicinity of the banks of the Kei River in the Eastern Cape Province. This historical setting must be considered fictional, as these two wars occurred in the Western Cape region in 1659–60 and 1673, respectively (S. A. History Online).[17] The conflict in the Eastern Cape involved nine frontier wars between the English and the amaXhosa between 1779–1878.

The story is a compelling account of the conflict between Makenna's sense of duty towards her Dutch employer and a sense of loyalty towards her Khoikhoin tribespeople. This inner conflict is, of course, exacerbated by the physical strife between the two races. Makenna is said to have heard her dying Dutch owner's voice at midnight, asking her to promise to raise her son. Makenna responds as follows:

Jarur, baa. Tamari ichcha mujab tamara balkne mari pase rakhis. Jivnu jokham khedi pan ene hu moto karish. Eni tandurastine khatar mari tandurastino bhog apta hu pachu farine nahi jou. (G. Patel 1982: 75)

[Indeed, mistress, as per your wish. I will keep your child always with me. I will risk my life, but I will raise him. I will sacrifice my health to nurture his health].

As a gesture of further assurance, Makenna repeats her pledge:

Baa, kaLaa shariroe aapelaa vachno paN kaLa nathi hotaa. toye goraa shariro-maa evi manyataa ghar kari bethi che to maanyataa bhulaavavaa khaatar paN hu vipattina vadala vacce tamne aapelu vacan purNa karish. (G. Patel 1982: 81)

[Madam, the pledges taken by black bodies are not black. It is white bodies that have such beliefs planted in their minds. I will risk my life and raise your son to clear such mistrust of my tribespeople. Moreover, I pledge to fulfill this vow].

Patel employs the word *black* for two purposes here. In the first instance, it relates to the colour of the body, whereas the second use of the word has a metaphorical meaning, implying preconceptions of falsehood and perjury. Listening to the ayah's pledge, the Dutch woman dies peacefully. This scene presents a melodramatic and romantic portrayal of courage, compassion and trust. Though Makenna was born poor and illiterate, she displays an intuitive understanding of Dutch views of the indigenous people and vice versa. Despite this political impasse and the possibility of violence by her tribespeople, Makenna risks her life to save the child. Subsequently, dissenters burn her hut, forcing her to flee into the woods with the child. Her pursuers find her and make clear their intention to kill the child. Makenna refuses to surrender, confronting her kinsmen with arguments such as 'Raising an orphan child is not against our race's principles' and 'Do butchers differentiate between sin and virtue?' (G. Patel 1982: 81). These statements are to no avail as she is murdered by her tribespeople, along with the child. Patel's use of a historical incident far removed in space and time forces his readers to contemplate the tragic consequences of the past and the time of writing – the early 1980s being at the height of apartheid and counter-struggles often cast in the form of racial conflict. Patel acknowledges the severity of the racial conflict through the child's death.

5.1 Plays and performances

Bhana and Shukla-Bhatta's (2011) compilation of literary materials excerpted and translated from *Indian Opinion* is valuable. The work gives a strong sense of poetic compositions that owe their inspiration to the oral tradition and whose performance was an essential part of the early passive resistance project. These poems, performed in open spaces, strongly indicate that Gujarati theatre and the performing arts tradition continued in South Africa. At the same time, they helped shape South African Gujarati poetry in a new political context. While the theatre is perhaps not so strong today, the Bollywood-song-based *Garba* (the clap dance) is during the Navaratri festival, incorporating Garba classes for the younger generations.[18] *Taare*, a Bollywood-based dance company, operates even today across the Western Cape and tours other provinces.

The community hosted theatre companies, dance troupes and Indian musicians from India to perform in South African cities regularly. For example, Shree Surat

Arya Sangeet Mandal performed Premabhai Patel's *Bhagyalakshmi* (The Goddess of Wealth) in the Patidar Hall in Lenasia (Johannesburg) on 25 June 1949. In 1953, the Navyuvak Vidya Mandir of Springfield, Durban, staged *Daridranarayana* (Service to the Poor) (written by G. Sewnarain and directed by G. Moonilal). A theatre group played Ramkumar Verma's *Samrat Samudragupta* (Emperor Samudragupta) on 5 June 1960 in Bharat Hall (Durban). In an event organised by the Natal Gujarat Parishad, Shree Lenasian Yuvak Mandal performed Vasant Kanitkar's *Ame Baraf Na Pankhi* (We Are Ice Birds) at the Joosub Hall at the University of Durban Westville. Additionally, the South African Gujarati community has toured nationally to raise funds for community projects. For example, the Camp Site Project of the Surat Hindu Scout Group coordinated performances by theatre companies at the Orient Hall (Durban) in 1987.

The Gandhi Hall and Bharat Hall of Durban were leading centres for theatrical activities. In addition, the community invested its creative energies in the annual Gujarati Eisteddfod. Taking their name from the Welsh choir festivals, these were annual national competitions for performing arts, including theatre, where the Gujarati and other Indian language communities (viz. Tamil, Telugu and Hindi) participated across South Africa. From 1969 on, the Gujarati Maha Sabha organised cultural festivities in which Gujarati schools, organisations and community members showcased their talents. Unfortunately, these events remain undocumented by way of scripts or audiovisual recordings. However, oral narratives, still pictures and private collections provide a glimpse into this rich theatrical history, including the scale on which the community organised Eisteddfods, despite their lack of trained professional actors, playwrights and directors.

The sub-genre of the theatrical skit, primarily inspired by Hinduism and Gandhian ideology, intersperses the moral element with comedy. Chaganlal Mistri (1990) wrote a comedy skit called *Bidi Nu Vyasan* (Smoking Addiction).[19] The story, set in an Indian context, revolves around a barber who confesses his smoking addiction to his father. This short skit revolves around a childhood incident recounted in Gandhi (1925: 47) when he had taken coppers from the family servants' pocket money to buy *bidi* (Indian cigarettes), later confessing it to his father.

In another skit, *Vachali Lejo Pakdi* (Hold the Middle One) Laxmiben Patel, a resident of Benoni, employs humour and linguistic ambiguity through wordplay in an Indian context. Three pilgrims beg for alms at a marketplace for their next pilgrimage. While two of them collect donations, the leader, seated at a corner place, shouts continuously: *aagli choDo, pachli choDo, vacli lejo pakDi* (Leave the child, leave the old aged one but grab the youth) (Patel 1979: 73). Passers-by – construing the pronunciation of the verb *choDo* 'leave' along with the adjective *vacli* (middle) with an obscene verb about sexual intercourse – set about to beat him. However, one of the pilgrims explains the intended religious message: 'Leave childhood behind as it is not a ripe age for devotion, old age is too weak for proper worship. Therefore, we should pray while we are young.' This wordplay revolves around the words *vacli* [middle] and the verb '*choDo*' (leave), which lead to a double entendre.

Kishore Dullabh's play *Ghar ane Samaaj Sevaa* (Home and Community Service), set in Gujarat, was written for the Patidar community's golden anniversary in South Africa in 1987. The play exists as an unpublished manuscript in possession of Shashi Daya, who played Hariprasad in the play and kindly made it available for this research. The play is a short family drama revolving around moral dilemmas facing Hariprasad, a trust-funded college lecturer. His family includes his wife, Parvati, a blind daughter, and an adolescent son, Vijal, who has aspirations towards a foreign education. His children study at the trust-run school, which does not charge fees. Hariprasad chairs a charitable organisation to which he devotes time and money. This service to society places his family at financial risk since his daughter requires an eye operation, over and above the costs of the son's educational aspirations. On the maturation of an insurance policy, Hariprasad donates 3,000 rupees to his charity-run orphanage. Unaware of her husband's charitable intentions, Parvati had been counting on the money to fulfil their family needs. Hariprasad had chosen society over family. This act of donation follows a Gandhian path concerning the concepts of ownership and trusteeship. Although family destitution is no longer an issue for Gujaratis in South Africa, the public versus family good themes are still relevant to the more than two dozen South African Gujarati organisations in South Africa. New immigrants (after 1994) have endeavoured to continue the tradition of Gujarati theatrical performing arts. The poet Mrs Nilam Narsee who had arrived as a bride and is now resident in Durban, has written two social satires, *Dhall* and *Whatsapp*, performed in Johannesburg and Durban. South African Gujarati theatre strongly reflects historical, social and cultural themes regarding their migration and exchanges between 'home' and 'host' culture.

A focus on Gujarati education and language is prominent in community-based magazines. Articles frequently occurred on Gujarati language pedagogy, covering general education, preschool education, the Montessori method, and the role of parents, especially mothers. There is also an emphasis on writing for and by children, which is discussed below. Regarding the language itself, Pandit Nardev Vedalankar provided an academic piece tracing the evolution, development of and changes to the Gujarati language about its *Apabhramsha* phase and periods of influence under Persian and English (Vedalankar 1989: 18–19). The gradual encroachment of English as lingua franca and later into informal domains – including the home – has long been a cause of concern to the community. Within South Africa, the language is said to be 'slowly' and 'surely' dwindling. K. C. Naik (1984: 20) considered this a 'hopeless and serious' situation to which 'no feasible solution has been found to date'. Many religious and cultural organisations, including the *Hindu Maha Sabha*, are still engaged in the attempt to bolster and possibly revive the spoken form of the language among the young.

Individuals such as K. C. Naik, Pandit Vedalankar and Umiyashakar Jokhakar proposed new teaching methods, including employing materials using transliteration in Roman orthography. In addition, organisations such as the Gujarati Maha Parishad (now inactive), the Mahatma Gandhi Centenary Committee (Lenasia), the Kendra (Durban) and many Gujarati schools run by Hindu temples have provided evening classes to young and old. However, these efforts seldom yield positive results regarding colloquial daily usage. The plight of the Gujarati language can be seen poignantly in an open request to the community by P. B. Patel (1991: 9), who pleads with readers of the *Diwali* magazine to speak in Gujarati, at least at home.

Gujarati children in South Africa typically attended two schools – i.e. state-run English-medium schools and community-run Gujarati-medium schools – with minimal overlap. The former pursued a secular curriculum common to all Indians in their province under various political dispensations, and now on a non-racial basis since 1994. The latter address matters of heritage and culture, offering Hindu-aligned cultural, social, political and religious material in Gujarati, including stories and songs for children. This dual school experience created a composite identity of being Gujarati and South African. Mesthrie (1995) proposes a nested sequence of identities for Indians in the 1990s, made up of a narrow language-based identity (e.g. Gujarati), a broader Indian South African identity (often expressed in a shared variety of local Indian English), a regional identity (e.g. KwaZulu-Natal or Western Cape) and a national South African identity.

While the *Diwali* annual magazines contained material primarily intended for adults, they also connected with children via special sections such as a *Student Section* in CHCS and *Aen Ken Diva Ghen* (Fun Section) in *Adarsh*. These segments included short stories, puzzles, riddles and occasional crossword puzzles in Gujarati created by teachers, children and other community members.[20] The children's sections include short biographies of religious, political and social personalities and a colouring section for children.[21] Padmaben Chotuben Patel (b. 1941), a resident of Simon's Town, Cape Town, wrote plays, poems and short stories for children between 1960 and 1990, published in CHCS. As it was unviable for the community to send their children from Simon's Town in Cape Town, Padmaben started writing in Gujarati to educate them. She used famous Bollywood tunes to write Gujarati educational, social and religious songs, some of which are reproduced in the *Diwali* magazines. For example, *Mari Mummy Bahu che Pyaari, Mara Pappa Bahu che Pyara* (My Mother is Adorable, My Father is Adorable Too) is based on the famous Hindi film song *Mera Juta Hai Japani* from the film *Shree 420*. In the new version, children observe their parents' routines (the mother in acts of praying and cooking and the father going to work and dropping the children at school). However, there is an interpolation in the last stanza in which the children sing:

> To run the family, my son
> Parents are needed
> To run the family, my daughter
> Parents are needed
> So are their blessings,
> My father is clever, and so is my mother. (P. Patel 1983: 99)

While open to charges of promoting gender stereotypes, the song's adaptation integrates and builds a strong sense of social, cultural and emotional identity among Gujarati children. This poem and similar writings give evidence of the community's efforts to preserve and instill their linguistic and cultural identity, with the traditional family as a basic unit. On the other hand, the secular daytime schools were preparing boys and girls alike for less traditional, less family-oriented professional roles.

Given the popularity of Indian cooking internationally, it is unsurprising that recipes have become a vital genre and cultural construct in the diaspora. The 'home' or Indian tradition of cooking also undergoes innovative adaptation to host country dishes, ingredients and methods. Moreover, published recipes contribute to a Gujarati identity in South Africa, stressing the value of tradition and social bonding in the present. Two notable classics of the international diaspora are UK resident

Yasmin Alibhai-Brown's *The Settler's Cookbook* (2009) and South Africa's Zuleikha Mayat's *Indian Delights*. Historians Goolam Vahed and Thembisa Waetjen (2010) captured the spirit of the latter in their book, also entitled *Indian Delights*, which centres around the producers of the cookbook viz. the Women's Cultural Group formed by Zuleikha Mayat in Durban in 1954. Vahed and Waetjen (2010) also discuss other civic associations and cultural societies formed by Muslim women, chiefly of Gujarati origin in Durban.

The recipes published in Gujarati in the *Diwali* magazines cannot compete with the specialised cookbooks. Despite an absence of narratives or anecdotes, these culinary practices became a mode of Gujarati cultural production, as they were not intended to sell as commercial books but to share everyday cooking. Some examples suggest innovative recipes cooked with new ingredients. These include *kela ni puri* (banana bread), *gajar nu pudding* (carrot pudding) and *dudhi na vada* (bottle gourd dumplings) as popular Gujarati side dishes.[22] Other innovative efforts include *Ghau na loT na bhajiya* (wheat flour dumplings), *gajar-kakdi nu khaman* (carrot and cucumber khaman), *karela nu sev bharelu sak* (stuffed bitter gourd with sev),[23] and *baTeka na gulab jambu* (mashed potato gulab jamun). Notably, while *gulab jamuns* are usually made of refined wheat flour, *suji* (cream of wheat) or *khoya* (a dairy product), this sweet item is presented in the magazine as a preparation with mashed potatoes – which exemplifies, at least as experimentation, a touch of vegan culture among Gujaratis as far back as 1974. Similarly, Rambhaben Vinaychandra Patel demonstrates her new recipe using gram flour paste on buns to make hybrid *dhebara* instead of traditional millet or wheat flour with fenugreek leaves or bottle gourd.[24] Examples of recipes such as *Chole BhaTure, Shahi Kofta* (both from Punjab),[25] *Idli and Masala Dosa* (from Southern India),[26] and *Daal BaaTi* (from Rajasthan), *Veg-Kabab* and *Eggless cakes* suggest the influence in South Africa of multi-religious diversity and different regional traditions of India less common in village India.[27]

There are some linguistic innovations of interest in the adapted recipes. Firstly, these published recipes retain some Gujarati words that are no longer employed by Gujaratis, at least in urban areas. These archaisms are *navTaank* (a little), *kanak* (dough), *sher* (500 grams) and *mon* (oil or ghee used in preparing dough). One example of an innovative translation of an English food term into Gujarati would strike an Indian reader as unusual: the translation of 'instant' as *taratna*. The Gujarati language has accepted *instant* as a loanword, referring to the Western concept of packaged food ready for quick cooking. A literal translation would be *jaldi, tvarit* and even *tatkalik*. The South African translation of 'Instant *Dhokla*' appears as *Taratna Dhokla*, which in Gujarat would invite bemusement as this loanword (*instant*) has been accepted in the Gujarati language. (*Taratna* is a literal translation of the word 'Instant' and is widely used regarding food. However, it is not used in the sense that it is used here as the recipe in question involves a long process.) These recipes overall give a sense of flexibility, adaptability and creativity in the diaspora.

6. Conclusion

This chapter has examined a representative selection of Gujarati literature during its heyday in South Africa. This research has expounded an aspect of what Green (2012) calls 'New South African literature' in the form of South African Gujarati Literature. At the other end of the spectrum are the folk and community contributions to magazines, giving a lively sense of diasporic life. However, there has been a noticeable decline in Gujarati political writing and translation activities in South Africa after 1990. This chapter has attempted to counter the erasure of knowledge of the South African Gujarati literary tradition: unknown in India and on the verge of being forgotten in South Africa. The Gujarati literary tradition in South Africa had a strong sense of agency in the early 1900s. The Gujarati community is not underrepresented in the world of books and writing compared to the indentured labourers. Despite little or no support from the agencies in Gujarat or wider India, the Gujarati community persevered in inserting itself into the field of Gujarati literature. Together with the work of Desai (1997), this chapter has provided the first steps in connecting South African writing to the Gujarati canon centred in India. The topic is worthy of further research to appreciate how these writings forged socio-cultural bonds between South Africa and Gujarat.

Notes

1. These statistics are taken from www.worldatlas.com (last accessed 2 May 2020).
2. We are thankful to Shree Radha Krishna Temple Library and Natubhai in Benoni (Johannesburg) for the loan of this book.
3. For the full Gujarati version of the poem see M. Chavda (2018: 87–96).
4. Some of them were M. A. Mehtar 'Farooqi', Nautam Mehta, A. M. Meer 'Alif', Indira Mistry, Yusuf Sheikhji, Karasandas Prajapati, Vijyoti Kara and Maulvi Saeed 'Akhtar', Kantilal Nayak, Kasim Hafeez, Govind Patel 'Anami', Mohmmad Lajpuria, Urmila Patel, and many others. We are thankful to Ms Bharati Vaidya Jokhakar for providing interesting insights into the life and literary writings of Pandit Umiyashankar Jokhakar. Jokhakar-Vaidya, B. (2017, 12 October), Pandit Umiyashankar Jokhakar (M. Chavda, Interviewer).
5. A Hindu deity for the Wind.
6. A detailed history of his press can be found on http://www.harryprinters.com/about.html (last accessed 2 May 2020).
7. For the full Gujarati version of the poem please refer to Chavda (2018: 88–9).
8. Many references appear to a *Kshatriya Centenary* (1882–1982) which is still to be located.
9. CHCS (1988), p. 75.
10. CHCS (1978), p. 63.
11. CHCS (1977), p. 53.
12. CHCS (1984), p. 81.
13. This mandal [organisation] was established on 15 August 1951.
14. *Adarsh* (1987), p. 63.
15. *Adarsh* (1986), p. 25.
16. *Adarsh* (1986), p. 31.
17. South African History Online, Treks and Lands Conflicts 1600s–1800s, 30 March 2011, www.sahistory.org.za/article/dutch-and-khoikhoi (last accessed 2 May 2020).
18. Navaratri is a nine-day Hindu festival worshipping the Female Power.

19. CHCS (1990), pp.73–5.
20. CHCS (1975) published a crossword on p. 75.
21. CHCS (1990) published a note on Gandhi on p. 63.
22. The list includes Surti dishes such as *khaja, mamna* or *panki* and *kakri lapsi* published in CHCS issues such as 1978 (p. 35), 1987 (p. 87) and 1974 (p. 41) respectively.
23. *Sev* is made of chickpea flour and is a fried savoury.
24. CHCS (1987), p. 73.
25. CHCS in 1991 (p. 71) and 1966 (p. 40) respectively.
26. CHCS in 1979 (p. 53) and 1982 (p. 63) respectively.
27. CHCS in 1991 (p. 75), 1966 (p. 40) and 1987 (p. 87) respectively.

References

Arya, H. 1967. Editorial. Jokhakar, Pandit U. *Kavya Guchcha: Bazme Adab*. Transvaal: Pandit U. Jokhakar.
Bhabha, Homi. 2002. Interrogating identity: The post colonial prerogative. In P. D. Gay, J. Evans and P. Redman (eds), *Identity: A Reader*. London: Sage Publications, pp. 94–101.
Bhana, Surendra and James Hunt. 1989. *Gandhi's Editor: The Letters of M. H. Nazar, 1902–1903*. New Delhi: Promilla and Co.
Bhana, S. and N. Shukla-Bhatt. 2011. Introduction. In S. Bhana and N. Shukla-Bhatt (eds), *A Fire That Blazed in the Ocean: Gandhi and the Poems of Satyagraha in South Africa, 1909–1911*. New Delhi and Chicago: Promilia/Bibliophile South Asia.
Bhatt, Dineshchandra. 1967. Imprisoned I. In Pandit U. Jokhakar (ed.), *Kavya Guchha*. Johannesburg: Buzme Adab, p. 19.
Bhatt, Naresh. 2002. *Sanskari Vyakti [Cultured Man]*. Johannesburg: Golden Era.
Bhatt, Naresh. 2003. *History of Transvaal Patidar United Society*. Johannesburg: Golden Era.
Bramdaw, Dhanee. 1939. *The South African Indian Who's Who and Commercial Directory*. Pietermartizburg: The Natal Witness.
Bulsara, Mohanlal. 1982. Bharat Darshan. *Diwali*, 52–7.
Bulsara, Mohanlal. 1995. Editorial. Trust, South African Kshatriya Mahasabha and South African Kshatriya Mahasabha. *Daan-Data Granth*. Port Elizabeth: South African Kshatriya Mahasabha and South African Kshatriya Mahasabha Trust, p. 221.
Bulsara, Mohanlal. 1995. Kshatriya-Mochi-Kshatriya. *Daan-Data Granth* (ed.) South African Kshatriya MahaSabha. Port Elizabeth, p. 216.
Chavda, Babar. 1991. *Svarachit Kavitao [My Poems]*. Cape Town and Port Elizabeth: Chotubhai Daya.
Chavda, M. 2018. Dakshin Africana Gujartiono Bhartiya Rashtravaad: Ek Zalak [Indian nationalism in South African Gujarati poets: A perspective]. *Sabdasrushti*, 421 (10): 87–96.
Desai, Gaurav. 2011. Asian literatures: Genealogies in the making. *Research in African Literature*, 42 (3): v–xxx.
Desai, Usha. 1997. *An Investigation of Factors Influencing Maintenance and Shift of the Gujarati Language in South Africa*. PhD dissertation, University of Durban.
Desai, Usha. 2000. Gujarati literature in South Africa. *Nidan*, 12: 53–72.
Dhupelia-Mesthrie, Uma. 1985. Reducing the Indian population to a 'manageable compass': A study of the South African Assisted Emigration Scheme of 1927. *Natalia*, 15: 36–56.
Dhupelia-Mesthrie, Uma. 2010. The Passenger Indian as worker: Indian immigrants in Cape Town in the early twentieth century." *African Studies*, 68 (1): 111–34.

Dhupelia-Mesthrie, Uma. 2012a. Cultural crossings from Africa to India: Select travel narratives of Indian South Africans from Durban and Cape Town, 1940s to 1990s. *South African Historical Journal*, 64: 295–312.

Dhupelia-Mesthrie, Uma. 2012b. Gujarati shoemakers in twentieth-century Cape Town: Family, gender, caste and community. *Journal of Southern African Studies*, 38 (1): 167–82.

Du Bois, Duncan. 2010. Towards a new labour dispensation: Background to the arrival of Indians in Natal in 1860. *Natalia*, 40: 12–19.

Ettlinger, Nancy. 2007. Precarity unbound. *Alternatives: Global, Local and Political*, 32 (3): 319–40.

Gandhi, M. K. 1925. *An Autobiography or My Experiments with Truth*. Ahmedabad: Navjivan Publishing House.

Gandhi, M. K. 1938. *Hind Swaraj or Indian Home Rule*. Ahmedabad: Navjivan Press.

Green, Nile. 2012. Urdu as an African language: A survey of a source literature. *Islamic Africa*, 3 (2): 173–99.

Gujarati Literature (Sahitya). n.d. Website. 26 December 2018. http://gujaratonline.com/arts/sahitya.htm.

Hall, Stuart. 2002. Who needs 'identity'? In P. D. Gay, J. Evans and P. Redman (eds), *Identity: A Reader*. London: Sage Publications, pp. 15–30.

Hiralal, Kalpana. 2008. Indian family businesses in Natal, 1870–1950. *Natalia*, 38: 27–37.

Hiralal, Kalpana. 2013. Caste in the diaspora: A case study of the Natal Rajput Association in Durban. *Man in India*, 93 (4): 591–606.

Hiralal, Kalpana. 2014. Women and migration in South Africa: Historical and literary perspective. *South Asian Diaspora*, 6 (1): 63–75.

Hiralal, Kalpana (ed.). 2018. *Global Hindu Diaspora: Historical and Contemporary Perspectives*. New York and Oxford: Routledge.

Holmes, E. C. 1944. The tyranny of colour: A study of Indian problems in South Africa. *Journal of Negro History*: 489–92.

Jokhakar, Umiyashankar. 1967. *Kavya Guchcha*. Johannesburg: Bazme Adab.

Jokhakar-Vaidya, B. 2017, 12 October. Pandit Umiyashankar Jokhakar (M. Chavda, Interviewer).

Joshi, P. S. 1942. Preface. In *The Tyranny of Colour: A Study of the Indian Problem in South Africa*. Durban: E. P. & Commercial Printing Ltd, pp. xv–xvi.

Joshi, P. S. 1945. *Verdict on South Africa*. Bombay: Thacker & Co.

Joshi, P. S. 1949. Literature of South African Indians. In E. Hellmann and L. Abrahams (eds), *Handbook on Race Relations in South Africa*. Cape Town: Oxford University Press, pp. 612–14.

Joshi, P. S. 1958. *Smruti Prasango [What I Recall]*. Johannesburg & Rajkot: Thacker & Co.

Lal, B. V. 2014. Review of coolie woman: The odyssey of indenture. *The Journal of Asian Studies*, 73 (4): 1146–7.

Majeed, Javed. 2005. Literary history: The case of South Asia. *History Compass*, 3 (AS(151)): 1–13.

Mehta, Kanti. 1967. *Baharo Phool Barsavo [An Anthology of Poems]*. Johannesburg: Kanti Mehta.

Mesthrie, Rajend. 1995. Reversing language shift: Problems and possibilities. *Journal of the Indological Society of South Africa*, 2 and 3: 1–20.

Mesthrie, Rajend. 2010. *A Dictionary of South African Indian English*. Cape Town: UCT Press.

Mesthrie, Rajend. 2015. Language shift, cultural practices and writing in South African Indian English. In C. Stroud and P. Mastin (eds), *Language, Literacy and Diversity: Moving Words*. Oxford and New York: Routledge, pp. 132–48.

Mukherjee, S. 1998. *A Dictionary of Indian Literature: Beginnings – 1850*. New Delhi: Orient Blackswan.

Naik, K. C. 1984. Gujarati Bhasha (Language): Quo Vadis? *Adarsh*: 20–3.

Pandya, Natwarlal. 1967. Foreword. In Kanti Pandya (ed.), *Baharo Phool Barsavo [An Anthology of Poems]*. Johannesburg: Kanti Mehta, n.p.

Patel, G. 1982. Vachanpalan. *Adarsh*: 75–81.
Patel, Laxmiben. 1979. Vachali Lejo Pakdi [Hold the middle one]. *Adarsh*: 73–5.
Patel, P. 1983. Mari Mummy Bahu che Pyaari, Mara Pappa Bahu che Pyaara. *Diwali*: 99.
Patel, P. B. 1991. Gujarati Bhasha Vishe. *Diwali*: 9.
Sheikhji, Yusuf. 1967. Ode to 1967 Kavi Sammelan. In Pandit Umiyashankar Jokhakar (ed.), *Kavya Guchha: Bazme Adab*. Transvaal: Pandit U. Jokhakar.
Shukla, Yashwant. 1977. Social ideals and patriotism in Gujarati literature 1900–1930. *Indian Literature*: 69–77.
Standing, A. 2014. *A Precariat Charter: From Denizens to Citizens*. London: Bloomsbury.
Tayob, A. 1995. *Islamic Resurgence in South Africa: The Muslim Youth Movement*. Cape Town: UCT Press.
Vahed, Goolam and T. Waetjen. 2010. Preface. In *Gender, Modernity and Indian Delights*. Cape Town: HSRC Press, pp. vii–xi.
Vedalankar, Pandit Nardev. 1989. Gujarati Bhasha ni Utpatti ane Vikas [Evolution and development of Gujarati language]. *Adarsh*: 18–19.

CHAPTER 12

Performing Language Alternation in Multilingual Mauritius: The Conversational Significance of Song Interludes in Everyday Interactions[1]

Tejshree Auckle

1. Introduction

Arguing for the conception of verbal performance as a creative expression of a speaker's masterful command over his linguistic repertoire, Bauman (1975) calls for an enhanced focus on performance-oriented features of conversation. According to Bauman (1975: 293), indexing a specific reflexive position that the speaker conversationally orients himself to, performance 'involves on the part of the performer an assumption of accountability to an audience for the way in which communication is carried out, beyond and above its referential content'. In other words, the shift in conversational frame from spontaneous chit-chat to a more histrionic style empowers participants to 'enregister' their speech by allowing 'linguistic forms [to] become ideologically linked with social identities' (Agha 2006, cited in Johnstone 2011: 657). In line with the above, this chapter reports upon and seeks to analyse multilingual participants' spontaneous lapses into song and dance sequences in the different languages which form part of their repertoire during casual interactional sequences. It aims to shed light on the pragmatic implications of language alternation phenomena during these 'vocal instrumentalising' sessions (Coupland 2011: 579).

Emphasis will be placed on the playful nature of code-switching – henceforth CS – resulting in speakers being endowed with the possibility of re-contextualising seemingly mundane conversations while simultaneously indexing increasingly hybrid ethnic identities. Consequently, this chapter will eventually attempt to view CS co-occurring during these song and dance sequences not simply as a reflection of the communicative competence of proficient multilinguals but also as an articulation of the resourceful ways in which language can be used to aid the sequential construction of meaning (cf. Auer 1984). Following Coupland (2011: 579), the social and stylistic effects of 'voice' as 'musical instrument, body, person and character' will be highlighted and their pragmatic significance explained with specific reference to the performance-oriented culture which prevails in multilingual Mauritius. In line with Kachru (1990) and Pandharipande (2019), the co-existence of CS with these more performance-oriented features will be seen as an externalisation of these speakers' 'creativity' which, according to Kachru (1990: 170) entails both 'the designing of a text which uses linguistic resources from two or more – related or unrelated – languages [...] and the use of verbal strategies in which subtle adjustments are made for psychological, sociological, and attitudinal reasons'.

This correlation between solidly entrenched multilingualism and creative and innovative forms of verbal expression is one which is highlighted by many researchers (cf. Simonton 2008, Kharkhurin 2012). This potentially could be the case for Mauritius, which due to three successive waves of colonisation offers a true picture of cultural and linguistic métissage. Indeed, Mauritius owes a big debt of gratitude to historical serendipity rather than to careful planning. Discovered by Arab and Portuguese sailors in the early sixteenth century, fitfully inhabited by the Dutch, it is following the takeover of the island by the French colonial powers in the eighteenth century that multilingualism became an intrinsic part of the linguistic fabric of the island (Miles 1999).[2] Slaves from 'Mozambique and elsewhere in East Africa (40–45 percent) and from Madagascar (30–35 percent) [as well as] Seychelles, Cape Verde, Rio de Janeiro, and West Africa' (Miles 1999: 213) interacted with sailors transiting through Mauritius to India (Vaughan 2005). With Port Louis serving as a base during French conflicts with India and playing host to large fleets of ships that needed repairs and reprovisioning, the early eighteenth century witnessed not only the genesis of Mauritian Creole (Kreol) but also the emergence of contact-induced phenomena such as CS (Vaughan 2005).

In addition to the slaves and slave-owners already cohabiting on the island, the big crews of the ships transiting through Mauritius 'constituted multicultural and multiracial microsocieties with their own naval patois, their own rules of conduct and their own hierarchies' (Vaughan 2005: 35). Ewald (2000: 70) provides more insight into the naval patois spoken by the crew members and labels them as 'boundary crossers' because of the ways in which they combined elements from East African and Indian vernacular languages during conversational exchanges. Further contributing to this picture of linguistic diversity was the fact that Governor, Mahé de Labourdonnais also imported both skilled and unskilled workers from India and other parts of the world. The demographic and linguistic heterogeneity of eighteenth-century Mauritius becomes particularly noticeable when the district registers presenting a consolidated list of maroon slaves are consulted. These record the presence of 'Abyssinians, Bambaras, Bengalis, Cafres, Guineans, Lascars, Malabars, Malambous, Malays, Talingas and Timorians among the country's fugitives' (Allen 1999: 42). Historically speaking, therefore, multilingual encounters were already the norm rather than the exception.

The above situation would be made even more complex with the successful takeover of the island by the British in 1810, thus contributing to the melting pot that is Mauritius today (Eriksen 1999, Allen 1999). Despite over a century and a half of British rule, English never became the main language of the land. Even today it has the paradoxical status of a de facto official tongue that is mostly shunned in daily life by most of the local population and an overwhelming majority of the written and the broadcast media (Miles 2000). Indeed, the terms of the 1810 Act of Capitulation, which officially bequeathed Mauritius to Great Britain, guaranteed minimal linguistic and cultural interference on the part of British colonial powers.[3] One immediate consequence of British rule was the abolition of the slave trade and subsequently of the institution of slavery itself. Finding itself short of labour, the newly established colonial power turned its attention to other horizons. In 1829, an experimental group of 'coolies' was brought in from India and its success led to the large-scale importation of Indian indentured labourers (Miles 2000, Eisenlohr 2006).

Consequently, Mauritian society underwent an important demographic and above all, linguistic revolution. Along with the European languages of French and – to a lesser degree – English and the by now popular Kreol tongue, the Indian languages of Bhojpuri, Marathi, Gujarati, Tamil and Telugu were integrated into the Mauritian linguistic mosaic, with Hindi and Urdu valued liturgically as well (Eriksen 1999). With the arrival of traders from mainland China, Chinese (especially Hakka Chinese) was also embraced by the populace. Of these Asian languages, Bhojpuri underwent the greatest evolution as it was adopted, and it emerged as the lingua franca amongst a large majority of the Indian immigrant population (Allen 1999). By the mid-nineteenth to early twentieth centuries, there emerged, according to Miles (2000: 217), a 'four-part harmony' of Mauritian languages:

> Kreol as the uncontested lingua franca; French as the inherited language of social and cultural prestige; English as the language of education, law, public administration and to a [small] degree commerce; and the panoply of Indian and Asian languages.

A similar situation prevails in contemporary Mauritius where multilingualism is still an inextricable part of the sociolinguistic fabric of the island.

2. Theoretical background

Pioneering research in the field of CS (Gumperz 1982, Auer 1984, Myers-Scotton 1988) tended to focus mainly on its orderliness and the pragmatic consequentiality of opting for one language out of the myriad others which form part of the repertoire of multilingual speakers. However, over the years attention has also shifted towards the creative and dynamic forms that language alternation phenomena such as CS can take in different contexts such as literature, drama, pop songs and public signs (Garcia and Li Wei 2014, Androutsopoulos 2013, Jonsson 2005, Shohamy and Gorter 2008), thus highlighting the need to see CS not simply as the juxtaposition of lexical and structural elements from multiple languages but as 'an expressive, creative, and often multimodal performance' (Kharkhurin and Wei 2015: 1). Indeed, while seminal work in the field of CS tended to view the juxtaposition of grammatical and structural elements from different languages as being pragmatically consequential (cf. Auer 1984, 1995, 1998, 2001 and Myers-Scotton 1988, 1993, amongst others), over the years, emphasis has also been placed on bi- and multilinguals' creativity – a term utilised by Kachru (1982) to refer to the verbal strategies adopted by speakers as they draw from the linguistic resources of two or more languages.[4] In such cases, the different forms that CS can take remain sensitive to the local linguistic 'ecosystems' (Thumboo 1985), revealing at both the written and the spoken levels the choices made by speakers in deference to the psychological, sociological and cultural contexts within which they operate.

The above perspective finds an echo in the work of Bhatia and Ritchie (2008) who maintain that CS should, in essence, be seen as an 'optimising' strategy allowing speakers to give voice to a wider array of meanings, which the individual languages are incapable of rendering when used in isolation. In keeping with the above, Li Wei (2011: 1222–3), drawing from the work of Garcia (2009), argues for the verbal performance of multilinguals to be viewed as being firmly inscribed within their respective 'translanguaging space'; that is, the social space created by multilingual users as they bring together 'different dimensions of their personal history, experience and environment, their attitude, belief and ideology, their cognitive and physical capacity into one coordinated and meaningful performance'. This translanguaging space, therefore, far from just celebrating the multiple discursive and semiotic practices in which multilinguals engage (cf. Garcia 2009), also becomes a realm where speakers can create 'new identities, values and practices' (Li Wei 2011: 1223) by using the different resources available to them. This is in keeping with Becker (1991) and Swain (2006) who argue for language – and by extension, languages – to be seen not just as a noun which indicates something relatively monolithic over which speakers display varying forms of mastery but as a verb which conceptualises the act of speaking as an ongoing process and 'a vehicle through which thinking is articulated and transformed into an artifactual form' (Swain 2006: 97).

As a matter of fact, the creative potential of CS in different translanguaging spaces can be seen in performance-related domains like fiction, poetry and songs where the artistic craftsmanship evidenced in multilingual artefacts such as song lyrics has been highlighted by researchers such as Y. Kachru (1989, 2006) and Omoniyi (2006), amongst others. In her study focusing on the language alternation mechanisms adopted by lyricists in Bollywood, Kachru (2006) focuses on the creative blending of Hindustani and English in an attempt to generate humour and to parody the adoption of a more Westernised lifestyle by Indian youngsters. She contrasts this Hindustani-English artefact with the one espoused by the more conservative middle-aged and elderly factions of the population who are more likely to prefer language alternation patterns between a more Sanskritised form of Hindi and Hindustani which, in turn, act as markers for a more traditional lifestyle. The fact that it is the more English-flavoured hybrid which is on the ascendance lends credence to her claims that the gradual urbanisation of India, coupled with the increasingly successful global distribution of Bollywood films in overseas territories, has led to a redefinition of language boundaries resulting in complex forms of language contact phenomena (Kachru 2006).

The above perspective is supported by Ganti (2004) who reveals that from the embryonic scriptwriting stage itself, CS remains the *maître mot*. Indeed, despite the popularity of both Hindustani and the newly nascent Hinglish, contemporary writers often opt to pen down the script in English itself. Dialogues are subsequently translated into Hindustani in order to bring in the local flavour. In fact, Ganti (2004) states that many cinema directors and producers encourage primary scriptwriters to work in tandem with a sidekick who is much better versed in Hindustani. During the filming process, the latter remains a quasi-permanent fixture on the sets and is frequently called upon to tone down any speeches that are deemed to be too anglicised through the strategic insertion of Hindustani words into an anglicised speech cluster. Empirical evidence for the above claims is offered by Y. Kachru (2006: 232) who provides the following extract, amongst others, from the 2002 movie *Kya Dil Ne*

Kaha (What the Heart Said) in an attempt to underscore the level of playful mixing displayed by lyricists:

> MaiN to bhaNwraa hoon *sorry*, kaliyon kii kartaa chorii
> BaaNdhe kyooN preet kii Dorii, rehne de thoRii duurii
> Rehne de thoRii sii duurii
>
> I am bumble bee, *sorry*; I steal buds
> Why are you tying threads of love; let some distance remain[5]

The above extract aims to depict the fickleness of the male lover since, as Kachru (2006) explains, in Indian poetic tradition, the analogy of the bumble bee flitting restlessly from one bud to the other is one that the media frequently uses to offer a stereotypical portrayal of the male lover as untrustworthy and inconstant. However, while the content of the song is, in itself, mundane and routinely articulated in countless romantic musicals, the conspicuous playfulness is displayed through the pronunciation of the word 'sorry' as the more Indianised [so:ri:] – a strategy adopted so that rhyming patterns between the lexical items *chorii*, *durii* and *dorii* can be maintained. In addition, the above extract is subsequently followed by a rejoinder from the female counterpart whose response contrasts with that of her lover as she reveals that irrespective of his fidelity or lack of it, she has 'tied threads for seven lives' (Kachru 2006: 232) between the two of them. While the above expression might elicit blank looks from Western native English speakers, an Indian audience, believing in the Hindi theological precept of reincarnation, would be familiar with the notion of romantic love as being a bond that lasts through a series of seven successive births. Thus, while the playful mixing of English and Hindustani has, on one hand, helped to ensure a harmonious phonetic co-existence between the two languages, on the other hand it has also resulted in a process of semantic extension whereby English words are bleached of their original meaning and are endowed with an enforced layer of double entendre and polysemy. B. Kachru (1985: 23) refers to these hybrid artefacts resulting from CS as being the driving force behind what he calls the 'expanded contextual loading of a text' that is the extension of the 'accepted literary and cultural norms' as users add additional meaning, drawn from the different languages that they master, to existing material.

Further corroboration regarding the versatility of the translanguaging space created by speakers is provided by Dewaele (2010) who views the act of swearing in multiple languages within one conversational encounter as being a further reflection of a multilingual speaker's creativity. Drawing from Jay (2009) who compares the act of swearing to that of using the horn on one's car to signify emotions as varied as anger, joy, surprise or frustration, Dewaele (2010) connects the verbal phenomenon of swearing in multiple languages to the emotional resonance that each language has for a specific speaker. Indeed, while the main purpose of swearing, according to him, remains the expression of emotions such as anger, the intensity of these feelings is often believed to be more aptly conveyed in one medium rather than the other. In deference to the context in which a particular language is usually acquired and utilised, it becomes endowed with a degree of emotional resonance that speakers can capitalise on during their own conversational encounters (Dewaele 2010). In the case of multilingual speakers, the emotional resonance of the different languages in their repertoire can prompt them to move from one to multiple others depending on the nature of a particular interaction. In addition, a sudden burst of emotion or 'emotional arousal' (Dewaele 2010: 600) brought about by some aspect of the conversation could easily 'force a speaker out of monolingual mode into a bilingual or trilingual mode' (Dewaele 2010: 600).

In keeping with the above perspective, this chapter will also investigate the significance of one particular multilingual artefact, namely the co-occurrence of CS with the insertion of song interludes derived from Bollywood films in casual, face-to-face conversational encounters in the Mauritian context. Speakers' creativity will be seen in the context of the translanguaging space within which they operate. The emotional resonance of these choices will also be explained by taking into account the socio-historical context of the island.

3. Methodology

This chapter reports upon the data collected between the months of October 2011 and March 2012 and subsequently between the months of October and December 2019 for the purposes of a bigger project investigating the different types of language alternation phenomena existing in multilingual Mauritius today. The findings obtained in this study, therefore, are quite incidental. However, they provide snapshots of the ways, not always cited in the existing literature, in which CS can be performed in some multilingual communities.

Participants were recruited via the friend-of-a-friend approach and through social media sites such as Facebook. As the administrator of the Facebook group *Langaz Kreol Morisyen* (Mauritian Creole Language), the interviewer was able to post messages on discussion forums and spread the word to a wide network of receptive group members. In addition to the above, messages requesting interested participants to get in touch were posted on the personal Facebook page of the interviewer. These, coupled with relevant messages shared on the Facebook profile of the interviewer's friends, helped to catch the interest of potential volunteers. Thus, word of mouth through the judicious exploitation of the friendship and kinship networks of friends and subsequently their acquaintances proved to be quite beneficial to the project, earning it much-needed exposure. Overall, fifty-five informants, aged between eighteen and twenty-two and from the Indo-Mauritian ethnic group, eventually took part in the recording process. These were split in groups of five, with a total of between fourteen to twenty hours of data collected per group, thus yielding an overall spoken corpus of about 200 hours.

Multi-party conversations were preferred because they allow informants the safety and comfort of interacting within a circle of close friends. Duranti (1997: 118) convincingly argues that speakers do not 'invent social behaviour, language included, out of the blue'. Patterns of linguistic variation are only transposed from the more private domain of friendship to the more public one of audio-recording. Psathas (1995: 2) concurs with Duranti (1997) and contends that locally salient conversational practices are easily highlighted through recordings of multi-party talk since such social interactions are often symbolically 'meaningful for those who produce them'. Consequently, the aim of the interviewer was to capture on tape the respondents' usual, everyday conversations while at the same time ensuring that their interpretation of their sequential contribution to the talk-in interaction was also heeded during the analysis phase of the project. According to Auer (1984: 6) prioritising the participants' 'interpretational leeway' through such an emic perspective allows for an enhanced focus on the verbal practices of informants. Concurring with Auer (1984), Li Wei (2011: 1224) calls for an enhanced focus on the 'momentary actions and performances of the individual'. Labelling the heightened attention to these small windows of creative performance as Moment Analysis (MA), Li Wei (2011) recommends for the recording of both naturally occurring conversational segments and 'metalanguaging data' such as comments made by the speaker regarding his/her own language practices. Coupled with the observation carried out by the fieldworker during the data collection process, MA allows the researcher to better understand the heat-of-the-moment verbal actions and reactions resulting in instances of multilingual creativity. The focus, therefore, remains on the individual and on the ways in which they choose to perform their multilingual selves. In essence, therefore, what this study provides is the double hermeneutic of 'participants [...] trying to make sense of their world [and] the researcher trying to make sense of the participants trying to make sense of their world' (Smith and Osborn 2008: 53).

In keeping with the above perspective, the selection and analysis of extracts from this medium-sized corpus of data take on board the input of the participants themselves and reports upon their attempts to create a translanguaging space of their own which is both informed by and feeds into a broader socio-historical and cultural matrix. The following subsections report upon the findings of this study.

4. Findings

The subsections below provide an insight into the ways in which CS and the insertion of Bollywood-inspired song sessions are creatively embedded into the routine face-to-face interactions of the informants taking part in this study. For ease of reference, Table 12.1 presents a summary of the different font styles associated with each language operating in the current multilingual matrix.

Although the current dataset consists of further examples of similar kinds of linguistic behaviour, this chapter explores only a few of the prototypical shapes that the performance of CS took in this study.

Table 12.1 *Font styles used to represent code-switching to specific languages*

Language	Matrix or embedded language	Font style
Kreol	Matrix	Normal style
French	Embedded	Single underline
English	Embedded	Double underline
Bhojpuri	Embedded	**Bold**
Hindustani[6]	Embedded	*Italics*

4.1 CS, songs and language play

Li Wei (2011: 1226) contends that multilinguals display their creativity by 'having fun with words'. This is exactly what the informants in this study appear to be doing as they shift from casual, conversational footings to brief song interludes during their everyday interactions with each other. Such occurrences of verbal play were, in fact, noticeable in the interactions of almost all the teams. Extract 1 is taken from one of the conversations of Team 5:

Extract 1
Gossip

Speaker 23: *Ek, do, teen, chaar, paanch*
Speaker 21: *Paanch paanch*
Speaker 22: *Paanch*
Speaker 23: *Che*

Speaker 23: *One, two, three, four, five*
Speaker 21: *Five five*
Speaker 22: *Five*
Speaker 23: *Six*

Far from being a simple list of consecutive integers, Extract 1, in fact, presents a transition point in an extended gossip and jocular session amongst the members of the team as the speakers gear up to move to another juicy tidbit of information after negotiating a satisfactory closure to the previous topic of conversation. While the conversations both preceding and following this segment are both in Kreol, this brief song interlude is completely couched in Hindustani and is accompanied by a change in prosody as participants adopt a sing-song voice quality. In conjunction with the interactional locus of topic shift, that of playfulness is also brought into salience as the verbal performance is inspired from a popular song of the same name from the 1988 Bollywood movie *Tezaab* (Chandra 1988). The success of the film hinged on the popularity of the song which propelled its lead performer, actress Madhuri Dixit, to stardom. Over the years, countless parodies and adaptations of both its lyrics and choreography have been carried out, thus bearing testimony to its enduring appeal amongst aficionados. In Extract 1, team members seem to be building on the iconicity of the song by using its catchy lyrics and fast tempo as a form of conversational scaffolding in order to mirror the liveliness and dynamism characterising their interactions. In fact, the change in prosody was also accompanied by a strategic shift in the body language as all of them sketched out a few tentative dance steps inspired by the original choreography of the song. CS, thus, is effectively linked with both phonetic skill and a high level of mastery of paralinguistic features such as non-verbal delivery.

Another example is provided in the extract below where speakers from Team 1 are discussing the quality of biscuits imported from various countries:

Extract 2
What to eat?

Speaker 1: **Kon dinwaa ke chaa piyat hay. Bouskouywa daalat hay. Niman nay rahal.**

Speaker 2: Pa bizin aste sa bann biskwi la. Zot sorti Thailand ha. Bizin aste bann biskwi ki sorti lafrans, langleter tou sa. Pa aste bann kitsoz sinwa, Thailand tou sa.

Speaker 3: Ki vre?

Speaker 2: Be ki to ti kwar twa? *Sach keh rahaa hai deewaanaa dil.*

Speaker 3: Al manz enn **bouskouy**. Dir to *dil* aret plorer.

Speaker 1: **This other day I was drinking tea. I was dunking a biscuit in it. It was not good.**

Speaker 2: You should not buy these types of biscuits. They come from Thailand. You should buy those biscuits which come from France, England and so on. There is no need to buy Chinese, Thai things and all.

Speaker 3: What really?

Speaker 2: So what did you think? *The smitten heart is telling the truth.*

Speaker 3: Go eat a **biscuit**. Tell your *heart* to stop crying.

In Extract 2, Speaker 1's complaint about the poor quality of the biscuit that she recently sampled is met with Speaker 2's advice of avoiding products imported from China and Thailand. Speaker 3's response, asking for a confirmation of the above recommendations, elicits a very brief lapse into Hindustani from the part of Speaker 2. The latter quotes the first line of the song from the same name from the movie *Rehnaa Hai Tere Dil Mein* (Menon 2001) to emphasise her point. This insertion serves a dual purpose: on the one hand, it provides Speaker 2 with an opportunity to overcome Speaker 3's scepticism regarding her recommendations. At the same time, the use of the adjective *deewana* ('smitten') allows her to put forward her own preferences and to underscore her own fondness for biscuits imported from France and England. The reaction of Speaker 3 is also particularly noteworthy. Not only does she switch to Bhojpuri to instruct Speaker 2 to please eat a biscuit and to, presumably, stop singing but she also opts to reuse the word *dil* (heart) from the song to indicate that she has taken on board the latter's advice and might, in the future, act on it.

In the two extracts above, both groups of speakers could have opted to couch their message in any one of the languages from their linguistic repertoire. Instead, they choose to switch to brief song interludes from Bollywood movies to get their message across. This could be seen as one way for them to bring to the fore their own identity as trendy, young multilinguals, aware of the possibilities afforded to them by Bollywood songs to convey their opinions, thoughts and feelings in ways which might be deemed to be both creative and innovative. Such co-associations between linguistic usage and the indexing of identity are believed to be characteristic of 'youngspeak' by Zimmermann (2009: 121) who provides a list of what he believes to be some of the key features and dimensions of youth language worldwide. Labelled as 'markers operating at the multimodal level' (Zimmermann 2009: 126), the creative merger of verbal and non-verbal features suggests that the construction of youth identity cannot be simplistically restricted to language. The emergence of 'emblematic markers' (Zimmermann 2009: 126) such as hairstyle, clothing, mimicry and kinesics such as dance can all be attributed to the need of youngsters to establish their emerging identity as 'little adults' (Andersen 2001) capable of maintaining their autonomy both at the social and linguistic levels. Acting as symbols of in-group solidarity and loyalty, markers of youngspeak are equally valuable in multilingual communities where the juxtaposition of myriad languages offers interactants with more opportunities to utilise heteroglossia as the sociolinguistic glue binding together a multi-ethnic and multicultural peer group.

4.2 CS in songs as pragmatic reinforcement to narratives

Examples of song interludes acting as pragmatic reinforcements can be noted in the interactions of other teams as well. For instance, the following performance (Extract 3) was provided by the members of Team 4 during their discussions of the plot lines of popular soap operas being screened by the Mauritius Broadcasting Corporation (MBC):

Extract 3
A discussion of Hindustani serials

Speaker 16: Sa Mandira la. Pa fasil ar li sa.
Speaker 17: Li kontan zis kas li.
Speaker 16: Mandira la li kontan zis kas li. So lizie lor kas ek bizou. Sa mem li bizin li. Mandira li nek kontan vin ris. Saem so problem. Enn fol sa. **Pagli. Pagli. Budhoo ha.** *Hey naa naa naa Shabaanaa. Hey bhuurii bhuurii aankhon mein ye khumaar hai kyun?* **Pagli budhoo.**

Speaker 16: That Mandira. She is unbelievable.
Speaker 17: She loves only money.
Speaker 16: That Mandira loves only money. She eyes only money and jewellery. That's all she needs. Mandira only wants to be rich. That's her problem. She's mad. **Mad. Mad. She's an idiot.** *Hey na na na Shabana. Why are your hazel eyes so intoxicating?* **Mad idiot.**

Extract 3 focuses on the storyline and characters of *Hitler Didi*, one of the innumerable Hindustani serials broadcast on the Zee Cable TV network in Mauritius. The first instance of CS occurs when Speaker 16 shifts from Kreol to Mauritian Bhojpuri, evidenced through the use of the Bhojpuri conjugated verb *ha* (is) as the latter offers a scathing evaluation of the character of one of the antagonists of the shows who is presented as being a gold-digger. This CS is immediately followed by a shift to the Hindustani lyrics of the title song of the more recent *Hum Tum Shabana* (Sagar 2011) movie before eventually reverting to Bhojpuri. What is of equal significance is the slight reworking of the lyrics from *'bholi bholi ankhon mein ye narazgi hain kyun'* (literally translated as 'why is there is anger in your innocent eyes?) to the description of the hazel eyes of the protagonist of the above-mentioned serial.

While the Bhojpuri insertions belong to the conversational locus of repetitions and seem to be highlighting the same point over and over again for emphatic purposes, the switch to Hindustani seems to function as an adjacency pair. Huang (2000) defines and elaborates upon the pragmatic consequentiality of adjacency pairs by stipulating their dual purpose in conversations. Firstly, adjacency pairs can be chained into a series of consecutive question-and-answer sessions where responses provided maintain the interactional code chosen by the asker. Secondly, in the words of Huang (2000: 313), 'adjacency pairs can [indicate] a relation of post-elaboration, where a subsequent "tying adjacency pair" functions as an elaboration of the content of a preceding, "tied to" adjacency pair'. Simply put, the second category of adjacency pairs allows a speaker to extend his/her conversational turn by delaying the progression to a Transition Relevance Place (Sacks et al. 1974).[7] In the above extract, Speaker 16's contribution elaborates upon Speaker 17's comments regarding the antagonist, Mandira's greed. In fact, the observations regarding the anger in the 'innocent' eyes of Shabana, the girl being serenaded in the song interlude, can be seen as a thematic extension of the topic of anger and resentment. While on the one hand, Shabana's eyes sparkle with anger, on the other hand, as Speaker 16 seems to be hinting, it is Mandira who, using the hypnotic beauty of her eyes, and, by extension, her own physical assets, is scheming against the unsuspecting protagonists – often futilely – to acquire wealth. Similar to Kachru (2006), code alternation through the song interlude, thus, acts as a stylistic device capable of enregistering connotations of greed to an otherwise innocuous statement regarding the intoxicating allure of a pretty lady.

In addition, the repetition of the discourse maker *na na na* in the song also becomes pragmatically powerful through its co-association with the homophonous negation marker *na* in Bhojpuri. Consequently, the song acts as a veiled admonition to the antagonist, negatively evaluating her behaviour and exhorting her to eschew her Machiavellian scheming in favour of a more righteous lifestyle. At this point, it needs to be kept in mind that such evaluative segments are not restricted only to multilingual interactions but, in actual fact, they are the staples of Personal Experience Narratives or PENs (Labov and Waletzky 1967) told by any speaker in a mundane conversation. According to them, any standard narrative can be broken down into six different phases namely the abstract, orientation, complicating action, evaluation, resolution and coda.

The abstract acts as the preface to the story while the orientation provides the required contextual information that would eventually facilitate the interpretation of the events unfolding in the subsequent narrative. The complicating action presents the climax of the story before progressing to its conclusion in the resolution and coda. Evaluation, on the other hand, is the only aspect of a narrative which does not follow any sequential order and can be inserted at the discretion of the speaker, at any given point in the narrative, in order to offer his/her observations regarding a particular turn of events. While the evaluation does not move the storyline further, it has a cathartic function since it provides participants with an outlet for their pent-up emotions. Jointly co-constructed by the teller and his/her addressees, an evaluation moves the narrative away from its referential function which 'gives the audience information through the recapitulation of the teller's experience' to its analytical function, thus 'communicat[ing] the meaning of the narrative by establishing some point of personal involvement' (Cortazzi and Jin 2001: 105).

Similarly, in Extract 3, the shift to the Bollywood song segments serves as an evaluative segment to the Personal Experience Narrative or PEN being spoken about by the participants. Based upon the major developments in a popular soap, it reveals the impact of such snippets from the media in the daily life of the interactants who regularly carry out analyses of defining moments. Extract 3, thus, showcases the normal closing segment of a PEN as the conversationalists move on from an abstract and complicating action, all voiced in Kreol, to an evaluation and eventually a coda (*pagli, budhoo*) provided in Bhojpuri. This change in code is accompanied by a slight rise in pitch and an increase in tempo, thus clearly denoting the move from the preliminary to the concluding stages of the narrative interlude. Consequently, the move from normal narrative mode to a song segment proves to be a strategic one since it coincides with the shift in footing in the conversation as conversationalists get into more judgemental territory by focusing on the ethical implications of the major events in their narrative.

4.3 CS, songs and multilingual puns

Such CS through the insertion of song interludes into narrative segments also took more complex forms. For instance, in Extract 4, Kreol is juxtaposed, firstly with English and secondly with Hindi as Bollywood is made to linguistically co-exist with Hollywood:

Extract 4
Bodyguard

Speaker 16: Bodyguard sa mem top fim ki line fer. Pena sa sante la? <u>I will always love youuuu</u>?
Speaker 18: *Bodyguard bodyguard aagayaa hai dekho bodyguard.*

Speaker 16: Bodyguard is the only nice film that she worked in. Isn't there that song? <u>I will always love youuuu?</u>
Speaker 18: *Bodyguard bodyguard see the bodyguard has arrived.*

Extract 4 is part of a much longer interactional segment discussing the demise of singer Whitney Houston in February 2012. In her attempt to pay a fitting tribute to the latter, Speaker 16 mentions one of her iconic films, the Kevin Costner-starred *Bodyguard*. However, instead of picking up the conversational thread and unspooling it further by elaborating upon the current topic, Speaker 18 opts for a pun on the word 'bodyguard' resulting in the creation of a conversational arc linking the Hollywood movie with its Bollywood counterpart of the same name. Released in 2011 and starring popular Bollywood actors Salman Khan and Kareena Kapoor, it proved to be a major commercial success as its songs and storyline all appealed to the masses. This is evidenced in the above excerpt as Speaker 18 cleverly juxtaposes a line from the Hindustani song (italicised text) to the catchy refrain of Houston's earlier version (underlined text). Thus, while the conversational locus of the conversation (cf. Auer 1984) shifts to that of playfulness through the insertion of the song sequence, so far as CS is concerned, a complex web of language alternation is created as English gives way to Hindustani. The change in code is accompanied by a modification in accent as speakers opt for the retroflex [ʈ] and [ɖ] sounds – for instance in the word 'bodyguard' – in order to make the move to another code more prominent and easily noticeable despite the obvious issues of homophony, given the similarity in the titles of both movies. The fact that this shift has been acknowledged, understood and ratified by other members of the conversational network is proved by the subsequent adoption of Hindustani for the remainder of the interaction as they carry out a minute vivisection of the movie's storyline.

Such instances of punning clearly bear testimony to multilingual speakers' creativity. Bell (2011: 631), following Agha (2003), also describes this process as one of enregisterment. Defined as the 'process in which a style registers in public space as indexing certain sociocultural values and positioning', the concept of enregisterment was first used by Agha (2003) in order to explain the establishment of RP over two centuries as particular styles became associated with specific social groups or personae. Agha (2003: 233) argues that certain speech styles may become instantly recognisable by a wide audience due to their association with individual 'characterological figures' ascribed a series of aesthetic and psycho-social values. For instance, Bell (2011) focuses on Hollywood icon, Marlene Dietrich, and argues that her enduring fame can be attributed to the success of this process of enregisterment since she can be considered as a characterological figure representing the sultry *femme fatale* figure that has come to be associated with characteristics such as otherness marked through the transgression of race and gender boundaries, a mesmerising personality and unattainability. Thus, subsequently, exotic accents in other movies have become enregistered as referring deictically to this *femme fatale* figure. In a similar vein, the co-association between Bollywood and Hollywood, in the above extract, shows the process of enregisterment at work as one conversational unit breaks down into multi-layered strands of narratives with each unit associated with its own characterological figure. In this instance, though, instead of being correlated with one specific character from a particular era or text, accents usually enregister, as in the case of Marlene Dietrich, specific characteristics that are embodied by particular stock characters. Indeed, owing to their strong diasporic links with India, stage shows carried out by famous Bollywood celebrities are common occurrences. Consequently, the popularisation of an Indian accent, adopted by Mauritian-born DJs, is noticeable on all major television and radio networks. This would explain the shift from an alveolar to a more retroflex place of articulation as the word 'bodyguard' is mentioned. Given that the Bollywood film uses the English borrowing as its title, it would have been initially difficult for the addressees to differentiate between the two languages and to locate the CS. However, due to the process of enregisterment through which the speaker adopts a stereotypical Indian accent, the change in code and footing is made all the more obvious.

Similar performances of enregisterment are common in the local media as CS is used as a strategy to nativise and add some local flavour to excerpts from the foreign media. One of the ways through which this is achieved is by dubbing original Hollywood and Bollywood clips with a medley of local *Sega* song – a rhythmic song and often dance number usually associated with members of the Creole community but massively popular in all parts of the island – and Bhojpuri songs. One example of such a hybrid mixture is the dubbing of the 'Swamp Song' from the first *Shrek* movie by Mauritian song enthusiasts. Titled as 'Shrekga' (a playful merger of Shrek and *Sega*),[8] it replaces all the original songs from the movie with an assortment of well-known *Sega* songs coupled with one snippet in Bhojpuri (the song played during the performance of the Robin Hood and gingerbread men characters). In fact, 'Shrekga' is not the only instance of creative jumbling being carried out by the local media. Other notable examples include the localised version of the Tamil song 'Kolaveri Di' from the movie *3* (2012).[9] A quick tour of video sharing websites such as YouTube brings to light a number of Mauritian DJs such as DJ Mirish offering their version of a 'Bhojpuri *Sega* Mix':[10] the number of overwhelmingly positive comments coupled with the tally of 'likes' achieved by such clips all hint at the popularity of such hybrid modes of expression by music aficionados in Mauritius. In the above song, for instance, Shrek and Princess Fiona croon snippets from Kreol *Sega* songs while Robin Hood and the gingerbread men sing in Bhojpuri. While it is hard to ascertain the pragmatic significance of attributing these specific codes to particular characters from the *Shrek* franchise, what comes to the fore is the creative potential of multilingualism which is exploited in myriad ways by speakers/ users of these languages. It should, therefore, come as no surprise that the participants interviewed for this study should display such innovative forms of playfulness. Conditioned by the media and connected to the internet through increasingly cheaper price packages, their performance enregisters and encapsulates the ability displayed by a large faction of the population to mix and match different codes in order to fit the contextual requirements of an interaction.

5. Discussion

As the findings of this study indicate, speakers make creative use of language alternation as a form of multilingual performance in relatively novel contexts such as while lapsing into song interludes. This indicates that, so far as the participants of this study are concerned, the judicious selection and maintenance of various languages appeared to be as crucial as the actual performance of those multilingual abilities. Indeed, while some of the ways in which multilingualism was performed might, undoubtedly, be unique to this study and its specific set of informants, the emphasis upon CS as a phenomenon endowed with the potential to also provide kinesthetic expression to the thoughts and emotions of its users is one which has been hinted at in the existing literature. Kachru (1982), for instance, elaborates upon what he considers to be the three key dimensions of a bi- or a multilingual's creativity namely the speaker's ability or instinct, the way it is expressed in various contexts and the way it functions in the specific sociolinguistic context within which it occurs.

The following subsection explores the latter point by Kachru (1982) in more depth by focusing on the ways in which the co-occurrence of performance-oriented features such as song interludes with various types of language alternation phenomena actually fit into the broader macrocosmic sociocultural and linguistic landscape of the island. As theorists such as Auer (1984) and Li Wei (1998) argue, CS cannot take place in a social vacuum; meaning is 'brought about' as a result of the particularities of a specific conversational interaction but this meaning-making process needs to be eventually understood from the perspective of a speaker who is as much a product of the community that (s)he operates in as the analyst is. In other words, while verbal strategies such as those presented in the previous section can help speakers create their own translanguaging space, their performance and the 'emotionality' associated with it is very much due to socio-historical reasons. CS is a reflection of the 'individual's cognitive capacity to understand and make use of the value differentials and give meaning to the choice and alternation between the languages' (Li Wei 2011: 1225).

5.1 The performance of multilingualism in Mauritius: the contribution of Bhojpuri and *Sega* songs

While the multilingual nature of Mauritius has been duly acknowledged by scholars (cf. Miles 1999), the performance of multilingualism in the daily life of Mauritians has, so far, remained largely under-studied. Indeed, in contrast to the Caribbean where the co-existence of multiple languages in popular forms of cultural expression such as its musical texts has been the focus of research – for instance, Myers's (1998) and Ramnarine's (2001) work on the music of countries like Trinidad and Guyana – Mauritian pop culture and the language(s) in which it is couched is still shrouded in mystery. Similar to its Caribbean counterparts, Mauritius also has a rich cultural and linguistic heritage. The two most popular forms of pop culture on the island are *Sega* and Bhojpuri songs which have, at both the prosodic and linguistic levels, undergone a process of hybridisation, resulting in increasing levels of similarity between both modes of expression. This merger has occurred not just at the level of sound and choreography but has also been impacted upon by the linguistic developments taking place on the island. Indeed, as the following paragraphs will illustrate, language has always been closely interrelated with issues of performance, and patterns of multilingual language use have always been shaped by and have, in turn, also shaped the performance of pop culture in Mauritius.

One of the earliest mentions with regards to the emergence of both a Creole and a popular form of expression on the then *Isle de France* is Baissac's (1888) seminal work on what he termed the 'folklore' of Mauritius. Based on his observations of the way of life of the enslaved population during the French colonisation era, it provides an insight into the socio-cultural and linguistic landscape of nineteenth-century Mauritius (Baissac 1888). Although it is usually his less than complimentary views about the Kreol language that are most frequently cited, his contribution to the field of pop culture is still relevant. Focusing on the traditional form of *Sega* known as *Sega Tipik* (literally translated as 'typical *Sega*'), Baissac (1888: 425–8) lists the following three specificities of this musical performance:

1. The lyrics were always couched in Kreol.
2. Three key musical instruments were played, namely the *ravann* (frame drum), the *maravann* (rattle) and the *triyang* (triangle).
3. It was always performed around a bonfire as the heat of the fire was used to heat the *ravann*'s top layer of goatskin so that it would produce a deeper percussion sound.

While the monolingual nature of *Sega Tipik* is often highlighted, labelling this emerging art form as the *Sega* testifies to the multilingual nature of the slave population

(Cangy 2012). In fact, following his visit to the island, Bernardin de Saint-Pierre (1773) described a type of slave performance that he had attended and named it *tchiega*. C. L. de Freycinet (1827) also follows suit using the term *chéga or tchéga* to refer to the performance of the slaves. French linguist Chaudenson (1979) has subsequently argued that the /tʃ/ sound in the word *tchega* was, actually, of Mozambican ancestry and that the term *Sega* itself is derived from Swahili and refers to the iconic act of female dancers who 'roll up' their clothes and gyrate their hips in rhythmically energetic movements. The change of /tʃ/ to /s/ and the adoption of Kreol-only lyrics in the embryonic stages of its development on the island bear testimony to the gradual nativisation of East African cultural forms as a result of the constant contact between slaves originating from diverse homelands. According to Baissac (1888), the strategic adoption of Kreol during *Sega* performances proved to be of immense benefit to the slave population of the island as it provided them with a common, homogeneous linguistic platform, allowing them to express the vicissitudes of slavery. In a world where the adoption of the *Code Noir* (Black Code) robbed them of both their basic human rights and their voice, performance became the only outlet for their pain and frustration (Baissac 1888). Although the actual voicing out of any kind of dissent was strictly prohibited, its performance through song and dance sequences was, at best, tolerated (Baissac 1888).

Moreover, as Baker and Hookoomsing (1987) argue, multilingualism also found its way into the world of the *Sega*. In the eighteenth century, as additional convoys of slaves were transported to Mauritius from South India and Bengal, allowances were made to accommodate their lack of proficiency in the Kreol tongue. Indeed, the *ravann*, a percussion instrument considered as being at the heart of all *Sega* performances is believed to be of South Indian origins (Baker and Hookoomsing 1987). Derived from the Tamil word *iravanum* (literally translated as 'a small tambourine'), the mere presence of the *ravann* in all performances of the *Sega* is firstly an overt acknowledgement of the contribution of all members of the slave population, irrespective of their country of origin. Secondly, it showcases the strong and reciprocal feelings of unity, love and respect that existed amongst them as they capitalised on their affinity for the *Sega Tipik* in order to survive the indignities of slavery (Baker and Hookoomsing 1987).[11]

Indentured labour brought with it not just much-needed relief to the understaffed plantation communities of Mauritius, but also a long tradition of Bhojpuri folk songs that are still performed, albeit in a more localised version, today (Servan-Schreiber 2011). The cultural and linguistic heritage of these Indian migrants is, at present, visible both in the Caribbean and in other parts of the word where indentured labour flourished (Myers 1998, Ramnarine 2001). Ramnarine (2001) focuses specifically on the emergence of chutney songs in Trinidad and Guyana and describes it as a reflection of the multicultural contexts of the Caribbean, culminating in the localisation of Indian forms of music to those that already existed on the local scene. Along similar lines, Myers's (1998) study of the music of Hindu Trinidad reveals a gradual erosion of the *dīpchandī* or *chachal tāl*, a tune consisting of fourteen beats in favour of a Bollywood-inspired *Kaharwa tāl*, a tune consisting of eight beats. The change in beat also makes it easier for the insertion of words that would not have, originally, fit a fourteen-beat tune. The possibility of such an occurrence was predicted by Grierson's (1884) seminal study of Bihari and Bhojpuri folk songs in late nineteenth-century

India when he had noted that for many performers, the actual lyrics of songs did not really matter. They would readily improvise and find words to fit the beat and metre of the song as the song progressed. He further added that 'the melody to which they are sung is the only guide, and so long as the accent and musical ictus is provided for, the author cared little whether his syllables were long or short' (Grierson 1884: 229). Such improvisation was also common amongst the indentured immigrants who mastered those folk songs. As one of Myers's informants (1998: 257) states: '[H]ere people sing their own texts on the same tune.' His complaint was against his fellow performers who felt empowered to change the lyrics of a song so long as they remained faithful to the original *tāl* or tune of the song. With a tune that has only eight beats instead of the usual fourteen, it is to be expected that performers would modify their lyrics in favour of words whose syllable structure and stress patterns would fit the requirements of an eight-beat song (Myers 1998, Ramnarine 2001). Consequently, in the long run, Bhojpuri folk songs gave way to more local forms which were both acoustically and linguistically different from their original versions.

A similar argument is made by Servan-Schreiber (2011) who believes that Bhojpuri songs in Mauritius have already undergone a process of hybridisation as they adapt to the rhythms of the *Sega* and the particularities of the Kreol language.[12] In so doing, they have opened themselves up to the sound, choreography and also the language choices made by *Sega* performers and the average Mauritian. The implications of these changes are manifold. While on the one hand, the localisation of Bhojpuri folk songs indicates the high levels of acculturation and integration of the descendants of the indentured labourers into the increasingly hybrid fabric of contemporary Mauritius society, on the other, it might explain the linguistic performance of the informants of this study. As shown in section 4 of this chapter, some of the participants of this study borrowed a Bollywood-inspired form of musical expression and integrated it within their own speech. Fluent in Hindustani and exposed to Bollywood films and music from a very early age, for them the shift from the fourteen-beat *dīpchandī* to the eight-beat *Kaharwa* of the Bollywood movie might not have been an altogether difficult one. In addition, given the nationwide popularity of *Sega* and other forms of storytelling performances, the blurring of the linguistic boundaries between Kreol, Bhojpuri, Hindustani, French, and to a much lesser extent English, would have been a staple of their daily interactions.

The use of multiple languages in a creative manner in public performances has been previously evidenced in the work of both *Sega* performers such as Ti-Frer and Nelzir Ventre (Cangy 2012) and Bhojpuri singers such as Sona Noyan (Servan-Schreiber 2011) who achieved national recognition for their songs and narrations of folk tales. During his fieldwork in Mauritius in the 1990s, Haring (2011) carried out a series of recordings with the now-late Ton (Uncle) Nelzir Ventre who constantly underlined the importance of the performance mode for most face-to-face interactions in Mauritius. Labelling 'obscure' non-Kreol words as *langaz* (language), he revealed that he viewed the process of performance-oriented, interactive and possibly multilingual forms of storytelling and singing as a process of 'translation' (Haring 2011: 186). In his words:[13]

> I had to have finished presenting [*tradwir*] the story – to present all the <u>words</u> to the people listening. Do you understand me? Drum players and musicians

accompany me. There is no dancing at that point. *Tradwir* means to tell the whole story beforehand, <u>while singing</u>. No dancing, just drumming. Everybody sits down and listens. (Interview with Venter 1990, cited in Haring 2011: 186, underlined emphasis mine)

As the island underwent a demographic change through the arrival of indentured labourers, the traditions developed by the slaves also experienced a gradual evolution. For Nelzir Ventre, multilingualism did not imply either an automatic loss of the tradition of *Sega* performance that evolved during the slavery era nor the exclusion of the Indian population from participating in this art form. Instead, it provided an opportunity for the both the Kreol and the Bhojpuri language to collide and combine, giving rise to a more hybrid product. With time, these storytelling sessions still made use of the percussion sounds generated by the *ravann*, but instead of the hip gyrations that a Creole-only audience would have been used to they utilised mainly a sing-song intonational pattern – an echo of the same prosodic particularities that would have been used by the *Sega* singer – and presented their now multilingual text in the form of a public performance. Haring (2011: 186) notes that he has often 'wonder[ed] how many other Southwest Indian Ocean story-tellers have been as expert translators as Nelzir Ventre'.

This emphasis upon the 'tension and excitement [caused by] the combination of speech and song' (Haring 1997: 217) has been the focus of previous academic work that has highlighted the strong role played by lapses into song sequences during narrative performances (cf. Richon 2009). Haring (1997) provides the example of Ton Nelzir Ventre's story of a young lady of marriageable age, who after refusing many eligible bachelors finally decides to marry a werewolf. She takes her brother TiZâ to live with them.[14] The latter soon discovers that Prince Lulu, his brother-in-law is, in fact, planning to eventually murder and eat up his sister (Haring 1997). In the next section Prince Lulu converses with his fellow wolves and TiZâ manages to stage an escape by casting a spell over a 'basket like a balloon' (Ventre, cited in Haring 1997: 217). Commenting upon Ventre's 'hybridization of speech and song' (Haring 1997: 217), Haring (ibid., emphasis in original text) asserts:

> The song of the wolves and Prince Lulu's answer ('Let's eat them!' 'Let them get fatter' in quick alternation) and TiZâ's song to the balloon are crucial moments in the narrative. The alternation yields a hybridization of 'two *individualized* language consciousnesses', as Bakhtin said. One is the rather impersonal consciousness of the narrator; the other is the 'individualized linguistic consciousness and will of the character represented'.

The above description has been cited in full because it makes the following two very important points:

1. Firstly, lapses to song sequences which, as Ventre has previously pointed out, are simply lines of speech that are accompanied by a few percussion sounds, occur at moments deemed to be important by the narrator.
2. Secondly, they can be considered as a stylistic device which allows the storyteller to flesh out his characters. In most cases, narrators will opt for verisimilitude and

will try to craft an individual voice that is as close to the sociocultural reality of the community that they represent.

Similarly, it can be argued that linguistic interaction in Mauritius displays a degree of intersection between speech and performance. In a speech community where both the descendants of the slaves and the indentured labourers shared the same space, it was to be expected that the performance of CS would draw from both their cultural traditions. Language alternation, in Mauritius, is therefore one that is deeply embedded within a socio-cultural reality that has been influenced by the demographic and linguistic changes brought about by centuries of colonisation, resulting in the emergence of an art form that merges elements from both speech and performance and is part of the socio-cultural ethos of the island.

As seen above, the versatility of speakers clearly bears testimony to the socio-cultural and linguistic framework within which they operate. It has also led researchers such as Coupland (2011: 573) to call for an enhanced theoretical emphasis upon what he labels as a 'sociolinguistics of performance' which considers 'voice [as] the repertoire of meaning-making options available to performers'. Subsuming within it issues of 'dialect indexicality, the management of singer identity and singer-audience relations through the performance of lyrics, rhythmic and bodily modalities' (Coupland 2011: 573), 'voice' also allows participants to create a new form of *'lingua franca* of musical expression' (Tagg 2006: 73), a functional resource which is activated in context-sensitive ways (cf. Hymes 1996). The above perspective finds an echo in Feld and Fox's (1994) work on the interconnection between music and language in which they draw attention to the interrelatedness between speech and song and reveal two categories of performance amongst others that fall squarely within the twilight zone that separates speech and song. These are, according to them, '*sprechgesang* (sung speech) and *Sprechstimme* (dynamically, rhythmically, and intonationally heightened speech)' (Feld and Fox 1994: 30–1). In the case of the speakers of this dataset, the presence of *sprechsang* and *Sprechstimme* can be detected as the interactants use their 'voice' in pragmatically consequential ways so that they can create their own musically expressive language that simultaneously allows them to project their own desired persona while maintaining the status quo that exists between them and their fellow co-conversationalists.

Further corroboration is provided by Bauman (2011) and Bell and Gibson (2011) who maintain that the sociolinguistic emphasis on 'natural, unselfconscious' speech should not render the analyst insensitive to other forms of context-specific and culturally-relevant vocal performances. To quote Bauman and Sherzer (1989: 7), performance consists of the 'interplay between resources and individual competence, within the context of particular situations'. In the case of individual speakers, this competence is honed through their continuous contact with the languages and the interactional norms prevalent in their own speech community. The linguistic and paralinguistic resources available to each speaker is then, subsequently, activated in specific situations which provide them with the opportunity to translate their competence into pragmatically loaded performances. A similar scenario appears to be at work in the Mauritian context as well. In a context which, as Haring (2011) points out, is deeply performance-oriented, the influence of *Sega* and Bhojpuri songs and interactive and polyphonic storytelling sessions would have, undoubtedly, shaped the linguistic competence of speakers, culminating in the final activation of these abilities in particular conversational contexts as they utilise their multilingual abilities in creative and impactful ways.

6. Conclusion

In essence, this chapter has attempted firstly to explore the translanguaging space of a group of informants in more detail by analysing spontaneous lapses into Bollywood-inspired song sequences in routine conversational encounters. Secondly, it has attempted to understand the 'emotionality' of these performances by situating them within the broader socio-cultural context of multilingual Mauritius. In so doing, it has attempted to correlate the creative forms of language behaviour of the participants taking part in this study with the socio-cultural and linguistic practices in contemporary Mauritius. Finally, in keeping with changes that have already taken place and are still taking place in other Creole- and Bhojpuri-speaking contexts such as the Caribbean, it has argued for the possible consideration of these innovative forms of language alternation as a form of 'chutnification'.

Notes

1. Some sections of this chapter are based on the author's unpublished doctoral thesis (Auckle 2015).
2. Except for the occasional place name along the lines of Plaine Wilhems and Flacq, very little linguistic evidence of the Dutch settlement has survived the test of time (Eriksen 1999).
3. As Miles (2000: 217) puts it, '[i]mplicitly, the French language was preserved. Mauritius thus continued to be a French and French Creole speaking society under the relatively unintrusive umbrella of British sovereignty. The one significant exception to Anglo-Saxon aloofness was the judiciary. In 1845 it was decreed that English would become the language of the higher courts.'
4. Kachru (1985: 20) also warns against seeing this creativity as a form of 'acquisitional deficienc[y] of the bilinguals in a particular language'.
5. The formatting provided in the original text has been maintained. Normal typeface is being used for Hindustani while italics have been adopted to highlight switches to English.
6. This article used Y. Kachru's (2009: 415) 'distinction between Hindi (Sanskritised variety), Urdu (Persianised variety) and Hindustani (neutral, colloquial variety)'. As per Y. Kachru (2009), while Sanskritised Hindi makes use of a number of borrowings, particularly at the lexical level, from Sanskrit, Persianised Hindi shows a degree of influence at the levels of lexis and syntax for instance from Perso-Arabic sources. The conversational Hindi used in Bollywood movies is labelled as Hindustani.
7. Sacks et al. (1974) define Transition Relevance Place (TRP) as points in a conversation where a turn at talk could be legitimately passed from one speaker to the next.

8. The full clip is available on: http://www.youtube.com/watch?v=DbumYf7KWmE (last accessed on 29 October 2020).
9. The Mauritian version of 'Kolaveri Di' is available on Skky Crew's YouTube channel on: http://www.youtube.com/watch?v=XuKLUD2eoWM (last accessed on 29 October 2020).
10. DJ Mirish's upload can be accessed on: http://www.youtube.com/watch?v=WzWdeAiy1U8&feature=related (last accessed on 29 October 2020).
11. It was hardly surprising, therefore, for slave-owners to view this emerging art form with deep mistrust. The disapproval of the colonial powers could be attributed to multiple factors such as the fear that such enhanced levels of conviviality could empower the slaves to stage a mutiny, the disdain towards the energetic hip gyrations deemed to be vulgar and, finally, their derision for the 'patois' used by the slaves (Baker and Hookoomsing 1987).
12. Manuel (1997, 2009) makes a similar point regarding the evolution of Bhojpuri songs in the Caribbean.
13. This translation is taken verbatim from Haring's (2011) work. The translation of Ventre's interview into English is his own. The original text which, in all likelihood, would have been in Kreol is not provided.
14. Haring (1997) makes use of the former orthographic system of Mauritian Creole. *Zâ*, written today as *Zan*, is pronounced as /zã/. On the other hand, *lulu*, written today as *loulou* and pronounced as [lulu], means 'wolf'.

References

Agha, A. (2003). The social life of cultural value. *Language and Communication*, 23 (3): 231–73.
Agha, A. (2006). Norm and trope in kinship behavior. *Texas Linguistics Forum*, 49: 1–21.
Allen, R. B. (1999). *Slaves, Freedmen and Indentured Laborers in Colonial Mauritius*. Cambridge: Cambridge University Press.
Andersen, H. (2001). Markedness and the theory of linguistic change. In H. Andersen (ed.), *Actualization: Linguistic Change in Progress*. Amsterdam and Philadelphia, PA: John Benjamins Publishing Company, pp. 21–57.
Androutsopoulos, J. (2013). Networked multilingualism: Some language practices on Facebook and their implications. *International Journal of Bilingualism*, 19 (2): 185–205.
Auckle, T. (2015). *Code Switching, Language Mixing and Fused Lects: Language Alternation Phenomena in Multilingual Mauritius*. D.Litt and Phil thesis, University of South Africa. https://uir.unisa.ac.za/bitstream/handle/10500/19832/thesis_auckle_t.pdf?sequence=1&isAllowed=y (accessed 25 August 2023).
Auer, J. C. P. (1984). On the meaning of conversational code-switching. In J. C. P. Auer and A. Di Luzio (eds), *Interpretive Sociolinguistics: Migrants, Children, Migrant Children*. Tübingen: G. Narr, pp. 87–112. http://www.freidok.unifreiburg.de/volltexte/4466/pdf/Auer_On_the_meaning_of_conversational.pdf (accessed 30 October 2020).
Auer, J. C. P. (1995). The pragmatics of code-switching: A sequential approach. In L. Milroy and P. Muysken (eds), *One Speaker, Two Languages: Cross-disciplinary Perspectives on Code-switching*. Cambridge: Cambridge University Press, pp. 115–35.
Auer, J. C. P. (1998). Introduction: Bilingual conversation revisited. In J. C. P. Auer (ed.), *Code-switching in Conversation: Language, Interaction and Identity*. London: Routledge, pp. 1–24.
Auer, J. C. P. (2001). Code-switching: Discourse models. In R. Mesthrie (ed.), *Concise Encyclopedia of Sociolinguistics*. Amsterdam and New York: Elsevier, pp. 443–6.

Baissac, C. (1888). *Le folklore de l'île Maurice*. Paris: Maisonneuve.
Baker, P. and V. Y. Hookoomsing. (1987). *Diksyoner kreol morisyen: Dictionary of Mauritian Creole*. Paris: l'Harmattan.
Bauman, R. (1975). Verbal art as performance. *American Anthropologist*, 77 (2): 290–311.
Bauman, R. (2011). Commentary: Foundations in performance. *Journal of Sociolinguistics*, 15 (5): 707–20.
Bauman, R. and J. Sherzer. (1989). *Explorations in the Ethnography of Speaking*. Cambridge: Cambridge University Press.
Becker, A. L. (1991). Language and languaging. *Language and Communication*, 11 (2): 33–5.
Bell, A. (2011). Falling in love again and again: Marlene Dietrich and the iconization of non-native English. *Journal of Sociolinguistics*, 15 (5): 627–56.
Bell, A. and A. Gibson. (2011). 'Staging language: An introduction to the sociolinguistics of performance. *Journal of Sociolinguistics*, 15 (5): 555–72.
Bernardin de Saint-Pierre, J. H. (1773). *'Voyage à l'Isle de France, à l'Isle de Bourbon, au Cap de Bonne-Experance etc.: Avec des observations nouvelles sur la nature & sur les hommes/par un officier du roi*. Paris: Band 1.
Bhatia, T. K. and W. C. Ritchie. (2008). The bilingual mind and linguistic creativity. *Journal of Creative Communications*, 3 (1): 5–21.
Cangy, J. C. (2012). *Le Sega, des origines à nos jours*. Mauritius: Edition Makanbo.
Chandra, N. (1988). *Tezaab* [Motion picture]. India: N. Chandra Films.
Chaudenson, R. (1979). A propos de la genèse du créole mauricien: le peuplement de l'île de France de 1721 à 1735. *Etudes Créoles*, II: 43–57.
Cortazzi, M. and L. Jin. (2001). Large classes in China: 'Good' teachers and interaction. In D. Watkins and J. Biggs (eds), *Teaching the Chinese Learner: Psychological and Pedagogical Perspectives*. Hong Kong: ACER, pp. 115–34.
Coupland, N. (2011). Voice, place and genre in popular song performance. *Journal of Sociolinguistics*, 15 (5): 573–602.
de Freycinet, C. L. (1827). *Voyage autour du monde*. Paris: Pillet.
Dewaele, J. M. (2010). Christ fucking shit merde!: Language preferences for swearing among maximally proficient multilinguals. *Sociolinguistic Studies*, 4 (3): 595–614.
Duranti, A. (1997). *Linguistic Anthropology*. Cambridge: Cambridge University Press.
Eisenlohr, P. (2006). *Little India*. Berkeley: University of California Press.
Eriksen, T. H. (1999). Tu dimunn pu vini Kreol: The Mauritian Creole and the concept of creolization. University of Oxford: Transnational Communities Programme. http://www.transcomm.ox.ac.uk/working%20papers/eriksen.pdf (accessed 30 October 2020).
Ewald, J. J. (2000). Crossers of the sea: Slaves, freedmen, and other migrants in the Northwestern Indian Ocean, c. 1750–1914. *American Historical Review*, 105 (1): 69–91.
Feld, S. and A. A. Fox. (1994). Music and language. *Annual Review of Anthropology*, 23: 25–53.
Ganti, T. (2004), *Bollywood: A Guidebook to Popular Hindi Cinema*. New York: Routledge.
Garcia, O. (2009). *Bilingual Education in the 21st Century: A Global Perspective*. Oxford: Wiley-Blackwell.
Garcia, O. and Li Wei. (2014). *Translanguaging: Language, Bilingualism and Education*. Basingstoke: Palgrave Macmillan.
Grierson, G. A. (1884). Art. XI.—Some Bihārī folk-songs. *Journal of the Royal Asiatic society of Great Britain & Ireland (New series)*, 16 (2): 196–246.
Gumperz, J. J. (1982). *Discourse Strategies*. Cambridge: Cambridge University Press.
Haring, L. (1997). The African challenge. In J. Harris and K. Reichl (eds), *Prosimetrum: Crosscultural Perspectives on Narratives in Prose and Verse*. Cambridge: D. S. Brewer, pp. 213–48.
Haring, L. (2011). Techniques of creolization. In R. Baron and A. C. Cara (eds), *Creolization as Cultural Creativity*. Jackson: University of Mississippi Press, pp. 178–97.

Huang, Y. (2000). Discourse anaphora: Four theoretical models. *Journal of Pragmatics*, 32 (2): 151–76.
Hymes, D. (1996). *Ethnography, Linguistics, Narrative Inequality: Toward an Understanding of Voice*. London: Taylor and Francis.
Jay, T. B. (2009). The utility and ubiquity of taboo words. *Perspectives on Psychological Science*, 4 (2): 153–61.
Johnstone, B. (2011). Dialect enregisterment in performance. *Journal of Sociolinguistics*, 15 (5): 657–79.
Jonsson, C. (2005). *Code-switching in Chicano Theater*. Umeå: Umeå University Press.
Kachru, B. B. (1982), *The Other Tongue: English Across Cultures*. Urbana: University of Illinois Press.
Kachru, B. B. (1985). Standards, codification and sociolinguistic realism: The English language in the outer circle. In R. Quirk and H. Widdowson (eds), *English in the World*. Cambridge: Cambridge University Press, pp 11–30.
Kachru, B. B. (1990). *The Alchemy of English: The Spread, Function and Models of Non-native Englishes* (reprint). Urbana: University of Illinois Press.
Kachru, Y. (1989). Code-mixing, style repertoire and language variation: English in Hindi poetic creativity. *World Englishes*, 8 (3): 311–19.
Kachru, Y. (2006). Mixers lyricing in Hinglish: Blending and fusion in Indian pop culture. *World Englishes*, 25: 223–33.
Kachru. Y. (2009). Hindi-Urdu. In B. Comrie (ed.), *The World's Major Languages*. London: Routledge, pp. 319–416.
Kharkhurin, A. V. (2012). *Multilingualism and Creativity*. Bristol: Multilingual Matters.
Kharkhurin, A. V. and Li Wei. (2015). The role of code-switching in bilingual creativity. *International Journal of Bilingual Education and Bilingualism*, 18 (2): 153–69.
Labov, W. and J. Waletzky. (1967). Narrative analysis: Oral versions of personal experience. In. J. Helm (ed.), *Essays on the Verbal and Visual Arts*. Seattle: University of Washington Press, pp. 12–44.
Li Wei. (1998). The *why* and *how* questions in the analysis of conversational code-switching. In J. C. P. Auer (ed.), *Code-switching in Conversation: Language, Interaction and Identity*. London and New York: Routledge, pp. 156–79.
Li Wei. (2011). Moment analysis and translanguaging space: Discursive construction of identities by multilingual Chinese youth in Britain. *Journal of Pragmatics*, 43 (5): 1222–35.
Manuel, P. (1997). Music, identity, and images of India in the Indo-Caribbean diaspora. *Asian Music*, 29 (1): 17–35.
Manuel, P. (2009). Transnational chowtal: Bhojpuri folk song from North India to the Caribbean, Fiji, and beyond. *Asian Music*, 40 (2): 1–32.
Menon, G. (2001). *Rehnaa Hai Tere Dil Mein* [motion picture]. India: Vashu Bhagnani Films.
Miles, W. F. S. (1999). The Creole malaise in Mauritius. *African Affairs*, 98 (391): 211–28.
Miles, W. F. S. (2000). The politics of language equilibrium in a multilingual society: Mauritius. *Comparative Politics*, 32 (2): 215–30.
Myers, H. (1998). *Music of Hindu Trinidad: Songs from the India diaspora*. Chicago: University of Chicago Press.
Myers-Scotton, C. (1988). Code-switching as indexical of social negotiations. In M. Heller (ed.), *Codeswitching: Anthropological and Sociolinguistic Perspectives*. Berlin: Mouton de Gruyter, pp. 151–86.
Myers-Scotton, C. (1993). Elite closure as a powerful language strategy: The African case. *International Journal of the Sociology of Language*, 103 (1): 149–64.
Omoniyi, T. (2006). Hip-hop through the world Englishes lens: A response to globalization. *World Englishes*, 25 (2): 195–208.
Pandharipande, R. V. (2019). 'Bilinguals' creativity and an argument for paradigm shift. *World Englishes*, 38 (1–2): 219–32.

Psathas, G. (1995), *Conversation Analysis: The Study of Talk-in-Interaction*. London: Sage Publications.

Ramnarine, T. K. (2001). *Creating their Own Space: The Development of an Indian-Caribbean Musical Tradition*. Kingston: University of West Indies Press.

Richon, E. (2009). *Sega: Témoignages anciens et récents*. Mauritius: Mauritiana.

Sacks, H., E. A. Schegloff and G. Jefferson. (1974). A simplest systematics for the organization of turn-taking for conversation. *Language*, 50 (4): 696–735.

Sagar, B. (2011). *Hum tum shabana* [motion picture]. India: Horseshoe Pictures Pvt. Ltd and Alliance Entertainment Pvt. Ltd.

Servan-Schreiber, C. (2011). Indian folk music and 'tropical body language': The case of Mauritian chutney. *South Asia Multidisciplinary Academic Journal* [online]. Free-Standing Articles, online since 24 January 2011. http://samaj.revues.org/3118 (accessed 30 October 2020).

Shohamy, E. and D. Gorter. (2008). *Linguistic Landscape: Expanding the Scenery*. London: Routledge.

Simonton, D. K. (2008). Bilingualism and creativity. In J. Altarriba and R. R. Heredia (eds), *An Introduction to Bilingualism: Principles and Processes*. New Jersey: Erlbaum, pp. 147–166.

Skky Crew YouTube channel. (2012). *Why this kolaveri di sega version by skkycrew from mauritius!* [video file]. http://www.youtube.com/watch?v=XuKLUD2eoWM (accessed 30 October 2020).

Smith, J. A. and M. Osborn. (2008). Interpretative phenomenological analysis. In J. A. Smith (ed.), *Qualitative Psychology: A Practical Guide to Research Methods*. London: Sage, pp. 53–80.

Swain, M. (2006). Languaging, agency and collaboration in advanced second language learning. In H. Byrnes (ed.), *Advanced Language Learning: The Contributions of Halliday and Vygotsky*. London: Continuum, pp. 95–108.

Tagg, P. (2006). Music, moving image, semiotics and the democratic right to know. In S. Brown and U. Volgsten (eds), *Music and Manipulation: On the Social Uses and Social Control of Music*. New York: Berghahn Books, pp. 163–86.

Thumboo, E. (1985). Twin perspectives and multi-ecosystems: Traditions for a commonwealth writer. *World Englishes*, 4 (2): 213–22.

Vaughan, M. (2005). *Creating the Creole Island: Slavery in Eighteenth-century Mauritius*. Durham, NC: Duke University Press.

Zimmermann, K. (2009). A theoretical outline for comparative research on youth language. In A. Stenström and A. M. Jørgensen (eds), *Youngspeak in a Multilingual Perspective*. Amsterdam and Philadelphia, PA: John Benjamins Publishing Company, pp. 119–36.

Index

accommodation, 10, 69, 73, 83, 149, 199
Afghanistan, 91, 216
Africanisation, 89
Afrikaans, 72, 75–6, 80, 82, 86, 171, 173, 176, 181, 183, 201
agent, 71, 77, 158, 176
ancestral
   homeland, 78
   language, 80, 90, 157
   villages, 75, 167–8, 170–1, 175–9, 189
Andhra Pradesh, 68
anti-immigration sentiment, 89, 94
Anu-Gandhi Yug, 206
Apartheid, 79, 83–4, 189, 203, 207, 209–10, 218
Arabian sea, 13, 20–1, 168
Arabic, 5, 9, 69, 72, 92–3, 114
areas of origin, 69, 73, 167, 173
Arya Samaj, 131–2, 214–15
asylum, 98
Australia, 1, 3, 5, 10, 125, 187, 203
authenticity, 109, 118–19, 122
Awadhi, 6, 53–4, 70, 73, 78, 84, 114

Bahasa Pasar, 129–30
bilingual, bilingualism 4, 6, 50, 75, 86, 90, 95–9, 100–3, 132–3, 153, 213, 232, 246
   active bilinguals, 95
   active repertoires, 102
   balanced, 103
   English dominant, 103
   stable, 6, 95, 103
Balochi, 98
Bangla, Bengali 4, 6, 7, 49, 50–2, 54–64, 70–1, 82–6, 90, 91–3, 102–3, 132–40, 145–6, 202
Bangladeshi, 82, 91–2, 102–3
barracks, 71, 77

Bazaar Hindustani, 125
Bengal Presidency, 68, 203
Bhil, 13–17, 20, 23–6
Bhili, 5, 14, 16–20, 24
Bhojpuri, 3, 6–8, 53–4, 61, 70–4, 76–80, 84–6, 134, 144–9, 151–5, 158, 163, 167, 183, 186–7, 203, 229, 233, 235–47
Biblical stories, 160
Bihar, 68, 77, 144, 147–8, 153–4, 163
Bihari, 54, 61, 69, 147, 152, 156, 242
Bollywood, 8, 161, 218, 221, 230–5, 238–9, 242–6
Bombay Presidency, 13
Boston philosophers, 109–10
boundaries, 48–9, 93, 206, 230, 239, 243
   boundary crossers, 228
   geopolitical, 206
Bourdieu, P., 50, 122
Braj, 54, 70, 151–3
Britain, 89, 90–3, 95, 97–9, 101–4, 148, 207, 228
British colonies, 4, 68, 127, 130, 147–8, 162–3
Buzme Adab, 210–12

Calcutta, 1–6, 49–52, 64, 68–71, 85, 163, 188; *see also* Kolkata
Calcuttia, Kalkatiya, 69–71, 73, 163
Canada, 1–2, 5, 10, 112, 125, 144
Cape Town, 7–8, 72–6, 79, 81–3, 86, 125, 167–75, 177–83
Caribbean, 3, 6–7, 68, 79, 143–5, 147–8, 152, 154, 156–8, 161–3, 207, 241–2, 246–7
Creole, 97
case-marking, 176, 180
caste, 1, 15, 20, 30, 68–9, 71, 98, 127–8, 149, 159, 173–4, 188, 190, 207, 210, 216
Central India 12–13, 26

chain shift, 8, 196–8
Charotari, 192, 195–6, 203
Chattisgarhi, 70
Chennai, 68, 98, 105
China, 127, 129, 229, 235
Chinese, 2, 54–5, 65, 93, 127, 132–4, 138, 229, 235
Christian missionaries, 72, 114–15, 159–61
Christianity, 110, 114–15
chutnification, 246
civic associations, 222
civil war, 98
code, 71, 103, 113, 118, 238–40, 242
   alternation, 6, 8, 237
   divergence, 78
   switching, 9, 39, 80, 95, 117, 201, 227, 233
colonisation, 241, 245; *see also* imperialism
   waves of, 228
Commonwealth citizens, 89
communicative context, 27, 101
community school, 126, 136, 140, 154
convicts, transported, 128, 129
Coolie, 1, 229
Coolie trade, 143
Creole, 7, 65, 97, 129, 144–6, 156–8, 160, 228, 232, 239, 241, 244, 246–7
cricket, 25, 79, 82–3, 86, 170
culture, 2, 26, 49, 53, 64–5, 84, 94, 97, 101, 111–12, 121, 126, 132, 140, 143, 153, 156–9, 161–2, 186, 193, 205, 207–9, 211–13, 216–7, 220–2, 227, 241
   cultural appropriation, 122
   cultural continuity, 83
   cultural practices, 12, 19, 26, 36, 37, 156
   and ethnicity, 127–9

Dakkhini Urdu, Deccani, 77–8
demographics, 6–7, 73, 80, 93, 103, 126, 133–9, 148, 163, 174, 182, 228–9, 244–5
derogatory words, 158
dialect, 6, 8, 69–80, 85, 97–8, 100, 103, 149, 153, 167, 173, 177, 183, 188–93, 195–203, 245
   ancestral, 75, 167
   accommodations, 73
   contact, 69, 72, 183
   input, 85, 167
   levelling, 76, 80, 147–8, 151, 183
   loyalty, 201
   retention of features, 167, 171, 175, 181–3, 188
   spread, 8
   village, 8
dialectology, 8, 186–8
diaspora
   creativity in, 222
   diasporic dialectology, 8, 187
   diasporic gap, 79–80
   diasporic idealism, 214
   diasporic styles, 103–4
   double, 9
   internal, 2, 5, 65
   multilingual context of, 246
   older, 82–3
digital media, 109, 118
   digital religion, 108
   digital/online rituals, 118–19
diglossia; *see also triglossia*, 50, 64, 137
   embedded, 92
displacement, 5, 12–15, 18, 24–9, 30–6, 42–5, 48
   development-induced, 12
   forced, 18
   internal, 12–13, 27
domain, 4, 25, 50–8, 60–4, 101, 154, 173, 232
   family, 171–2
dominant community, 24, 125
double migration *see* migration
Dravidian, 77
   languages, 14, 70, 72, 89, 91, 134–5, 137
   politics, 131
Durban, Port Natal, 8, 68, 76, 144, 187–9, 191–2, 195, 198–203, 208, 211, 219–22

East Africa, 4, 89, 187, 205, 228
   East African Indians, 94, 187
East India company, 89
East Indians, 143–4, 147, 161
ecology of language, 5
economic opportunities, 99, 129
education, 7, 9, 25, 45, 52, 70, 78, 89–94, 98–99, 115, 126, 130–5, 137–40, 147, 157–9, 161–2, 173, 189, 205, 213–14, 220, 229
emic perspective, 233
English, 3, 7, 8, 21, 38–40, 44, 50–2, 55–65, 71–2, 75–7, 80, 82–4, 90–2, 94–5, 97, 100–5, 109–11, 113, 115–18, 128–31, 133–4, 138–9, 143–7, 154, 156–8, 160–4, 171–3, 179–83, 191, 201, 205–11, 213–17, 220–2, 228–33, 238–9, 243, 246–7
enregisterment, 27, 239
ergative, ergativity, 77, 153, 156, 176, 180–1

Index

ethnic, ethnicity
  category, 91
  and diversity, 4
  marked variety, 95
  multi-ethnic networks, 100, 103, 236
  tensions, 89

Fanakalo, 71, 82
feature-factor matrix, 126, 139
festivals, 5, 37, 44, 114, 158, 211, 219
Fiji, 1, 3, 6, 10, 65, 68, 77, 125–6, 147–8, 152–3
food preferences, 71
French, 7, 54–5, 65, 100, 104, 125, 144–5, 147, 156, 228–9, 233, 241–3, 246
French Guiana, 144–5
fugitives, 228
future tense, 149–2, 75–8

Gandhi, M. K., 8, 71, 187, 189, 205–10, 213–15, 217, 219, 220, 224
German, Germany, 3, 98, 100–2, 110, 209
girmitya, 147; *see also* indenture
globalisation, 82, 90
Godaveri, 75
Grierson, G. A., 70, 76, 149, 163, 173–4, 190–2, 194–5, 199–201, 243; *see also* Linguistic Survey of India
Group Areas Act, 207
Guadeloupe, 6, 144–5
Gujarat, 1, 12–15, 20, 23–4, 69–70, 76–8, 85, 186, 188–191, 194–201, 205–8, 211–16, 219, 222–3
Gujarati, 6–8, 14, 23, 54–5, 61, 72, 76–9, 81–3, 89–93, 103, 114, 127, 132, 134–7, 139–40, 145–6, 167, 183, 186–98, 200–03, 205–23; *see also* Surti, Kathiawadi
gurdwaras, 131
Gurmukhi, 94
Guyana, 3, 7, 65, 125–6, 143–5, 147–9, 152–5, 157–9, 161, 163, 188, 241–2

habitual, 75, 149, 215
Hajratwala, M., 1, 187
heritage language, 8, 24, 75, 90, 99–2, 143, 147, 156–60, 162–3, 183
heritage research, 186
heteroglossia, 64, 236
hierarchical marginalisation, 27
Hindi (Hindustani), 6–8, 14, 23, 36–7, 44, 51–65, 70–3, 76–80, 85, 89, 92–5, 104, 113–14, 117, 122, 125–6, 129–32, 135–40, 144–56, 158–9, 161–63, 186–7, 196, 202–3, 207, 210–11, 219, 221, 229–31, 234–9, 243, 246
  Contact Hindi, 77
  Caribbean, 155
  Dravidian Hindi-Urdu, 77
  Fijian Pidgin Hindi, 77
  movies, 147, 154
  South African, 76–7
Hindus, Hinduism 5, 7, 19, 31–2, 37, 64, 71, 76–8, 82–3, 94, 108–19, 121–3, 144–7, 157, 188–9, 207–17, 219–23, 242
  Hindu temple, 109, 111–14, 117–18, 144, 146, 157, 220
  pan-Hindu identity, 109, 114, 122
  Punjabi Hindus, 93
Hinglish, 230
homeland, 1–4, 6, 27–9, 32–3, 36, 38, 42–4, 48–50, 52, 64–5, 69, 79–80, 86, 90, 110, 112, 128–9, 140, 157–9, 198, 212, 215, 242
  ancestral, 78
  new, 79, 112, 157, 159
homophones, 237, 239
horizontal communication, 70–1
hybridity, 35, 38, 43
  and diasporic styles, 103–4
Hyderabad, 50, 75, 77, 78

identity, 1–2, 8–10, 12, 20, 26, 29–32, 35–40, 42–5, 49, 65, 71–6, 78–80, 82–3, 86, 109, 111–14, 122–3, 132–4, 138–40, 143, 149, 157–9, 179, 188, 191, 211–17, 221, 235–6, 245; *see also* ethnicity
  marker, 112, 122
  nested sequence of, 79, 221
ideology, 79, 93, 109, 110–11, 209, 219, 230
Immigration Act, 89, 112
immigration laws, 168
Imperial Gazetteer of India, 68, 85–6
imperialism, 159, 168
indenture, 1–5, 7–8, 68–70, 72–5, 81, 83–86, 125–8, 140–3, 147–8, 161, 168–70, 186–8, 207, 211, 223, 229, 242–5
index, indexicality 6, 13, 20, 26–7, 36, 52, 69–70, 74, 97, 167, 175–7, 181, 227, 235, 239, 245
Indian
  grammatical tradition, 111
  heritage, 71, 85
  nationalism, 131, 212
  restaurant, 94, 144–6

253

Indian (*cont.*)
  South African, 3, 78–80, 84–5, 205–7, 211
  vernacular language education, 130
  and Eastern perception of reality, 111
Indian Opinion 8, 207–9, 213, 217–18
Indianisation, 231
Indo-Aryan, 8, 14, 70, 89, 151, 194, 202
Indo-European, 134, 209
Indo-Mauritian, 227–9, 232
In-group solidarity, 97, 236
innovative grammatical forms, 77
institutional embedding, 90
interdialect, 73
inter-tribal communication, 24
Islam, 32–4, 41–2, 114, 208
  Kokni Muslims, 167–70, 173–4, 179–82
  Panjabi Muslims, 93
  Tamil Muslims, 127, 130

Jamaica, 143, 145
Johannesburg, 76, 187–8, 209–11, 215–17, 219–20

Kacchi, 54–5, 187–8, 203
Kalkatiyā, 69–71, 73
kangani system, 128, 140
Kannada, 4, 54–5, 59, 61, 71, 134, 180
karma, 110, 121
Karnataka, 49, 85
Kashmiri Pandits, 30–43
Kathiawad, 8, 76, 188, 191, 194, 198–9
Kathiawadi, 8, 76, 188–90, 192, 194–201, 203
Kenya, 89, 112, 187
Khandesh, 13–14, 18, 26
Khari Boli, 53–4, 153
kinship network, 12, 15, 232
Kiswahili, 187
koine, koineization, 6–7, 73–6, 78–9, 85–6, 104, 148–9, 151–3, 183
Kokni, 6–8, 72, 75–6, 79–83, 167, 168–83
Kolkata, 1, 5–6, 49–52, 64, 68, 71, 85; *see also* Calcutta.
Kollywood, 100, 105
Konkan, 8, 69–70, 75–6, 82, 86, 98, 168, 170–5, 178–9, 181–2, 186
Konkan standard (Marathi), 173–4, 178
Konkani, 4, 6, 54–5, 98, 168, 173–4

language
  choice, 50–1, 55–61, 63–5
  continuum, 6, 14, 70–1, 85, 148–50, 154, 203

heritage, 7–8, 24, 75, 90–1, 99, 101–2, 104–5, 143–7, 156–63, 183, 187
hierarchies, 90
ideologies, 6, 92, 103
maintenance, 7, 23, 55, 93–4, 98, 103, 108, 123, 139, 159, 162–3, 186–7, 205
prestige, 83, 92–4, 114, 117
revival, 109, 118, 120, 163
shift, 7, 23–4, 83, 90, 133, 157–8, 162
lingua franca, 51, 63–4, 70, 104–5, 125, 130–1, 134, 138, 144, 148–9, 151, 220, 229, 245
linguistic and cultural landscape, 7, 108, 127, 129, 135, 137–8, 240–1
linguistic convergence, 148
linguistic repertoire, 23, 27, 69, 97, 227, 235
Linguistic Survey of India, 68, 149, 173–4, 177–8, 180–3
link language, 15, 24
London
  Multicultural English, 103
  vernacular, 97

Madhya Pradesh, 12–13, 23, 25, 85
Madras, Madras Presidency, 68–9, 71, 74, 128, 147
Madrasi, 69
Magahi, 54, 70, 73–4, 152, 203
Maharashtra, 12–13, 24, 49, 76, 85, 114, 168–9
Maithili, 54–5, 70, 73–4, 152–3
Malawi, 187
Malay, 4, 7, 127–9, 132–5, 138
Malayalam, Malayali, 54–5, 59, 61, 71–2, 91, 98, 114, 129–32, 134–7
Mandarin, 7, 132–5, 138
Marathi, 14, 23–7, 54–5, 114, 122, 125, 173–4, 178–80, 188, 202, 229
markedness
  marked feature, 179
  marked forms, 73–4, 77
  markedness reduction, 180
marriage customs, 71; *see also* weddings
Martinique, 144–5
Marwari, 53–4, 61, 202
Massachusetts, 110, 120
Mauritius
  Mauritian Bhojpuri, 152–3, 229, 233, 236–42
  Mauritian Creole, 228, 232, 247
Meman, 188, 203

Index

metathesis, 76, 200
Mewati, 202
migrant workers, 4; *see also* indenture
migration
   catenaic, 70
   circular, 4, 8, 70, 168, 170, 181, 183
   double, 6, 102
   and middle-class professionals, 98
   out-migration, 134, 139, 168, 174
   records, 68
Mirpuri, 92
mixing *see* code-switching
mobility, 26, 29, 31, 33, 48–9, 51, 68–9, 127–8, 157
moment analysis, 233
monolingual framing, 92
Mozambique, 187, 228
multilingualism
   functional, 24, 26
multimodal performance, 229, 235

named varieties, 70
naming practices, 21, 72
Nandurbar, 12–16, 20, 22, 24
Narmada River, 5, 12–26
narratives of personal experience, 237, 238
national language policy, 126
Navsari, 1, 76, 188, 191, 203
Netherlands, 3, 98, 144, 161–2
New Zealand, 1, 3, 10
non-official language, 134–5, 140
non-resident Indians (NRIs), 2, 126
non-standard variability, 193
North Indians, 68, 70–1

onomastics, 82
oral tradition, 18, 80, 119, 218
Oriental studies, 111
Oriya, 54–5, 59, 61, 70
Oudh, 68, 147

Pahari, 53–4, 92, 98
Pakistan, 2–3, 30–3, 41, 44, 91–3, 140, 216
Panjabi, Punjabi, 3–4, 6–7, 36–8, 54–5, 61, 70, 89–98, 100, 103, 114, 127–9, 131–2, 134–7, 139–40, 145
Passenger Indians, 68–70, 75, 168, 188, 207, 211
People of Indian Origin (PIOs), 2, 143–4
personal experience narratives *see* narratives of personal experience

pidgin, 5, 71, 77, 82, 129–30
plantation contexts, 69–72, 77, 127–8, 147, 152, 188, 204, 242
Pondicherry, Puducherry, 144
pop culture, 241
port cities, 69, 74, 127, 128
Port Elizabeth, 8, 76, 86, 187, 191–2, 195, 198–9, 201, 213
post-indenture societies, 126; *see also* indenture
post-independence, 7, 12, 98, 132
post-war period, 89, 94, 131
prestige
   high, 57, 59, 63–4, 92, 117
   language, 83, 92–4, 114, 117
   low, 57–9, 63–4
protest writing, 205

racial classification, 132
Raigad, 168, 173–5, 178, 180–2
Rajasthani, 14, 54, 70, 202
Ratnagiri, 168, 173–5, 177, 180–2
reallocation, 148, 151
recitation, 113, 115, 117–18
re-contextualisation, 227
referential function, 237
refugees, 12, 34, 48, 98–9
religion
   choice of, 112
   religious ceremonies, 71
   religious context, 111–13
   religious experience, 109, 119
   religious practices, 27, 44, 108, 119, 149
resettlement, 12, 15–16, 19, 21–3, 26–7, 144
retroflex, 8–9, 44, 74, 76, 148, 190–5, 200–202, 239
   boosting, 192–3
return to India, 72, 161, 168
rituals, 5, 18, 32, 37, 44, 109, 113–18, 122, 158, 214
   and life cycle, 113

Sanskrit, 4, 6–7, 31, 43–4, 69, 108–23, 125, 162, 202, 214, 246
   Sanskritised, 230, 246
   hybrid Sanskrit, 109
Sarnami, 145, 151, 153, 155, 159–63
Satpuda mountains, 12–13, 15–16
Saurashtri, 4
scaling, 42–3, 126
   rescaling, 24, 71–2

schools, 9, 17–18, 24–5, 37–8, 52, 56–9, 63, 83, 126, 130–6, 140, 147, 156–9, 202, 209, 214, 220–1
   school policies, 94
scriptures, 109–11, 113, 115–19, 121, 214
Second World War, 130
semiotic practices, 230
sending area, 24, 168–9, 186
settlers, 2, 127
shared cultural knowledge, 97
shibboleths, 77
signified, 119
signifier, 114, 119
Sikh, Sikhism, 3, 83, 95, 114, 130, 132
Sindhi, 4, 7, 54–5, 98, 127, 132, 144–6
Singapore, 3, 7, 65, 112, 125–33, 135–9
Sinhala, 98
slavery, 110, 143, 147, 163, 188, 207, 228, 242, 244
social
   class, 6, 103
   networks, 2, 9, 75, 92, 182–3
   semiotic resources, 13, 26
   structure, 167
   vacuum, 240
socio-
   cultural factors, 90, 126,139–40
   demographic factors, 103
   economic factors, 89, 127–8, 157
   historical factors, 5, 9, 74, 85, 186, 191, 232–3, 241
sojourner, 127
South Africa, South African, 1–11, 68–88, 167–226
   Indian writing, 205
   languages, 68–88, 167–226
South Asia
   language dominance, 103
   literary cultures, 206
South Indians, 68–9, 71, 78, 98, 100–2, 125, 144, 188, 242
Southeast Asia, 4, 127
speech accommodation, 1, 69, 73, 83, 149, 199
speech continuum *see* language continuum
speech repertoire, 3, 5–6, 70, 79, 81
Sri Lanka, 2–3, 9, 72, 83, 89–91, 93, 98–100, 103, 112, 131
stance alignments, 97
State Reorganisation Act, 49
stereotype, 49, 72, 221, 231, 239
story-telling, 19, 217, 243–4, 246

Straits settlements, 128
stylistic device, 237, 244
Summer Institute of Linguistics, 159–60
Surat, 8, 76, 188–91, 195, 203, 207, 211, 214, 216–19
Suriname, 3, 7, 143–5, 147, 153–5, 158–63
Surti, 8, 76, 79, 188–92, 194–203
survey methods, 102
sustainable languaging, 90
Swiss–German, 100–2
Switzerland, 98
Sylheti, 90–3, 102
symbolic domination, 50
symbolic value, 108–9, 111, 114, 122

taluka, 16, 27, 168
Tamil, 4, 6–7, 54–5, 59, 61, 65, 68–9, 71–2, 74–5, 77, 79, 80–1, 83–6, 89, 91, 93, 98–105, 113–14, 122, 125–7, 129–40, 145–6, 167, 183, 187, 207, 219, 229, 240, 242
   Singapore & Malaysia, 125–42
   South African, 6, 74
   Sri Lankan, 9, 93, 98–9, 103, 131
Tamil Nadu, 4, 68, 85, 101, 105, 127, 131
Tanzania, 187
Telugu, 6, 54–5, 72, 75, 77, 79, 86, 125, 129, 130–2, 134, 137, 145, 167, 183, 219, 229
third space, 36, 38, 40, 43, 78
topic shift, 234
transcendentalism, 110–11
translanguaging space, 230–3, 241, 246
transnationalism, 8, 75, 86
Tribal communities, 12–14, 25
triglossia, 92
trilingualism, 95, 232
Trinidad & Tobago, 3, 5, 7, 65, 125, 143–5, 147, 152–4, 157–9, 161, 163, 241–2

Uganda, 89
United Kingdom, 6, 89, 103–4, 125, 144
United Provinces, 144, 147, 153, 188
Urdu, 6–7, 14, 32, 53–5, 70–2, 76–9, 89, 92–5, 114, 125, 129, 132, 135–7, 139–40, 146–7, 151, 153–4, 188, 203–5, 209–13, 229, 246
USA, 2, 5–7, 9–10, 126, 108–24
Uttar Pradesh, 32, 68, 144, 148

Valsad, 76, 188, 191
verb agreement, 156, 180
verbal practices, 233
vertical communication, 70–1

village
    ancestral, 75, 167–8, 170–1, 175–9, 189
    dialect, 8, 167–85
virtual space, 119
vocal instrumentalising, 8, 227

weddings 1, 18–9, 97, 109, 113, 115–17, 122, 158

West Africa, 228
West Bengal, 49, 68, 82
Western Ghats, 168
Women's Cultural group, 222

yoga, 7, 108–9, 120–2

Zulu, 71, 77, 80, 81

EU representative:
Easy Access System Europe
Mustamäe tee 50, 10621 Tallinn, Estonia
Gpsr.requests@easproject.com

www.ingramcontent.com/pod-product-compliance
Lightning Source LLC
Chambersburg PA
CBHW060231240426
43671CB00016B/2912